Philipp von Weitershausen

Web Component Development with Zope 3

Philipp von Weitershausen

Web Component Development with Zope 3

With 39 Figures and 10 Tables

 Springer

Philipp von Weitershausen
Goebenstraße 14
16548 Glienicke
Germany
e-mail: philipp@weitershausen.de

Library of Congress Control Number: 2004114750

ISBN 3-540-22359-2 Springer Berlin Heidelberg New York

Springer is a part of Springer Science+Business Media

springeronline.com

© Springer-Verlag Berlin Heidelberg 2005
Printed in The Netherlands

Cover design: KünkelLopka, Heidelberg
Typesetting and Production: LE-TeX Jelonek, Schmidt & Vöckler GbR, Leipzig
Printed on acid-free paper 33/3142/YL - 5 4 3 2 1 0

Dedication

Für Mami und Papi.

Preface

A common gateway linked code to the net,
Its limitations plain for some to see.
While on a plane an engineer set
This common gateway object-orientedly.

Created through a clown's principia,
All built upon acquisitive ideals:
Dark reservoirs of content will see a
Great framework that an acqueduct reveals.

Alas, ideals of acquisition fall
Beneath the weight of complex modes of use.
Who listens to the new religion's call?
How many will the purer creed seduce?

Foundations that we took such pains to mold
Support a new world better than the old.

Steve Alexander, inspired by
Aroldo Souza-Leite's *Sonnets from Pythia*

Contents

Part I Beginner

1 Introduction   3
   1.1 Is this book for me?   3
   1.2 What is Zope?   3
   1.3 The history of Zope   6
   1.4 The Python Programming Language   6
   1.5 About the examples   8

2 Installing Zope 13
   2.1 Requirements 13
   2.2 Download, compilation and installation 15
   2.3 Setting up a Zope instance 16

3 The Zope 3 Component Architecture 25
   3.1 Introducing components 25
   3.2 Interfaces 27
   3.3 Content components 29
   3.4 Views 30
   3.5 Adapters 32
   3.6 Utilities 33
   3.7 Services 34
   3.8 Configuring components 35
   3.9 Security 36

4 Interfaces 41
   4.1 Interface jargon 41
   4.2 Defining interfaces 42
   4.3 Declaring that an object provides an interface 45

    4.4   Verifying implementations 48
    4.5   Schemas.. 49

5   **Content Components** 55
    5.1   Content types.. 55
    5.2   Schema-based content.................................... 59
    5.3   Configuration 63
    5.4   Advanced: Factories 65

6   **Persistency** 71
    6.1   The problem of object storage.......................... 71
    6.2   Making persistent objects 72
    6.3   Rules of persistency.................................... 75

7   **Presenting components on the web** 79
    7.1   Schema-based browser views 79
    7.2   Page Templates 82
          7.2.1   TAL 83
          7.2.2   TALES 84
          7.2.3   Variable namespaces and scopes 86
    7.3   Simple view Page Template 90
    7.4   Advanced: Customizing automatically generated forms 94

Part II Intermediate

8   **Customizing a site's layout** 105
    8.1   Layers and skins 105
    8.2   Page Template macros 108
    8.3   Stylesheets and other resources........................ 116

9   **Internationalization**.................................... 121
    9.1   Overview 121
    9.2   Message IDs and translation domains 123
    9.3   Internationalizing an application 127
          9.3.1   Python code 127
          9.3.2   Page Templates 128
          9.3.3   ZCML 133
    9.4   Message catalogs 137
    9.5   Advanced: Localization.................................. 141

10 **Adapters** 147
    10.1 Size.. 147
    10.2 File representation..................................... 151
    10.3 Customizing an existing adapter........................ 157

11 Automated testing 161
  11.1 Introduction 161
  11.2 Unit tests 163
  11.3 Doctests.. 167
  11.4 Integration tests.................................... 172
  11.5 Running tests 180

12 Views 185
  12.1 Enhanced browser pages............................... 185
  12.2 Complex views implemented in Python.................. 188
  12.3 Browser menus 197
  12.4 Other HTTP protocols 201
      12.4.1 WebDAV 201
      12.4.2 XML-RPC 203

13 Metadata 211
  13.1 Annotations 211
  13.2 The Dublin Core 215
  13.3 Custom metadata 223

14 Containers... 233
  14.1 Containers, containment, and location................ 233
  14.2 Constraints and preconditions....................... 239
  14.3 Names of contained objects 245
  14.4 File representation.................................. 250

Part III Expert

15 Events 257
  15.1 Introduction 257
  15.2 Object events 259
  15.3 Sending emails for event notification 266

16 Vocabularies 279
  16.1 Simple choices 279
  16.2 Theory and applications of vocabularies 280
  16.3 Using vocabularies................................... 286

17 Sites 291
  17.1 Introduction 291
  17.2 Local utilities 295
  17.3 Virtual hosting 303

18 Security 309
     18.1 Overview 309
     18.2 Permissions 315
     18.3 Roles 317

19 Authentication and user management 323
     19.1 Credentials 323
     19.2 Managing principals 330
     19.3 Principal metadata 342

Part IV Appendices

1   ZAPI Reference 351

2   ZCML Reference 391

References 457

Index 463

Foreword

Zope 3 is here! Congratulations to Jim Fulton, the Zope Pope, and the global team that made it happen. Now the rest of us can start putting its power to use. Truly, with the arrival of the component architecture, Zope can now change its tagline from "Brilliant but clunky" to just "Brilliant".

The world of Zope and its offspring such as Plone have now matured to the point of mainstream legitimacy. In fact, one major European telecom recently told me, "If you bid on a government CMS project, and you don't use Zope, you have to explain why." Incredible!

The world of Zope is big. There are hundreds of add-on packages that integrate into the system in ways that other architectures simply don't anticipate. However, the full potential of Zope's broad basis for business has been held back by limitations that we didn't expect when Zope 2 was designed.

Enter the component architecture! With these lessons from Zope 2, and particularly from the trail blazed by the CMF, software packages can be plugged in and replaced on a more robust and industrial-strength basis. This will help raise the level of basic capabilities common to all Zope-based software, thus accelerating a trend towards enterprise-class services such as versioning.

Most exciting, though, is the business integration. Small companies are specializing in certain platform services and working together for full solutions. The component architecture is crucial for making this work to level of quality demanded by consulting deployments. Also, the often-overlooked upside of Zope 3's test-oriented culture gives us all a boost into better ways of working.

Just like Zope 3 will prove indispensible to the business of Zope, so too will this book. Zope 3 is a commercial-class platform for application services. This book is an in-depth guide to Zope 3, written by one of the most important developers of Zope 3 itself. The overview of core concepts in Chapter 3 is, alone, worth the price of the book. And because the writing style is thoroughly instructive, while also entertaining, the book makes getting started with Zope 3 a pleasure.

This book appears only shortly after a first version of Zope X3 has been released. This is a monumental accomplishment, serving as a testimony to several factors: the discipline of the author, the dedication of the team of developers that managed the last phase of the project in a professional way, and the now-provable wisdom of Jim Fulton's design decisions. Compared to the early days of Zope 1 and 2, the upside of having this book to accompany Zope 3's launch cannot be overstated. It's a big deal.

I've been lucky to know Philipp for a few years, even working with him on some consulting projects. Not only is he great fun to be around, he is also a real leader in the world of Zope. He has the credibility, the reliability, and the right touch for working with the far-flung army of volunteers that are producing Zope. And atop all that, he has written for us the guide to developing killer apps for Zope 3.

I hope you enjoy this book as much as I have, and good luck in your start on Zope 3.

Paul Everitt, co-founder of Zope Corporation

Part I

Beginner

1

Introduction

1.1 Is this book for me?

This book is not for beginners. It does not cover XHTML, HTTP, and all those other standards on the web; it requires the knowledge of them. This book is for web developers. No matter whether you are migrating from Zope 2 or have prior experience in competing technologies, like J2EE or Vignette StoryServer, or even Python-based frameworks like Webware and CherryPy – this book is for you! It certainly is not if you are looking for a thorough introduction to web applications developing.

This book is not a cook book. It does not present recipes for specific tasks nor solutions for specific problems. Rather, it introduces the web applications developer step-by-step to the world of Zope 3 and its component architecture and tries to give the reader the necessary skill for building web applications. It does not cover advanced tips and tricks such as fine-tuning applications or making applications scale better in large environments.

1.2 What is Zope?

Zope is
- a collection of free software
- jointly developed by Zope Corporation and a large community of software developers
- that you can use in whole or in part
- to manage complexity in gluing software components together,
- securely publish objects on the web and other systems,
- and make it easy to do Quality Assurance.

Steve Alexander at EuroPython 2004

a collection of free software: Zope is freely distributable software, it comes free of charge. That does not mean it does not have a value, it just means that you do not have to pay to use it. This successful concept is commonly called *Open Source*. Please consult the website of the Open Source Initiative for a definition of Open Source [7] and the Zope community website for a copy of the *Zope Public License* [21] under which Zope may be distributed.

jointly developed by Zope Corporation and a large community of software developers: After Zope Corporation opened Zope 2's source code to the public, it also started propagating an open development model, encouraging other developers to contribute. Zope 3 too has been a community effort from the beginning, with the majority of the contributions coming from a large community of software developers around the globe. The benefits for the single developer, the whole community as well as the quality of the software have proven to be enormous.

that you can use in whole or in part: Zope is very modular. It is possible to use just certain functionality from Zope and it is not even necessary to install all parts of Zope. Zope is a *collection* of many software modules.

to manage complexity in gluing software components together: Requirements for web-based applications are increasingly complex and the need for systems that can handle such complexity is growing. Zope solves this problem elegantly by separating responsibility into many different components. The way these components are then "glued together" determines the behaviour of the overall application.
Secondly, complex applications require a lot of planning and resources. Zope divides responsibilities into components which also allows *you* to divide up responsbilities when working in a team. Zope is an excellent platform for collaborative development.
Last but not least, the distinction between components with different responsibilities allows easy refactorings since only certain components have to be interchanged. A common example is the customization of presentation and layout components, meaning HTML pages and CSS style sheets, while the underlying software components are not touched.

securely publish objects on the web and other systems: Zope is about objects – it is object-oriented – and about the web. As the points before stated, one can use many Zope components in applications that are not web-specific. However, Zope's main intention is to allow people to manage objects that are published on the web as part of a larger application, not just a website.
Zope is about security, too. Compliance to international IT security norms is a major part of the Zope 3 philosophy. Zope 3 is therefore undergoing

a development-concurrent examination process run by an official IT security agency in Germany. As a result, the Common Criteria Certificate (ISO-15854), a security certificate accepted in Europe, North America and many other countries, will be issued to Zope as one of the first open source products. An invaluable by-product of this will also be that Zope's security model in its full extent is being documented in an ISO-compliant manner.

and make it easy to do Quality Assurance: The developers of Zope 3 have enforced a high level of quality during development. Zope itself is tested by several thousand automated tests; any modifications need to assure that the tests still pass, any new feature needs to be covered by new tests. This has not only lead to a great quality of the software itself, but makes Zope a great platform to do quality assurance with.

Zope runs on all major Unix platforms, including Mac OS X, as well as Microsoft Windows operating systems. It comes with its own webserver but can interoperate with an existing webserver software such as Apache.

Content Management

As an object-oriented web application server with features such as object persistency, Zope provides an excellent platform for building content management systems (CMS). Additional open source party libraries jointly developed by content management vendors allow one to easily construct a custom CMS built on Zope. It is important, though, to note that Zope itself is *not* a content management system. Yet, its whole machinery is geared toward managing content which is why the main focus of this book is the construction of applications that manage content.

Zope X3 vs. Zope 3

When we talk about Zope 3 as a software product, we are usually talking about *Zope X3*. When the development of Zope 3 was launched as a rewrite of Zope 2 from scratch, the goal was to first provide a software collection based on the new concepts and principles that led to the rewrite, *Zope X3*. Only later maybe a form of backward-compatability will be provided which should allow the porting of old Zope 2 packages. This will eventually lead to *Zope 3*. It is uncertain yet, when that will happen and what it will look like. As it was intended, Zope X3 is perfectly suitable for developing new applications, as demonstrated in this book. Packages that are developed with Zope X3 now will run on Zope 3 without modification.

1.3 The history of Zope

The Zope community might have been small when I joined it, but it certainly already had its myths. "Jim wrote the first Zope on a plane" the Zope birthing myth said. Fact is that Jim Fulton was not happy with the status-quo of web development in Python when he returned from the International Python Conference in 1998. Noone can blame him since he had just given a tutorial on CGI programming at the conference, certainly not the nicest way of web developing. Back at Digital Creations, he started writing Bobo, an object database and object request broker capable of publishing Python objects over the web. Later, the commercial Principia, Zope's predecessor, joined its little brother Bobo. Until today, method and attribute names like bobobase_modification_time or isPrincipiaFolderish in the Zope 2 API still tell that history of Zope's parents.

In 1998, Hadar Pedhazur of the venture capital firm Verticality Investment Group invested into Digital Creations and convinced them to make their successful web applications open source. Paul Everitt, CEO of Digital Creations at the time, announced the opening of the sources at the Python Conference 1998. That same year, Bobo and Principia became Zope, the *Z Object Publishing Environment*, which was released under the Zope Public License.

Zope's path of success began with version 2.0 which was released in 1999. It was the basis for all stable releases for around five years until Zope 3 was released. During that time, instead of selling Bobo and Principia, Digital Creations – later renamed to Zope Corporation – successfully sold its services as a software consultant and implemented solutions based on open source Zope, just like many other companies around the globe who started basing their services on Zope. Many successful open source Zope applications such as Plone, Silva, and CPS originally come from these companies and make up for a great part of the Zope community now. The wide-spread network of solution providers ensure every level of support that one can expect from an enterprise solution system.

1.4 The Python Programming Language

> *Zope magic is Python magic.*
> Jim Fulton at the EuroZope Conference Berlin 2002

Zope profits from Python's supremity. Even more, Zope would be impossible without Python. Python is a quick, easy-to-learn, Swiss Army knife-like scripting language – but so is Perl. Python also is an industrial strength, highly dynamic, object-oriented, interpreted programming language – but so is Java. What makes Python special then?

Python is easy to learn. It took me one afternoon to go through the Python tutorial [9]. Sure, I bought a few books on Python afterwards, but not for learning the language. I merely wanted to know what it was capable of.

Python is easy to read. Go and open an arbitrary python source code file in Zope 3. Chances are good that you will understand most of what is going on without actually having seen Python before. Using indentation for marking blocks certainly is the most aesthetic aspect of the language, but also the one many people have to get used to first. Obviously, it is still possible to write cryptic code in Python, but less likely.

Python is easy to write. I rarely need the library reference when programming. When developing Java, I constantly find myself looking up standard library interfaces, abstract classes, etc. Python is not as wordy as Java, but it is not as cryptic as Perl, either.

Python is easy to develop with. Not having complicated package names and large names in standard library classes, Python can easily be developed without an IDE that would ease the development process. In fact, the Zope contributor community is more or less equally split into those who use emacs and those who use vi. Moreover, Python does not require a compiler. That abandons long compiling sessions.

Python comes with batteries included. The regular Python distribution comes with a rich library of useful modules, ranging from parsers for several text file formats to email messaging and processing. That means you can get started with Python very quickly without having to collect the basic modules yourself. In case you are looking for third party packages you can use the *Python Package Index*[1] to find the software package of your desire. There are numerous third party packages available as open source which can easily be used in Zope applications, too.[2]

"Python – it fits your brain" a popular Python t-shirt reads; it sums up my programming experience with Python in one sentence. If you are new to it, you are sure to be converted to Python by the end of this book. In case you are looking for a Python book to accompany your Zope 3 development, the author can strongly recommend the excellent *Dive Into Python* by Mark Pilgrim [3].

---

[1] Python Package Index <http://www.python.org/pypi>

[2] In Chapter 12, for example, we will use *ReportLab*, a third party library for PDF generation, to generate PDF documents out of Zope content objects.

1.5 About the examples

Whenever possible, the examples in this book follow a common theme, an example application. This example application is to drive the fictitious *World Cookery* website, a website where hobby cooks from around the globe can share their recipes with each other. This particular application was chosen because it incorporates the most important characteristics of the majority of Zope-based web applications:

- There is a limited set of content object types. In the case of our example application, the primary type of content object is a *recipe*.
- Content is added in a management interface accessible through-the-web using a web browser.
- The layout of the application follows a common theme, for example a *corporate identity*.
- The application has to cope with multiple or even numerous users.
- The target audience is international, thus internationalization is required.
- Existing features must easily be extensible and new functionality easily be addable.

Because the example application is extended throughout the book, there is a version of it available for each chapter. To work with the example code of a particular chapter, simply copy the corresponding directory from the examples archive to a directory in your Python modules search path, for example your instance's `lib/python` directory, and rename it to `worldcookery` so that the package is found under the right name. See Chapter 2 for more information on installing Zope and add-on packages.

You may download an archive containing the example application from the book's website[3].

Interactive interpreter examples

As an interpreted language, Python provides us with an interactive interpreter, which is invoked by running the `python` program without arguments. This interpreter shell allows us to test code or conduct quick experiments on it. Thus you will find examples of code being typed in at the Python interpreter prompt. These lines start with >>>. If you choose not to type the sometimes admittedly lengthy example listings into your computer, but to download them, consider at least typing in these interactive interpreter sessions. It will give you a better understanding of what is going on.

You can invoke the Python interpreter usually by typing `python` at the command line. On Windows, you often need to explicitly call it from the directory it is installed in; that means you can either type something similar to `C:\Python23\python` or put the `C:\Python23` directory in the command line search path (`PATH` environment variable).

---

[3] Book website <http://www.philikon.de/book>

Also make sure that Zope's Python packages are in the interpreter's search path. This should not be a problem for Windows users, only on a Unix system you will probably have to set the PYTHONPATH environment variable, depending on where you installed the Zope software files. To test whether the interpreter can find the Zope libraries, invoke the interpreter and try to import the zope package:

```
philipp@bender:~$ python
Python 2.3.4 (#1, Jun 12 2004, 15:25:34)
[GCC 3.3 20030304 (Apple Computer, Inc. build 1640)] on
darwin
Type "help", "copyright", "credits" or "license" for
more information.
>>> import zope
Traceback (most recent call last):
  ...
ImportError: No module named zope
```

If you see this error message, then you need to set the search path variable. Quit the interpreter by hitting **Ctrl–D** and enter the following command:

```
~$ export PYTHONPATH=/usr/local/ZopeX3-3.x.y/lib/python
```

Now try again invoking the Python interpreter and importing the zope package.

Some interactive interpreter examples in this book require you having started the interpreter from your Zope instance directory. See Chapter 2 for more information on instances.

Conventions

When you encounter a particular example listing, the caption of the listing states the name of the file whose contents in shown in parentheses. For example, if an example is titled *Configuring a content type (configure.zcml)*, then look for the code in the configure.zcml file within that chapter's examples directory. If you installed the chapter's examples directory as the worldcookery package in the Zope instance, the path relative to the instance directory will be lib/python/worldcookery/configure.zcml.

The coding style and naming conventions of the Python code follow the Zope 3 coding style and naming conventions [2], Guido van Rossum's recommendations [8], and the author's personal taste (in that order).

Features in future releases

Zope is under constant development. An active community of developers constantly enhance and improve its. That means that features that are used and documented now might become obsolete in upcoming versions because they are replaced with other, better features. Alone by the time of this writing, a hand full of features were deprecated or about to be deprecated for future versions.

Why am I documenting them here? Because Zope X3.0, the Zope 3 version that this book is based on, can be used *now*. Unlike the development code, X3.0 is being used in production successfully. Even though a couple of features have been deprecated, they are known to work well and satisfy existing needs. Constant improvement is a good thing. It shows that Zope development is not standing still. Having stable versions to work with is important, too, though. The Zope 3 development cycle guarantees us both.

The following features, some well known to Zope 2 users, are still being developed on and are very likely to appear in upcoming versions of Zope 3 and if possible in upcoming editions of this book:

Indexing and searching The successor to the famous Zope Catalog and the necessary indices were still being developed at the time of this writing.

Sessions A thread-safe session framework has been added to Zope 3 already and will be released with the next release, most likely X3.1.

Relational database access Zope X3.0 already supports some functionality that allows access to relational databases. Most functionality that makes RDB integration a lot easier is not in the Zope core, though, and thus out of this book's scope.

Workflow A rudimentary workflow implementation already exists in the development tree of Zope 3. It is probably not usable for production systems, though. Different concepts of modelling workflow are being discussed and implemented for trial which might eventually lead to a usable workflow framework.

XML Even though Zope 3 itself uses XML in quite a few places (Page Templates, ZCML, etc.), it does not yet have a framework dedicated to XML processing. There have been initial prototypes, however, which were by the time of this writing being developed in external projects.

It's Open Source!

If you think that a vital feature is missing from Zope, do not hesistate to participate in development. Everyone can contribute and the community welcomes even the smallest contribution.

2

Installing Zope

Before we can start, we need to set up our environment, most importantly Zope itself. Luckily, a working Zope instance can be set up within minutes.

2.1 Requirements

Zope 3 runs on all major platforms: Microsoft Windows , Linux , Apple Mac OS X and other Unix flavours. Its disk usage of about 50 megabytes installed size is minimal compared to today's harddrive sizes. For production systems as well as development environments, a machine with a processor not too slow and a fair amount of RAM is recommended, though. This, of course, depends on the extent and complexity of the applications that are to be developed and run.

Python

Zope usually requires a specific version of Python to be used, which may change from release to release. Therefore, make sure you have the Python version installed that is mentioned in the release notes or README.txt file of your Zope 3 distribution.

Unix and Unix-like systems

Many software distributions, such as Linux and BSD distributions and Mac OS X provide default installation of Python. You can find out its version number by issuing the following command line:

```
$ python -V
Python x.y.z
```

If you do not have Python installed yet or an older version than required by Zope, please consult the packaging system of your Linux or BSD distribution to retrieve a more recent version. On Mac OS X, there are third party packaging systems available, such as Fink[1] and DarwinPorts[2].

Alternatively, you can easily install a recent Python version from source. The source packages are procied on the Python website[3]. First, download the source archive and extract it in a temporary directory, such as /tmp:

```
/tmp$ tar xzf Python-x.y.z.tgz
/tmp$ cd Python-x.y.z
```

On most systems, you can then simply enter the following three typical commands to compile Python:

```
/tmp/Python-x.y.z$ ./configure
/tmp/Python-x.y.z$ make
/tmp/Python-x.y.z$ make install
```

If you would like to install Python into a different location than the standard one in /usr, you can specify extra parameters to the configure script. Enter ./configure --help for a detailed help on the script parameters.

Windows

If you are on Windows, you can simply download the installer executable from the Python website and run it. The installer will first ask you where to install Python and its libraries. We will assume that this is the default location at C:\Python23 (depending on the Python version) here, though you are free to choose any other location. Before the actual installation begins, you can choose which components you wish to install apart from the interpreter and libraries. None of these extra items are required but some of them might be useful during development.

C compiler for source downloads

A few parts of Zope 3 are written in C, mostly for optimization. Therefore, unless you are planning to use a binary distribution of Zope, you will also need an ANSI C compiler, such as gcc. Linux and Unix systems should be equipped with the GNU compiler. On Mac OS X, you will have to install

---

[1] Fink website <http://fink.sourceforge.net>

[2] DarwinPorts website <http://darwinports.opendarwin.org/>

[3] Python website <http://www.python.org>

the Xcode utilities. On Windows, you may use the cygwin[4] collection of Unix tools which provides a Windows version of gcc, or, alternatively use Microsoft Visual C++ to compile Zope.

2.2 Download, compilation and installation

A Zope 3 distribution can be downloaded from the Zope community website[5]. On Unix systems, it may also be possible that your operating system distribution already contains a packaged version of Zope 3. In that case, please consult your packaging system in order to install this package.

Source installation (Unix)

Unless you are on a Windows system or your packaging system provides a binary install package, you will need to download the source archive. The compilation and installation follows the standard Unix procedure using a configuration script and the make program.

After having downloaded the archive, extract it in a temporary directory, such as /tmp and invoke the configure script to generate a Makefile:

```
/tmp$ tar xzf ZopeX3-3.x.y.tgz
/tmp$ cd ZopeX3-3.x.y
/tmp/ZopeX3-3.x.y$ ./configure
Configuring Zope X3 installation

Testing for an acceptable Python interpreter...

Python version x.y.z found at /usr/bin/python

The optimum Python version (x.y.z) was found at
/usr/bin/python.
```

If the configure script is given no parameters, it will try to detect any installed Python versions and use the optimum one. You can force it to use a specific Python version using the --with-python parameter, for example:

```
./configure --with-python=/usr/local/bin/python2.3
```

The Python libraries and executable scripts of Zope will be installed into the *software home*, by default /usr/local/ZopeX3-3.x.y/. This can be changed using the --prefix parameter, for example:

---

[4] Cygwin website <http://cygwin.com>
[5] Zope community website <http://zope.org>

```
./configure --prefix=/opt/ZopeX3
```

Now that the Makefile is generated, there is only left to call the make program, once to compile the Zope libraries and once more to install it into the various locations:

```
/tmp/ZopeX3-3.x.y$ make
/usr/bin/python install.py -q build
/tmp/ZopeX3-3.x.y$ make install
/opt/bin/python install.py -q build
/opt/bin/python install.py -q install
--home "/usr/local/ZopeX3-3.x.y"
```

Windows

On a Windows system, it is recommended to download the binary archive which comes in the form of a handy installer program. When you execute the installer, it will search the Windows registry for any installed Python versions. In case you have more than one installed, you can select the appropriate version and advance by clicking the *Next* button. To begin the installation, click on *Next* once more. The installer program will then install the Zope libraries into Python's library directory, usually C:\Python23\Lib\site-packages, and the executable scripts to the scripts directory, usually C:\Python23\Scripts.

Zope can be deinstalled like any other Windows program. To remove Zope from your system, go to the *Add or Remove Programs* section in the *Control Panel*, select the entry concerning Zope and invoke the *Change/Remove* button.

2.3 Setting up a Zope instance

Installing Zope itself is only one half of the whole setup. To run Zope and develop with it you will need to set up at least one *instance* which is a server instance and a database instance running together with a specific configuration and in a specific location. You can create as many parallel instances from one Zope installation as you wish and, provided the servers listen to different TCP/IP ports, run as many as you wish in parallel. We will only be needing one here, but when developing several applications simultaneously, it is often useful to create separate instances for each project. Similarly, in a server environment, different instances can be used to give different users control over their Zope applications.

On a production system, Zope instances are typically installed where other large datafiles occur, since instances contain the database files. A good place on Unix systems is /var/lib/zope. On a development system, however,

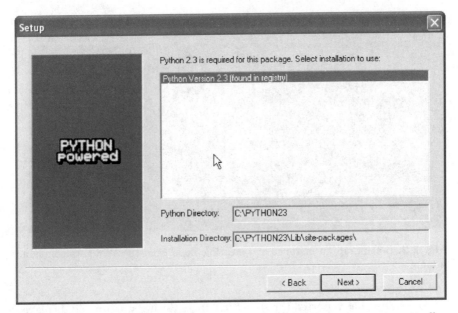

Fig. 2.1. The Windows installer detects installed Python versions automatically.

one would really like to work out of one's home directory. It is therefore recommended to simply create a Zope instance in your home directory. To do that, use the mkzopeinstance script that was installed into the executables directory:

```
~$ /usr/local/ZopeX3-3.x.y/bin/mkzopeinstance
-d Zope3Instance -u manager:secret
```

This will create an instance in the Zope3Instance directory below the current one with an initial admistrator user account manager, password secret. You can start it up by running the runzope script inside the instance's bin directory:

```
~$ cd Zope3Instance
~/Zope3Instance$ bin/runzope
```

On Windows, use the *Command Prompt* (available in the Start Menu under *Accessories*) to type in these commands. Note that the location of the scripts is different and that you have to explicitly call them with the Python interpreter:

```
C:\> C:\Python23\python C:\Python23\Scripts
\mkzopeinstance -d Zope3Instance -u manager:secret
C:\> cd Zope3Instance
C:\Zope3Instance> C:\Python23\python bin\runzope
```

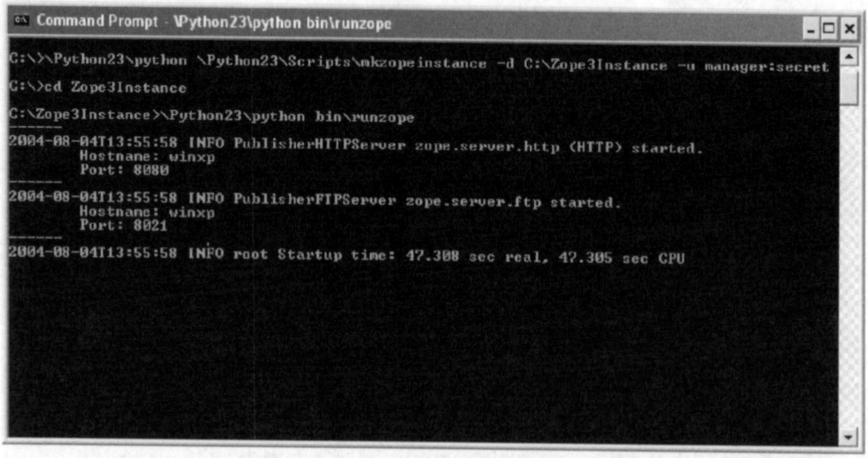

Fig. 2.2. Setting up an instance and starting Zope from the Windows command prompt.

Once Zope has reported the server instances during startup and displayed a message about the startup time, the instance is ready for request. To test whether Zope is operational, open http://localhost:8080/manage in a web browser and login with the administrator user account you provided when creating the instance. You should now see the *Zope Management Interface* (ZMI) which will be explained with more detailed further down. To stop the Zope instance, hit *Ctrl+C* in your terminal or command prompt window.

Controlling an instance

For development purposes, the runzope script is perfectly sufficient to start and terminate an instance. In a server environment, however, one often needs to start a server instance that detaches from the terminal so it will keep on running even after the terminal has been closed. This is especially useful when the server is administrated from a remote location. This functionality and more is provided for each instance in a small script, bin/zopectl. It works similarly to Apache's apachectl program or even System V init scripts. It accepts the following parameters:

start starts the detached server daemon or does nothing in case it is already running.

stop stops the detached server daemon or does nothing in case it is not running.

status shows the status of the server process, for example if it is running or not.

reload reloads the server configuration.

restart first stops and then starts the daemon again.

foreground, fg starts the server process without detaching. This is equals to calling bin/runzope.

logtail [logfile] follow the specified logfile on the terminal, equivalent to tail -f. Use *Ctrl+C* to exit.

kill [signal] sends a signal, by default SIGTERM to the daemon process.

wait wait for daemon process to finish when shutting down.

show {options|python|all} prints options about the controller script itself, the Python environment or both.

help [command] prints a list of available commands or displays information about a specific command if given.

Note that because of its nature, bin/zopectl only works on Unix-style operating systems.

Instance configuration

By default, a Zope instance's default configuration contains

- an HTTP server listening on port 8080,
- an FTP server listening on port 8021,
- a FileStorage database stored in var/Data.fs,
- an access log written to log/access.log as well as *standard output*,
- and an error log written to log/error.log as well as *standard output*.

These and other settings can be changed in the instance's configuration file, etc/zope.conf. You can use a text editor of your choice to edit this file. The syntax is similar to Apache's configuration files.

Moreover, you can and probably should configure the initial user accounts that mkzopeinstance created for you. They can be changed by editing etc/principals.zcml, an XML file containing ZCML markup. We will cover ZCML in all of the coming chapters quite extensively. Also refer to Appendix 2, ZCML Reference for a detailled reference of ZCML directives.

Zope Management Interface (ZMI)

Zope has an online, web-based administrative user interface called the *Zope Management Interface* (ZMI). It can be used not only to manage the content stored in Zope but also to administer run-time settings of the Zope instance. To log into the ZMI, open the following URL in your web browser: `http://localhost:8080/manage`, provided your Zope instance is in fact listening to port 8080 on the same machine. Zope will then ask you for authentication; use the initial user account for the administator which you provided when setting up the instance here. You will then be presented a screen similar to what Figure 2.3 shows.

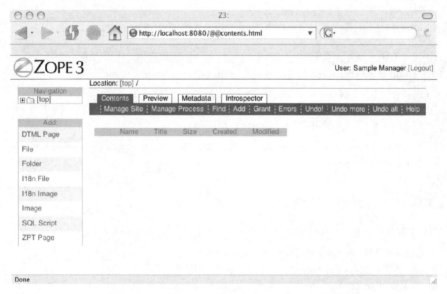

Fig. 2.3. The *Zope Management Interface* (ZMI).

For server administration, the management screens of the process controller are of particular interest. Click on *Manage Process* or enter the URL `http://localhost:8080/++etc++process/` in your web browser to view them. You can review runtime information, shutdown or restart the Zope server, and do other administrative tasks in separate screens. Note that restarting Zope only works when started using `bin/zopectl`.

We will use the ZMI in the future mostly to manage our content which can be added, edited, and deleted in ZMI screens. It is a good idea to familiarize yourself with the ZMI a bit before starting with the example application.

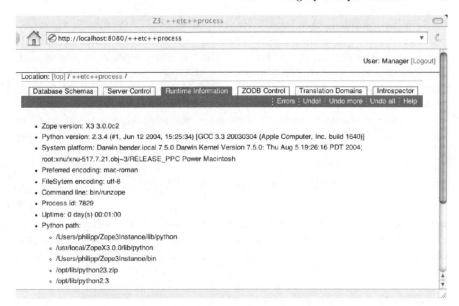

Fig. 2.4. The process administration screens of the ZMI.

Installing additional packages

A Zope instance not only has its own server and security configuration, but also its own software configuration. Apart from a small set of core packages, Zope mainly consists of more or less independent packages which, though they are installed together with Zope, are configured independently. Furthermore, applications running on Zope come as add-on packages that need to be installed and configured together with the instance.

Add-on packages that are to be used in more than once instance can be installed into Python's add-on package directory (usually `/usr/lib/python/site-packages` or `C:\Python23\Lib\site-packages`). If the package comes with a `setup.py` installation script, it will install it there by default. Instance-specific software, on the other hand, is best installed into the instance's `lib/python` directory. You can tell the `setup.py` script to use a different directory with the `--home` parameter, for example:

```
python setup.py --home=~/Zope3Instance
```

This would install the package in our instance's `lib/python` directory where it would automatically be importable for Python code running in that instance.

Each package, whether part of Zope core, the instance installation or the global Python environment, needs to be configured so the components are actually registered with Zope. Software configuration happens through ZCML, a Zope-specific XML dialect which will be introduced later in the book. When started, the Zope instance processes ZCML files in its `etc/package-includes` directory. Typically, this directory contains one file per package ending in `-configure.zcml` which simply tells the ZCML processor to process the configuration of the package in question. In rare cases, packages need to register their own ZCML directives; then they have an additional file in `etc/package-includes` ending in `-meta.zcml`.

To make an instance aware of a package, you simply need to drop one of those small ZCML files into the `package-includes` directory containing the line

```
<include package="my.python.package" />
```

where `my.python.package` is the dotted name of the package to be included. To disable the configuration of a certain package, simply rename the corresponding include file so that it does not end in `-configure.zcml` or remove it alltogether.

Installing the example application

As mentioned in the introduction, the example application will accompany us throughout the book. Since it is modified and extended in each chapter, there is a version of the `worldcookery` package available for every chapter.

To work with the example of a particular chapter, copy the corresponding directory from examples archive to your instance's `lib/python` directory, e.g. `~/Zope3Instance/lib/python` and rename it to `worldcookery`. Then, to tell Zope that is should load the package, create a file called `worldcookery-configure.zcml` in the instance's `etc/package-includes` directory, e.g. `~/Zope3Instance/etc/package-includes`, with the following contents:

```
<include package="worldcookery" />
```

When moving on to a new chapter, simply delete the `worldcookery` directory from the instance, copy over the directory from the examples archive that corresponds to the new chapter, and rename it to `worldcookery` again.

Summary

- Zope instances are created using the `mkzopeinstance` script.
- An instance's server and database configuration can be found and adjusted in `etc/zope.conf`.
- A Zope server instance is either started using the `runzope` script (Windows or development environment) or the `zopectl` program (Unix only).

- Additional packages, if instance-specific, are installed into the instance's
  lib/python directory. All add-on packages need to be configured using
  ZCML one-liners in etc/package-includes.

Flashback

Products vs. packages

The treatment of additional packages in Zope 3 is fundamentally different
in Zope 3 than it is in Zope 2. The latter does not support loading pure
Python packages that are installed somewhere in Python's package search
path. It requires add-on software to be located in a special directory called
Products. This led to the confusion of Zope 2 addons being called *products*,
which would imply that they have some sort of an economic value. That is as
incorrect as it is confusing. After all, a product is something that is sold to
a customer. A piece of software, on the other hand, deals with other pieces
of software, such as *plug-ins*, *add-ons*, etc., which is independent from the
fact whether those are sold as products or not. In Zope 3, we therefore call
software add-ons *packages* because that is what they are – Python packages.

As a consequence of Zope 3 add-ons being regular Python packages, their
location is arbitrary as long as they are in the package search path of the
Python interpreter. Of course, it is still preferrable to install software for just
a particular instance, which is what an instance's lib/python directory
is used for. Again, as the name suggests, the contents are regular Python
packages.

One a last note, it is important to realize the difference in semantics
between Zope 2 *products* and Zope 3 *packages*. Zope 2 picks up whatever is
dropped into that Products directory. While that makes it easy to install
add-ons, it makes it difficult to disable a certain add-on temporarily, for
example. In Zope 3, package configuration is explicit, meaning that you have
to explicitly tell Zope 3 to load a package. That is done using small ZCML
one-liners in an instance's etc/package-includes directory, as discussed
above.

Focus of the ZMI

Zope 2 developers will have heard the name *ZMI* before. In Zope 2, it is the
name of a user interface that allows software developers to persistently add
and manage mostly software objects, such as Python scripts, DTML methods
and Page Templates. In a few but rare cases, Zope 2's ZMI was even used
to manage content, though usually a completely new user interface was built
for this. The CMF and Silva are prominent examples of that.

The focus of the ZMI has changed in Zope 3. It is now an interface for all
purposes, but with a strong focus on content management. Only certain sections like the *Site Management* screens go beyond this scope. However, most

importantly, one must realize that the ZMI is not used for development any-more. Especially in the early days of Zope 2, through-the-web development using the ZMI was very popular, but also had little to do with developing in Python. This has changed with Zope 3 which gives pure Python development on the file system a much higher priority.

3

The Zope 3 Component Architecture

Components are not a new idea. Many other systems, for example in the Java world, have come up with their component architectures already. Is the Zope world behind its time then when it is introducing a component architecture now? Certainly not. Zope 2 was already very successful without the help of a component architecture. The persistent object database, the browser-viewable management interface which allows rapid through-the-web development, and the availability of numerous addon products convinced many web developers to build solutions using Zope and helped them attract customers from all industries all over the world. As you will see further down the line, all these features are not missing from Zope 3, either.

After a short introduction to components themselves, this chapter will cover all Zope 3 component types. You will also see that in the end, Zope 3 *is* innovative by surpassing the traditional Model-View-Controller (MVC) concept. This chapter is very theoretical compared to others. Feel free to fast forward whenever cross references to other chapters with example code are made. Still it is necessary to understand the basic concepts explained here.

3.1 Introducing components

Breaking an application down into components means dividing up responsibilities into different objects. In monolithic approaches, like original Zope 2, an object would be responsible for processing, storing, and presenting data. A powerful application with numerous objects would only be useful as long as the developer would not want to modify a certain behavior or display the stored data differently. Or what if the way data was presented were really good, but the storage not? Or the data processing?

Subclassing

Object-orientation provides two solutions for tackling this problem. A common one subclassing. A subclass derived from one or more super classes inherits all their functionality, unless it decides to override it. That certainly is a very powerful concept, allowing you as the developer to mix as many functions together in one class as you like[1]. That is a very common scheme in Zope 2. Many classes only exist because they are being "mixed in" into actual classes. Some of them even carry a `Mixin` suffix in their name. A problem with subclassing is, that you have to create a new class for every change in functionality. Often, you find your mixin classes are relying on functionality that are to be implemented by subclasses, an error-prone scheme. Moreover, changing even presentation behavior would mean writing Python code (a new subclass) even if only an HTML template has to be customized.

Delegation

The other concept is delegation. Instead of inheriting functionality from super class, work is delegated among several separate objects called *components*. Each component takes a responsibility in a complex action. For example, a presentation component is responsible for presenting data, while a content component is reponsible for storing data, and so on. When a component is not satisfactory anymore for whatever reason, it can be replaced by a better implementation, usually without impacting other components. For example, a presentation component could be exchanged without any modifications of the underlying content component. That is one of the key ideas of the Component Architecture. A common scheme is to divide components into three categories: Model, View, and Controller (MVC). The model component holds the data. It knows about its structure and often where and how to store it, if necessary. The view component presents the data. More generally, it is responsible for all user interaction. Finally, controller components implement the logic behind an application, for example sort algorithms, calculations, database lookups etc. Later in this chapter, you will see that Zope's Component Architecture knows more than just Model, View, and Controller.

Apart from exchangeable implementations of components, a large benefit of the Component Architecture is the ability to use already existing components with little or almost no modification. There are numerous Python packages providing data handling, processing and presenting functionality, why should Zope prevent you from using them? Consider a web application for handling email messages. Python already has excellent support for handling emails. The `email` package provides, apart from others, a content class `Message` which represents an email message. The `smtplib` package provides the `SMTP` utility for sending emails. In your application, you really want to

---

[1] As long as the language supports multiple inheritance, which Python does.

reuse those components instead of reinventing the wheel all over again. You really only want to add the Zope specific parts to it, meaning presentation components that would allow an email message to be displayed as HTML. Zope 2 only lets you do this by subclassing, because it expects Zope-aware objects to subclass certain mixin classes, often even in the correct order. In Zope 3, you simply add functionality, like HTML presentation or support for another network protocol like FTP, by adding components.

Summary

- Zope 3 is based on a component architecture.
- Different responsiblities are covered by different components.
- The component architecture gives developers the ability to replace implementations with better or different ones later in the development process.
- It is easy to reuse non-Zope specific third party components or make Zope-specific components usable outside Zope, respectively.

Flashback

Zope 3 is the first Zope version completely based on a component architecture, but a so-to-speak prototype was introduced with the Content Management Framework (CMF). The CMF already separates content objects from application logic and presentation. But since it is based on Zope 2, it suffers from its very limitations. For example, content objects, software components ("tools") and presentation layers still persist in the same folders and namespaces, making the developer rely on naming conventions everywhere in order to avoid name clashes.

On the other hand, the CMF allows the developer to completely customize the default application. In fact, it was designed to be customized, which probably every developer is happy to do when facing the "beauty" of the default presentation skin. A now famous third party product was born out of a customized CMF skin: Plone. It uses the CMF's architecture and many CMF default components, customizing them to the extent of hiding the CMF beneath from the user completely (the developer unfortunately still has to deal with the CMF). Ironically, the Plone documentation nowadays tells developers to customize Plone, just like CMF does.

3.2 Interfaces

When a company delegates work to another company, a legal contract listing features, conditions and most importantly the price is produced and signed by both parties. While the company providing the service has to fulfill what it promised in the contract, the customer company has the contract as a guarantee that the service provider actually does so. Both parties need the contract in order to know what service to provide or to what extent, and what service to expect, respectively. Components are no different in that respect. Components need to know what other components promise. For example, a presentation component needs to know what kind of data a content components provides.

Many programming languages have come up with a formalization of the contract concept: interfaces. Interfaces describe the methods and attributes and object provides, in other words: the API. They describe the *what* of a component (as in "what can I do with it?"), but not the *how* (as in "how does it do it"). Python sadly does not have built-in support of interfaces. One may ask whether that is even necessary or makes sense for a dynamically-typed language. Still, it forces Python products which need formalizations in the form of interfaces to come up with their own solutions. Zope 3 interface support resides in the `zope.interface` package.

Different semantics

It is important to understand the way interfaces are used in Zope, for the semantics are different than in other languages (such as Java). Thus the name *interface* might be misleading, especially for people coming from languages with different interface sematics.

While in other languages, interfaces are often used to cope with the lack of multiple inheritance, they more than often only have a symbolic value in Zope. It is important to remember that classes or objects implementing interfaces are not required to comply with what the interface promises. Interfaces cannot and do not change the semantics of the Python language, especially the dynamic typing. As we will see in the following sections, interfaces identify components by what functionality they promise to provide. In that case, they are nothing more than markers or identifiers. Other uses of interfaces are data schemas where interfaces are used to describe a data format rather than functionality.

Interfaces also serve for API documentation. If one needed to replace a component with another one, if is enough to look at the interface, which usually looks clearer and cleaner than the implementation.

Summary

- Interfaces are the contracts by which components work together.
- They are not a part of the standard Python distribution.
- Semantics differ from other languages, for example interface compliance is not enforced but implied.
- Interfaces often serve as markers/identifiers and API documentation.

How to define and declare interfaces as well as more uses than just for markers or identifiers will be covered in Chapter 4.

3.3 Content components

In general, content components are objects containing data. All they should provide is functionality to store and update that data. Data presentation (such as in HTML, XML, etc.) and processing (sorting, interpreting, transforming, etc.) should not be part of their responsibilities. Just like all other components, content components should be exchangeable as long as the new component implements the same interface, while other parts of the application should not be affected.

The majority of all applications built with Zope are content management systems. Of course, these applications revolve around content components, but even other applications need to deal with content once in a while. Undoubtedly, content components play an important role in Zope development. Fortunately, it is very easy to reuse existing content components in Zope, so the application developer can focus on the presentation and application logic. As discussed above, one of the benefits of the Component Architecture is the reusability of already existing components. That includes third party components, but also those you write yourself. Writing a content component therefore is usually not much more work than writing a simple Python class for any other application.

A simple example for a content component has already been mentioned, the `email.Message` class. Since it resides in a standard Python library package, there cannot be anything Zope specific about it. That component's uses are limited though. For example, it is not persistent in any sense. That means, instances will only be available while the thread invoked by a certain user request is being processed. After the response has been written to the user client, non-persistent objects created during that request will be garbage-collected. Unless a content object makes the data or itself persistent, the data stored in it will be lost after the request has been served out.

Object vs. relational database

Many of today's web content management systems use a relational database for data storage. They provide a reliable, efficient, scalable, and often cost-effective way to store amounts of complex data. Scripting languages like Perl and PHP make database access easy and allow the developer to build an application in a reasonable short amount of time. Unfortunately, it is very hard to evolve an application based on a relational database once the data schema is set in stone (and scripting languages with their degenerated object model additionally limit the reusability of software). Zope has come up with a better idea for storing data permanently, an object-oriented one. After all, it is called the Z *Object* Publishing Environment.

Zope's solution to the storage problem is the ZODB, the Zope Object Database. It allows one to create persistent Python objects without nearly any additional code and much knowledge about object persistency. The

ZODB is transactional, supports undo and versioning and has a pluggable backend storage architecture. All that is nearly transparent to the developer of content objects (those are the most common persistent objects) and can be used outside of Zope just as well. The ZODB, its features as well as the implementation of persistent objects and rules thereof will be covered in depth in Chapter 6.

Summary

- Content components ideally are simple Python classes usable outside Zope applications.
- Their responsibility is only to store data, not to presenting or processing it.
- Typically, content components are persistent, using the transparent object storage ZODB.

3.4 Views

Views present components in a for the user understandable way. They make the bridge between application components and the user because a user obviously does not know how to talk to a component using a Python API, even if it were documented in an interface. Actually, the end user in Zope is represented by two related objects: the request invoked by the user application, for example the HTTP request of a web browser, and the response that will be sent back to it[2]. Therefore, a view presents components in a for the *user application* understandable way. For example, if the user application were a web browser, that way were HTML. Looking at it the other way, the view should be the only part of an application that deals with the request and response objects.

Obviously views are components, too. That inevitably makes them subject to the rule that they should be replaceable by other implementations, as much as the content components they present. The common denominator, the "contract" that holds both sides together, is of course the interface the content object promises to implement and the view relies upon to present. That means in general, views cannot rely on being used with a certain class; they are *registered for interfaces*. As we will see later, this registration is not done in Python, but in special configuration files, allowing the site administrator to enable and disable, among others, view registrations without having to dive into code.

---

[2] This is not meant in the sense of user authentication, where users are indeed represented differently.

Different views for different user interfaces

Views are not solely characterized by the interface they present. For as much as there are different types of user interfaces, different types of views are necessary. Thus, apart from the interface they present, views are also registered for a certain type of request. The type of request is expressed through its interface. Zope knows the following request types[3]:

- HTTP (request interface zope.publisher.interfaces.http. IHTTPRequest), including the subprotocols WebDAV and XML-RPC.
- FTP (request interface zope.publisher.interfaces.ftp. IFTPRequest).

Additionally, different operations require different views. Some views solely display data, others allow the user to change it, for example via an HTML form. Therefore views are usually given names, so they can be identified uniquely. Those names appear in a URL, for example:

http://www.worldcookery.com/recipes/miso/@@edit.html

The path to the content object to be displayed is recipes/miso. The @@ is a shortcut for ++view++ and indicates that a view name follows and not another element in an object traversal graph[4]. What follows is the name of the view, in this case edit.html.

Summary

- Views are components that present other components.
- They are nearly the only parts in an application that deal with request and response objects.
- A view's characteristics are
  - the interface it presents
  - the type of presentation it provides
  - its name
- Views are looked up for the object they are supposed to present (the context), the view type and their name.

Flashback

Zope's view concept is roughly derived from the CMF. However, the CMF only knows the concept of views on content objects. Zope 3 generalizes that idea and allows views for any kind of component, be it content object or utility.

Views will be covered in depth in Chapter 7 and Chapter 12.

---

[3] Of course, it is possible to extend Zope's view machinery to deal with other request types.

[4] Think of the @@ as two eyes, as Jim Fulton suggested once.

3.5 Adapters

As you might have noticed, no special requirements are made on content components. They do not have to implement a special interface; nor a certain method or attribute is required in order to be used in Zope. On one hand, that lets us use nearly any third party component in Zope. On the other hand, it makes it hard for other components to expect certain functionality. For example, a directory listing often displays the size of objects listed. How would the component responsible for generating the directory listing (typically a view) know how to retrieve an object's size (if the object had a size at all)? The answer lies in adapters, a very powerful feature of the component architecture.

Plugging components together

Adapters work like adapters for a stereo. Imagine you have some strange music recorder, for example an old European tape deck, and you want to hook it up to your modern amplifier. Of course, the amplifier expects RCA plugs, but all the tape deck provides is the European five prong DIN interface. In that case, you would go into an electronics shop and buy an adapter from DIN to RCA or, if you had the parts and the tools, would solder one yourself. As expected, you will hear the ancient sounds from the tape deck when you plug it all together. To the amplifier, it frankly does not matter what device the music is coming from nor the interface it originally provided. All it cares about is that it comes in over RCA plugs. One could say, the amplifier accepts any source device which provides RCA plugs or for which an adapter to RCA is available.

If we reconsider the directory listing example, we know the answer to it now. We simply require objects to implement a certain interface that promises to be able to tell us about the object's size. If that object does not provide that interface (which is likely to be the case), we look for an adapter that adapts the object to it. Whenever we introduce some new type of component and want the directory listing to show its size, we need to supply an adapter to the expected interface. It is quite obvious now that adapters let us extend existing components as much as we like without having to change any of the original code. Adapters almost never depend on a certain implementation but only on the interfaces they adapt and provide.

Looking back at views now, we see that views are like adapters in a way. In fact, the view and adapter machinery in Zope use the same underlying logic. Views are so-called multi-adapters. Instead of adapting a single object, they adapt an object and a request. That way, different views are invoked for different requests, just as we discussed above. Like views, adapters are also registered and configured using configuration files, allowing them to be enabled, disabled, or exchanged easily.

Summary

- Adapters extend the functionality of existing components without code modifications.
- They are registered for the interface they adapt and the one they provide.
- They are looked up for the object they are supposed to adapt (the context) and the target interface.
- Views are special adapters.

Adapters will be covered in depth in Chapter 10.

3.6 Utilities

Utilities are small software components providing a certain type of limited functionality. They do not rely on any context component like views or adapters do.

Singletons

There are two typical use-cases for utilities. In the first one, a certain type of functionality is needed in an application for which one utility is registered as a singleton (meaning there is only one instance per site or application). They are registered and looked up solely by interface for, again, exchangeability of implementations. Examples for this type of utilities are:

- database connectivity, indexing, searching
- encoding/decoding, encryption/decryption
- mail delivery, browser sessions, translation negotation
- sorting, randomizing, etc.

Named utilities

Secondly, small components that occur more than once and are looked up by name within their group of components are often treated as utilities. The components are registered and looked up as utilites by *name and interface*, which identifies the type of component that is to be looked up. Typical use-cases include:

- permissions and roles
- factories
- content types
- translation domains

Summary

- A utility is a small software component that provides a certain type of limited functionality.
- A singleton is a utility that occurs only once; it is simply registered and looked up by its interface.
- Many named components of the same kind can be registered as *named* utilities; they are looked up by name and interface.

3.7 Services

Services provide fundamental functionality. The component architecture itself is based on a few services to manage the different types of components. Services are looked up with well-known names with the *service service*, a service that manages service lookups. Table 3.1 lists the standard services of the Component Architecture.

Table 3.1. Standard global services of the Component Architecture

Service name	Description
Services	Global service manager, used to define, register and look up global services.
Utilities	Used to register and look up utilities, both singletons and names utilities.
Adapters	Used to register and look up adapters, named adapters and multi-adapters.
Presentation	Used to register and look up views, multi-views, providing views and resources.

Usually you do not even have to get in touch with services at all. The zope.app.zapi package combines common look-up functionality in form of functions. Using these, you can easily look up components such as utilities and views without having to go through the extra services. We will use the zapi quite frequently in our example application. For a detailed reference, please refer to Appendix 1, ZAPI Reference.

Summary

- Services provide fundamental functionality, such as the registration and look-up of other components.
- The zope.app.zapi package combines the most essential service functionality and exposes it through a set of functions.
- Global services are available always and everywhere. Local services are registered in site managers and used to customize certain parts of an application.

3.8 Configuring components

As we have seen in the previous section, many components need to be registered with certain services in order to be used in an application, otherwise the component architecture will not know about them. Views need to be registered with the presentation service, adapters with the adapter service, etc. Where should this registration take place? It certainly is not the reponsibility of the component itself. How would a component know where and how it was going to be registered, or if it was going to be registered at all? That question really is a matter of configuration and configuration often is not even the responsibility of the site developer, but the site adminsitrator. This rules out using Python for the configuration wiring because site administrators do not want to get involved with Python code. While it might be quite comfortable for developers to use Python, it would also be tempting to mix logic and configuration, or component code and configuration. That would make the component hardly reusable outside that configuration context.

Zope Configuration Markup Language (ZCML)

Zope 3 uses an XML-based configuration language for global component configuration: the Zope Configuration Markup Language, ZCML. Since a form of text and not code is used for configuration, developers will not be tempted to mix configuration into their implementations and viceversa. XML is an web standard and many of today's text editors ease markup editing. That should justify the additional knowledge the developer has to provide, while at the same it makes it easier for the site administrator who does not have to touch Python code for enabling, disabling or exchanging a component through configuration.

Naming conventions

By convention, configuration files are named `configure.zcml`. They can be placed in any Python package. Global objects, like classes in modules or packages, are referred to using dotted names that describe their full package path, for example `email.Message` or `worldcookery.recipe.Recipe`
[5]. When an object in the same package as the configuration file is referred to, the short syntax `.recipe.Recipe` (when used in a configuration file in the `worldcookery` package) can be used. Apart from that, dotted names are often used to indicate namespaces in identifiers, for example `zope.View` (permission) or `worldcookery.Visitor` (role).

---

[5] think: `from email import Message` or `from worldcookery.recipe import Recipe`, respectively.

Summary

- Component registration is a matter of configuration.
- Zope 3 uses the XML-based ZCML language for configuration.
- Global objects are referred to using a dotted path. Both absolute and relative module paths are supported.

We will see examples of configuration entries and whole file listings in all of the following chapters.

3.9 Security

Storing, presenting, and processing data is one part of an application. Granting or denying certain functionality based on authentication is another. Especially for web applications, of which the majority is accessible over the internet, handling security plays an extremely important role. Zope promotes flexible and agile application development, therefore it needs to be equipped with a security system just as flexible and agile. This chapter introduces the key concepts of the Zope security system.

Permissions

The smallest "unit" of security assertions Zope knows is a *permission*. Most components require a certain permission for being used. Different actions require different permissions, too. While accessing a content object's data usually only requires a view permission, storing data naturally requires a different one. Who or what is in the possession of those permissions fortunately is not the components' concern, but totally in the hands of the developer or site developer.

Permissions are identified by ids (dotted names), for example zope.View (the typical view permission). One permission is always available to everybody, zope.Public. A component that is protected with this permission is practically accessible by anyone. In order to allow fine-grained security control, it is recommended to use your own set of permissions when developing custom components or whole applications. Before being used, new permissions must be defined via the ZCML directive permission.

Principals

In short, principals in Zope are entities with certain access privileges. Typically, when we speak of principals we mean users with accounts. Other applications might want to stick additional metadata on principals, for example when the data is retrieved from a directory service such as LDAP that contains not only full names but also addresses, phone numbers and the location

Table 3.2. Zope's default permissions (excerpt)

ID	Title	Description
zope.Public	Public	No security checking, available to everyone.
zope.View	View	Necessary to view objects.
zope.ManageContent	Manage Content	Add, edit and delete content objects.
zope.Security	Change security settings	Grant/revoke permissions and assign roles.
zope.ManageCode	Manage Code	Manage executable code, including Python, SQL, ZPT, etc..
zope.ManageServices	Manage Services	Add and configure services and service managers.
zope.ManageApplication	Manage Application	Manage the Zope Application, such as Restart/Shutdown or packing the ZODB.

within an organization. Then again, a principal does not necessarily have to have a login account. The *unauthenticated principal*, a principal that is always available in Zope and represents users that have not authenticated with the system, does not have a login account. You do not have to login to be unauthenticated. You simply are.

Principals are provided by a principal source, a component that is queried by the authentication service. Thus, with a custom principal source, principals can be defined almost anywhere, whether in a file on the filesystem or in tables of a relational database system. They are identified through a request which is taken care of by special, request-specific login views. For example, HTTP provides a basic authentication system, but some people prefer cookie-based authentication when using a browser. A custom login view could identify principals using cookies instead of using HTTP's authentication mechanism.

Security policy

Zope's default security policy can be summed up in one sentence: Everything is denied unless explicitly allowed. Thus, whenever you encounter a ForbiddenAttributeError, it is most of the time a lacking configuration directive explicitly allowing the attribute in question.

In Zope, security policy is a piece of machinery that decides when to allow and when to deny certain privileges. When doing so, it has to check whether the active principal has permission to perform an action or not. The default security policy, provided by the zope.app.securitypolicy package, introduces a third, very useful concept to the security machinery for this: roles

Roles

When people join in collaborative processes to do a certain job, they divide up their responsibilities among themselves. Who is reponsible for what is often given by a certain hierarchy within the group or the different abilities of the participants. It also happens more than often, people are responsible for two or more separate things. Zope calls that responsiblity a *role*.

You can also think of roles as different hats. A person might possess several hats but can really only wear one at a time (anything else would look very silly). It is the same with roles. A principal in an application might have several roles assigned, but can carry out only one at a time. A good example are the roles *Editor* and *Publisher* in a simple content management or publishing system. A person might actually have both, but before publishing something, it has to be written first! Thus the person will first wear the "editor hat" and then the "publisher hat", maybe even the "reviewer hat" while proofreading in between.

Question

What do you think are the "hats" in our *World Cookery* application ?

In terms of security assertions, a role is a logical grouping of permissions. Instead of granting or denying each individual permission to a principal, you simply assign a role. Other security policies might locate their principals in hierarchical groups and determine their permissions that way. Security policies are replaceable and can be custom implemented according to an application's needs.

Summary

- Components are secured using permissions. Different actions may require different permissions.
- The abstraction of a user in Zope is called a princpal.
- Principal sources and principal identification views can be customized for application-specific security contexts.
- A security policy determines whether a principal has permission to perform an action. The default security policy denies everything unless it is explicitly allowed.
- The default security policy abstracts user responsibilities as roles which represent a certain set of permissions and can be assigned to principals.

Flashback

The concepts of permissions and roles should sound quite familiar to the Zope 2 developer. A few semantics have changed though. Permissions are identified by IDs now and can optionally have a title and description; the same applies to roles. Permissions need to be explicitly defined through ZCML now before they can be used in security declarations. Thus, typos in security declarations do not generate new permissions anymore like it is possible in Zope 2.

Zope 2 only knows the concept of a user, whereas the CMF and Plone extend that notion and talk about Members. In order not to be limited in narrow concepts such as users or members, Zope 3 deals with principals. Zope 2 looks for users in special user folders under the ID acl_users. This service is now provided by custom principal sources. The CMF member data tool additionally could save metadata of portal members, such as fullname and email address. Zope 3 uses a standard way to store metadata on objects, annotations, which apply to principals as well (see Chapter 13).

4

Interfaces

We looked at the fundamental Zope concepts in the last chapter, largely based on the Component Architecture. Let us now start with our example application, the *World Cookery* website. First thing we need is a component to store information about recipes from all over the world in. As we have discussed in the previous chapter, components that store data are content components. Before we are going to write such a component, we need to define what kind of data it shall store and provide: we need to write an interface!

The saying "There's more than one way to do it" applies to Zope, too. In this chapter you will see how even the first step of a typical development cycle, the modelling of interfaces, can be tackled with many different approaches, of which we will discuss a few here. Considering these discussions, we will improve the implementation in each iteration. We will apply this process called *refactoring* a number of times in this book to constantly improve and adjust the code.

4.1 Interface jargon

The semantics of interfaces in Zope are a bit different than in other object-oriented languages. It therefore helps to understand the jargon typically used with interfaces, since it is also used throughout Zope's API. The main difference between Zope's interface model and others is that it is more object-centric than class-centric. In general, one does not care as much about the implementation of an object but only about the functionality a certain object provides.

In interface jargon, we say that an object *provides* an interface, just like a machine providing functionality or somebody providing a service. Objects in this case is meant in a general sense: class instances, Python modules or even interfaces themselves (since interfaces provide functionality, too!). Yet, it would be tiresome having to declare what interface each object we encounter provides. It is often easier to declare what instances of a class provide. We then say, a class *implements* an interface, which is equivalent to saying that all of the class's instances provide that interface.

Summary

- Interface jargon reflects the semantics of interfaces in Zope.
- The functionality an object provides is usually more of interest than its particular implementation.
- Classes *implement* interfaces so that their instances *provide* them.

4.2 Defining interfaces

An interface is defined by using the `class` statement and inheriting from `Interface`, which is imported from the `zope.interface` package. By convention, interface names are written in `CamelCase`[1] like classes, but with a proceeding I to indicate the difference between classes and interfaces. Standard Python syntax is used, like when defining a class with methods. Interfaces and their methods are documented using standard Python docstrings. A simple docstring as class or method body satisfies the Python syntax, meaning you do not have to use the `pass` keyword. When declaring methods for the interface, the `self` parameter is not declared either, because the interface describes how the method is used, not its implementational details.

It is another convention to put all interfaces of a package in a module called `interfaces.py`, or in case of a larger software product, in modules which reside in a package called `interfaces`.

The `IRecipeInfo` interface from Example 4.2.1 only defines methods for retrieving information about the recipe. If one needed a recipe object whose values can be set, one would either have to extend `IRecipeInfo` to provide those methods or derive a new interface from it. Deriving an interface from another works like subclassing, as demonstrated in Example 4.2.2.

With both examples, we have two interfaces of which one of them provides the information contained in a recipe, the other one additionally lets us set the data. Dividing getters and setters up into two separate interfaces certainly has its advantages. There might be components that provide recipe information but do not allow to set it. Also, as we will see later on, it is useful to separate read and write functionality when declaring permissions (reading data obviously requires different permissions that writing it). However, unless you have the before mentioned reasons for the separation, you might as well put everything in one interface with both getters and setters.

---

[1] Two or more words are concatenated to one and their first letter is capitalized. Upper and lower case letters in the resulting word suggest the image of a camel, thus CamelCase.

Example 4.2.1 An example interface (`interfaces.py`)

```
1    from zope.interface import Interface
2
3    class IRecipeInfo(Interface):
4        """Give information about a recipe.
5        """
6
7        def getName():
8            """Return the name of the dish described.
9            """
10
11       def getIngredients():
12           """Return a list of ingredients.
13           """
14
15       def getTools():
16           """Return a list of necessary kitchen tools.
17           """
18
19       def getTimeToCook():
20           """Return the time necessary for preparing the meal in
21           minutes.
22           """
23
24       def getDescription():
25           """Return the description of the recipe.
26           """
```

1. The "base" interface must be imported from the `zope.interface` package.

3. Although the `class` statement is used here, there is no class being defined. That is because `Interface` is not a class, but an object, an interface object to be exact. The `class` statement is really abused here, because it always creates a new object of the same kind as the object to extend, in this case an interface object.

7. As with the `class` statement, the `def` statements suggest a method being defined. The contrary is the case. Since `IRecipeInfo` is not a class but an interface object, the method definitions end up as special definition objects on the interface. Since these method definition objects solely *describe* real callable methods, you should omit the otherwise obligatory `self` parameter, too.

8. A Python docstring fullfills the function body syntax. It is not required to use `pass` or to even raise `NotImplemented` or similar. Any code put in the method definitions will not be executable because no method is being defined (if you want to see for yourself, try to call an interface method at the interactive interpreter shell; you will see it fails).

Example 4.2.2 Deriving from an interface (`interfaces.py`)

```
1    ...
2
3    class IRecipe(IRecipeInfo):
4        """Give and store information about a recipe.
5        """
6
7        def setName(name):
8            """Set the name of the dish provided in the 'name' parameter.
9            """
10
11       def setIngredients(ingredients):
12           """Set the ingredients necessary for this recipe provided in
13           the 'ingredients' parameter."""
14
15       def setTools(tools):
16           """Set the list of necessary kitchen tools.
17           """
18
19       def setTimeToCook(time_to_cook):
20           """Set the time necessary for preparing the meal in minutes.
21           """
22
23       def setDescription(description):
24           """Set the description of the recipe.
25           """
```

3. The `class` statement allows us to let interfaces derive from interfaces the same way classes can derive from other classes. Method and attribute definitions are inherited and can be overriden in the derived interface.

Attribute definitions

Using getters and setteres is not very pythonic, though. In Python, it is allowed to set attributes on an object from the outside. Why not declare the data as gettable and settable attributes? Consider Example 4.2.3.

As you can see in the rewritten `IRecipe` interface example, attributes are declared using instances of `Attribute` which is provided by the `zope.interface` package as well. Of course, attribute and method definitions can be mixed in an interface.

Example 4.2.3 An interface with attribute declarations (`interfaces.py`)

```
1   from zope.interface import Interface, Attribute
2
3   class IRecipe(Interface):
4       """Store information about a recipe.
5       """
6
7       name = Attribute("Name of the dish.")
8
9       ingredients = Attribute(
10          "List of ingredients necessary for this recipe.")
11
12      tools = Attribute("List of necessary kitchen tools.")
13
14      time_to_cook = Attribute(
15          "Necessary time for preparing the meal described.")
16
17      description = Attribute("Description of the recipe.")
```

Summary

- Interfaces are defined by using the `class` statement, although no class is created.
- Extending an interface works like extending a class (subclassing syntax).
- Docstrings are used to satisfy the Python block syntax and to document the API that is being defined.
- Attributes are defined using `Attribute` objects.

4.3 Declaring that an object provides an interface

When a component wants to promise to provide a certain interface, it needs to do so explicitly, otherwise the component machinery in Zope will not know so. The most common case is declaring that a class implements an interface so that its instances provide it. That is usually done using the `implements()` function in the class declaration. Consider the simple implementation of `IRecipeInfo` in Example 4.3.1.

Note that, unlike in other programming languages with interfaces, no actual checking is enforced. `RecipeInfo` may choose to implement less than it promises through the interface. That per se will not let the application fail. However, if other components rely on `RecipeInfo` implementing the whole interface, the application will sooner or later break at the point where components are trying to use the part of the interface the class does not implement. In conclusion, interface compliance is *assumed*, not enforced, though the interface machinery provides utilities for verification (see below).

Example 4.3.1 A simple implementation of the `IRecipeInfo` interface (`recipe.py`)

```
1   from zope.interface import implements
2   from worldcookery.interfaces import IRecipeInfo
3
4   class RecipeInfo(object):
5       """Give information about a recipe.
6       """
7       implements(IRecipeInfo)
8
9       def __init__(self, name, ingredients, tools, time_to_cook,
10                      description):
11          self.name = name
12          self.ingredients = ingredients
13          self.tools = tools
14          self.time_to_took = time_to_cook
15          self.description = description
16
17      def getName(self):
18          return self.name
19
20      def getIngredients(self):
21          return self.ingredients
22
23      def getTools(self):
24          return self.tools
25
26      def getTimeToCook(self):
27          return self.time_to_cook
28
29      def getDescription(self):
30          return self.description
```

7.   The `RecipeInfo` class promises to implement the `IRecipeInfo` interface by using the `implements()` function in the class body. `implements()` takes an arbitrary number of arguments, thus you can use it to declare several interfaces at one time.

17 – 30.   Below the constructor method (`__init__`), you find the implementations of the five methods promised by the interface.

There also are other ways of declaring that a component implements an interface. The `classImplements()` function declares an interface on an already existing class. This is useful when third party components are being used in Zope 3 and source code modification is not possible or unwanted. The `directlyProvides()` function declares an interface on an object that has already been instantiated. This is mostly used for marker interfaces which are interfaces that do not promise any methods or attributes to be implemented but mark the object that implements them in a certain way. Zope 3 makes use of a few marker interfaces as we will see later on. Consider the follow-

ing example code for classImplements() and directlyProvides(),
typed in at the Python interpreter prompt:

```
>>> class RecipeInfo:
...     pass
...
>>> from worldcookery.interfaces import IRecipeInfo
>>> IRecipeInfo.implementedBy(RecipeInfo)
False
>>> chilaquiles = RecipeInfo()
>>> IRecipeInfo.providedBy(chilaquiles)
False
```

Here we actually see a proof for why interfaces are not classes but special objects, because they have implementedBy() and providedBy() methods
which return True when the argument implements or provides the interface, respectively, and False otherwise. Interfaces have many more methods
which are all documented in (surprise!) an interface, IInterface. In the
example, the chilaquiles object as an instance of the RecipeInfo class
does not implement the IRecipeInfo interface, just as we expected.

```
>>> from zope.interface import directlyProvides
>>> directlyProvides(chilaquiles, IRecipeInfo)
>>> IRecipeInfo.providedBy(chilaquiles)
True
```

Now the chilaquiles object, and only this object, provides the interface,
as the providedBy method verifies:

```
>>> posole = RecipeInfo()
>>> IRecipeInfo.providedBy(posole)
False
>>> from zope.interface import classImplements
>>> classImplements(RecipeInfo, IRecipeInfo)
>>> IRecipeInfo.implementedBy(RecipeInfo)
True
>>> IRecipeInfo.providedBy(posole)
True
```

This last example demonstrates how to declare an interface on a whole class
afterwards. The instance posole at first does not provide IRecipeInfo.
But when the interface is declared on its class, the instance automatically
provides the interface.

Note that although it is the common case, interfaces do not necessarily have to describe what a certain *class* implements. We have already seen that it is possible to say that only a certain object provides an interface without its class implementing it. Moreover, interfaces can be used to describe what functions a Python module provides. In order to declare an interface on a module, use the `moduleProvides()` function. Those and other functions provided by the `zope.interface` package are documented in the `IInterfaceDeclaration` interface in `zope/interface/interfaces.py` (which is, by the way, the best example of an interface describing what a Python module or package provides.).

Summary

- Classes *implement* interfaces so that their instances *provide* them.
- Interfaces are typically declared on classes using the `implements()` function in the class body.
- It is also possible to declare that a single object or even a Python module provides an interface.
- An interface's `providedBy()` method informs whether an object provides that interface.

4.4 Verifying implementations

As mentioned before, interfaces are a Zope-specific addition and not part of Python, thus declarations in interfaces are not enforced. The interface package though provides a way to verify whether a class or an object conforms with the interface it implements when needed.

```
>>> from zope.interface.verify import verifyClass
>>> from zope.interface import implements
>>> from worldcookery.interfaces import IRecipeInfo
>>> class NotARecipeInfo:
...     implements(IRecipeInfo)
...
>>> verifyClass(IRecipeInfo, NotARecipeInfo)
Traceback (most recent call last):
  File "<stdin>;", line 1, in ?
  ...
zope.interface.exceptions.BrokenImplementation:
  An object has failed to implement interface
  <InterfaceClass interfaces.IRecipeInfo at 3008cfd0>

      The getName attribute was not provided.
```

As expected, `verifyClass` finds that `NotARecipe` does not implement the `IRecipeInfo` interface. The contrary is the case with the `RecipeInfo` class we defined in Example 4.3.1; it fulfills the interface:

```
>>> from worldcookery.recipe import RecipeInfo
>>> verifyClass(IRecipeInfo, RecipeInfo)
True
```

Sometimes classes cannot implement an interface right away, because the constructor method (`__init__`) might have to set some initial attributes. In this case, the `zope.interface.verify` module provides the `verifyObject` function which verifies an object instance against the interface specified. It is used like `verifyClass` as shown above, only with an object as argument.

Summary

- Interface compliance is implied and not enforced at runtime.
- The `zope.interface.verify` module provides a tool for the developer to verify that implementations concurr with what the interface defines.

4.5 Schemas

As we have seen previously, simple content objects usually do not need methods because all they are responsible for is storing data. That can easily be done in instance attributes; defining setters and getters is not complicated but quite verbose and frankly very unpythonic. We have also seen that we can describe required attributes in interfaces using `Attribute` objects. However, even in the simple `IRecipeInfo` example above, it is quite obvious that one could supply much more information about each field than just a docstring. For example, we see that name should be a one line text string while `time_to_cook` should store an integer. Even though Python is dynamically-typed, we are absolutely certain that these attributes should only contain values of a certain form.

If we continue that thought and define the type of each attribute we have defined in the interface before, we end up with what is called a *schema*. Much like in a table schema known from relational databases, each property is called a *field*. Different fields imply different type constraints. Integer fields imply that values in those fields must be integers, for example. Sure you can think of many other field types.

Defining schemas

Schemas are defined exactly like interfaces. There is no special schema object to derive from. However, instead of using `Attribute`, we now use fields provided by the `zope.schema` package to describe attributes. Table 4.1 lists the standard field types provided by Zope 3 and the type they describe. Since schemas and interfaces are semantically and syntactically the same thing, an interface with method definitions can just as well contain schema fields and

Table 4.1. Schema fields from `zope.schema`[2]

Field type	Type constraint
Abstract fields (mostly used for subclassing)	
Field	Simple field without any type contraint (unless a custom one is provided), base class for all other fields.
Container	Object supporting the in operator, meaning it has to provide either __contains__ or __getitem__.
Iterable	Object supporting iteration, meaning it has to provide either __iter__ or __getitem__.
Fields for standard python types	
Bool	Boolean value (bool).
Int	Integer (int).
Float	Float (float).
Text	Unicode text (unicode).
TextLine	Like Text, but without newline characters.
Bytes	Byte string (str), useful for binary data.
BytesLine	Like Bytes, but without newline characters.
Tuple	Tuple (tuple).
List	List (list).
Dict	Dictionary (dict).
Set	Set (sets.Set).
Date	Date value (datetime.date).
Datetime	Date and time value (datetime.datetime).
Fields with special contraints	
Password	A TextLine used for storing passwords.
SourceText	A Text field that holds the source of some computed output.
ASCII	A string containing only ASCII characters.
InterfaceField	Interface (zope.interface.Interface).
Object	Arbitrary object providing a schema.
URI	A BytesLine that holds a Uniform Resource Identifier (URI).
DottedName	A BytesLine that contains a dotted name.
Id	A BytesLine that contains either a URI or a dotted name.

---

[2] This list does not aim at being complete. It only tries to give an overview over the most important fields.

Table 4.2. Schema field parameters/attributes

Name	Type	Description
`title`	`TextLine`	Label for the field.
`description`	`Text`	Longer description.
`required`	`Bool`	Require the existance of the value exclusive with (mutally `default`). Defaults to `True`.
`readonly`	`Bool`	Determine whether the field's value can be changed.
`default`	`Field`	The default value if none was provided (mutually exclusive with `required`).
`missing_value`	`Field`	In the case of missing input value, the value provided here is used.
`order`	`Int`	Gives information about the order in which fields in a schema are defined. This is a readonly attribute.
`min, max`	`Int or Float`	Limit the numeric range of `Int` and `Float` fields.
`min_length, max_length`	`Int`	Require a minimum and/or maximum length. Applicable to all sequence and string fields.
`allowed_values`	`Container`	The field value can only contain one of the specified values. Applicable to all enumerated fields.

viceversa. It is all interfaces to Zope. Example 4.5.1 demonstrates what a schema definition looks like.

In Example 4.5.1, we see that all fields are passed nearly the same arguments, such as `title` and `description`. Table 4.2 gives an overview over possible field arguments. All arguments to the field constructor listed below are also attributes of the field instance. We see that field parameters/attributes are defined through a schema as well, since they have to comply with certain field constraints (e.g. `title` has to be a `TextLine`, that is why we have to pass a unicode string)[3].

All arguments to the field constructor are optional and only have to provided to the necessary extent. However, providing at least the title and a longer descriptive text is useful not only for documentation, but also for application purposes, such as automatically generated forms (see Chapter 7).

Introspecting schemas

Sometimes it is useful to introspect schemas, for example when you want to retrieve a list of the fields a schema carries. Since schemas are just plain interfaces and could contain, apart from fields, standard method or attribute

---

[3] Like interfaces, schemas also "eat their own dogfood" by using a schema to define what fields must look like while schemas are composed of fields.

declarations, an interface's names() or namesAndDescriptions() methods would not only return fields, but the other declarations, too. That would not be too useful. For the case that you would only like to know about a schema's fields, the zope.schema package provides a few functions for introspecting schemas as listed in Table 4.3.

Table 4.3. Schema introspecting functions provided by zope.schema

Function	Parameters	Description
getFieldNames	*schema*	Returns a list of the fields' names defined in *schema*.
getFields	*schema*	Returns a dictionary containing a mapping of field names to fields defined in *schema*.
getFieldsInOrder	*schema*	Returns a list of (name, field) tuples in the order the fields are defined in *schema*.
getFieldNamesInOrder	*schema*	Returns a list of the fields' names in the order they are defined in *schema*.

Summary

- Interfaces can be used to describe data schemas.
- Instead of attribute declarations, fields usually expressing type constraints are used to describe the schema.
- The zope.schema package provides many basic field types.

Writing content objects that provide a schema and the automatic validation of schema compliance will be covered in Chapter 5. Vocabularies, an advanced schema-related feature, is the subject of Chapter 16.

Flashback

The ones among you with experience in Plone development are probably already familiar with schemas from the Archetypes product. Archetypes is, among other things, a framework for rapid development of content objects for Plone. Like in Zope 3, a schema describing the data layout of the content type using fields is defined. That schema is just like any object, though, while in Zope 3, a schema is an interface. Since Zope 3 uses interfaces as formal contracts between components, or even for practical things like security assertions, the developer benefits from schemas being an interface everywhere. There are also large differences in the implementation of schema-based content types as we will see in the next chapter.

Example 4.5.1 Defining a schema (`interfaces.py`)

```
1  from zope.interface import Interface
2  from zope.schema import List, Text, TextLine, Int
3
4  class IRecipe(Interface):
5      """Store information about a recipe.
6      """
7
8      name = TextLine(
9          title=u"Name",
10         description=u"Name of the dish",
11         required = True
12         )
13
14     ingredients = List(
15         title=u"Ingredients",
16         description=u"List of ingredients necessary for this recipe.",
17         required=True,
18         value_type=TextLine(title=u"Ingredient")
19         )
20
21     tools = List(
22         title=u"Tools",
23         description=u"List of necessary kitchen tools",
24         required=False,
25         value_type=TextLine(title=u"Tool")
26         )
27
28     time_to_cook = Int(
29         title=u"Time to cook",
30         description=u"Necessary time for preparing the meal described, "
31         "in minutes.",
32         required=True
33         )
34
35     description = Text(
36         title=u"Description",
37         description=u"Description of the recipe",
38         required=True
39         )
```

2.   The zope.schema package provides field types for the most common types of objects, such as Python lists, integers, and unicode strings.

4.   As mentioned before, Zope does not distinguish between interfaces and schemas, the difference is pure nomenclature.

8–39. Fields on the schema are specified like Attribute definitions on a regular interface, however with a rich set of parameters that document the field and describe the constraints.

5

Content Components

5.1 Content types

The previous chapter demonstrated what interfaces of content components can look like. Schemas have proven to be most suitable for this kind of component, since we often think in terms of data schemas. Yet to Zope, a content component's interface (or schema, respectively) is just another interface, even though we imply more than a formal contract between components. By defining an interface for content components, we really mean to define a new *content type*. The interface then works as a content type identifier. Following our example, recipes would be of the content type `IRecipe`. Note that not the name "IRecipe" is the identifier but the interface itself!

Content types are interfaces with the added notion that they are meant to be for content components. A component might provide several interfaces, but it typically only provides one content type. We also say "the object is of the type *content type*" or "the object's type is *content type*". Of what type an interface is is declared via the ZCML `interface` directive:

Example 5.1.1 Configuring a content type (`configure.zcml`)

```
1  <configure xmlns="http://namespaces.zope.org/zope">
2
3    <interface
4        interface=".interfaces.IRecipe"
5        type="zope.app.content.interfaces.IContentType"
6        />
7
8  </configure>
```

The ZCML code in Example 5.1.1 is equal to providing `IContentType` directly on `IRecipe`:

```
>>> from zope.interface import directlyProvides
>>> from interfaces import IRecipe
```

```
>>> from zope.app.content.interfaces import \
...       IContentType
>>> directlyProvides(IRecipe, IContentType)
```

It is perfectly okay to stumble at this point. An interface that provides
an interface? Sounds complicated. But if we think about it for a minute,
it makes perfect sense. Interfaces provide IInterface, which promises
methods we have already used, like providedBy and implementedBy.
IContentType merely extends IInterface, it does not declare additional
methods or attributes. Interface providing IContentType only promise to
be content types. Since IContentType only implies that promise and cannot
express it in terms of methods and attributes, we call it a *marker interface*.
That way, checking whether an interface is a content type or not is simply a
matter of checking whether it provides IContentType.

Querying an object's content type

When you deal with content components, you often might want to know its
content type. For example, when you have a tabular folder listing containing
a number of different content objects, you might want to display each object's
name and type. You could use the providedBy from the zope.interface
package to retrieve a list of interfaces each object provides. The only problem
is that objects can provide many interfaces at a time. It would be quite
complicated having to figure out every time which one of them is a content
type.

Zope has a shortcut for this problem. The zope.app.content package
provides the queryContentType function. It takes an object as argument
and returns its content type. In case the object has more than one content
type, it returns the first one it finds; in case the object does not provide a
content type at all, it returns None. The following example demonstrates
the usage of queryContentType. Note that for it to work, IRecipe must
be a content type, meaning it must provide IContentType. The previous
example from the Python interpreter shows you how to set that up.

```
>>> # load configuration; start Python in your Zope
instance directory
>>> from zope.app.debug import Debugger
>>> debugger = Debugger(db="var/Data.fs",
...                      config_file="etc/site.zcml")
>>>
>>> from zope.interface import implements, providedBy
>>> from zope.app.content import queryContentType
>>> from zope.app.interfaces.annotation import \
...       IAttributeAnnotatable
>>> from interfaces import IRecipe
>>>
```

```
>>> class Recipe:
...        implements(IAttributeAnnotatable, IRecipe)
...
>>> meatballs = Recipe()
>>> list(providedBy(meatballs))
[<InterfaceClass zope.app.interfaces.annotation.
IAttributeAnnotatable at 3023df90>,
<InterfaceClass interfaces.IRecipe at 30096330>]
>>> queryContentType(meatballs)
<InterfaceClass interfaces.IRecipe at 30096330>
```

The example demonstrates the difference between providedBy and query-
ContentType. Instances of the Recipe class do not only provide IRecipe,
but also the marker interface IAttributeAnnotatable. We will cover
later what that means, for now it is just important that recipes provide two
interfaces. But only one of them is a content type, as the different outputs of
providedBy and queryContentType demonstrate.

Browsing interfaces in the ZMI

By marking IRecipe as a content type, we have also registered it as a
named utility providing IContentType. The Zope Management Interface
(ZMI) lets us browse through all registered interfaces (utilities providing
IInterface), which includes content types (as IContentType extends
IInterface). Click on *Manage Site* in the blue bar to enter the site management area. Then click on the *Interface Browse* tab. You should see a screen
like the one shown in Figure 5.1. If you find IRecipe in this list and click on
it, you will be shown a page listing detailed information about the interface,
including the schema fields, their types and their description, as shown in
Figure 5.2.

The ZMI interface browser is one of Zope's interactive documentation
tools. You can use it whenever you need to information about a certain interface and prefer not to read the source code itself. As you can see, we have
discovered yet another advantage of interfaces – interactive API documentation.

Summary

- When interfaces describe pure content objects we call them content types.
- Content type interfaces provide IContentType, which is derived from
  IInterface.
- Interfaces are made content types through ZCML configuration using the
  interface directive.
- queryContentType returns an object's content type interface, if it has
  one.

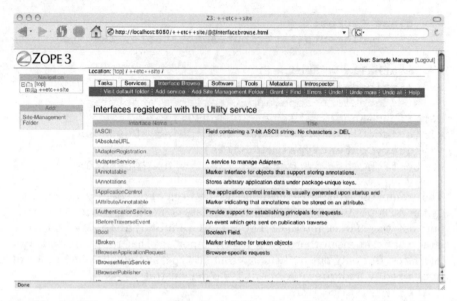

Fig. 5.1. The interface browser in the site management section of the ZMI.

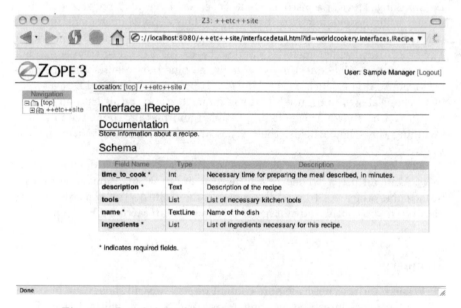

Fig. 5.2. Detailed display of the IRecipe interface in the ZMI.

Flashback

Zope 2 distinguishes kinds of objects by their *meta type*, a simple string attribute of the objects. In order to make objects work with Zope 2, they need to carry that attribute. Since Zope 2 by itself does not distinguish between application objects such as a session manager and content objects, the Content Management Framework (CMF), gives content objects yet another mandatory attribute, the *portal type*.

Zope 3 has neither meta type nor portal type. It uses a more subtle and at the same time meaningful way: interfaces. Plain interfaces can be seen as the Zope 3 equivalent of the meta type, while content types (which are interfaces, too) replace the portal type attribute.

5.2 Schema-based content

In Example 4.3.1, we have seen what an implementation of a regular interface looks like. It is pretty straight-forward. All you have to do is implement every method as described in the interface. Implementing a schema is even easier, at least most of the time. All you have to do is provide sane default values for the fields described in the schema, as Example 5.2.1 demonstrates.

Example 5.2.1 Implementing a schema (`recipe.py`)

```
1   from zope.interface import implements
2   from worldcookery.interfaces import IRecipe
3
4   class Recipe:
5       implements(IRecipe)
6
7       name = u''
8       ingredients = []
9       tools = []
10      time_to_cook = 0
11      description = u''
```

That class could not be simpler. Except for the import of the `zope.interface` package, this class could be perfectly usable outside Zope. Maybe you might want to give it a constructor that sets some initial values, but that is not even necessary. The fact that it implements a schema, does not mean that its attributes are constrained to conform with the schema, though. Remember, interfaces are not enforced! Consider the following example of a schema violation on this class:

```
>>> from recipe import Recipe
>>> strudel = Recipe()
```

```
>>> strudel.time_to_cook
0
>>> strudel.time_to_cook = "Well, about an hour"
>>> strudel.time_to_cook
'Well, about an hour'
```

The class defines default attributes with the correct types as specified in the schema. But then some "bad application code", like the above, sets the time_to_cook attribute, which is supposed to be an integer, with a string. Since Python is a dynamically typed language and Zope 3 interfaces definitions are not enforced on implementations, no error is raised. However, your application depending on time_to_cook being an integer could fail horribly. Imagine that in one part of the application you would have to sum up the necessary time for preparing several recipes, for example the aperitif, main dish and dessert of a large meal. Then your application would break and the problem would not even be in the aggregation code.

Luckily, Zope has a solution for that. First of all, the form widget framework which allows one to change a schema-based content object's data through the web, validates all input against the schema and if it has validated, converts it to the right data type. Thus, most of the time you do not even have to worry about that problem and you can rely on these very simple implementations of a schema. However, if you do need explicit validation, for whatever reason, here are your options:

Validate parameters passed to a method

Let's take Recipe and extend it with a method that validates incoming values according to the schema (Example 5.2.2).

We can now use the update method to update instances of Recipe. When we pass a string for the time_to_cook attribute like before, we expect an error to be raised, while it should let us set an integer:

```
>>> from recipe import Recipe
>>> strudel = Recipe()
>>> strudel.time_to_cook
0
>>> strudel.update(time_to_cook="Well, about an hour")
Traceback (most recent call last):
  File "<stdin>", line 1, in ?
  File "recipe.py", line 21, in update
    IRecipe[key].validate(value)
  ...
zope.schema._bootstrapinterfaces.ValidationError:
(u'Wrong type', 'Well, about an hour', (<type 'int'>,
<type 'long'>))
```

```
>>> strudel.update(time_to_cook=45)
>>> strudel.time_to_cook
45
```

As we see, keyword parameters passed to update() are validated. A field's
validate method raises ValidationError when validation fails. Validation-
Error can be imported from the zope.schema package.

Example 5.2.2 Using a schema's fields for validation (recipe.py)

```
 1  from zope.interface import implements
 2  from zope.schema import getFieldNames
 3  from worldcookery.interfaces import IRecipe
 4
 5  class Recipe:
 6      implements(IRecipe)
 7
 8      name = u''
 9      ingredients = []
10      tools = []
11      time_to_cook = 0
12      description = u''
13
14      def update(self, **kw):
15          # retrieve a list of the names of the schema's fields
16          field_names = getFieldNames(IRecipe)
17          for key, value in kw.items():
18              if key not in field_names:
19                  raise TypeError, "Invalid field to set: %s" % key
20              field = IRecipe[key]
21              field.validate(value)
22              setattr(self, key, value)
```

20. Declarations in interfaces, such as schema fields, can be accessed using
    the index notation, also known as the __getitem__ protocol. For exam-
    ple, IRecipe['time_to_cook'] refers to the integer field describing the
    time_to_cook attribute (see Example 4.5.1, line 28.)

21. Every field has a validate method that validates an object against the field
    constraint. A ValidationError exception is raised if the value does not val-
    idate.

Validation upon attribute setting

We can now validate values according to schema fields, but we have to do so
manually, by calling a special update method. It would really be much nicer
if we could simply set the attributes on instances and still have the values

validated, in case bad application code would ignore the update method.
Python allows such validation upon attribute setting through property
objects. They allow us to execute any business logic when an attribute is
read from or written to an instance, such as validation.

Fortunately, the Zope schema machinery already provides us with a vali-
dating property implementation. FieldProperty, provided by the zope.
schema.fieldproperty module, also returns the default value if an attribute has not yet been set on the instance. With it we can now rewrite our
Recipe implementation, as shown in Example 5.2.3.

Example 5.2.3 Using the schema machinery to auto-validate instance attributes (recipe.py)

```
1   from zope.interface import implements
2   from zope.schema.fieldproperty import FieldProperty
3   from worldcookery.interfaces import IRecipe
4
5   class Recipe(object):
6       implements(IRecipe)
7
8       name = FieldProperty(IRecipe['name'])
9       ingredients = FieldProperty(IRecipe['ingredients'])
10      tools = FieldProperty(IRecipe['tools'])
11      time_to_cook = FieldProperty(IRecipe['time_to_cook'])
12      description = FieldProperty(IRecipe['description'])
```

That implementation is quite compact. There are two things to note about
it. First, Python's property feature only works with *new-style classes*[1]. That
is why we have to subclass from object now. Otherwise, FieldProperty
cannot assume control over the attribute. Second, FieldProperty needs
to know which field to validate against. Thus, we have to pass it the corresponding field each time, which we can get from IRecipe using the index
notation, as already discussed above.

Let us now try out the new implementation:

```
>>> from recipe import Recipe
>>> strudel = Recipe()
>>> strudel.time_to_cook = "Well, about an hour"
Traceback (most recent call last):
  File "<stdin>", line 1, in ?
  ...
```

---

[1] New-style classes were introduced in Python 2.2. They are a new implementation
of classes in Python supporting a number of new features, such as slots, properties
and a new class inheritance resolution. Please refer to A. M. Kuchling's *What's
New in Python 2.2* [19] for more information.

```
zope.schema._bootstrapinterfaces.ValidationError:
(u'Wrong type', 'Well, about an hour', (<type 'int'>,
<type 'long'>))

>>> strudel.time_to_cook = 45
>>> strudel.time_to_cook
45
```

As expected, setting a string to the integer attribute time_to_cook fails as
a ValidationError is raised. Setting an integer works as expected and the last
two lines prove that the instance is storing the value correctly.

Summary

- A simple implementation of a schema is straightforward since it is only
  about storing a certain set of attributes.
- For some applications, it is necessary to validate the values to be stored.
  Fields provide a validate method for that.
- A schema's fields can be accessed through the index notation, a.k.a.
  getitem protocol.
- FieldProperty allows one to transparently validate the attributes that
  are set on a class.

5.3 Configuration

We now have several implementations for recipes, each of them good for
different purposes. For future examples however, we will only rely on the
implementation shown in Example 5.2.3. If you would like, you can also
use the shorter implementation shown in Example 5.2.1. The only difference
between them is that the latter does not validate attributes being set to its
instances, an aspect which shall not be of importance in future examples.

So how do we make this implementation usable in Zope now? The answer
is simple: We need to configure it! First of all, we need tell Zope about the
class and restrict its use with security declarations. Remember that in Zope,
everything is forbidden unless explicitly allowed.

As we see in Example 5.3.1, the content directive is used to configure
content components. It is a *complex directive*, meaning it expects subdirectives. The only subdirective used in this example is the require directive.
It is used to configure a class's security. The first require directive tells the
security proxy wrapping recipes to require the zope.View when accessing
the given set of attributes, which happen to be the attributes defined in the
IRecipe schema. A method in a security context is treated like an an instance's attribute and is protected the same way. Attributes obviously cannot
only be read, but also written. Thus, the second require directive protects

Example 5.3.1 Configuring a content component's security (`configure.zcml`)

```
1   <configure xmlns="http://namespaces.zope.org/zope">
2
3     <interface
4         interface=".interfaces.IRecipe"
5         type="zope.app.content.interfaces.IContentType"
6         />
7
8     <content class=".recipe.Recipe">
9       <require
10          permission="zope.View"
11          attributes="name ingredients tools time_to_cook description"
12          />
13      <require
14          permission="zope.ManageContent"
15          set_attributes="name ingredients tools time_to_cook description"
16          />
17      </content>
18
19  </configure>
```

10 and 14. Notice the usage of dotted names. The ones used here refer to *permissions* which have been registered with that identifier.

8.   Here we also use a dotted name, but this time it refers to a global python object located in a module or package. The leading dot stands for the package the configuration file is located in, in this case the worldcookery package. This way, we can write .recipe.Recipe instead of worldcookery.recipe.Recipe. This is a real space saver when you have deep package structures, since absolute package paths can get pretty long.

attribute setting on Recipe instances with the zope.ManageContent permission.

In case we decide to extend the IRecipe schema with another field, we would have to update both require directives to list that additional attribute. Also, some schemas can be quite large, which would make configuration quite inconvenient. The ZCML machinery luckily provides a shortcut. In Example 5.3.2, we configure the class's security using the schema. The ZCML machinery knows how to inspect the schema and thus knows which attributes we mean.

Summary

- Content components are configured using the complex content ZCML directive.
- A class's attributes, including its methods, are configured using the require subdirective.

Example 5.3.2 Using interfaces/schemas for security declarations (`configure.zcml`)

```
1   <configure xmlns="http://namespaces.zope.org/zope">
2
3     <interface
4         interface=".interfaces.IRecipe"
5         type="zope.app.content.interfaces.IContentType"
6         />
7
8     <content class=".recipe.Recipe">
9       <require
10          permission="zope.View"
11          interface=".interfaces.IRecipe"
12          />
13      <require
14          permission="zope.ManageContent"
15          set_schema=".interfaces.IRecipe"
16          />
17    </content>
18
19  </configure>
```

Flashback

Zope 2 supports several ways of protecting a class's methods and attributes with security declarations, of which the newest one, *declarative security* using the `ClassSecurityInfo` class, is perceived to be the most elegant way. Either way enforces one to mix security declarations right into the code that is to be protected. That makes it impossible to use and protect third party classes in Zope 2 and to use classes written for Zope 2 outside Zope applications. Also, security checking is only activated if the special function `InitializeClass`, formerly `default_class_init_`, is called on the class. It is a common mistake to forget to call this function, thus leaving class instances openly accessible.

5.4 Advanced: Factories

Factories are not specific to content objects, but are typically used and configured with them, so it makes sense to cover them here. A factory is another component type in the Component Architecture, but a less important one. Factories are responsible for making instances of a particular class. In plain Python, a class itself is usually used to make instances. That is still true in Zope, but sometimes you might want to do something before or after an instantiation of a class, or you might simply regulate permissions for instantiation of a particular object. For those cases, factories can be used to instantiate objects. The simplest case is using a *factory from class*, using the class itself to instantiate new objects, like in plain Python. The content directive supports a factory subdirective for this which registers a new factory for the component.

Example 5.4.1 Defining a factory for content components (configure. zcml)

```
1   <configure xmlns="http://namespaces.zope.org/zope">
2
3     <interface
4         interface=".interfaces.IRecipe"
5         type="zope.app.content.interfaces.IContentType"
6         />
7
8     <content class=".recipe.Recipe">
9       <factory
10          id="worldcookery.Recipe"
11          title="Create a new recipe"
12          description="This factory instantiates new recipes"
13          />
14      <require
15          permission="zope.View"
16          interface=".interfaces.IRecipe"
17          />
18      <require
19          permission="zope.ManageContent"
20          set_schema=".interfaces.IRecipe"
21          />
22    </content>
23
24  </configure>
```

9–13. The factory subdirective allows us to set descriptive title and description parameters, apart from the mandatory ID. We do not set a permission because factories are *code components*, meaning they neither store, present or process data. Code components are not protected, rather the objects the code works with. In case of the factory, the component that gets created is protected, not the factory itself.

Example 5.4.1 defines a factory from class with the id worldcookery .Recipe. Factories from class make instances by directly calling the class (in this case the Recipe class). If the class has a constructor method (__init__), it may not take any arguments. Using the factory instead of the class, we can now make new recipe instances without having to import the Recipe class. This indirection allows us to decouple the implementation of recipes from the instantiation in the following application code:

```
>>> from zope.app.debug import Debugger
>>> debugger = Debugger(db="var/Data.fs",
...                         config_file="etc/site.zcml")
```

```
>>>
>>> from zope.component.interfaces import IFactory
>>> from zope.app import zapi
>>> recipe_factory = zapi.getUtility(
...     IFactory, u"worldcookery.Recipe")
>>> weisswurst = recipe_factory()
>>> weisswurst
<worldcookery.recipe.Recipe object at 0x30469c30>
```

Note how factories are not a special type of component. They are named utilities. That is why we use getUtility to acquire the factory. We can also instantiate recipes in a shorter way by using the createObject function:

```
>>> weisswurst = zapi.createObject(
...     None, u"worldcookery.Recipe")
>>> weisswurst
<worldcookery.recipe.Recipe object at 0x308d8210>
```

This is much shorter since neither IFactory has to be imported nor a factory be instantiated. The createObject function takes a location as first argument, which is only interesting when dealing with local component defintions. Since we are currently working in a global context, the location argument is None.

Custom factories

Note that in the above examples, the recipe class or module is not imported, yet we end up with a Recipe object. This code solely relies on a factory with the id worldcookery.Recipe, not on the implementation itself. We could now implement a custom factory, for example one that allows us to set initial attribute values of the recipe. (We would normally extend the Recipe class with a constructor to do that, but let us implement a factory here for demonstration purposes.)

As Example 5.4.2 demonstrates, a factory is a usually a very simple type of component. All factories have to provide the IFactory interfaces from the zope.component.interfaces module. This interface requires implementors to carry two methods, __call__ and getInterfaces. While former is responsible for doing the actual factory work (making new instances), the latter simply returns an iterable object of the interface that will be provided by instances. Also note that factories are *instances* of a class, not the class itself. The last line therefore makes a singleton instance of the RecipeFactory class.

Now we can use the *standalone* factory directive (as opposed to the subdirective) to register our factory component. There is even less of a connection between the factory and the recipe implementation now. The code example from above can be modified slightly so that it passes initial values for recipe attributes:

```
>>> from zope.app.debug import Debugger
>>> debugger = Debugger(db="var/Data.fs",
...                      config_file="etc/site.zcml")
>>>
>>> from zope.component.interfaces import IFactory
>>> from zope.app import zapi
>>> recipe_factory = zapi.getUtility(
...       IFactory,
...       u"worldcookery.RecipeWithInitialValues")
>>> weisswurst = recipe_factory(
...       name=u"Weisswurst",
...       ingredients=[u"Weisswurst", u"Sweet mustard",
...                    u"Pretzels"],
...       time_to_cook=30,
...       description=u"..."
...       )
>>> weisswurst
<worldcookery.recipe.Recipe object at 0x30cd6050>
>>> weisswurst.name
u'Weisswurst'
```

Again, we can shorten this by a few lines by using the createObject function:

```
>>> weisswurst = zapi.createObject(
...       None,
...       u"worldcookery.RecipeWithInitialValues",
...       u"Weisswurst",
...       ingredients=[u"Weisswurst", u"Sweet mustard",
...                    u"Pretzels"],
...       time_to_cook=30,
...       description=u"..."
...       )
>>> weisswurst
<worldcookery.recipe.Recipe object at 0x30fe3320>
```

Note that the name parameter for the recipe may not be passed as a keyword argument here since it would conflict with the name of the factory, worldcookery.RecipeWithInitialValues.

Example 5.4.2 Implementing a custom factory (`recipe.py`)

```
1    ...
2
3    from zope.component.interfaces import IFactory
4    from zope.interface import implementedBy
5
6    class RecipeFactory:
7        implements(IFactory)
8
9        def __call__(self, name=u'', ingredients=[], tools=[],
10                     time_to_cook=0, description=u''):
11           recipe = Recipe()
12           recipe.name = name
13           recipe.ingredients = ingredients
14           recipe.tools = tools
15           recipe.time_to_cook = time_to_cook
16           recipe.description = description
17           return recipe
18
19       def getInterfaces(self):
20           return implementedBy(Recipe)
21
22   RecipeFactory = RecipeFactory()
```

Example 5.4.3 Configuring a custom factory (`configure.zcml`)

```
1    ...
2    <factory
3        component=".recipe.RecipeFactory"
4        id="worldcookery.RecipeWithInitialValues"
5        title="Create a new recipe with initial values"
6        description="This factory instantiates new recipes with initial
7        values" />
8    ...
```

Summary

- Factories are named utilities providing `IFactory`; they are responsible for making new instances of a class, typically, but not limited to content objects.
- Factories are *code components*, thus they are not protected by a permission but publicly usable; the objects they create a security-aware and protected.
- Simple factories are *factories from class* which are configured when configuring the corresponding class. Custom factory components need to provide `IFactory`.
- Factories are instances, not classes. Typically a singleton instance is created in the same module namespace as the class.

6

Persistency

In the previous chapters, we have seen what content objects can look like. You can store and provide data with getters and setters, or you can use the pythonic attribute approach. In either case, the values were stored in the object's instance dictionary. That means when the instance is gone, the data the instance is holding is gone, too. That is obviously not a practical approach. When we make a content component that is to store data over a period of time, we would like to be able to restart our application without losing that data. This chapter will show you how to do that.

If you are already familiar with the Zope's persistency mechanisms, you can skip this chapter and continue with Chapter 7.

6.1 The problem of object storage

Many web applications driven by scripting languanges (PHP, ASP, etc.) use relational databases to store and query data. Other systems, such as Cocoon, widely use XML in storage and component interaction. By making use of Python database connectors, Zope supports relational database connectivity very well, but we do not want to lose the simplicity of content objects. After all, Python is completely object-oriented, so it would only feel natural if there was a way to store objects transparently.

Zope's solution is the *Zope Object Database*, the ZODB. Python itself already provides mechanisms to represent objects as character streams so they can be saved to files or sent over a network connection in the `pickle` module. The ZODB is an object database built around object pickling with the following features:

Transparency. The fact that an object is persistent is nearly completely transparent to it and other components working with it. No special methods have to be called to store or retrieve data nor does one have to implement a special interface for persistency compliance. That makes it possible to persist any pickable object[1].

Transactions. Data can be written to the database any time, but if an error occurs somewhere along that process, data might only be partially written; the whole database might be in an inconsistent state. The answer to this problem is transactions. In Zope's case, a transaction is started whenever a request is received and to be processed. In case an error occurs, Zope aborts the transaction, thus making any already written data invalid. This, again, is completely transparent to the developer.

Undo. Even when a transaction has long been committed and written to the database, one might want to undo the changes. The ZODB not only supports a simple undo like this, it can actually keep every revision of every stored object, thus allowing simple revision control of stored data.

Pluggable Storages. The ZODB can store persistency data in many ways. The most common storage is `FileStorage` which stores data in a file usually called `Data.fs`. By using a different storage backend, you can choose where and how you would like to store persistent objects. ZODB even supports a network storage system called ZEO where one or many Zope servers, the ZEO clients, delegate storage to a central storage server, the ZEO server over the network. This environment is typically used in high-availability, scaling or distributed environments.

Summary

- Since Zope deals with objects (e.g. content components), it is desirable to store data as objects as well.
- Zope's object database ZODB is based on Python's support to serialize objects as pickles.
- The ZODB is a database framework providing features generally expected from an industrial strength database.

6.2 Making persistent objects

It is not possible to make just a single instance persistent. The persistency machinery needs to take advantage of certain Python hooks which is the reason for persistency needing to happen at the class level. Classes of persistent objects need to derive from a special base class, `Persistent` from the `persistent` package. This package is part of the ZODB and can be used outside Zope.

---

[1] Pickable objects include all class instances except file objects, network connection objects, and the like.

Let us look back at our recipe class as we defined it in Example 5.2.1. To make its instances support persistency, we simply have to derive from `Persistent` now (Example 6.2.1).

Example 6.2.1 Simple persistent class (`recipe.py`)

```
1   from persistent import Persistent
2   from zope.interface import implements
3   from worldcookery.interfaces import IRecipe
4
5   class Recipe(Persistent):
6       implements(IRecipe)
7
8       name = u''
9       ingredients = []
10      tools = []
11      time_to_cook = 0
12      description = u''
```

1 and 5. By deriving from the `Persistent` base class, we automatically make all recipe instances persistent. Because of its simplicity the rest of the class does not have to be changed.

Since we have not changed anything except a base class, the configuration of this class is identical to the one in the previous chapter, as defined in Example 5.3.2. But now that we have persistent recipes, we could start adding them to a folder in the object database without having to worry about the side-effects. The most convenient way to do that is through an entry in the *Add* browser menu as shown in Example 6.2.2.

Note that browser menus such as the *Add* menu are browser specific features. A menu would not make much sense in an FTP or WebDAV context. That is why we usually speak of *browser menus* and use the `browser` XML namespace in ZCML like for all browser-related configuration. Browser menus are covered in Chapter 7 and Chapter 12.

If you start Zope and go to a folder's *Contents* view, for example in the root folder, you will now discover that there is a new content type to add: Recipe. When you click to add one, Zope will ask you for a name of the new object in that folder, much like a filename. Zope will create a new recipe object and add it to the folder when you hit enter after having provided a valid name.

Summary

- Persistent classes need to inherit from `Persistent` provided by the `persistent` package.
- Configuration of a persistent class is identical to its non-persistent equivalent.
- A convenient way to add (persistent) objects to a folder is using the *Add* browser menu.

Example 6.2.2 Configuring a persistent class (`configure.zcml`)

```
1   <configure
2       xmlns="http://namespaces.zope.org/zope"
3       xmlns:browser="http://namespaces.zope.org/browser"
4       >
5
6     <interface
7         interface=".interfaces.IRecipe"
8         type="zope.app.content.interfaces.IContentType"
9         />
10
11    <content class=".recipe.Recipe">
12      <factory
13          id="worldcookery.Recipe"
14          title="Create a new recipe"
15          description="This factory instantiates new recipes"
16          />
17      <require
18          permission="zope.View"
19          interface=".interfaces.IRecipe"
20          />
21      <require
22          permission="zope.ManageContent"
23          set_schema=".interfaces.IRecipe"
24          />
25    </content>
26
27    <browser:addMenuItem
28        title="Recipe"
29        class=".recipe.Recipe"
30        permission="zope.ManageContent"
31        />
32
33  </configure>
```

11 – 25. The configuration of a content class does not have to be changed when it is made persistent. That is one of the aspects of transparent persistency.

27 – 31. This configuration directive registers an entry for the Recipe class in the *Add* menu. It allows us to add persistent recipe instances to folders through the web interface.

Flashback

Except for those versions that were released in parallel to Zope 3, Zope 2 provides the Persistent class only in the Persistence package or, for convenience, in the Globals module. Zope 3 exclusively provides the persistent package, thus Zope 2 code potentially needs to be adjusted. Both syntax and semantics of ZODB persistency have not changed, though.

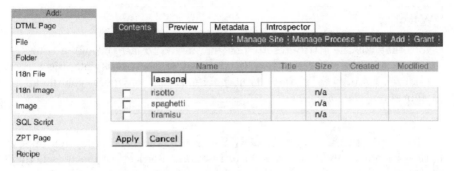

Fig. 6.1. Adding recipes through the web. **a)** The *Add* menu now containing an entry for recipes. **b)** Providing a name for the recipe in the container

6.3 Rules of persistency

Even though the persistency machinery aims to be as transparent as possible, it can not keep track of everything. Therefore, there are a few simple rules to be followed to ensure consistent data storage.

Because the ZODB facilitates Python's *pickling* mechanism to serialize objects, all attributes on an object need to be pickable themselves. In case you absolutely need to store a non-pickable object as an attribute, you need to mark it *volatile*, in other words non-persistent. Volatile attributes are prefixed with _v_ and always need to be used for file handle objects, network connections or cached values whose change shall not invoke a persistency transaction. Consider the following short example:

```
>>> from persistent import Persistent
>>> class File(Persistent):
...     def __init__(self, filename):
...         self.filename = filename        # persistent
...         self._v_file = file(filename)    # volatile
...     def read(self):
...         self._v_file.read()
```

The objects this class instantiates are persistent, since it derives from Persistent. The filename attribute is also persistent, since it would normaly be a simple string or unicode object. However, the file handle object needs to be stored as a volatile attribute and is thus prepended with a _v_.

> **Warning**
>
> Note that volatile attributes are not guaranteed to last through a trans-
> action. When a subtransaction is triggered or the persistent object is
> serialized again because there is no reference to it anymore, volatile at-
> tributes may be lost.

To ensure the a great deal of transparency, the persistency machinery
notices whenever an attribute is set or reset on an object, no matter whether
that happens inside an object's method using self, for example self.name
= u"Risotto" or outside to the object, risotto.name = u"Risotto".
Yet, it is not able to keep track of any changes to the attributes that will not
result in a re-setting of them. Consider the following example:

```
>>> from recipe import Recipe
>>> risotto = Recipe()
>>> risotto.ingredients
[]
>>> risotto.ingredients.append(u"Rice")
>>> risotto.ingredients
[u"Rice"]
```

Here, we have successfully added an ingredient to our recipe object. However,
the problem is that the recipe object itself was not modified at all; all we did
was append something to the ingredients list. The persistency machinery
would not notice anything.

There are two solutions for this common problem. The less transparent
one is to set a special attribute called _p_changed on the object. This will
let the persistency machinery know that the object has changed for sure:

```
>>> risotto._p_changed = True
```

The problem with this solution is that one loses a great deal of transparency.
One has to make sure to always set the _p_changed attribute. While that
is not so much of a problem when encountering such cases inside object
methods, it is from the outside of an object. When would some code know
that it is dealing with a persistent component or not?

The better solution is to make those attributes that can be changed independently persistent themselves. That way, the persistent machinery gets
notified when those change automatically and transparently to outside code.
For two of the built-in data structures in Python, lists and dictionaries, the

persistent package provides persistent flavours: `PersistentList`, provided by the `persistent.list` module, and `PersistentDict`, provided by the `persistent.dict` module. Using those, we can update our recipe class to use `PersistentList` instead of Python's built-in list (see Example 6.3.1).

Example 6.3.1 Persistent attributes (`recipe.py`)

```
1   from persistent import Persistent
2   from persistent.list import PersistentList
3   from zope.interface import implements
4   from worldcookery.interfaces import IRecipe
5
6   class Recipe(Persistent):
7       implements(IRecipe)
8
9       name = u''
10      ingredients = PersistentList()
11      tools = PersistentList()
12      time_to_cook = 0
13      description = u''
```

BTrees

An advanced feature of the ZODB are balanced binary trees called *BTrees*. A BTree object is a persistent mapping object that stores its items in a tree form. Using this special form of storage and an appropriate search algorithm, BTrees perform much better than regular dictionaries when looking up items. While the mean time needed to look up an item from a dictionary increases linearly with the number of items stored in the dictionary, BTrees perform the search proportionally to the logarithm of the number items stored. This makes BTrees the perfect data storage when managing thousands of items in a dictionary-like object.

In computer science literature, the BTree implementation that comes with the ZODB is sometimes referred to as B^+ trees. There are four different flavours of BTrees that you can use depending on your needs. All of the following can be imported from their subpackage below the `BTrees` package:

`IIBTree` A BTree whose keys and values are integers.

`IOBTree` A BTree whose keys are integers and whose values are abritrary objects. This kind of BTree can be used to mimic a sequence of objects that is persistent and has the fast look up capabilities of BTrees.

`OIBTree` A BTree whose keys are abritrary objects and whose values are integers. This kind of BTree is useful for keeping count of object occurrences or similar use-cases.

OOBTree A BTree whose keys and values are arbitrary objects. This is the most general kind of BTree and commonly used for object containers.

Apart from the regular mapping API, BTrees also support operations known from mathmatical sets, such as unions, intersections and differences. Consider the following small example using IOBTree:

```
>>> from BTrees.IOBTree import IOBTree, union, \
...       intersection
>>> odd = IOBTree({1: 'one', 3: 'three'})
>>> even = IOBTree({2: 'two', 4: 'four'})
```

The union of these two BTrees obviously contains all four numbers, while the intersection is empty:

```
>>> union(odd, even)
IOSet([1, 2, 3, 4])
>>> intersection(odd, even)
IOSet([])
```

It is not only convenient that these operations are already implemented so that one can use an existing implementation when it is needed; because of the underlying BTree storage, these operations are also relatively fast.

Summary

- The persistency machinery only takes notice of direct changes to persistent objects; in cases of indirect change, setting the _p_changed attribute on the persistent object invokes the machinery manually.
- It is usually preferable to make sub-objects persistent as well, using PersistentList and PersistentDict as a replacement for Python's data structures.
- BTrees are an implementation of persistent mappings that can efficiently store and look up large amounts of items.
- Attributes that are not to be persisted need to be prefixed with _v_.

7

Presenting components on the web

What can we do with recipes now? We know how to describe their API and data structure using interfaces or schemas, respectively; we have found a minimal implementation as a Python class which we have even made persistent so its instances can be stored in the ZODB. We can also add recipes to a Zope folder through-the-web using a browser.

What we cannot do yet is displaying the data stored inside a recipe to a web browser, or allowing users with a web browser or some other client to modify recipes that are stored inside the ZODB. Our content component is only useful for interaction on a Python API level. We are now looking for components responsible for user interaction: Views.

7.1 Schema-based browser views

Having used a schema to describe the recipe API now pays off because Zope has several mechanisms to provide automatic views for such components. The reason is because in the schema we have given detailed information about each property a recipe has. That way, Zope knows how to ask the user for input regarding each field, which again means that little or no code is necessary for schema-based views.

Furthermore, Zope can do automatic validation of the user input. In Chapter 4, we have validated an object according to a schema using the Python interpreter. Here, the form machinery uses the very same mechanism to validate the user's input. The object in question is not modified if the input does not validate according to the schema. That way, we can be sure that the time_to_cook variable only contains an integer, and so on. If the user enters something that does not validate, the form machinery will present an error message next to the input field.

Adding and editing

Zope's *form* machinery provides two flavours of automatic schema-based views: one used when adding objects, one for editing objects. Enabling them is a matter of one ZCML directive each, as Example 7.1.1 demonstrates. This example certainly is a lot to digest. The `browser:editform` and `browser:addform` directives are probably the most verbose configuration directives in Zope and we have not even used all available parameters. Yet, they are very powerful and allow a great deal of automation.

As you maybe have noticed from the location of the configuration file, we are now using a subpackage of the `worldcookery` package for these browser-specific directives, `worldcookery.browser`. It is a Zope convention to separate components that are specific to a certain type of representation into different modules or, when the amount of code is substantial, into different packages. Since we will be adding many more components and files in this and subsequent chapters that are browser-specific, it makes sense to start this subpackage now. Note that the configuration file of the subpackage will have to be loaded explicitly, though. Therefore, add the following line to the bottom of `configure.zcml`:

```
<include package=".browser" />
```

When we now click on the entry in the *Add* menu to add a recipe, we are not asked for a name directly. Instead, we are presented the automatically generated form shown in Figure 7.1. There we can specify the *Object Name* on the lower right.

Configuring an editing form works analogous to the add form, except that there is no need to specify a content factory. Instead we configure an entry in another browser menu, the `zmi_views` menu. ZMI views are browser pages that make up the *Zope Management Interface* (ZMI). These typically include pages for editing an object's data or metadata, adding contents to a container, etc. The `zmi_views` menu provides a visible list of such ZMI pages for an object. We want our editing page appear in this menu for recipes, so we add the menu and `title` parameters to the `browser:editform` to directive. The `title` parameter describes the title of menu entry.

Summary

- Zope can render HTML forms based on the type specifications in a schema.
- User input is automatically validated according to the schema.
- Forms for adding and editing objects can be enabled with just one ZCML directive each.
- The Zope Management Interface (ZMI) consists of browser pages usually registered in the `zmi_views` menu, which is presented as management tabs.

Example 7.1.1 Configuring schema-based browser views (`browser/` `configure.zcml`)

```
1   <configure
2       xmlns="http://namespaces.zope.org/zope"
3       xmlns:browser="http://namespaces.zope.org/browser"
4       >
5
6     <browser:addMenuItem
7         title="Recipe"
8         class="worldcookery.recipe.Recipe"
9         permission="zope.ManageContent"
10        view="AddRecipe.html"
11        />
12
13    <browser:addform
14        schema="worldcookery.interfaces.IRecipe"
15        content_factory="worldcookery.recipe.Recipe"
16        label="Add Recipe"
17        name="AddRecipe.html"
18        permission="zope.ManageContent"
19        />
20
21    <browser:editform
22        schema="worldcookery.interfaces.IRecipe"
23        label="Edit"
24        name="edit.html"
25        menu="zmi_views" title="Edit"
26        permission="zope.ManageContent"
27        />
28
29   </configure>
```

14.   `browser:addform` defines and configures a form that is presented to us when we add recipes. For that it needs to know the schema out of which it shall generate the form, for which we use our `IRecipe` schema, of course.

15.   It also needs to know the class it shall construct and save the information onto after having collected the latter. We use the persistent `Recipe` class from the previous chapter here.

16.   We can then also give the form a `label` which will be shown when presenting the form.

17.   Naturally, the HTML form page needs to have a name that will be part of its URL.

18.   Last but not least, we have to set a `permission` that is required to use the form.

6–11.   With the lengthy `browser:addform` directive, we have the form, but we still need to tell Zope when to present it to us. When we look back to the last chapter, Example 6.2.2 already involved the configuration of an entry in the *Add* browser menu.

10.   Now that we have the add form, we can extend the *Add* menu entry to specify the add form we have just registered under the name of `AddRecipe.html`.

25.   The menu and `title` parameters register the edit form with a browser menu.

Fig. 7.1. An automatically generated add form.

7.2 Page Templates

We can now add and edit recipes, but there is one essential functionality still missing: displaying them. In a web application, the displaying of content components is typically done by generating HTML for a web browser. The essential structure of these HTML pages is mostly the same and only the actual content coming from the component is inserted automatically. Assembling small HTML pages is often not too complicated, but one would not want to do it in Python. Especially when it comes to larger tasks, one usually would like to use an appropriate templating facility.

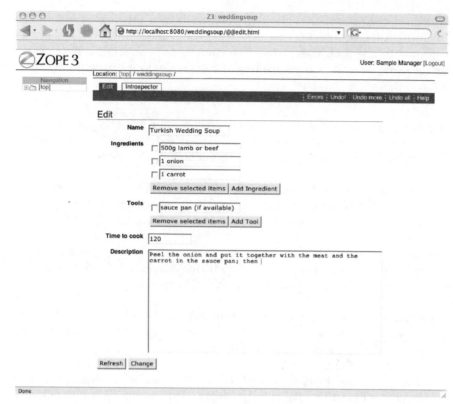

Fig. 7.2. An automatically generated edit form with an entry in the manage interface tabs menu.

7.2.1 TAL

In Zope, dynamic XML pages and especially XHTML are rendered using *Page Templates*, also referred to as ZPT (Zope Page Templates). Page Templates contain the basic markup structure of the output page, but also special commands that are executed when the page is invoked, thus making the output dynamic. For the dynamic commands, the *Template Attribute Language* (TAL) is used. As its name says, the commands are element attributes; they are placed on the element they are supposed to modify. By putting these commands into a special namespace[1], Page Templates remain valid XHTML documents and can thus still be edited using a WYSIWYG editor or directly viewed in a browser.

XML does not know an order of attributes. Even though one attribute can be defined before another one in an XML text, this order is arbitrary. For the same reason it does not matter to the TAL interpreter which attribute

---

[1] http://xml.zope.org/namespaces/tal

is defined first; it will execute TAL commands in a pre-defined order. The following list gives an overview over TAL commands in the order they are executed by the TAL interpreter. Note that some commands cannot occurr on the same element at the same time, for example `content` and `replace`. TAL COMMANDS

`define` defines new variable(s) with the return value(s) of the corresponding expression(s) in the current namespace. If a definition is preceeded by `global`, the variable is available throughout the whole template.

`condition` removes the element from the output if the expression evaluates to false; the element will only appear if the expression evaluates to true. Values are evaluated according to Python boolean rules.

`repeat` Repeat the current element for every item in the sequence returned by an expression. The current item in the sequence is bound to a local variable within the repeated element's namespace.

`content` Fills the contents of the element with the return value of an expression. The element and its attributes are preserved, only its contents including all child elements is replaced.

`replace` replaces the element with the return value of an expression. The element will not be appear in the result. This command is mutually exclusive with the `content` command on the same element.

`attributes` defines or replaces attribute(s) on the current element with the value(s) of the corresponding expression(s).

`omit-tag` removes the element itself from the output but leaves its contents and child elements in if the given expression evaluates to true. True is assumed for the expression value if no expression is provided.

`on-error` inserts the return value of an expression if an error occurrs in subelement processing.

7.2.2 TALES

As you have probably noticed, most TAL commands deal with expressions. The values of expressions determine the outcome of a condition or what is inserted into the template, either as a text node or an element attribute. Expressions follow the *TAL Expression Syntax* (TALES), which allows multiple types of expressions. The following list gives an overview over them: TALES EXPRESSIONS

Path expressions allow the access of attributes, items and methods through a filesystem or URL path-like notation. If the resulting object is callable (meaning a method, function or class), it will be called with no arguments. Examples:

```
<!-- Call the values() method of the my_recipes
folder -->
<p tal:repeat="recipe context/my_recipes/values">
  Name of the dish: <span tal:replace="recipe/name"/>.
</p>
```

String expressions allow the direct insertion of text. They also allow the result of path expressions to be inserted within an expression. Example:

```
<div tal:define="global message string:
    The ${recipe/name} recipe was modified" />
```

Python expressions make it possible to evaluate a piece of Python code in a TALES expression. This is especially useful for boolean expressions in a condition or for calling functions explicitly or functions that require parameters. Examples:

```
<p tal:condition="python: recipe.time_to_cook
&lt; 60">
  Cooking <span tal:replace="recipe/name/title" />
  will take less than an hour.
</p>
```

Expressions can also be preceded by a modifier that changes its behaviour or result: EXPRESSION MODIFIERS

not : negates the boolean value of an expression. In Python, everything except the number 0, an empty string, list, tuple, or dictionary and None are treated as False in a boolean expression. Example:

```
<div tal:define="takes_little_time python:
recipe.time_to_cook < 60">
  <p tal:condition="takes_little_time">
    Cooking will take less than an hour.
  </p>
  <p tal:condition="not:takes_little_time">
    Make time for more than hour to prepare this
dish!
  </p>
</div>
```

`nocall:` prevents the following path expression from potentially calling a function, method or class. Examples:

```
<div tal:define="pop nocall:recipe/ingredients/pop;
                 lastitem pop"
     tal:content="lastitem">last ingredient goes here
</div>
```

`structure` lets the result of an expression be inserted unquoted. Normally, all characters sensible to XML are quoted using entities. In some cases, one would like to prevent that (for example when directly inserting HTML markup). Notice that structure is separated from the expression by a *space*, not a colon. Example:

```
<p tal:define="html string:<b>bold</b>"
   tal:content="structure html">insert html here</p>
```

`|` (pipe, or) allows the specification of a fallback if a path expression fails. It is not an *or* operator in a boolean sense since the result of the expression to its left is still returned even if it evaluates to `False`. The operator only becomes active when the path expression to its left cannot be resolved.

```
<div tal:define="name_of_dish recipe/name | string:
Unknown dish"
     tal:content="name_of_dish">name of the dish goes
here</div>
```

7.2.3 Variable namespaces and scopes

Much like Python, a Page Template provides a namespace where all variables that are used in expressions are looked up. Path expressions that allow us to traverse to an object or one of its attributes obviously need to start their traversal with one object. Similarly, Python expressions often need to work with objects which come from the variable namespace.

In ZPT, variable namespaces have a scope, much like in Python. A new scope begins with each new XML child element. Child element namespaces inherit everything defined in a higher namespace. Using the TAL command `define`, you can set new variables in a namespace. Unless these definitions are preceded by a `global` statement, they are only effective in the current namespace and the ones of child elements. Consider the following example:

```
<div tal:define="recipe_name string:Kebab"></div>
<p tal:condition="python: recipe_name=='Kebab'">
  Yummy, Kebab!
</p>
```

This will obviously fail because the variable recipe_name is defined in the div element, thus not accessible in the paragraph element. This could easily be fixed by making the div element the parent element so that the p will inherit its namespace:

```
<div tal:define="recipe_name string:Kebab">
  <p tal:condition="python: recipe_name=='Kebab'">
    Yummy, Kebab!
  </p>
</div>
```

or even simpler:

```
<p tal:define="recipe_name string:Kebab"
   tal:condition="python: recipe_name=='Kebab'">
   Yummy, Kebab!
</p>
```

Alternatively, we could have made recipe_name a global variable:

```
<div tal:define="global recipe_name string:Kebab" />
<p tal:condition="python: recipe_name=='Kebab'">
   Yummy, Kebab!
</p>
```

Of course, with just being able to define our own variables we will not get far. Luckily, a Page Template provides some useful variables in the root namespace, thus accessible everywhere in the template: GLOBAL DEFAULT VARIABLES

request is an object representing the request from the browser, usually a HTTP request. It can be used to access CGI variables passed in from the browser or even the authenticated principal, for example:

```
<p>You are
<span tal:replace="request/principal/title" />
using
<span tal:replace="request/HTTP_USER_AGENT" />
</p>
```

nothing represents a false and empty value. It is useful in conditions whenever a false value is needed and in string insertions whenever "nothing"
should be inserted, for example:

```
<p tal:condition="nothing">This paragraph will not be
printed</p>
<p tal:replace="nothing">Neither will this one</p>
```

default is a marker that indicated that the provided default value should
be used. This is usually used in a fallback when a path expression fails
to lookup up an object or attribute, for example:

```
<p>
  You are using
  <span tal:content="request/HTTP_USER_AGENT |
default">
    a browser
  </span>
</p>
```

This is a variation of an example used above. The difference is that this
will not fail if the browser did not send the CGI variable HTTP_USER_AGENT
with the request. In that case, the standard text ("a browser") will be
printed to the user as a fall-back.

repeat provides auxiliary functionality in loops invoked by the repeat
TAL command, such as the current number of repetition both in arabic
and roman numbers:

```
<p>You will need the following tools to prepare this
dish:</p>

<div>
  <p tal:repeat="tool recipe/tools">
    <span tal:replace="repeat/tool/number" />.
    <span tal:replace="tool" />
  </p>
</div>
```

Of course, in a real Page Template, we could simply use the HTML
element ol which automatically makes an ordered list.

modules makes it possible to import Python modules in a Page Template. Since Page Templates are not intended to execute heavy application logic, this should generally be avoided. Example:

```
<p tal:define="IRecipe
    modules/worldcookery.interfaces/IRecipe"
    tal:condition="python:
                        IRecipe.providedBy(context)">
  The object is indeed a recipe.
</p>
```

context is the object that the Page Template is supposed to display. Page Templates are generally used to present a particular type of object's data to the browser, thus acting as mediators between the browser and the object. In Component Architecture terms, we say that the Page Template is a *view* for the object. The object that a view is displaying is always called its context. Example:

```
<h2 tal:content="context/name/title">recipe name goes
here</h2>

<p>Cooking <span tal:replace="context/name" />
will take
<span tal:replace="context/time_to_cook" />
minutes.</p>
```

view represents the view component that the Page Template is part of in case the Page Template is used as a view. Page Templates are usually used without an extra view component. Then such a component is created for them automatically. However, if you specify such an extra component in the configuration, you can have access it to through this variable. Enhanced view components will be covered in Chapter 12.

Summary

- Zope is equipped with an extensive HTML/XML templating system called *Page Templates* or *ZPT*.
- Page Templates interoperate with any HTML/XML capable application, such as WYSIWYG editors, as they remain well-formed XML documents.
- ZPT's templating language, TAL, uses attributes in a special namespace to specify commands.
- Page Templates interact with other components by means of various expressions, most importantly *path expressions*.

Flashback

Page Templates are a part of Zope since version 2.5 and probably one of the greatest innovations of Zope 2. The implementation shipping with Zope 3 is nearly identical to its Zope 2 pendant. Therefore, if you are already familiar with Page Templates, you can apply all of that knowledge in Zope 3, too. The few and minimal differences include

- partially different set of global variables, for example `here` is now called `context`,
- traversal namespaces like in URLs, for example `@@` for traversing to views,
- TALES namespace adapters as described in Chapter 13.

Note that DTML is not used for rendering HTML markup at all anymore.

7.3 Simple view Page Template

We now know everything we need to know to present recipes as HTML to a web browser. Let us do so then and write a Page Template that shows us the information we have saved in a recipe (see Example 7.3.1).

As we have said, Page Templates remain valid XHTML documents, so nothing would prevent us from viewing them in a regular browser off of the filesystem. Figure 7.3 shows `recipeview.pt` being displayed in a browser. Since the browser does not interpret TAL, we see the default text we put

recipe name goes here

Time needed for preparation: xyz mins
Ingredients: • ingredients go here
Needed kitchen tools: • tools go here

Longer description goes here.

Done

Fig. 7.3. Web browser displaying `recipeview.pt` off of the filesystem.

Example 7.3.1 View Page Template for displaying recipes (browser/recipeview.pt)

```
1   <html xmlns="http://www.w3.org/1999/xhtml"
2          xmlns:tal="http://xml.zope.org/namespaces/tal">
3   <head>
4     <title tal:content="context/name/title">recipe name goes here</title>
5   </head>
6   <body>
7
8     <h2 tal:content="context/name/title">recipe name goes here</h2>
9
10    <table>
11      <tbody>
12        <tr>
13          <td>Time needed for preparation:</td>
14          <td><tal:var replace="context/time_to_cook">xyz</tal:var> mins</td>
15        </tr>
16
17        <tr>
18          <td>Ingredients:</td>
19          <td>
20            <ul>
21              <li tal:repeat="ingredient context/ingredients"
22                  tal:content="ingredient">ingredients go here</li>
23            </ul>
24          </td>
25        </tr>
26
27        <tr>
28          <td>Needed kitchen tools:</td>
29          <td>
30            <ul>
31              <li tal:repeat="tool context/tools"
32                  tal:content="tool">tools go here</li>
33            </ul>
34          </td>
35        </tr>
36
37      </tbody>
38    </table>
39
40    <p tal:content="context/description">Longer description goes here.</p>
41
42  </body>
43  </html>
```

2.   In order to let the Page Template remain a valid XHTML document,
          we define an XML namespace for TAL commands. By convention, the
          namespace prefix is tal.

4 and 8. We use the global context variable to access the current recipe's values.
          Thanks to path expressions, it is quite obvious even to non-programmers
          what is inserted into the markup.

21 and 31. Recipes store two lists: a list of ingredients and a list of tools. Here in the Page Template, we want to display these lists as *unordered lists* (ul), each entry being a list item (li). Therefore, we generate an li element for each item in the list and display the item value inside.

in instead of actual values of a recipe. It would not have been necessary to fill elements with a default text, but it makes it easier to view the template without a TAL interpreter, for example off of the filesystem. Furthermore, as the template in its current form is obviously not very pretty, we could send it to a designer who could edit it with a regular HTML design software; the default values will give the designer an idea where the real text will appear in the dynamic version. As long as the TAL commands we put into the template remain there, a designer is free to work with any HTML-capable tools, which is another benefit of Page Templates being valid XHTML documents.

Example 7.3.2 Configuring a default view for displaying recipes (browser/configure.zcml)

```
1    ...
2    <browser:page
3        for="worldcookery.interfaces.IRecipe"
4        name="index.html"
5        template="recipeview.pt"
6        permission="zope.View"
7        />
8    ...
```

3. As with any type of view, we register it for an *interface*, not a particular implementation. That way we can replace the implementation and still have the view.

4. As with browser:editform and browser:addform, the page needs to have a name under which it will be accessible in a URL. By convention, the name for the default view of an object is index.html; in other words, when Zope is given the URL of an object without any view postfix, it will try to use the index.html view.

5. The template parameter refers to the file containing the template to be used. This filename is looked up relative to the configuration file (browser/configure.zcml).

6. Once again we have to provide a permission that will be required for viewing the page. Since this page does not expose an editing form or any other management functionality, we can protect it with a less restraining permission. Typically, all anonymous users (unauthenticated users) have the permission zope.View which allows them to view most content.

As with any other component so far, views have to be registered and configured as well. Since we usually refer to web *pages* when we mean browser views, the browser:page ZCML directives takes care of configuring views for browser requests. Example 7.3.2 shows us how to do so.

We can now easily display a recipe by simply pointing a web browser at its URL. Zope will by default look for the index.html view for the object[2], which means it will find our recipeview.pt template. Figure 7.4 shows us what the recipe we have added and edited before looks like when displayed.

Fig. 7.4. Displaying a recipe using the simple view Page Template.

As a bonus, we can also add another management interface tab that lets one preview a newly added or edited recipe. Zope already provides a template called preview.pt for this in the zope.app.preview package. Example 7.3.3 shows how to configure the *Preview* page.

---

[2] This behaviour can be changed with the browser:defaultView directive. See Appendix 2, ZCML Reference for a detailed reference.

Example 7.3.3 Configuring a *Preview* page. (`browser/configure.zcml`)

```
1    ...
2    <!-- Preview page - requires zope.app.preview -->
3    <configure package="zope.app.preview">
4      <browser:page
5          for="worldcookery.interfaces.IRecipe"
6          name="preview.html"
7          template="preview.pt"
8          permission="zope.ManageContent"
9          menu="zmi_views" title="Preview"
10         />
11   </configure>
12   ...
```

3. The `preview.pt` file lies in the `zope.app.preview` package. Since files are found relative to the current package, we wrap the following `browser:page` directive in another `configure>` directive and set the current package explicitly. This way, `browser:page` will look in `zope.app.preview` and not in `worldcookery.present` where the configuration file actually is located.

9. Just like with the edit form we configured earlier, we would like the *Preview* page to appear in the manage interface tabs. Like `browser:editform`, `browser:page` allows one to automatically define a menu entry for the registered page, which we here do for the `zmi_views` menu, the menu that contains management tabs.

Summary

- Simple Page Templates can be viewed off of the filesystem for preview or demonstration purposes.
- View Page Templates are configured using the `browser:page` ZCML directive.
- Files in ZCML directives are found relative to the current package.

7.4 Advanced: Customizing automatically generated forms

Having add and edit forms generated is enormously convenient. Not only is the rendering of the form automated, which by itself would already be a tiresome task if more than just a few forms where involved, but validation is also handled automatically. Despite all this automation, one can still customize certain behaviour. In the following advanced section, we will customize our add and edit form by changing the way we edit sequences.

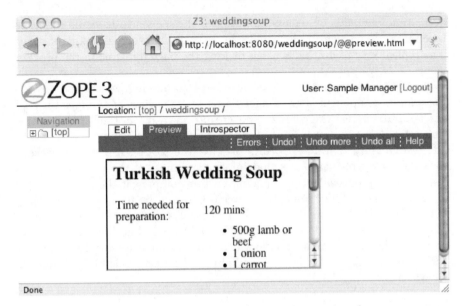

Fig. 7.5. A *Preview* page in the management interface.

Widgets

An automatically generated form is composed of components called *widgets* which are representations of schema fields. Widgets are *views* for schema fields, because they are a request-specific representation of them and are mediators between the field and the user. Since widgets are views, thus standard components, they can be customized. Widgets are not regular views, though, because they are not looked up by name; they are looked up by the type of functionality they provide. Widgets that display field data to the client, be it browser or something else, provide IDisplayWidget from the zope. app.form.interfaces module. Widgets that provide editing functionality and retrieve input from the user, provide IInputWidget. Views providing an interface are looked up with zapi.getViewProviding rather than zapi.getView.

Browser widgets are typically represented using HTML form fields; simple browser widgets facilitate the text input field, more complex ones use radio buttons, checkboxes and/or other input fields. In the forms we have seen so far, the browser widget for TextLine and Int fields use a simple text input box; the List field, however, which is used to describe a recipe's ingredients and tools, requires a much more complex browser widget.

A better sequence widget

Since the default list widget provided by Zope tries to be as general as possible, it is very complex and not too user-friendly. The form has to be reloaded every time one adds or removes an item of the sequence. It would really be much more convenient if one could add, remove, and sort entries right away. The typical way to do this is using making the page dynamic in the browser using *ECMAScript*.

But before we can dive into client-side programming, we need to provide the widget component. Our widget needs to be a view *of the type* browser (zope.publisher.browser.BrowserRequeset) *for* the list field (zope .schema.List) *providing* input functionality (zope.app.form .interfaces.IInputWidget). Luckily, the zope.app.form package provides us with a base class that implements most of the functionality required by an input widget, making our custom component shown in Example 7.4.1 quite short. Since Page Templates do a much better job at assembling HTML than Python, we delegate all the actual widget markup off to a template whose source code is shown in Example 7.4.2. The Page Template in turn tells the browser to load a file which contains the necessary ECMAScript functions to make the widget dynamic in the browser. This file's contents is shown in Example 7.4.3.

Example 7.4.1 Custom sequence widget class (browser/widget.py)

```
1   from zope.app import zapi
2   from zope.app.form.interfaces import IInputWidget
3   from zope.app.form.browser.widget import SimpleInputWidget
4   from zope.app.pagetemplate.viewpagetemplatefile import
    ViewPageTemplateFile

5
6   class DynamicSequenceWidget(SimpleInputWidget):
7       """Widget for (simple) sequences that does not require the form to be
8       reloaded for every change."""
9
10      template = ViewPageTemplateFile('widget.pt')
11
12      def __call__(self):
13          """Display the widget by invoking the page template"""
14          return self.template()
15
16      def getData(self):
17          """Provide the current field data to the page template"""
18          # self._data and self._data_marker are set by
19          # SimpleInputWidget
20          if self._data is self._data_marker:
21              return []
22          return self._data[:]
23
24      def _getFormInput(self):
25          """Retrieve the input value from the form
26
```

```
27      Make sure that we always retrieve a list object from the
28      request, even if only a single item has been entered."""
29      value = super(DynamicSequenceWidget, self)._getFormInput()
30      if not isinstance(value, list):
31          value = [value]
32      return value
33
34  def hidden(self):
35      """Render the widget as hidden fields"""
36      s = ''
37      for value in self._data:
38          widget = zapi.getViewProviding(self.context.value_type,
39                                         IInputWidget, self.request)
40          widget.name = self.name
41          widget.setRenderedValue(value)
42          s += widget.hidden()
43      return s
```

3 and 6. We import and subclass SimpleInputWidget since it already provides most of the basic functionality for a browser input widget. It also already implements IInputWidget.

10 – 14. When widgets are rendered, they are called as if they were functions; the returned HTML is pasted into the form. To support callability, we implement a __call__ method. However, instead of assembling the HTML ourselves here, we use a Page Template file called widget.pt, which is bound to the class under the template variable.

24 – 33. Sometimes browser widgets need to be rendered as hidden fields, for example when only a part of the overall form should be editable, for example in a wizard. The hidden method takes care of this by getting a widget for all elements in the sequence and having their hidden field rendered.

Note

Not all browsers support ECMAScript equally well. Microsoft's Internet Explorer, for instance, is known for its erratic behaviour especially regarding DOM manipulations. The provided widget implementation uses certain ECMAScript functionality that is unfortunately known to cause problems on this browser. It has been tested successfully on browsers with better support for the ECMAScript standard, such as Mozilla Firefox, Opera and Apple's Safari. Even though browsers like the former two are available for different platforms, the Internet Explorer is still predominant in the browser market. One should therefore consider less client-side scripting when cross-browser compatability is required.

Example 7.4.2 Custom sequence widget template (`browser/widget.pt`)

```
1   <div xmlns:tal="http://xml.zope.org/namespaces/tal">
2
3   <script type="text/javascript" src="sequence.js"
4           tal:attributes="src context/++resource++sequence.js">
5   </script>
6
7   <p>
8     <select name="foo" id="foo" size="5"
9             tal:attributes="name view/name; id view/name;
10                            size python:min(max(len(view.getData()), 5),
    12)">
11      <option tal:repeat="item view/getData" tal:content="item">item</option>
12    </select>
13    <script type="text/javascript"
14            tal:content="string:registerSequenceElement('${view/name}')">
15      registerSequenceElement('foo')
16    </script>
17  </p>
18
19  <p>
20    <input
21        type="text" id="input"
22        tal:attributes="id string:input.${view/name}"
23        value="Click here to add an item" onfocus="this.value=''"
24        />
25  </p>
26  <p>
27    <button
28        type="button" onclick="sequenceAddItem('foo', 'input')"
29        tal:attributes="onclick string:sequenceAddItem('${view/name}',
    'input.${view/name}')">
30      Add
31    </button>
32
33    <button
34        type="button" onclick="sequenceRemoveItem('foo')"
35        tal:attributes="onclick string:sequenceRemoveItem('${view/name}')">
36      Remove
37    </button>
38
39    <button
40        type="button" onclick="sequenceMoveItem('foo', -1)"
41        tal:attributes="onclick string:sequenceMoveItem('${view/name}', -1)">
42      Move Up
43    </button>
44
45    <button
46        type="button" onclick="sequenceMoveItem('foo', 1)"
47        tal:attributes="onclick string:sequenceMoveItem('${view/name}', 1)">
48      Move Down
49    </button>
50  </p>
51  </div>
```

3 – 5.   As mentioned before, we want to make our widget dynamic in the browser; we therefore need to use a set of ECMAScript functions that we load from a separate file (see Example 7.4.3), a browser resource. For more information on browser resources, please refer to Section 8.3.

8 – 12.   As a container for the items of the sequence we use a `select` box which we pre-fill with the sequence data if there is any available.

13 – 16. In order for the ECMAScript to do its dynamic actions on the entered values, we need to register the `select` box with it.

20 – 24. One can enter a new item into this input field. When the *Add* button is pressed, it will be added to the above `select` box.

27 – 49. Four buttons allow one to edit the sequence items in the `select` box dynamically. When a button is clicked, a corresponding ECMAScript function is called to operate on the items, such as adding or deleting one, or moving them around.

Example 7.4.3 ECMAScript functions for the custom sequence widget (`browser/sequence.js`)

```
1   function sequenceAddItem(select_id, input_id) {
2       var select = document.getElementById(select_id);
3       var input = document.getElementById(input_id);
4
5       var item = new Option(input.value);
6       select.options[select.length] = item;
7       input.value = '';
8   }
9
10  function sequenceRemoveItem(select_id) {
11      var select = document.getElementById(select_id);
12      select.remove(select.selectedIndex);
13  }
14
15  function sequenceMoveItem(select_id, direction) {
16      var select = document.getElementById(select_id);
17      var old_position = select.selectedIndex;
18      var new_position = old_position + direction;
19      if (new_position < 0 || new_position >= select.length ) return;
20
21      var array = new Array();
22      for (var i=0; i<select.options.length; i++)
    array.push(select.options[i]);
23
24      for (var i=0; i<array.length; i++) {
25          if (i==old_position) select.options[i] = array[new_position];
26          else if (i==new_position) select.options[i] = array[old_position];
27          else select.options[i] = array[i];
28      }
29  }
30
```

```
31   if (!sequence_elements)
32       var sequence_elements = new Array();
33
34   function registerSequenceElement(id) {
35       var el = document.getElementById(id);
36       sequence_elements.push(el);
37   }
38
39   function sequenceSubmit(form) {
40       for (var i=0; i<sequence_elements.length; i++) {
41           sequence_elements[i].multiple = true;
42           for (var j=0; j<sequence_elements[i].options.length; j++) {
43               sequence_elements[i].options[j].selected = true;
44           }
45       }
46   }
47
48   document.forms[0].setAttribute("onsubmit", "sequenceSubmit(this);");
```

1 – 8.   sequenceAddItem responds to the *Add* button and adds the item entered in the text input field to the select box.

10 – 13.   Equally, sequenceRemoveItem responds to the *Remove* button and removes the selected item from the select box.

15 – 29.   sequenceMoveItem moves the selected item in the select box up or down, depending on the direction parameter. If direction is positive, the item will be moved up; if it is negative, it will be moved down. Since the ECMAScript API does not support moving items in select boxes by itself, this function is a little more complex since it needs to do the shift manually.

39 – 46.   A select box widget usually only submits the items to the server that have been selected. In our widget, we are "abusing" select boxes as list containers and therefore want all of the items be sent. sequenceSubmit tricks the browser into sending all items by selecting all of them before the form is submitted.

48.   In order for sequenceSubmit to be called when the form is submitted, we need to install a hook on the form object.

Even though the widget's Page Template is technically not a full HTML document (it is lacking the required document and body elements), most browsers will be able to display it. Since we again provided sensible default values where TAL commands make the widget dynamically work in a form, we can view it in a browser without a problem. Even better, the dynamic features provided by the ECMAScript functions work, too, so we can actually test the widget in a browser before embedding it into a form, as shown in Figure 7.6.

To enable the new widget in the forms we now only need the right kind of configuration. Fortunately that is very easy. The browser:addform and browser:editform ZCML directives simply grow a subdirective called

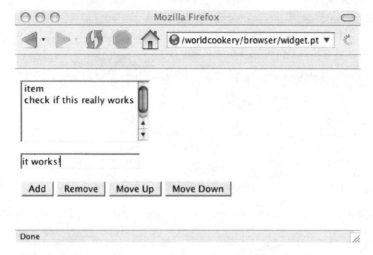

Fig. 7.6. Testing the widget's functionality from the filesystem.

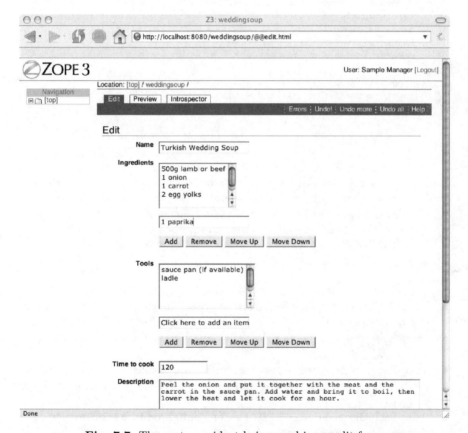

Fig. 7.7. The custom widget being used in an edit form.

widget that specifies our custom widget component, as you can see in Example 7.4.4. After reloading the edit form of the recipe in your browser, you should see a page like shown in Figure 7.7.

Example 7.4.4 Configuring the custom widget (browser/configure.zcml)

```
1     ...
2     <browser:addform
3         schema="worldcookery.interfaces.IRecipe"
4         content_factory="worldcookery.recipe.Recipe"
5         label="Add Recipe"
6         name="AddRecipe.html"
7         permission="zope.ManageContent"
8         >
9       <widget field="ingredients" class=".widget.DynamicSequenceWidget" />
10      <widget field="tools" class=".widget.DynamicSequenceWidget" />
11    </browser:addform>
12
13    <browser:editform
14        schema="worldcookery.interfaces.IRecipe"
15        label="Edit"
16        name="edit.html"
17        menu="zmi_views" title="Edit"
18        permission="zope.ManageContent"
19        >
20      <widget field="ingredients" class=".widget.DynamicSequenceWidget" />
21      <widget field="tools" class=".widget.DynamicSequenceWidget" />
22    </browser:editform>
23
24    <browser:resource name="sequence.js" file="sequence.js" />
25    ...
```

9 – 10 and 20 – 21. We simply add two subdirectives to each form configuration directive, one to set the alternate widget for the ingredients, one for the kitchen tools. The widget component is referenced using a dotted name as usual.

24. As mentioned before, the ECMAScript functions are loaded from a separate file, a resource. Like browser pages, resources are configured through ZCML and given a name by which they are looked up.

Summary

- Automatically generated forms are composed of widget components which can be customized.
- Widgets represent schema fields; they are unnamed *views* providing functionality.
- SimpleInputWidget from the zope.app.form.browser.widget module provides most of the functionality needed for a browser input widget.
- Automatically generated forms can be configured to use custom widgets through the widget subdirective.

Part II

Intermediate

8

Customizing a site's layout

Our small application lets us do quite a lot already and that with a rather limited amount of code. We can add and edit recipes to the object database where they are persisted and later displayed to the visitor – time to start thinking about a proper appearance of the overall application. Fortunately, Zope lets us worry about that independently of component code. That means we can delay the layouting of the application as far back in time as we want to. We can also hire a designer to do the layouting for us. We only have to integrate the design back into the application. This chapter shows you how to do that.

8.1 Layers and skins

Views determine how objects are represented. In many cases, different views for a particular component, although they essentially present the same information, may want to do the presentation in a different layout. Especially with respect to browser views, it is necessary to present the application in a certain design, sometimes even two separate designs within the same application are required, for example one for visitors and one for editors. In Zope jargon, the look of a site, its layout or design is called a *skin*; in other systems, the same concept is sometimes called a *theme*. You can imagine skins as wallpapers that give the naked objects an appearance, or as wrapping papers that wrap dull boxes to make them look pretty.

Experience has shown that skins have to provide a lot of basic infrastructure that is common to all of them. In order to be able to share this common groundwork, skins are broken down into *layers*. A skin then is essentially a list of layers. That way, skins can share those layers that provide the basic functionality they need and then provide their specific custom look and feel in layers on top of that.

When Zope 3 needs to look up a view, it does the following steps:

1. Ask the request for the presentation skin to be used. If the request does not contain information about which skin is to be used (for example through a hint in the URL or a browser cookie), it falls back to the configured default skin.
2. Look up which layers the skin is composed of.
3. Try to look up the requested view in one of the layers of the skin, beginning with the first or topmost layer. If the requested view is not defined for any of the layers the skin consists of, the look up fails with an error.

A typical way to take advantage of the skin and layer concept is to override only very few essential places in a custom layer and falling back to another skin's layers otherwise. Example 8.1.1 shows how to define a new layer and a new skin based on it and already existing layers. Note that we use a yet another subpackage of worldcookery.browser to place all components related to the *WorldCookery* skin in. That means we have to make sure we load the subpackage's configuration, too. Add the following line to the bottom of browser/configure.zcml:

```
<include package=".skin" />
```

Example 8.1.1 Defining a custom layer and skin (browser/skin/configure.zcml)

```
1  <configure
2      xmlns="http://namespaces.zope.org/zope"
3      xmlns:browser="http://namespaces.zope.org/browser"
4      >
5
6    <browser:layer name="worldcookery" />
7    <browser:skin name="WorldCookery" layers="worldcookery rotterdam
   default" />
8
9  </configure>
```

6. Layer names are lower case by convention.

7. Skin names are upper case or camel case by convention. The list of layers a skin consists of is space-separated and ordered from topmost layer to bottom one.

We can now view Zope's Management Interface using the *WorldCookery* skin by opening the following URL in our browser:

```
http://localhost:8080/++skin++WorldCookery/
```

Of course, this will look exactly like the *Rotterdam* skin because we haven't overriden any components in our worldcookery layer yet. To make the *WorldCookery* the default skin from now on and prevent visitors from having to type in the long and complicated URL above, we can use the browser:

defaultSkin directive. However, zope.app already sets this value to *Rotterdam*. If we were to use this directive again, we would get a configuration conflict. To avoid that, we need make sure that when we use the directive, it overrides zope.app's value. ZCML provides such an override mechanism; all directives that reside in an instance's etc/overrides.zcml are executed to override any directives that they would conflict with otherwise. The short listing in Example 8.1.2 shows what is needed to be included in the overrides file.

Example 8.1.2 Overriding Zope's default skin with a custom one (etc/overrides.zcml)

```
1   <configure xmlns="http://namespaces.zope.org/zope"
2              xmlns:browser="http://namespaces.zope.org/browser">
3
4      <!-- Provide local overrides of standard configurations -->
5      <!-- Copy this file to your instance's etc directory -->
6
7      <browser:defaultSkin name="WorldCookery" />
8
9   </configure>
```

Table 8.1. Layers defined in Zope packages

Name	Defined in	Description
default	zope.component	If not specified otherwise, all views are registered for this layer. Always put this layer as the last one in your skin definition so that view lookup will work normally.
rotterdam	zope.app.rotterdam	Layer for the *Rotterdam* skin, Zope's standard skin
debug	zope.app.debugksin	Provides views for exceptions to improve error debugging.
statictree	zope.app.tree	Provides a static navigation tree, meant to be layered over rotterdam's dynamic tree which requires JavaScript.

Summary

- Skins determine the look and feel of an application's views.
- Views are registered for layers which, in an ordered definition, make up a skin.
- Zope's default skin is *Rotterdam*. It provides a lot of basic infrastructure and is thus a good basis for custom skins.
- A different skin than the default skin can be invoked using the skin traversal namespace (for example ++skin++WorldCookery); the default skin can be changed in an override ZCML directive.

Table 8.2. Skins defined in Zope packages

Name	Layers	Defined in	Description
default	`default`	`zope.component`	Fallback skin that is used when the request does not report a preferred skin and the default skin has not been set.
Basic	`default`	`zope.app.basicskin`	Extremely rudimentary skin.
Rotterdam	`rotterdam, default`	`zope.app.rotterdam`	Zope's standard skin.
Debug	`debug, rotterdam, default`	`zope.app.debugksin`	Identical to the *Rotterdam* skin except that exceptions are displayed with their traceback, as provided by the debug layer.
StaticTree	`statictree, rotterdam, default`	`zope.app.tree`	Identical to *Rotterdam* except that the dynamic navigation tree is replaced by a static version.

Flashback

The skinning concept was first introduced to Zope in the *Content Management Framework* (CMF) and is extensively used in deriving applications such as *Plone*. What in Zope X3.0 is the responsibility of the *Presentation service* is handled by the *skins tool* in the CMF. Like in Zope 3, CMF skins are defined as an ordered list of layers. CMF layers, however, exist as sub-folders of the tool object in which the view objects, such as Page Templates or Python Scripts are located. In Zope 3, layers are simply an identifier for which views are registered. That gives us the advantage to register views for a layer from many different packages, whereas in CMF, each *Product* would typically register its own layer and all skins to include it upon installation. That is not necessary anymore; in most cases, views are registered for the `default` layer, meaning no layer is specified upon registration.

8.2 Page Template macros

When presenting data to a browser, views within one skin generally share a lot of common markup. For example, views in the ZMI always have the same basic HTML structure, only a few parts are unique to each view, most significantly the body of the view. Obviously, we would only want to define the general HTML structure once and reuse it everywhere. Page Templates allow us to do that using *macros*.

A macro is a piece of HTML markup that is meant to be reused in other Page Template views. Markup within macros is not limited to static HTML but can contain regular TAL statements. Those parts of a macro that can change with each view are called *slots*. Macros and slots in Page Templates are defined using the *Macro Expression Template Attribute Language* (METAL). METAL works like TAL in the sense that it uses attributes in a special name-space[1] for commands. It defines the following commands:

define-macro defines the markup tree starting below the current element as a macro.

define-slot defines the markup tree starting below the current element as a slot.

use-macro inserts the contents of a macro into the current template.

fill-slot fills a slot of the current macro with contents.

As an example, consider a simple macro that applies a certain formatting to arbitrary text. To save the time of writing a file system-based template and registering it via ZCML, we can simply create a *ZPT Page* in the ZMI. ZPT Pages are persistent Page Templates that are added like regular content objects. They allow quick mockups of Page Templates without the extra hassle of configuration. Simply go to an arbitrary folder in the ZMI and add a *ZPT Page* by clicking on the corresponding entry in the *Add* menu on the left hand side. Enter the following source code and give the object the name macro.html:

```
<html xmlns:metal="http://xml.zope.org/namespaces/metal"
      metal:define-macro="page_with_text">
<head>
  <title metal:define-slot="title">title</title>
</head>
<body>
  <p style="font-weight:bold;">
    <span metal:define-slot="text" />
  </p>
</body>
</html>
```

As you can see, in this Page Template there is a macro that is called page_with_text and starts with the html element. There are two slots in the macro that allow views to fill in custom information: title for the page's title and text for the text that is to be displayed. We can now provide a simple Page Template-based view that uses the macro. Add another ZPT Page called page.html in the same folder with the following source code:

---

[1] http://xml.zope.org/namespaces/metal

```
<div xmlns:metal="http://xml.zope.org/namespaces/metal"
     metal:use-macro="context/macro.html/macros/
page_with_text">
<title metal:fill-slot="title">Hello world!</title>
<span metal:fill-slot="text">Hello world!</span>
</div>
```

This page's markup structure has little to do with the one above. It is not even valid HTML as far as the structure is concerned. However, all that matters is that the macro from above is used. All markup that occurs within a use-macro is ignored and superseded by the macro itself, unless a slot is filled. If you open the preview of page.html in your browser now, you will see the following HTML being presented:

```
<html>
<head>
  <title>Hello World!</title>
</head>
<body>
  <p style="font-weight:bold;">
    <span>Hello world!</span>
  </p>
</body>
</html>
```

As you can see, the result has the markup structure of the macro but the slots contain the data from view.

Macros as part of a skin

In the quick demonstration above, the macro was exposed by the ZPT Page under the macros attribute. We could reference the macro by giving the path of the template containing it. This is not practical for macros that are part of a Zope skin. These are exposed through a special view called standard_macros. Every Zope skin should provide at least the following macros through this view:

page provides markup structure for a regular page without management capabilities (a regular browser page).

view is the macro for an object view as part of the ZMI. These pages are typically also registered in the zmi_views browser menu.

dialog, addingdialog allow pages to display themselves as dialogs or special variants of dialogs. These pages typically have little framework around the main content. In Rotterdam, they are identical to page.

Knowing this, we can revise the Page Template we use for displaying recipes. Example 8.2.1 shows a revised `recipeview.pt` now using the `page` macro provided by the current Zope skin. When you now view a recipe, compare the result as shown in Figure 8.1 with the way it looked before we involved the macro (Figure 7.4).

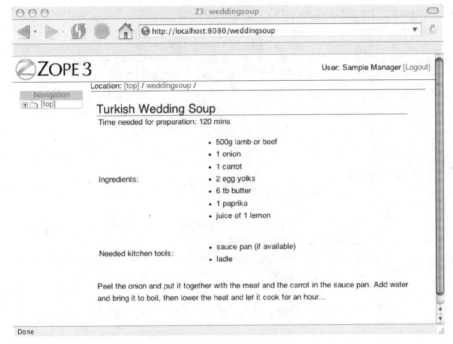

Fig. 8.1. Displaying a recipe with a template using a standard Zope skin macro.

Customizing a skin macro

Ideally, a page's layout is solely determined by the styling that is applied to it, for example through the use of CSS. More than often, though, one has to adjust the markup structure of a skin, too. Typical cases of that are when additional stylesheets have to be loaded, a different logo image is to be used, or the markup simply has be restructured so that it can be referenced better in CSS.

Changing the markup structure of a skin essentially means customizing the `page` macro. Before we can do that, we need to understand how skin macros are looked up. We have already seen in Example 8.2.1 that this happens through a special view called `standard_macros`. This view, on the other hand, looks up macros in a well-defined set of Page Template views. So, if we were to override the page macro, we would also have to customize the standard_macros view and tell it to include our new Page Template in the lookup list first. Example 8.2.2 shows the customization of the standard_macros view, Example 8.2.3 a custom page macro.

Example 8.2.1 View Page Template using a standard Zope skin macro (browser/recipeview.pt)

```
1   <html xmlns="http://www.w3.org/1999/xhtml"
2         xmlns:tal="http://xml.zope.org/namespaces/tal"
3         xmlns:metal="http://xml.zope.org/namespaces/metal"
4         metal:use-macro="context/@@standard_macros/page">
5   <head>
6     <title metal:fill-slot="title"
7            tal:content="context/name/title">recipe name goes here</title>
8   </head>
9   <body>
10  <div metal:fill-slot="body">
11
12    <h2 tal:content="context/name/title">recipe name goes here</h2>
13
14    <table>
15      <tbody>
16        <tr>
17          <td>Time needed for preparation:</td>
18          <td><tal:var replace="context/time_to_cook">xyz</tal:var> mins</td>
19        </tr>
20
21        <tr>
22          <td>Ingredients:</td>
23          <td>
24            <ul>
25              <li tal:repeat="ingredient context/ingredients"
26                  tal:content="ingredient">ingredients go here</li>
27            </ul>
28          </td>
29        </tr>
30
31        <tr>
32          <td>Needed kitchen tools:</td>
33          <td>
34            <ul>
35              <li tal:repeat="tool context/tools"
36                  tal:content="tool">tools go here</li>
37            </ul>
38          </td>
39        </tr>
40
41      </tbody>
42    </table>
43
```

```
44    <p tal:content="context/description">Longer description goes here.</p>
45
46    </div>
47    </body>
48    </html>
```

3. All macro-related commands are contained in this namespace which is abbreviated with the `metal` prefix by convention.

4. Since this Page Template is not a management screen or exposes any other kind of management facility, the `page` macro is to be used. It is acquired by means of the special `standard_macros` view.

6 – 7. One of the slots that the `page` macro provides for customization is the `title` slot. It allows overriding Page Templates to set the title of the HTML page.

10 and 46. Templates using the `page` macro are supposed to fill the body slot with the main contents of the page. Here we basically wrap the essential recipe display in a `fill-slot` command.

Example 8.2.2 Customizing the `standard_macros` view (`browser/skin/standardmacros.py`)

```
1    from zope.app.rotterdam.standardmacros import StandardMacros as BaseMacros
2
3    class StandardMacros(BaseMacros):
4        macro_pages = ('worldcookery_macros',) + BaseMacros.macro_pages
```

1 and 3. To make things easier, we simply inherit from Rotterdam's `StandardMacros` view. We have to import it under a different name, though, so it will not conflict with the class we are creating.

4. The base class we inherit from the Rotterdam skin already takes care of the macro lookup. We only have to provide it with a list of Page Template views to look for the macro; here we simply extend the list from the base class by the name of the Page Template view whose listing is shown in Example 8.2.3. This way, `StandardMacros` will first look in `worldcookery_macros`, then in other Page Templates, for example the ones defined in Rotterdam.

Both the `standard_macros` view and the template defining the `page` macro need to be configured now. There is no magic to that, both are defined like regular browser pages. Example 8.2.4 shows a revised version of `browser/skin/configure.zcml`.

Example 8.2.3 Customizing the page macro (browser/skin/worldcookery_macros.pt)

```
1  <metal:macro define-macro="page">
2    <metal:macro use-macro="context/@@skin_macros/page">
3
4  <metal:slot fill-slot="style_slot">
5    <link
6      href="worldcookery.css" rel="stylesheet" type="text/css"
7      tal:attributes="href context/++resource++worldcookery.css" />
8
9    <link
10     href="worldcookery_mgmt.css" rel="stylesheet" type="text/css"
11     tal:attributes="href context/++resource++worldcookery_mgmt.css" />
12
13     <metal:slot define-slot="style_slot" />
14  </metal:slot>
15
16  <metal:slot fill-slot="global">
17    <metal:slot define-slot="globals">
18    <div id="global">
19      <img src="worldcookery.png" alt="WorldCookery" class="toplogo"
20          tal:attributes="src context/++resource++worldcookery.png" />
21    </div>
22    </metal:slot>
23  </metal:slot>
24
25  <metal:slot fill-slot="breadcrumbs">
26    <metal:slot define-slot="breadcrumbs">
27    <div id="breadcrumbs">
28      <div id="userDetails" metal:define-slot="user_details">
29        <metal:macro metal:use-macro="context/@@skin_macros/logged_user" />
30        <metal:slot define-slot="login_logout">
31          <metal:macro use-macro="context/@@skin_macros/login_logout" />
32        </metal:slot>
33      </div>
34    </div>
35    <div metal:use-macro="context/@@skin_macros/breadcrumbs" />
36    </metal:slot>
37  </metal:slot>
38
39  <metal:slot fill-slot="body">
40    <metal:slot define-slot="body" />
41  </metal:slot>
42
43    </metal:macro>
44  </metal:macro>
```

1–2. In the first line we obviously have to define the page macro as this is what we are customizing. To save ourselves some work, we reuse the page macro from Rotterdam which is provided by a Page Template view called skin_macros.

Note that when a whole element is in either the tal or metal namespaces, it is stripped from the output; TAL or METAL attributes do not have to carry the namespace prefix. For example,

```
<metal:macro define-macro="page">...</metal:macro>
```

is equal to

```
<span metal:define-macro="page" tal:omit-tag="">
...</span>
```

4–14. The page macro has a style_slot slot which can be used to load additional CSS styles. Anticipating that we later would like to provide some custom CSS sheets we add corresponding directives here, not forgetting to re-provide the style_slot so that pages using this macro can add custom stylesheets, too.

16–37. Here we override the global and breadcrumbs slots to override the main logo on top of the page and rearrange the login/logout buttons to fit the layout better.

39–41. Finally, we have to provide the most important slot, body, for pages to fill.

Example 8.2.4 Configuring the custom macro template and the macros view (browser/skin/configure.zcml)

```
1  <configure
2      xmlns="http://namespaces.zope.org/zope"
3      xmlns:browser="http://namespaces.zope.org/browser"
4      >
5
6    <browser:layer name="worldcookery" />
7    <browser:skin name="WorldCookery" layers="worldcookery rotterdam
   default" />
8
9    <browser:page
10      for="*"
11      name="standard_macros"
12      permission="zope.View"
13      class=".standardmacros.StandardMacros"
14      layer="worldcookery"
15      allowed_interface="zope.interface.common.mapping.IItemMapping"
16      />
17
18    <browser:page
19      for="*"
20      name="worldcookery_macros"
21      permission="zope.View"
22      layer="worldcookery"
23      template="worldcookery_macros.pt"
24      />
25
26  </configure>
```

10 and 19. All skin-related views should always be registered for *any* object which is expressed through an asterisk (*).

a   b

Fig. 8.2. a) Logo for the *World Cookery* application (`browser/skin/`
`worldcookery.png`). **b)** Icon for recipe objects (`browser/skin/recipe_icon.`
`png`).

Summary

- Page Templates can inherit the markup structure of other Page Templates through the *macro* functionality. *Slots* allow the insertion of content into the provided structure.
- The common layout of browser pages in Zope is provided by a few skin macros, most importantly the `page` macro.
- Skin macros are looked up through a special view called `standard_macros`.

8.3 Stylesheets and other resources

A browser skin's look and feel is ideally determined only by the styling of the HTML markup and not the markup itself. Using CSS, it is possible to give the same HTML a completely different layout. Even though modifications to the HTML markup are admittedly necessary sometimes, most of a website's layout is still determined by CSS. Although stylesheets play an important role in a skin then, they are not views, though, since they do not present a particular type of object. They are really more like auxiliary files that need to be loaded together with the website. These types of components are called *resources*.

A browser resource is typically static and can be any type of file. Common use-cases are:

- stylesheets such as CSS and XSLT files,
- images that are part of the layout,
- scripts to support dynamic web pages, such as ECMAScripts or even Java Applets, MacroMedia Flash and ActiveX controls.

To provide a unique layout for our *World Cookery* application, we will customize the CSS stylesheets that determine the HTML display. The two files for which we already provided links in our custom `page` macro (Example 8.2.3) are shown in Example 8.3.1 and Example 8.3.2, respectively.

Additionally, we provide a custom logo which was also already referenced in the macro. To perfect the new look and feel of the *World Cookery* application, we also provide an icon for recipes. All of that is configured using four ZCML directives listed in Example 8.3.3.

Example 8.3.1 CSS stylesheet for layout customization of regular pages (browser/skin/worldcookery.css)

```
1   body    { background: #fdfdfd; color: black; }
2   table   { width: 100%;}
3   iframe { min-width: 600px; min-height: 400px; border: 1px solid #003366; }
4
5   a          { color: #003366; }
6   a:hover    { text-decoration: underline; }
7   a:visited { color: #519fbd; }
8
9   textarea            { border: 1px solid #003366; background-color: #f4f4f4;}
10  textarea:active,
11  textarea:hover    { background-color: #fdfdfd; min-width: 300px;}
12  input, button     { background-color: #f4f4f4; border: 1px solid #003366;}
13  input[type=text] { min-width: 300px; }
14  input[type=text]:hover, input[type=text]:active { background-color:
    #fdfdfd;}
15  select            { background-color: #f4f4f4; border: 1px solid #003366;
16                      min-width: 300px; }
17
18  #global      { height: 60px; border-bottom: 1px solid #116692;
19                  background-color: #003366; }
20  #global #userDetails,
21  #global .toplogo { float: right; padding-left: 0.5em; }
22  #actions     { background: #196692; }
23  #actions a   { color: White; float: left; padding: 0 0.7em;
24                  border-left: 1px dotted white; }
25  #breadcrumbs { padding: 0.1em 1em; border-bottom: 1px dotted #003366; }
26  #navigators { padding: 0; border: 1px solid #116692;
27                  border-style: None solid solid None; min-width: 15%; }
28  #workspace   { width: 75%; background-color: #fdfdfd; margin-left: 0.4em;}
29  #sortable, #sortable th, #sortable td { border: 1px solid #fe8700; }
30  #sortable thead th { background-color: #ffed7b; color: black; }
31
32  div.box h4       { border: 1px solid #003366; border-style: solid None;
33                      color: #fdfdfd; padding: 0.5em;
34                      text-align: left; background-color: #116692; }
35  div.box div.body { border: none }
36  div.box .even    { background-color: #f4f4f4; }
37  .itemViews a     { background: #cecece; color: #7f7f7f;
38                      padding: 0.1em 0.5em; border: 1px solid #dddedd;
39                      border-bottom: 0; }
40  .itemViews a.selected { background: #196692; border: none;
41                      font-weight: bold; padding: 0.1em 0.5em; }
```

Example 8.3.2 CSS stylesheet for layout customization of site management pages (`browser/skin/worldcookery_mgmt.css`)

```
1   .itemViews a:hover { background-color: #fe8700; }
2   .itemViews { border-bottom: 1px solid #cecece; }
3   #navigators h4 { background-color: #519fbd; }
4   #actions, .itemViews a.selected{
5       background-color: #519fbd; border-left: 0; border-right: 0; }
6   h2 { border-bottom: 1px solid #003366; }
```

Example 8.3.3 Configuring resources and icons (`browser/skin/configure.zcml`)

```
1      ...
2      <browser:resource
3          name="worldcookery.png"
4          image="worldcookery.png"
5          layer="worldcookery"
6          />
7
8      <browser:resource
9          name="worldcookery.css"
10         file="worldcookery.css"
11         layer="worldcookery"
12         />
13
14     <browser:resource
15         name="worldcookery_mgmt.css"
16         file="worldcookery_mgmt.css"
17         layer="worldcookery"
18         />
19
20     <browser:resource
21         name="arrow.png"
22         image="arrow.png"
23         layer="worldcookery"
24         />
25
26     <browser:icon
27         name="zmi_icon"
28         for="worldcookery.interfaces.IRecipe"
29         file="recipe_icon.png"
30         layer="worldcookery"
31         />
32     ...
```

2–24.   Resources are configured using the browser:resource directive. For image resources, specify the filename in the image attribute; for regular files, use the file attribute.

26–31. Icons are not exactly resources. They are more like views because they are registered for a specific interface. Icons used by the ZMI carry the name zmi_icon. Custom UIs might use different icon names.

Conclusion

We have managed to centrally customize the layout of Zope views by providing a custom skin macro and two custom CSS stylesheets. This is the minimum work one has to do to customize a skin. To save time, we have based our skin largely on Rotterdam. The more you want to change the way Rotterdam does things, the more customization work you have to do, obviously.

Many developers, including the author, prefer the actual software development over the designing, mostly because of the lack of ability and creativity in such matters. It is not uncommon, therefore, to hire a designer to do the customization. With the ability to customize macros and register resources, you should be able to integrate your designer's work into your Zope application easily.

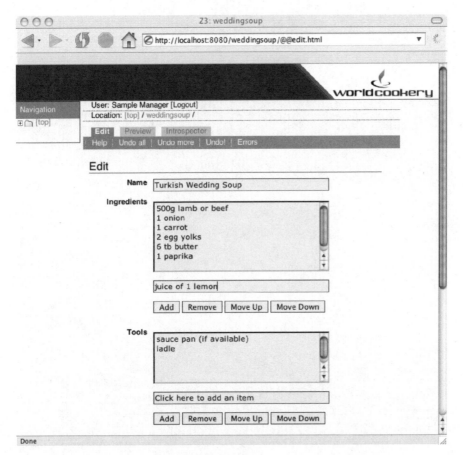

Fig. 8.3. A recipe's edit form displayed in the *WorldCookery* skin.

Summary

- Static files CSS stylesheets mostly determine the look and feel of HTML markup.
- Files that are not views but still part of a skin (like CSS stylesheets) are called *resources*.
- Resources are configured using the `browser:resource` directive.

9

Internationalization

The web is a multilingual and multicultural medium. Many websites and services offered over the web already need to cope with a user base from different language backgrounds. It is common that European websites deal with four languages or more at a time. Even in large countries like the United States, an increasing amount of national websites provide their content in Spanish next to English.

Internationalization does not only include the language aspect. Time and dates are displayed differently in different countries, as well as numbers. Web applications that deal with these things need to be aware of the differences. Fortunately, Zope provides an excellent framework for internationalization (*i18n*) and localization (*l10n*) which is the subject of this chapter.

9.1 Overview

When internationalizing an application, it is usually the application itself that needs to be translated, not the data the application works with. In Zope terms, that means content objects are often not i18n-aware; views, on the other hand, are. In the context of our *World Cookery* application, it would make little sense to request a translation to many different languages for every recipe that is added to the site. However, the application that lets us add recipes should be available in the language the user prefers.

Most of the text that would be subject to translation is part of a browser view, such as a Page Template. Sometimes, though, text comes from different components that are not view-specific per-se. In case of auto-generated forms, for example, the schema carries descriptive strings that are used to construct the form. Even configuration carries text that is visible in a user interface and thus subject to translation. In all cases, it is necessary to tag the strings that are to be translated so that the Zope machinery can pick them up.

Messages

In i18n jargon, strings that need to be translated are referred to as *messages*. They are identified by a *message id* which can be the string itself or an abstract but unique value. The message id is used to look up the translation of the message, the *message string*. If the lookup fails, the translation machinery typically falls back to a *default value*. Furthermore, message strings are looked up by a certain context, the *domain*. Different domains usually hold messages for different groups of messages. In Zope, it is the convention that every add-on package or application, respectively, uses its own domain. Zope itself uses the `zope` domain. In our example application, we will use the `worldcookery` domain.

To demonstrate the concept of messages, consider the translation of the English word *view*. This word has several different meanings in Zope; people can usually find out the proper meaning from the context, but a translation machinery cannot. In Zope, *view* is used as

- the name of components that take care of presentation, *view components*,
- the title of a permission that represents the action of viewing, the *view permission*,
- the actual action of viewing, as displayed on buttons or management tabs.

The dilemma here is two-fold. Not only are slightly different meanings involved; the English language also often does not distinguish between nouns and verbs, as in this case. To allow the proper translation of terms like these, the application developer needs to clarify using unique message ids. For example, one could use

- `view-component` to identify the message for the component type,
- `view-permission` for the permission title,
- `view-button`, `view-tab`, etc. whenever the action of viewing is described.

Of course, all these messages would default to *view*.

Fortunately, this example is an edge case. The longer the message that needs to be translated is, the more likely it is that it is unique in its meaning. Whole sentences are usually unique and can be used as their own message ids. In any case, it is preferrable to include as much context in the message as possible. For programmers, it is often tempting to use shortcuts when assembling user strings, especially when they are similar and can easily be computed. Such a behaviour, however, is not constructive for translators and can even make proper translation impossible.

Most of the actual translation in Zope happens in an automated manner because browser presentation usually works through Page Templates. Once a portion of text is marked as a message, Page Templates automatically do the translation. To know which language they actually need to translate to, they ask the request. Most of today's browsers send a special HTTP header, `Accept-Language` in which they tell the server which languages they prefer. That value is usually determined by the user's locale setting of the operating system. A special type of component, an adapter, is used to build a set list of preferred languages from the HTTP header value. Then, a negotiator component compares the list of preferred languages with the list of available languages and chooses the best match. Both components can, of course, be overridden with custom ones to change the language lookup or negotiation policy.

Summary

- Zope's translation machinery can be used to automatically translate messages that are part of an application's presentation.
- Messages are identified by their message id, which is usually the string itself.
- Explicitly unique message ids can be used to distinguish ambiguous messages.
- For browser views, an adapter extracts the user preferences regarding languages from the request and a negotiator finds the optimum language to be translated to.

9.2 Message IDs and translation domains

To give you an overview over the Zope components that handle translation, it is probably best to "play" with them on the interactive interpreter shell. It is not that one gets directly in touch with them that often, but knowing how they work helps understanding the concepts behind them.

In order to be able to work with messages, we need to setup some basic machinery. In Zope, translation domains are components that carry the mappings between message ids and message strings. The underlying machinery is not important; domain objects can acquire their data from a collection of *gettext*[1] files or from data stored in the ZODB, for example. What is important is that they provide the same API as documented in the `zope.i18n.interfaces.ITranslationDomain` interface. So, translation domains provide a certain functionality (translating strings) which is documented in that interface and they have names. That makes them *named utilities* in Zope, just like permissions and factories (see Section 5.4).

For our experiments on the interactive interpreter shell, we can use a demo implementation of translation domains called `SimpleTranslationDomain`. Instead of reading data from a file or anything like that, we can simply pass in a mapping of message ids to message strings:

---

[1] *gettext* is a Unix library for internationalization and localization. Python has built-in *gettext* support.

```
>>> from zope.i18n.simpletranslationdomain import \
...        SimpleTranslationDomain
>>> from zope.i18n.interfaces import ITranslationDomain
>>>
>>> messages = {
...        ('es', u'Time to cook'): u'Tiempo para cocinar',
...        ('de', u'Time to cook'): u'Zeit zum Kochen',
...        ('es', u'Necessary kitchen tools'):
...        u'Herramientas necesarias',
...        ('de', u'Necessary kitchen tools'):
...        u'Benoetigte Kuechengeraete'
...        }
>>> worldcookery = SimpleTranslationDomain(
...        'worldcookery', messages)
```

We now have a domain object, but in order for the translation machinery
to find it, we need to register it as a named utility. To have access to the
utility service, we also have to load Zope's configuration. Similar to the zapi
module which provides the common API functions for Zope code, the ztapi
(Zope *test* API) module provides useful functions that are frequently needed
in automated test, but also in interactive sessions like here:

```
>>> # load configuration; start Python in your Zope
instance directory
>>> from zope.app.debug import Debugger
>>> debugger = Debugger(db="var/Data.fs",
...                      config_file="etc/site.zcml")
>>>
>>> from zope.app.tests import ztapi
>>> ztapi.provideUtility(ITranslationDomain,
...        worldcookery, 'worldcookery')
```

Now we can start our interactive session with messages. In order to make a
string or a unicode object aware of translation, it needs to be converted into a
MessageID object. These objects represent the message within Zope; apart
from the message id, they also carry the domain they belong to and a default
value. Since the domain of messages in one Python module is generally the
same and making an instance of MessageID for every string in the module is
tiresome, it is common practice to use a factory for message ids as a shortcut.
The factory creates message ids of the same domain and is simply named _
(underscore) by convention:

```
>>> from zope.i18nmessageid import MessageIDFactory
>>> _ = MessageIDFactory('worldcookery')
```

It is fairly easy now to convert regular unicode to message ids, and even though they still appear to be unicode objects, they now carry the domain they are part of and a default translation:

```
>>> time_to_cook = _(u"Time to cook")
>>> time_to_cook
u'Time to cook'
>>> time_to_cook.domain
'worldcookery'
>>> time_to_cook.default
u'Time to cook'
```

We have successfully tagged a user string as a message and can have it automatically translated now. The zope.i18n package provides the necessary function for this:

```
>>> from zope.i18n import translate
>>> translate(time_to_cook, target_language='es')
u'Tiempo para cocinar'
>>> translate(time_to_cook, target_language='de')
u'Zeit zum Kochen
```

Since we did not provide a message string for French, the translate function will simply return the default value for the message when we request a French translation:

```
>>> translate(time_to_cook, target_language='fr')
u'Time to cook'
```

Variable interpolation

Sometimes, messages are not static but have to include some dynamic values. Imagine the sentence "It takes x minutes to cook" where x is a number to be dynamically inserted. This trivial task turns into a real problem when you need to translate the string. What do you translate? Just "It takes" and "minutes to cook"? That is unlikely to work because the order of a sentence is different in other languages. There is no guarantee that it will always be at the same place of the sentence.

Fortunately, the translation machinery provides a solution since it is a common problem. You can define placeholders in your message strings that will later then be interpolated automatically. The message id object carries the values to be interpolated. The placeholder syntax follows the one of embedded path expressions in Page Templates' string expressions.

So, let us take the above sentence and turn it into a message id:

```
>>> time_report = _(u'time-report',
...      u"It takes ${time_to_cook} minutes to cook")
>>> time_report
u'time-report'
>>> time_report.default
u'It takes ${time_to_cook} minutes to cook'
```

Because it is a rather long sentence, we now use an abstract message id, time-report and provide an English default value which carries a placeholder for x called time_to_cook. Now, let us provide some translations for this message, making sure that we include the placeholder there, too:

```
>>> messages = {
...     ('es', u'time-report'):
...       u'Necesita ${time_to_cook} minutos para cocinar',
...     ('de', u'time-report'):
...       u'Es werden ${time_to_cook} Minuten zum Kochen
...         benoetigt'
... }
>>> worldcookery = SimpleTranslationDomain(
...       'worldcookery', messages)
>>> ztapi.provideUtility(ITranslationDomain,
...       worldcookery, 'worldcookery')
```

Now, before requesting a translation, we need to fill the placeholder with a value. Message id objects carry a mapping attribute which can hold the necessary values for the variable interpolation. We fill it with a value for the time_to_cook placeholder; then we can ask for a translation:

```
>>> time_report.mapping['time_to_cook'] = 45
>>> translate(time_report, target_language='de')
u'Es werden 45 Minuten zum Kochen benoetigt'
>>> translate(time_report, target_language='es')
u'Necesita 45 minutos para cocinar'
```

As you can see, the translation machinery replaced the placeholder with the actual value we provided in the message id's mapping. Of course, it will do the interpolation even when a translation is not found and the fallback value has to be used:

```
>>> translate(time_report, target_language='fr')
u'It takes 45 minutes to cook'
```

Summary

- The translation functionality is provided by translation domain components which are registered as *named utilities*.
- Unicode strings are turned into message id objects using *message id factories*, which create message ids of the same domain.
- Apart from the message id itself, message id objects carry the domain they belong, a default value and a mapping for variable interpolation.
- Dynamic messages can be achieved by placing placeholders in message strings which are then interpolated using the message id's mapping.

9.3 Internationalizing an application

9.3.1 Python code

With the knowledge we have gained in the previous tour through the translation components we can now make our Python code "i18n-aware". Python code is probably the most difficult of all three (Python, ZPT, ZCML) to internationalize because it can be difficult to find out which strings are actually shown to the user and which are not. A rule of thumb is that whenever a string does not hold some identifier but real words or even a whole sentence, it should be made translatable. Examples include

- titles, labels, and description, for example in schema fields or browser widgets,
- report and status messages, such as "Your changes have been saved",
- error messages, even when raising exceptions (exceptions, too, are displayed to the user through views such as Page Templates).

When we have to internationalize our Python code now, we do exactly the same as we have done in the interactive interpreter session: we create a message id factory for our translation domain and then convert all strings with it. It is important now that we follow the convention to call the message id factory _ (underscore) because Zope provides us with automatic extraction utilities that search our source code for occurrences of message ids and compile a message catalog for us (more on that later). Consider the following technically correct but unuseful piece of code:

```
if successful:
    msg = u"The recipe has successfully been saved"
else:
    msg = u"An error has occurred while saving"
return _(msg)
```

Here, the programmer was aware of the fact that all messages that are to be displayed to the user need to be turned into message strings. However, the automatic extract utility will not be able to collect the message ids because they were defined above and do not appear when the message id is created. The following code fixes the problem:

```
if successful:
    return _(u"The recipe has successfully been saved")
else:
    return _(u"An error has occurred while saving")
```

Here, the strings are directly turned into message ids, allow the extract utility to pick them up. Even though this code might seem less elegant since the same action – turning a string into a message id – is spelled out twice, it is the more functional one.

After this bit of theory, we can finally internationalize the Python code we have written in the previous chapters. Fortunately, there is currently only one place where user strings appear in – the IRecipe schema. Though by now you can probably predict what it has to look like, Example 9.3.1 shows you what the internationalized version should look like.

With a translation provided for the message ids in the schema, the automatically generated add and edit forms for recipes are now translated as Figure 9.1 shows.

9.3.2 Page Templates

As mentioned in the introduction to this chapter, Page Templates typically contain many strings that need to be internationalized and are prominent places to look for them. Similar to *TAL* and *METAL* which are used to modify the XML output tree, a third command set in another namespace[2] is used to tag internationalized values. The namespace prefix here is i18n by convention. The following list gives an overview over the i18n command set in Page Templates:

---

[2] http://xml.zope.org/namespaces/i18n

Example 9.3.1 Internationalized schema (`interfaces.py`)

```
1   from zope.interface import Interface
2   from zope.schema import List, Text, TextLine, Int
3   from zope.i18nmessageid import MessageIDFactory
4   _ = MessageIDFactory('worldcookery')
5
6   class IRecipe(Interface):
7       """Store information about a recipe.
8       """
9
10      name = TextLine(
11          title=_(u"Name"),
12          description=_(u"Name of the dish"),
13          required = True
14          )
15
16      ingredients = List(
17          title=_(u"Ingredients"),
18          description=_(u"List of ingredients necessary for this recipe."),
19          required=True,
20          value_type=TextLine(title=_(u"Ingredient"))
21          )
22
23      tools = List(
24          title=_(u"Tools"),
25          description=_(u"List of necessary kitchen tools"),
26          required=False,
27          value_type=TextLine(title=_(u"Tool"))
28          )
29
30      time_to_cook = Int(
31          title=_(u"Time to cook"),
32          description=_(u"Necessary time for preparing the meal described, "
33                        "in minutes."),
34          required=True
35          )
36
37      description = Text(
38          title=_(u"Description"),
39          description=_(u"Description of the recipe"),
40          required=True
41          )
```

`translate` tells the TAL interpreter to translate the contents of the element, using for a message id either an explicitly given one or the existing element contents. Examples:

```
<h1 i18n:translate="heading-objective">The objective
</h1>
```

```
<p i18n:translate="">The goal of the World Cookery
website is to provide a place for hobby cooks to
share their favourite recipes.</p>
```

For the heading, an explicit message id is given, heading-objective. For the paragraph, the paragraph contents will be used as the message id. In both cases, the element contents serve as default fallback values when translation fails.

domain sets the translation domain for the current element and all child elements. Examples:

```
<div i18n:domain="worldcookery">
  <span i18n:translate="">This is looked up in the
worldcookery domain.</span>
  <span i18n:translate="" i18n:domain="zope">This is
not.</span>
</div>
```

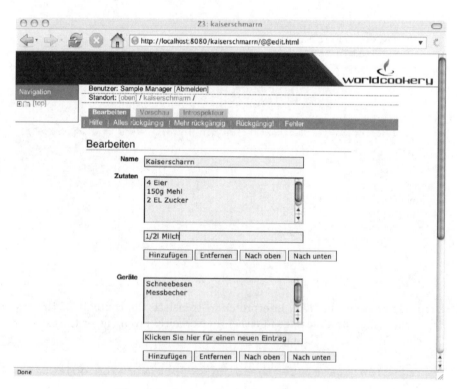

Fig. 9.1. A recipe's edit form in German.

attributes specifies which attributes, whether static or dynamically inserted, are to be translated. As with tal:attributes, several entries are separated by semicolon. Specifying a message id is optional. Example:

```
<form>
  <input type="text" name="country"
         tal:attributes="value context/country"
         i18n:attributes="value" />
  <input type="submit" title="Save form data"
         value="Save"
         i18n:attributes="title;
         value button-save" />
</form>
```

In this example the first form element, a text input box, receives a dynamically set attribute, value which is also to translate. The second form element, a submit button, has two static attributes which should be translated. The message id for title is the value itself, the message id for value is explicitly set to button-save. In both cases, the static attribute contents is assumed as the default fallback value when translation fails.

name marks an element as a variable placeholder. Like in message ids generated in Python code, Page Template message ids often need the placeholder functionality too. Example:

```
<p i18n:translate="time-report">
  It takes
  <span tal:replace="context/time_to_cook"
        i18:name="time_to_cook" />
  minutes to cook
</p>
```

This would be the TAL equivalent of

```
>>> time_report = _(u'time-report',
...      u"It takes ${time_to_cook} minutes to cook")
>>> time_report.mapping['time_to_cook'] = \
...      context.time_to_cook
```

as covered in Section 9.2.

Example 9.3.2 Internationalized View Page Template (browser/ recipeview.pt)

```
1   <html xmlns="http://www.w3.org/1999/xhtml"
2         xmlns:tal="http://xml.zope.org/namespaces/tal"
3         xmlns:metal="http://xml.zope.org/namespaces/metal"
4         xmlns:i18n="http://xml.zope.org/namespaces/i18n"
5         metal:use-macro="context/@@standard_macros/page"
6         i18n:domain="worldcookery">
7   <head>
8     <title metal:fill-slot="title"
9            tal:content="context/name/title">recipe name goes here</title>
10  </head>
11  <body>
12  <div metal:fill-slot="body">
13
14    <h2 tal:content="context/name/title">recipe name goes here</h2>
15
16    <table>
17      <tbody>
18        <tr>
19          <td i18n:translate="">Time needed for preparation:</td>
20          <td i18n:translate="">
21              <tal:var replace="context/time_to_cook"
22                       i18n:name="time_to_cook">xyz</tal:var> mins
23          </td>
24        </tr>
25
26        <tr>
27          <td i18n:translate="">Ingredients:</td>
28          <td>
29            <ul>
30              <li tal:repeat="ingredient context/ingredients"
31                  tal:content="ingredient">ingredients go here</li>
32            </ul>
33          </td>
34        </tr>
35
36        <tr>
37          <td i18n:translate="">Needed kitchen tools:</td>
38          <td>
39            <ul>
40              <li tal:repeat="tool context/tools"
41                  tal:content="tool">tools go here</li>
42            </ul>
43          </td>
44        </tr>
45
46      </tbody>
47    </table>
48
```

```
49    <p tal:content="context/description">Longer description goes here.</p>
50
51    </div>
52    </body>
53    </html>
```

4.   For XML validity we need to define the namespace of the i18n command
         set. The prefix used is i18n by convention.

6.   Because all of the messages in this Page Template should be part of the
         worldcookery domain, we set it at the topmost place.

19, 27, As stated previously, the i18n:translate attribute invokes translation
and 37. of the elements contents. Here we leave the attribute value empty, so the
         implied message id is the element contents itself.

21 – 22. This is a good example of placeholders within translation messages in Page
         Templates. The actual time that is necessary to prepare a dish is inserted
         into the message, thus requires a named placeholder. This is accomplished
         with the i18n:name attribute.

With this we can now internationalize our Page Templates. So far, we only
wrote two: the one used to display recipes (browser/recipeview.pt)
and the one used for the dynamic sequence widget (browser/widget.pt).
Example 9.3.2 and Example 9.3.3 list their internationalized versions. Note
that the Page Templates are still valid XML documents and can still be
viewed in a browser directly off of the filesystem.

9.3.3 ZCML

The least problematic part of the whole internationalization process is ZCML
configuration. Because of the way the configuration machinery works, it
knows what values are expected for which directive parameters. That means
that there is no need to specify what needs to be translated and what not
– ZCML already knows! The only thing left for us to do is set a translation
domain. Because we have not done this, Zope has warned us before with a
message similar to the following:

```
zope/configuration/fields.py:380: UserWarning:
    You did not specify an i18n translation domain for
the 'label'
    field in worldcookery/browser/configure.zcml
```

That means we have used configuration directives that take translatable
strings but do not know in which domain they should be translated. That
can easily be fixed by setting the domain on the configuration context of the
corresponding file, meaning the configure document element of a ZCML
file or a context higher up in the ZCML tree. In our case, it would make
sense to add it to the topmost ZCML file of our package, configure.zcml
so that all included files, such as browser/configure.zcml inherit the
setting. Simply replace the opening document element tag with the following:

Example 9.3.3 Internationalized widget template (`browser/widget.pt`)

```
1   <div xmlns:tal="http://xml.zope.org/namespaces/tal"
2         xmlns:i18n="http://xml.zope.org/namespaces/i18n"
3         i18n:domain="worldcookery">
4
5   <script type="text/javascript" src="sequence.js"
6           tal:attributes="src context/++resource++sequence.js">
7   </script>
8
9   <p>
10    <select name="foo" id="foo" size="5"
11            tal:attributes="name view/name; id view/name;
12                            size python:min(max(len(view.getData()),5),12)">
13      <option tal:repeat="item view/getData" tal:content="item">item</option>
14    </select>
15    <script type="text/javascript"
16            tal:content="string:registerSequenceElement('${view/name}')">
17      registerSequenceElement('foo')
18    </script>
19  </p>
20
21  <p>
22    <input
23        type="text" id="input"
24        tal:attributes="id string:input.${view/name}"
25        value="Click here to add an item" onfocus="this.value=''"
26        i18n:attributes="value"
27        />
28  </p>
29  <p>
30    <button
31        type="button" onclick="sequenceAddItem('foo', 'input')"
32        tal:attributes="onclick string:sequenceAddItem('${view/name}',
    'input.${view/name}')"
33        i18n:translate="button-add">
34      Add
35    </button>
36
37    <button
38        type="button" onclick="sequenceRemoveItem('foo')"
39        tal:attributes="onclick string:sequenceRemoveItem('${view/name}')"
40        i18n:translate="button-remove">
41      Remove
42    </button>
43
44    <button
45        type="button" onclick="sequenceMoveItem('foo', -1)"
46        tal:attributes="onclick string:sequenceMoveItem('${view/name}', -1)"
47        i18n:translate="button-move-up">
48      Move Up
49    </button>
50
```

```
51    <button
52        type="button" onclick="sequenceMoveItem('foo', 1)"
53        tal:attributes="onclick string:sequenceMoveItem('${view/name}', 1)"
54        i18n:translate="button-move-down">
55      Move Down
56    </button>
57  </p>
58  </div>
```

22.   Translating the default value of a text input box in a form is the typical example for i18n:attributes; even the examples earlier on introduced it this way. Here we see a perfect application of this example.

29, 36, 43, and 50.   Since the button labels are only one or two words each and often do not provide enough context to ensure a unique translation, we use explicit message ids here just to be sure.

```
<configure
    xmlns="http://namespaces.zope.org/zope"
    i18n_domain="worldcookery"
    >
...
```

Now, the ZCML interpreter knows in which domain translation messages are to be created and the extractor utility can correctly extract the messages. This will be, among others, the subject of the next section.

Finally, it is possible to explicitly specify a message id in ZCML, too. Here, we have to rely on a special syntax because everything needs to be contained in the attribute value; the explicit message id, if given, is included in square brackets before the message text:

```
[label-edit] Edit
```

This will set the message id explicitly to label-edit while retaining the message text and default translation as Edit. In the special case that a leading word enclosed in square brackets is intended to be part of the message text and not the message id, preprend the attribute value with an empty set of square brackets, like so:

```
[] [top]
```

To ensure proper translation of our application, we can now specify some explicit message ids for some configuration values. Example 9.3.4 lists an internationalized version of browser/configure.zcml. Note that not all string parameters passed to a ZCML directive can be translated text. Typically only those that will appear in a browser presentation, such as form labels, menu entry titles, etc.

Example   9.3.4   Internationalized   configuration   file   (browser/
configure.zcml)

```
1    <configure
2        xmlns="http://namespaces.zope.org/zope"
3        xmlns:browser="http://namespaces.zope.org/browser"
4        >
5
6      <browser:addMenuItem
7          title="[label-recipe] Recipe"
8          class="worldcookery.recipe.Recipe"
9          permission="zope.ManageContent"
10         view="AddRecipe.html"
11         />
12
13     <browser:addform
14         schema="worldcookery.interfaces.IRecipe"
15         content_factory="worldcookery.recipe.Recipe"
16         label="[label-add-recipe] Add Recipe"
17         name="AddRecipe.html"
18         permission="zope.ManageContent"
19         >
20       <widget field="ingredients" class=".widget.DynamicSequenceWidget" />
21       <widget field="tools" class=".widget.DynamicSequenceWidget" />
22     </browser:addform>
23
24     <browser:editform
25         schema="worldcookery.interfaces.IRecipe"
26         label="[label-edit] Edit"
27         name="edit.html"
28         menu="zmi_views" title="[label-edit] Edit"
29         permission="zope.ManageContent"
30         >
31       <widget field="ingredients" class=".widget.DynamicSequenceWidget" />
32       <widget field="tools" class=".widget.DynamicSequenceWidget" />
33     </browser:editform>
34
35     <browser:resource name="sequence.js" file="sequence.js" />
36
37     <browser:page
38         for="worldcookery.interfaces.IRecipe"
39         name="index.html"
40         template="recipeview.pt"
41         permission="zope.View"
42         />
43
44     <!-- Preview page - requires zope.app.preview -->
45     <configure package="zope.app.preview" i18n_domain="zope">
46       <browser:page
47           for="worldcookery.interfaces.IRecipe"
48           name="preview.html"
49           template="preview.pt"
50           permission="zope.ManageContent"
51           menu="zmi_views" title="Preview"
```

```
52              />
53      </configure>
54
55      <include package=".skin" />
56
57  </configure>
```

7, 16, 26,   Where messages might be ambigious, such as for short labels and menu
and 28.   entry titles, we provide an explicit message id using the square bracket
               syntax.

45.   Because the preview page comes from a Zope package and the config-
               uration directive we used, including the title, is generic to the preview
               page, we tell ZCML to use the zope domain. That way, it will use the
               translation that is already available in Zope's message catalogs, which
               means one message less for us to translate.

Summary

- In Python, a message id factory, named _ (underscore) by convention, is
  used to create message id objects. It is important that message ids are
  created from string constants, not from possibly dynamic variables so that
  the extractor utility can pick them up.
- In Page Templates, yet another command set is used to identify translated
  text. The contents of an element or an attribute can be translated, with
  or without an explicitly given message id. The placeholder functionality
  is available as well.
- ZCML directives already know for which values they expect translatable
  messages or not. The ZCML interpreter only needs to know which translation domain they belong to. Once set, the domain setting is inherited
  in included files until overridden.

9.4 Message catalogs

We have now successfully made our application aware of translation. Only a
few files had to be changed and the changes were mostly small adjustments.
Thanks to the internationalization framework Zope provides, writing translatable software requires very little overhead compared to the benefits. What
we have not done yet, though, is to provide the translations. Although developers usually do not provide translations themselves but acquire them from
professional translators, they do need to know how to tell the translators
what is to be translated. Finally, a translated set of messages needs to be
integrated back into the application so that automatic translation can do its
job.

The translation system in Zope uses a well known backend for retrieving
translations for a certain message id, the *GNU gettext* system. The *gettext*

library provides access to message ids and their message strings stored in files called *message catalogs*. Message catalogs are plain text files but the library itself can only work with a binary representation of the files. You will need the *gettext utilities*, the msgfmt program in particular, to compile the text files to the binary catalogs. The *gettext utilities* can be retrieved from the GNU project homepage[3]; packages for your operating system might also exist.

The extractor utility

As mentioned earlier, Zope comes with an extractor utility called i18n-extract.py which can extract all message ids from Python code, Page Templates and ZCML files. It writes the result into a message catalog *template* (file extension .pot). i18nextract.py takes the following arguments:

-p, --path specifies the path of the package that is to be searched. All Python modules, ZCML files and Page Templates in this package and subpackages are searched for message ids.

-d, --domain specifies the translation domain for which the message catalog is to be created. Only message ids from this domain will be included in the catalog template, except for the ones found in Python code; message ids found in Python code are included regardless of their domain (this is a limitation of the extracing algorithm). If not set, the domain defaults to zope, thus needs to be given for all third-party packages.

-o specifies a directory *within* the given package where the catalog template file is to be written to. It is a convention that all internationalization-related files of a package reside in a subdirectory called locales. The filename of the catalog template will be <domain>.pot. If this option is not specified, the extractor writes the file to the current directory.

By passing the right arguments to those parameter options, we obtain the template file for message catalogs, locales/worldcookery.pot:

```
~/Zope3Instance$ bin/i18nextract -p lib/python/
worldcookery -d worldcookery -o locales
base path: '~/Zope3Instance/lib/python/worldcookery'
search path: '~/Zope3Instance/lib/python/worldcookery'
domain: 'worldcookery'
output file: '~/Zope3Instance/lib/python/worldcookery/
locales/worldcookery.pot'
```

---

[3] GNU project homepage <http://www.gnu.org/software/gettext/>

This generates catalog template contains all the message ids we have defined in the source code throughout our package. The syntax follows the *gettext* message catalog syntax. In the template file, the message string is simply left empty. This is what an entry in the file looks like for example:

```
#: ~/lib/python/worldcookery/browser/configure.zcml:13
# Default: "Add Recipe"
msgid "label-add-recipe"
msgstr ""
```

You can now give the catalog template to a translator who will translate each message id by filling in the translation for the empty message string. This can be achieved with a simple text editor or a specialized tool, like *KBabel*[4] and *gtranslator*[5] which are available for Unix/X11 systems and *poEdit*[6] which is available for all major platforms. Using such a tool is recommended because these tools are capable of writing non-ASCII text (usually in UTF-8) and ensure that the syntax of the catalog files is still valid.

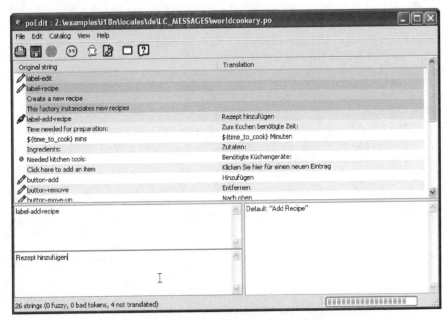

Fig. 9.2. Translating the worldcookery domain to German with *poEdit*.

---

[4] KBabel homepage <http://i18n.kde.org/tools/kbabel/>

[5] gtranslator homepage <http://gtranslator.sourceforge.net/>

[6] poEdit homepage <http://poedit.sourceforge.net>

Message catalogs in their text version have the file extension .po. When we retrieve such a file from a translator, we have to install it in the locales directory and compile it. The *gettext* system expects a subdirectory of locales for each language that is available. So, if we had a Spanish translation, we would create a directory called es inside locales; in that directory, we create another directory called LC_MESSAGES in which we put our Spanish message catalog file, worldcookery.po. We then have to compile it to its binary version as *gettext* only works with the compiled catalogs. This is achieved with the msgfmt program of the *gettext utilities*. Compiled catalogs carry the .mo file extension:

```
.../locales/es/LC_MESSAGES$ msgfmt -o worldcookery.mo
worldcookery.po
```

Note that the translation tools mentioned above often aid the translator here, for example *poEdit* automatically compiles message catalogs upon saving.

For a detailed description of the *gettext* system and the *gettext utilities*, please refer to the *gettext manual* [5].

As a final step, we need to tell the translation machinery where to find the translations we provided. We do that using a ZCML directive called registerTranslations of the http://namespaces.zope.org/i18n namespace. Change the document element of configure.zcml to the following:

```
<configure
    xmlns="http://namespaces.zope.org/zope"
    xmlns:i18n="http://namespaces.zope.org/i18n"
    i18n_domain="worldcookery"
    >
```

and insert the following line somewhere in the file:

```
<i18n:registerTranslations directory="locales" />
```

Zope will then pick up the message catalogs that you can provide under locales/<language>/LC_MESSAGES as compiled *gettext* files. Note that the filenames *must* be of the form <domain>.mo. You can check whether Zope has found the message catalogs in a ZMI screen in the process management area (see Figure 9.3).

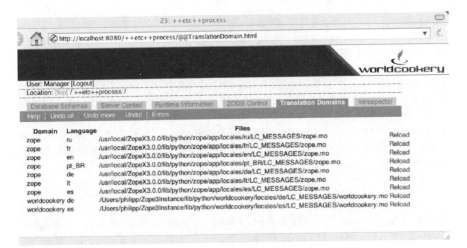

Fig. 9.3. Filesystem-based translation domains can be reloaded on the fly through the ZMI.

Summary

- Translation messages are stored in message catalogs, one for each translation domain and language.
- Zope comes with an automatic extractor utility that extracts message ids from Python code, Page Templates and ZCML files and writes them into a message catalog template file.
- Zope uses the *GNU gettext* system as a backend for retrieving translation messages. The *gettext utilities* are needed to compile message catalogs from their editable text format to the required binary format.
- The compiled message catalogs are managed in a standard *gettext* directory structure below a directory usually called `locales`.

9.5 Advanced: Localization

Internationalization is not always just a matter of translating everything literally. Different countries have different cultural background which primarily includes differences in calendars and dates on one hand and numbers and currencies on the other one. To give you examples:

Calendars

In the western Christian societies, the Gregorian calendar[7] is predominant, whereas in Islamic countries, the Ismalic calendar[8] is used. *1 Muharram AH 1423* and *16 March 2002* are the same day, but in different calendars. Even within the Gregorian calendar there are subtle differences between different societies. In the United States, a date is commonly given in the order of *Month/Day/Year* and the week starts on Sunday. In Europe, on the other hand, the week starts on Monday and dates are given in the form of *Day/-Month/Year*.

Numbers

In the Anglo-Saxon world, numbers and currencies are written differently than in Europe, too. Decimal numbers in Europe use a *comma* for the decimal separator and commonly a *dot* for the thousand separator. In English-speaking countries, it is the reverse way. Furthermore, the position of the currency symbol changes its position. A million dollars are commonly written as *$1,000,000*, whereas in Europe a million euros would be written as *1.000.000 €*.

Localization

Adjusting an application to be sensible towards these kinds of internationalization issues is commonly referred to as *localization* (l10n). As you can imagine, there are many subtle differences that would be impossible to take care of manually. Fortunately, Zope provides a rich localization API as part of the zope.i18n.locales package. Central to the API design are *locale objects*. A *locale* represents the localization aspect of a particular language or region and is referred to by the typical two letter code combinations. For example, es stands for the Spanish locale, es-ES for Spanish in Spain and es-MX for Spanish in Mexico.

Just like translation, localization is a pure presentation matter. What is stored in a database are floating point numbers and datetime objects. They contain the abstract values, so to speak. When presenting those values to a user, such as in form of an HTML page, you will have to make sure to apply the right formatting. Formatting is conveniently done by formatters which are retrieved from the locale object. The locale object, on the other hand, is usually retrieved from the request, since, after all, formatting is part of the presentation.

---

[7] Named after Pope Gregory XIII, who introduced it in 1582; succeeded the the Julian calendar of the Roman empire.

[8] A pure lunar calendar counting the years since the prophet Muhammad emigrated to Medina.

Numbers

As a simple example, we shall consider a Page Template that has to display different kinds of numbers in localization-sensible environment. Because our *World Cookery* application does not need to deal with numbers or dates, it is difficult to provide an example in the context of this application. To try the localization features of Page Templates out, though, we can use the persistent, content space-based *ZPT Page*, which is perfect for trying out features like this. Go to an arbitrary folder in the ZMI and add a *ZPT Page* by clicking on the corresponding entry in the *Add* menu on the left. For the source of the template, enter the code listing shown in Example 9.5.1 and provide a name for the object on the bottom, for example `locales.html`. After you have saved, click on the *Preview* tab to see the result of the localization. You should be shown something similar to Figure 9.4, depending on your browser's locale.

Example 9.5.1 Demonstration of localization in a Page Template (`locales.html`)

```
1   <html>
2   <head>
3     <title>L10n formatting examples</title>
4   </head>
5
6   <body tal:define="locale request/locale">
7
8   <p>
9     The number pi has the value of
10    <span tal:define="pi         modules/math/pi;
11            formatter python:locale.numbers.getFormatter('decimal')"
12          tal:replace="python:formatter.format(pi)">3.14</span>
13  </p>
14
15  <p>
16    The speed of light is
17    <span tal:define="c           python: 3e8;
18            formatter python:locale.numbers.getFormatter('scientific')"
19          tal:replace="python:formatter.format(c)">3*10^8 m/s</span>
20    metres per second.
21  </p>
22
23  <p>
24    In order to be a millionaire, you need possess
25    <span tal:define="million    python:1e6;
26            formatter python:locale.numbers.getFormatter('currency')"
27          tal:replace="python:formatter.format(million)">$1,000,000</span>.
28  </p>
29
30  </body>
31  </html>
```

6.   The preferred locale of the browser is available as an attribute on the request.

11, 18, In order to format numbers, one has to retrieve a *formatter* from the
and 26. `numbers` attribute of the locale object. There are four different categories of formatters:

- `decimal`
- `percent`
- `scientific`
- `currency`

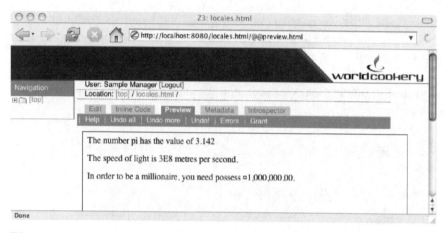

Fig. 9.4. Rendering locale-sensitive information with Page Templates (here in the English/U.S.A. locale).

Dates and times

For the demonstration of localizing date and time values we will use the interactive interpreter shell once more. The reason is because now `date` or `datetime` objects are involved and these cannot be created as easily in web-based *ZPT Pages*. To get started, let us first create a `datetime` object. We can use the convenient class method `utcnow` to create an object that reflects today's date and the current time:

```
>>> from datetime import datetime
>>> now = datetime.utcnow()
>>> now
datetime.datetime(2004, 7, 23, 15, 46, 36, 911803)
```

Now we can acquire different locales, for example one for English and one for German:

```
>>> from zope.i18n.locales import locales
>>> english = locales.getLocale('en')
>>> german = locales.getLocale('de', 'DE')
```

Similar to number formatting, we have to retrieve formatters from the locale's dates attribute. As with number formatters, there are again different categories:

- date
- time
- dateTime

So if we wanted to format the datetime object we just created with today's date and the current time, we would probably want to the use the dateTime formatter:

```
>>> formatter = english.dates.getFormatter('dateTime')
>>> formatter.format(now)
u'Jul 23, 2004 3:46:36 PM'
```

In a German environment, the same date would be printed differently:

```
>>> formatter = german.dates.getFormatter('dateTime')
>>> formatter.format(now)
u'23.07.2004 15:46:36'
```

Dates can be written in different forms; one could spell out the name of the month or just use the numbers, for example. We can use one of the following identifiers to set the length of a date format:

- short
- medium
- long
- full

For example, one could print all of the available date and time information, including the time zone, for example, by acquiring the formatter that produces output in the full length:

```
>>> formatter = english.dates.getFormatter(
...         'dateTime', length='full')
```

```
>>> formatter.format(now)
u'Friday, July 23, 2004 3:46:36 PM +000'

>>> formatter = german.dates.getFormatter(
...        'dateTime', length='full')
>>> formatter.format(now)
u'Freitag, 23. Juli 2004 15:46 Uhr +000'
```

As you can see, localized times and dates are already translated, so there is
no need to invoke the translation machinery for this again.

Summary

- Internationalization not only includes the translation of static text, but
  also the localization (l10n) of sensible information such as numbers, dates
  and times.
- Zope's localization API comes in form of *locale* objects which represent
  the formatting of numbers, dates, and times in a certain language and
  region.
- Formatting of localization-sensible values is achieved through formatter
  objects which are acquired from the locale object; different formatters
  exist for different formatting categories and presentation lengths.

10

Adapters

It is one of the dedicated concepts of the Component Architecture to divide different types of functionality into different components and to keep the amount of functionality provided by a single component small. Its strength lies in combining these components into a powerful application. In Chapter 3, *adapters* were defined as components that allow one to extend the functionality of existing components. It is obvious at this point that adapters play a *major* role in the Component Architecture and the software based on it, Zope.

Adapters are useful in every-day tasks when a component needs to work with a certain framework. Instead of requiring the objects the framework works with to provide a certain API, the framework usually tries to adapt the object to one of its own APIs. If such an adapter exists for the object, then the framework can work with the object through the adapter. This chapter will demonstrate implementing adapters by introducing a few of such frameworks here. Since adapters are such an integral concept of the Component Architecture, they will frequently reoccur in subsequent chapters.

Note that we have already worked with a framework that adapts objects: the presentation framework. Views are nothing but named adapters that make Zope's presentation framework, the Zope publisher, work with objects. In a broad sense, views can be perceived as adapters between objects and user interaction, for example through a web browser request.

10.1 Size

A quite common problem in a user or management interface is to display the size of stored objects. Zope has its own API for handling size information, formalized in the ISized interfaces provided by the zope.app.size package. Obviously, no object is required to implement this interface directly. You usually provide an adapter to it.

Adapters *adapt* objects of one interface to *provide* another one. In this case, we want to adapt `IRecipe` objects and provide `ISized`. Adapters are typically simple classes. An adapter factory – for a class it is the `__init__` method – needs to take exactly one argument, `context`, which is the object that is to be adapted. This object should be stored on the adapter object in the `context` attribute.

Even though it might seem awkward to compute a size of a recipe, we shall provide a size adapter here. The reason is that it is not only a very common one for content components; it is also a rather simple one and therefore serves well as an example. The `ISized` interface only expects two relatively simple methods which can easily be implemented. Example 10.1.1 shows the implementation for recipes.

Example 10.1.1 Adapter to display a recipe's size (`size.py`)

```
1   from zope.interface import implements
2   from zope.i18nmessageid import MessageIDFactory
3   from zope.app.size.interfaces import ISized
4   _ = MessageIDFactory('worldcookery')
5
6   class RecipeSize(object):
7       implements(ISized)
8
9       def __init__(self, context):
10          self.context = context
11
12      def sizeForSorting(self):
13          """Compute a size for sorting"""
14          chars = 0
15          chars += len(self.context.name)
16          chars += sum(map(len, self.context.tools))
17          chars += sum(map(len, self.context.ingredients))
18          chars += len(self.context.description)
19          return ('byte', chars)
20
21      def sizeForDisplay(self):
22          """Generate a displayable size report"""
23          unit, chars = self.sizeForSorting()
24          msg = _('${chars} characters')
25          msg.mapping['chars'] = chars
26          return msg
```

7.   Once created, the adapter is supposed to provide `ISized`. The easiest way to ensure that is by having the class implement it, just like any other class we wrote before implements the promised interface.

9–10.   A factory that instantiates an adapter takes exactly one argument, the object that is to be adapted. Most of the time, an adapter's factory is the class's `__init__` method. The object that is to be adapted should then be stored on the adapter as the `context` attribute so that the methods of the adapter have access to it.

12 – 19. This method is used by management views and similiar facilities when objects are to be sorted by size. Because objects may not necessarily be able to tell their size in a uniform way, e.g. number of bytes, different basic units are supported:

- 'byte' for file-like objects,
- 'item' for objects that contain a number of items, such as containers,
- 'line' for textual components, like objects holding plain text or source code.

For our recipe, we simply add the length of all strings that are stored inside the recipe and return that as the number of bytes. This, of course, can only serve as a rough estimate, because the size of a unicode encoded into a string varies depending on the encoding you choose.

21 – 26. This method is supposed to generate a small message that can be used when displaying the size of objects. This message, of course, needs to be a message id so that it can be translated. Then we simply let the sizeForSorting method compute the number of characters and fill the placeholder value on the message id.

As with any other type of component, we need to configure the adapter now. This is easily achieved with the adapter ZCML directive. Add the following lines to configure.zcml:

```
<adapter
    for=".interfaces.IRecipe"
    provides="zope.app.size.interfaces.ISized"
    factory=".size.RecipeSize"
    />
```

This directive is straight-forward. The adapter is supposed to adapt recipes, so we register it *for* IRecipe. It will *provide* ISized. For a factory, we simply use the class itself by using its dotted name.

Testing

We can now test the adapter on the interactive interpreter shell like we have done with other components in previous chapters. First, we create a recipe object and provide some initial data:

```
>>> from worldcookery.recipe import Recipe
>>> falafel = Recipe()
>>> falafel.name = u"Falafel"
>>> falafel.ingredients = [u"beans", u"peas", u"garlic"]
```

Now, before we can do anything, we need to load the configuration so that the adapter is registered. As usual, we do that by creating an instance of the Debugger. Then, we can adapt our recipe object to ISized. That is achieved by calling the interface with the object as an argument. Think of this like a type casting known in other programming languages. We "cast" (read: adapt) the recipe object to ISized:

```
>>> # load configuration
>>> from zope.app.debug import Debugger
>>> debugger = Debugger(db="var/Data.fs",
...                         config_file="etc/site.zcml")
>>>
>>> from zope.app.size.interfaces import ISized
>>> size = ISized(falafel)
```

We now have an object that provides ISized, so we can call the two methods promised by this interface. Of course, we know that this is really our adapter for the recipe object, so we know what output to expect. To enable the variable interpolation for the message id the sizeForDisplay returns, we have to use the familiar translate function:

```
>>> size.sizeForSorting()
('byte', 22)
>>> from zope.i18n import translate
>>> translate(size.sizeForDisplay())
u'22 characters'
```

To prove that the adapter is indeed working within the Zope application server, we can go to the Zope management interface and view the contents of a folder that contains one or more recipes. A recipe's size in characters should now be shown in the *Size* column of the folder listing, as shown in Figure 10.1.

Summary

- Object listings frequently need to list the size of objects. The zope.app.size package provides a small general framework for this problem.
- The functionality of providing the size of an object is implemented as an adapter from an interface the object provides to ISized.
- Adapter factories take a single argument, context, the object that is to be adapted.
- Objects are adapted to a particular interface by calling the interface with the object as an argument, making adaptation syntactically similar to type casting.

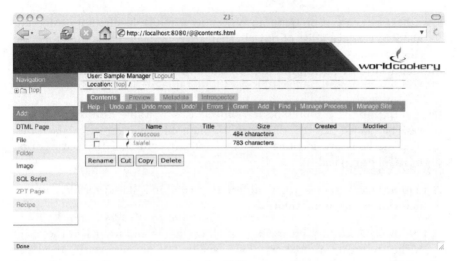

Fig. 10.1. The *Contents* screen in the ZMI uses `ISized` adapters to display the size of objects.

10.2 File representation

Apart from publishing objects to web browsers over HTTP, Zope knows a variety of other protocols, such as WebDAV, XML-RPC and FTP. The former ones are covered in Chapter 12, the latter shall be the subject of this section. As the name already suggests, the *file transfer protocol* (FTP) is about files (and directories). Zope, however, does not work with simple files, it works with objects. The different aspects of objects are easy to communicate to a browser through different views, as we have seen. An FTP client still expects a structure of simple files and directories. How can we connect both sides?

A Zope developer like you, with the experience of this chapter and the previous ones, already knows the answer – adapters! Not unlike in the previous section, a Zope package provides a collection of interfaces that make up a file representation API. Using this API, other components such as generic FTP views can adapt objects so that they are representable as files or directories. The file contents or directory listings can then be sent to the client which does not know that it is looking at objects; it only sees files.

The `zope.app.filerepresentation` package defines the following API interfaces:

`IReadFile` represents an object as a readable file. Methods allow access to the contents of the file representation and its size.

`IWriteFile` represents an object as a writable file. The `write` method allows writing data to the file.

IReadDirectory represents an object as a readable directory. Methods
   allow to retrieve a list of objects that are contained in the directory and
   can be represented as files or directories themselves. The methods are
   identical to IReadContainer of the zope.app.container package.

IWriteDirectory represents an object as a writable directory. Objects
   can be added to the directory through file and directory factories.
   The methods are identical to IWriteContainer of the zope.app.
   container pacakge.

IFileFactory creates a new object in a container based on file contents
   and content type information.

IDirectoryFactory creates a new object in a container when the client
   wishes to create a directory. This usually, but not necessarily results in
   creating a container-like object.

   By providing adapters to the appropriate interfaces above, we can easily enable file representation for our content components, thus allowing access through FTP. When we provide adapters for IReadFile and IFile-
Factory, we will also be able to issue an HTTP *PUT* request to save the
object data.

A limited example

The way we defined the recipe content type in IRecipe makes it hard to
find a sensible file representation for recipe objects. If one really wanted a
one-to-one relationship between recipe objects and their file representations,
one would have to to find a way to encode all data stored in a recipe in a
text file, for example using XML, and to decode that data again. Given the
right tools, this is quite possible, but out of the scope of this chapter.
   As a demonstration of the file representation API, we will only provide
adapters that allow us to edit a recipe's *description* as a normal text file.
That means we will have to write adapters that provide IReadFile and
IWriteFile. Additionally, we can write a factory that creates new recipes
when an FTP or WebDAV client uploads a text file that ends in .recipe.
Example 10.2.1 shows the code for the three adapters.
   File factories are adapters for containers in which they should be responsible for creating new objects. When a file is uploaded to a container,
the FTP or WebDAV view tries to turn it into an object by acquiring a
IFileFactory adapter. However, the type of the file that is uploaded can
be anything, an image, a text file or something else. Obviously, one would
want different file factories for each type of object that can be created. Which
factory is chosen is determined by the extension of the file that is uploaded.

Example 10.2.1 Adapters for file representation (`filerepresentation.py`)

```
1   from zope.interface import implements
2   from zope.app.filerepresentation.interfaces import IReadFile, IWriteFile
3   from zope.app.filerepresentation.interfaces import IFileFactory
4   from worldcookery.recipe import Recipe
5
6   class RecipeReadFile(object):
7       implements(IReadFile)
8
9       def __init__(self, context):
10          self.context = context
11          self.data = self.context.description.encode('utf-8')
12
13      def read(self):
14          return self.data
15
16      def size(self):
17          return len(self.data)
18
19  class RecipeWriteFile(object):
20      implements(IWriteFile)
21
22      def __init__(self, context):
23          self.context = context
24
25      def write(self, data):
26          self.context.description = data.decode('utf-8')
27
28  class RecipeFactory(object):
29      implements(IFileFactory)
30
31      def __init__(self, context):
32          self.context = context
33
34      def __call__(self, name, content_type, data):
35          recipe = Recipe()
36          recipe.name = name.title()
37          recipe.description = data.decode('utf-8')
38          return recipe
```

13 – 17. The interface requires us to provide `read` and `size` methods for the data which in this case is the description text of the recipe. In the `IRecipe` schema, we defined `description` as text which means it is a unicode string. However, we have to return a string here, so we encode the data to UTF-8, an encoding that can handle the whole unicode range. This data is pre-computed in the constructor of the adapter.

25 – 26. The `IWriteFile` adapter is even easier to implement, we just have to provide a `write` method. As much as we encoded unicode to UTF-8 in the `IReadFile` adapter, we have to *decode* incoming strings with it to obtain a unicode object.

34 – 38.   File factory adapters have to be callable which we accomplish here by
providing a __call__ method. In that we create a new recipe object, store
the data we are given from the caller and return it. The object will then
be added to the container the factory adapter was acquired for.

The appropriate factory adapter is then looked up *by name* which corresponds to the extension of the file. Example 10.2.2 shows the configuration

Example 10.2.2 Configuring file representation adapters (`configure.
zcml`)

```
1     ...
2     <adapter
3         for=".interfaces.IRecipe"
4         provides="zope.app.filerepresentation.interfaces.IReadFile"
5         factory=".filerepresentation.RecipeReadFile"
6         permission="zope.View"
7         />
8
9     <adapter
10        for=".interfaces.IRecipe"
11        provides="zope.app.filerepresentation.interfaces.IWriteFile"
12        factory=".filerepresentation.RecipeWriteFile"
13        permission="zope.ManageContent"
14        />
15
16    <adapter
17        for="zope.app.folder.interfaces.IFolder"
18        provides="zope.app.filerepresentation.interfaces.IFileFactory"
19        name=".recipe"
20        factory=".filerepresentation.RecipeFactory"
21        permission="zope.ManageContent"
22        />
23    ...
```

6, 13,   The directive we use to configure the file representation adapters looks,
and 21.   of course, the same way as with the size adapter. However, since these
adapters serve in the context of FTP and WebDAV views and modify
objects, we need to make sure their usage is restricted to users with correct
permissions.

17.   IFileFactory adapters are registered for containers in which they
should be responsible for creating new objects. In our case, we want to be
able to add new recipes to folder objects so we register the adapter for the
folder interface.

19.   File factory adapters are an example of *named adapters* because there exist
more than one of them. In this case, different factories are responsible for
different file extensions which are also the names of the adapters. Here we
make our factory responsible for all files with the .recipe extension.

for the factory adapter which is registered as a *named adapter*, as well as configuration directives for the read and write adapters.

Testing

Just like the size adapter, we can test the file representation adapters in the interactive interpreter shell, too. First, we need to load Zope's configuration as usual:

```
>>> # load configuration
>>> from zope.app.debug import Debugger
>>> debugger = Debugger(db="var/Data.fs",
...                       config_file="etc/site.zcml")
```

Let us first create a recipe object through a file factory. In order to acquire the factory, we need a folder object since we registered the factory as an adapter for folders. We can throw the folder away afterwards. Even though the factory is an adapter, we cannot look it up by calling the interface anymore because that will not take the adapter name into account. We need to use getAdapter from the zapi now:

```
>>> from zope.app.folder import Folder
>>> from zope.app.filerepresentation.interfaces \
...       import IReadFile, IWriteFile, IFileFactory
>>> from zope.app import zapi
>>> folder = Folder()
>>> factory = zapi.getAdapter(folder, IFileFactory,
...                            ".recipe")
```

Now we can call the factory with some made-up data. We expect to get a recipe object back, of course, and that the recipe's description equals to the data we passed to the factory.

```
>>> data = "Add spices to the water and bring it to boil.
Then add the couscous"
>>> couscous = factory("couscous", "text/plain", data)
>>> couscous
<worldcookery.recipe.Recipe object at 0x27d9770>
>>> couscous.name
'Couscous'
>>> couscous.description
```

u'Add spices to the water and bring it to boil. Then add
the couscous'

Now we can get a file representation for the recipe again and read its data.
Note that the file representation returns a string object, not a unicode object,
since only the former can be written to a file stream.

```
>>> readfile = IReadFile(couscous)
>>> readfile.size()
67
>>> readfile.read()
'Add spices to the water and bring it to boil. Then add
the couscous'
```

Finally, we can adapt the recipe object to a writeable file and store new data
on it. The recipe will be changed accordingly, of course:

```
>>> writefile = IWriteFile(couscous)
>>> writefile.write("Couscous consists of grains made
from semolina")
>>> couscous.description
u'Couscous consists of grains made from semolina'
```

To see the file representation in action, you can also use an FTP client
to connect to Zope and retrieve a recipe's description as a file or upload an
existing textfile to a recipe. When adding new files to a folder, you can give
them the .recipe extension and the files will be turned into Recipe objects.
Not only the generic FTP views use the file representation adapters, though.
The WebDAV view for the HTTP *PUT* command uses file factories as well,
so you could also try adding a recipe with a WebDAV client.

Summary

- Zope has support for the file-based protocols FTP and WebDAV.
- Objects can be represented as files using adapters, allowing them to be
  read and written through file-based protocols.
- File factories create new objects based on file data. They are named
  adapters registered for the type of container the file is supposed to be
  created in.

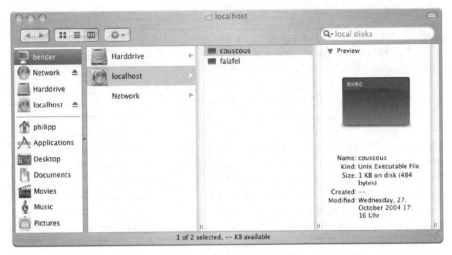

Fig. 10.2. A Zope folder with recipes mounted under Mac OS X via WebDAV.

Flashback

Adapters are a truly innovative and special concept compared to Zope 2. In previous Zope versions, it is very difficult and nearly impossible to extend existing components with functionality. To make an object FTP or WebDAV-aware in Zope 2, one has to provide special methods, such as manage_FTPget, PUT, or PUT_factory; the same goes for providing size information. In Zope 3, it is now a simple matter of providing the right adapters. Adapters and views allow us to seaminglessly integrate components that originally were not even designed to work in Zope, something that is nearly impossible in Zope 2. This is a big deal because it helps us reduce duplication and re-inventions of the wheel.

The file factory idea, on the other hand, is not that new and already exists in the CMF, in a smiliar way at least. There, the *Content Type Registry* tool inside the CMF site matches file extensions, file names or MIME types with content type factories which are invoked when a file is created through FTP or WebDAV inside a CMF site. By using adapters for this functionality, Zope 3 makes the creation of objects based on file representation more flexible because each factory can decide what kind of object is to be created based on the given circumstances (container, name, and MIME type).

10.3 Customizing an existing adapter

Adapters will cross our paths in coming chapters again. As a final dedicated adapter example as part of this chapter, we will customize an already existing adapter.

Zope has many components that provide a certain default behaviour. Especially when the policy induced by these components should be exchangeable, the functionality is factored out into a separate, exchangeable component, such as a view, an adapter or a utility. It is therefore quite frequently necessary to replace an existing component with a custom one to achieve a different behaviour of the application. In some cases, such as with browser skins, one is even *supposed* to customize the default components.

In Chapter 9, we learned that Zope automatically deduces the preferred language from an HTTP header sent by the browser in the request. Browsers either allow setting a list of preferred languages or they acquire the value from the locale setting of the environment they are running in. In either way, the preferred language the browser exposes to Zope might not match the user's preferences at all. Just the fact that somebody is using a computer running a German version of Microsoft Windows would not necessarily mean that that person would also prefer to operate our web application in German.

If we would want to allow users to choose the language they are viewing the web application in, we would have to change the language deducing behaviour of Zope, which comes in form of an adapter for the request to the IUserPreferredLanguages interface. Zope provides the default adapter which inspects the *Accept-Language* HTTP header in the zope.publisher.browser module. We will override it with our own one which should give a user setting in form of a form variable or browser cookie precedence over the HTTP header. In case such a value is absent, the expected behaviour of evaluating the HTTP header should still be intact, of course.

Example 10.3.1 A custom preferred languages adapter (browser/adapter.py)

```
1   from zope.publisher.browser import BrowserLanguages
2
3   class BrowserFormLanguages(BrowserLanguages):
4
5       def getPreferredLanguages(self):
6           langs = super(BrowserFormLanguages, self).getPreferredLanguages()
7           form_lang = self.request.get("ZopeLanguage", None)
8           if form_lang is not None:
9               langs.insert(0, form_lang)
10          return langs
```

6. Using the super functionality, we retrieve the language values from the base class's implementation of getPreferredLanguages.

7. Here we retrieve possible language values from the request which could either be sent by the browser as a form variable or a cookie under the name ZopeLanguage. If we retrieve a valid value (in other words, not None), we put at the top of the list of preferred languages, telling the negotiator that this would then be the most preferred language.

Since adapters are classes, we can simply subclass the existing adapter, thus inheriting the existing functionality. Example 10.3.1 demonstrates the brevity of the adapter code.

Overriding existing configuration

Because Zope already defines an adapter from `IBrowserRequest` to `IUserPreferredLanguages`, we cannot simply register our own adapter in `configure.zcml`. We want our adapter to *override* the existing one, hence we have to make another entry in our instance's `etc/overrides.zcml` file. Its contents is shown in Example 10.3.2, including the setting of the default browser skin as introduced in Chapter 8.

Example 10.3.2 Overriding an existing adapter configuration with a custom one (`etc/overrides.zcml`)

```
1   <configure xmlns="http://namespaces.zope.org/zope"
2              xmlns:browser="http://namespaces.zope.org/browser">
3
4     <!-- Provide local overrides of standard configurations -->
5     <!-- Copy this file to your instance's etc directory -->
6
7     <browser:defaultSkin name="WorldCookery" />
8
9     <adapter
10        for="zope.publisher.interfaces.browser.IBrowserRequest"
11        provides="zope.i18n.interfaces.IUserPreferredLanguages"
12        factory="worldcookery.browser.adapter.BrowserFormLanguages"
13        />
14
15  </configure>
```

You can now open a browser page in Zope and append `?ZopeLanguage=es` to the URL, for example. This will cause our custom adapter to find the necessary form variable in the request and thus let the whole page appear in Spanish. In Chapter 12 we will see how we can offer the user a more comfortable way of choosing the language.

In conclusion, we can say that this example is probably one of the best ones to demonstrate the Component Architecture at work. We have changed the behaviour of a core framework of Zope by writing only third party software and four lines of configuration! Keep in mind, though, that this is not just a consequence of the Component Architecture itself. It is possible to write code that makes use of the Component Architecture and is still hard to customize. Zope 3 has been written from ground up to be based on customizable components. The functionality of extracting preferred languages from a request does not *have* to be an adapter, but it is obvious at this point that only by being one it gives us a maximum of flexbility. Thus try to follow Zope's rule and factor out additional functionality into separate components as soon as possible. It will also be easier when the time comes that you yourself will have to adjust or customize your own code.

Summary

- The translation machinery uses an adapter to retrieve a list of preferred languages from the browser request.
- Zope's default implementation for such an adapter interprets the values sent by most of today's browser in the *Accept-Language* HTTP header.
- By overriding the adapter with a custom one, it is possible to adjust the existing behaviour or change it alltogether.

11

Automated testing

In the introduction, Zope was advertised as a product that makes it easy to do Quality Assurance. To be honest, we have not done much to reflect that. That is mostly because we were rather busy walking our first steps through the Component Architecture. Now that we have covered even the most advanced and powerful type of component of the them all, adapters, it is time to start thinking about those things that ensure not only a good development process but also a high-quality product.

11.1 Introduction

So far, each time we wrote a new component, added a new feature to our example application or changed something else, we had to see for ourselves whether what we did was actually working. Apart from that, it probably would also have been wise to test whether the rest of the application was still working as usual or whether the change had affected the existing code in any way. A small application, such as ours is right now, might still be easy to test manually. Yet, there comes a moment where you would like to automate all that testing because your application is growing and it takes an increasingly large amount of time to go through the manual tests.

Different flavours

Traditionally, automatic tests are distinguished by the following categories:

Unit tests isolate a specific component and test only this component's functionality. This is the most common and most effective kind of test because environmental circumstances do not influence the functionality of the component and its testing.

Relying on other components for testing means that any potential bugs these components contain would let the test fail, even if the component that was to be tested was fine. Unit tests avoid these dependencies; if a component has to rely on other components because of its nature (for example adapters or views), it is common practice to write *mock objects* that pretend to be the necessary components while in fact they are very dull implementations.

Integration tests make sure that components interaction works as expected. While unit tests cover the individual component's responsibility, integration tests cover a whole set of components integrated into an application sub-process. Of course, integration tests only make sense when you already have unit tests of the components that are interacting, because if you would not have unit tests and an integration test would fail, you would not be able to tell whether it failed because of one of the components and which component it was that made the test fail, or whether it failed because the integration was not working.

Integration tests in Zope are sadly called *functional tests*, making it difficult to differentiate them from real functional tests.

Functional tests treat an application like black box and do not take implementation details into account. They see what the user sees and exercise everything a user would do with the application, ideally through the user interface itself. In a case of a web application, the test could simply pretend to be a web browser operated by a user, for example.

Functional tests are independent of the development platform and programming language of the application, especially in the case of web applications. There are numerous web testing kits for functional testing web applications available, most of them being commercial software.

The right philosophy

Having automatic tests is not a guarantee for a higher quality software product per se. Test cases can be ineffective and thus useless if they do not cover realistic circumstances. On the other hand, tests that do not exercise possible edge-cases may easily hide bugs. Within the Zope community, the following testing philosophy has proven to be quite successful to circumvent such cases:

- Each time a change is made to the application, the whole test suite is run to check whether all of the application is still working.
- When a new feature is added, a test case has to be written that makes sure that all of the new functionality is covered by tests. That not only ensures that the code works right now but also in the future.
- When despite the automatic tests a bug is found and a bugfix is applied, the tests covering that particular feature should be revised and extended

to exercise the action that led to the discovery of the bug. This ensures that the bugfix actually does what it is intended to do.

As you can see, it is the right combination of leveraging the given tools and a solid philosophy that makes up good Quality Assurance. In this chapter we shall only be introduced to the tools Zope provides us with. As for the philosophy, you will have to find one that suits best you, your team and the software you are developing. This is sadly beyond the scope of this chapter, but further reading is encouraged, such as [18].

11.2 Unit tests

As mentioned in the introduction, unit tests are the most common test flavour. They are not a particular feature of Zope, though; Python itself comes with unit test support in the unittest module, a contribution from the *PyUnit* project. It manages tests by grouping them in different levels:

- A *test* is a minimal, atomic test for one particular functionality of a component.
- A *test case* is a group of the tests that test the functionality of one particular component.
- A *test suite* is a collection of test cases, usually the ones from the module or package.

Because the other types of tests that will be introduced further down this chapter rely on the infrastructure provided by the unittest module, these categories also apply to them.

In the test infrastructure based on the unittest module, test cases are classes that derive from unittest.TestCase. Every method on such a class that begins with test is a test and will be called when the test case is executed. Furthermore, TestCase provides a number of useful methods for asserting values and other circumstances. Consider a very simple test case typed in at the interactive interpreter shell:

```
>>> import unittest
>>> class SimpleTestCase(unittest.TestCase):
...        def test_one_plus_one(self):
...                self.assertEqual(1 + 1, 2)
...                self.failIfEqual(1 + 1, 3)
...
>>> unittest.main()
.
------------------------------------------------------------
```

```
Ran 1 test in 0.002s

OK
```

We will cover the Zope-specific parts of unit tests next. For general information about *PyUnit* and its unittest module, please consult the *PyUnit* website[1].

Unit testing a component

We could write a unit test for the Recipe class now. However, it provides almost no functionality other than being persistent and providing some default values. If you think that this is still worth testing, consider it an exercise to write a test for it.

In the following example, however, we want to test a component that provides functionality worth enough to be tested. The adapters we wrote in the previous chapter are perfect for that. Example 11.2.1 shows a unit test for the ISized adapter. Note that unit tests typically go into a tests. py module or, if there are many tests that should be split up into their own modules, a tests package.

To run the unit test, simply execute the test_size.py file as a Python script from the command line. Make sure that both the Zope 3 libraries and the instance's library directory are in your *python path*:

```
~/Zope3Instance$ export PYTHONPATH=./lib/python:/usr/
local/ZopeX3-3.x.y/lib/python
~/Zope3Instance$ python lib/python/worldcookery/tests/
test_size.py
..
----------------------------------------------------------
Ran 2 tests in 0.078s

OK
```

On Windows, the commands look a slightly different, but the outcome is the same:

```
C:\Zope3Instance> set PYTHONPATH=.\lib\python
C:\Zope3Instance> C:\Python23\python lib\python\
worldcookery\tests\test_size.py
..
```

---

[1] PyUnit project website <http://pyunit.sourceforge.net>

Example 11.2.1 Unit test for the size adapter (tests/test_size.py)

```
1   import unittest
2   from zope.i18n import translate
3   from zope.app.tests.placelesssetup import PlacelessSetup
4
5   from worldcookery.recipe import Recipe
6   from worldcookery.size import RecipeSize
7
8   class RecipeSizeTestCase(PlacelessSetup, unittest.TestCase):
9
10          def setUp(self):
11              self.recipe = recipe = Recipe()
12              recipe.name = u"Fish and Chips"
13              recipe.ingredients = [u"Fish", u"Potato chips"]
14              recipe.description = u"Fish and Chips is a typical British dish."
15              self.size = RecipeSize(recipe)
16              super(RecipeSizeTestCase, self).setUp()
17
18          def test_size_for_sorting(self):
19              unit, size = self.size.sizeForSorting()
20              self.assertEqual(unit, 'byte')
21              self.assertEqual(size, 71)
22
23          def test_size_for_display(self):
24              msg = self.size.sizeForDisplay()
25              self.assertEqual(u"71 characters", translate(msg))
26
27  def test_suite():
28      suite = unittest.TestSuite()
29      suite.addTest(unittest.makeSuite(RecipeSizeTestCase))
30      return suite
31
32  if __name__ == '__main__':
33      unittest.main()
```

3 and 8. Apart from the mandatory TestCase class, we also inherit from PlacelessSetup which is provided by the zope.app.tests package. It takes care of loading the most essential Zope services before running each test. This would not be required for the ISized adapter itself, however the translate function we use in line 25 for variable interpolation of the message id depends on the utility service.

10–16. A test case's setUp method is called before each test is executed. It can be used to instantiate test objects, for instance a Recipe object and a size adapter for that recipe.

16. Note that we must not forget to call the super class's setUp method which in this case comes from PlacelessSetup and will take care of service initalization. If our test did something of a global effect that could change the outcome of subsequent tests, we would also have to provide a tearDown method that reverted this change after every test has been executed. PlacelessSetup already provides such a method in which it destroys all the services it has created in setUp.

18 – 21   With the recipe object and the size adapter already instantiated in setUp,
and   the actual tests are quite simple. We provide a test for each method the
23 – 25. ISized interface promises and test the behaviour of each method inde-
          pendently.

27 – 33. At last, the "boiler plate" code at the bottom allows us to run the tests
          from the command line and independently from the test runner while
          providing the test runner with a test suite when running the test as part
          of a large test run.

```
----------------------------------------------------------------

Ran 2 tests in 1.192s

OK
```

As the test framework reports both tests are passing. The adapter is working
correctly, just like we expected, of course.

Summary

- Unit tests are based on *PyUnit*, Python's unit test implementation which
  is provided in the unittest module.
- Test cases are classes inheriting from unittest.TestCase whos methods starting with test are the tests of the test case.
- A special mixin class, PlacelessSetup, initializes Zope's basic services in its setUp method and provides the corresponding cleanup in its
  tearDown method. Tests for components that depend on global services
  should subclass PlacelessSetup.

Flashback

Compared to Zope 2, testing in Zope 3 has become a lot more sophisticated,
but also a lot easier. That is because the Zope 3 developers have made software testing part of the development cycle from the beginning.

   In Zope 2, one can easily write unit tests for a component using the
ZopeTestCase package. Using it is necessary because Zope 2 packages are
placed in the Products directory of a Zope instance which is not a regular
Python packages even though it is used as one from the code. Also, many Zope
2 objects need additional machinery in place in order to function properly.
The degree of dependency on other objects is very in Zope 2, mostly induced
by relying on implicit acquisition.

For these reasons it is almost impossible to write unit tests for Zope 2 software without using *ZopeTestCase*. The problem with this is that these tests are never real unit tests because they depend on too much Zope infrastructure. In fact, *ZopeTestCase* loads almost a whole Zope instance with a volatile ZODB database instance to execute the tests. Thus they should probably be considered integration tests, not unit tests.

Zope 3 on the other hand is as light-weight as you want it to be. For simple components, special test setup is not even required. For components requiring Component Architecture functionality, tests can use the `PlacelessSetup` mixin class which only sets up basic services. As you can see, testing is one of the places where Zope 3's modularity pays off since you only have to load as much as you need and not the whole thing.

11.3 Doctests

While unit tests provide a good way for testing a component's functionality in isolated test cases, they have obvious deficiencies. To the Python programmer, first of all, they feel quite unnatural to write. One has to call various methods for test assertions, for instance. The *PyUnit* package cannot deny its heritage from the Java world there. To a Python programmer, it feels much more natural to play with components on the interactive interpreter shell first and see if the component behaves as expected. If you look back, you see that this is exactly what we have been doing! What is more natural than to use the interpreter as a test harness then?

The idea behind *doctests* also includes another aspect. A unit test is most often the first piece of code in which the component is used in all of its extent. For someone who wants to know how a component behaves, a unit test is generally a good place to find out. The problem is that the unit tests the way we wrote them in the previous section are quite hard to read and maybe even difficult to find. This problem is what doctests want to solve. They allow the developer to test a component while documenting it in a for another developer understandable form. Or, reversely, they allow one to document a component and provide a test at the same time.

The right place for documentation

Python itself has a very neat way of providing documentation inside code – *docstrings*. We have already used them, for example when satisfying the Python syntax for a function body in interfaces. Docstrings were invented so that developers can document components for other developers, including themselves, in a uniform way. Since doctests are understood as a type of component documentation, their place is the component's docstring, as the name already suggests. Example 11.3.1 shows the modified size adapter now carrying a docstring with a doctest.

Example 11.3.1 The size adapter with a *doc test* (`size.py`)

```
1   from zope.interface import implements
2   from zope.i18nmessageid import MessageIDFactory
3   from zope.app.size.interfaces import ISized
4   _ = MessageIDFactory('worldcookery')
5
6   class RecipeSize(object):
7       """Provide size functionality for recipes
8
9       For a demonstration of this adapter, consider the following
10      recipe object, providing some demo data:
11
12        >>> from worldcookery.recipe import Recipe
13        >>> recipe = Recipe()
14        >>> recipe.name = u"Fish and Chips"
15        >>> recipe.ingredients = [u"Fish", u"Potato chips"]
16        >>> recipe.description = u"Fish and Chips is a typical British dish."
17
18      Now we instantiate the adapter.  For sorting, the adapter computes
19      a recipe's size in the 'bytes' unit (number of characters):
20
21        >>> size = RecipeSize(recipe)
22        >>> size.sizeForSorting()
23        ('byte', 71)
24
25      It also provides a message id for displaying size in a UI.  In
26      order to display the message correctly, we have to set up some
27      basic services so we can use the translation facilities:
28
29        >>> from zope.app.tests.placelesssetup import setUp, tearDown
30        >>> from zope.i18n import translate
31        >>> setUp()
32        >>> translate(size.sizeForDisplay())
33        u'71 characters'
34
35      At last, we must clean up after ourselves:
36
37        >>> tearDown()
38      """
39      implements(ISized)
40
41      def __init__(self, context):
42          self.context = context
43
44          ...
```

7–38.   The docstring of the adapter class now contains explanation of what it does and how it can be used. Code demonstrations are inserted as if they were printouts from the interactive interpreter. The doctest machinery parses the doctest, executes those statements, and compares their return values with possibly expected return values that are printed out in the doctest. To make the doctest easier to follow, we explain what we are doing in the test after every couple of lines.

29, 31,   We cannot subclass PlacelessSetup in a docstring, yet we need the
and 37.   global services to be initialized for the translate function. Luckily the
           same package provides us with two functions that handle the equivalent
           intialization procedures and are intended to be used in doctests and similar
           testing environments. Note that we now must not forget to clean up after
           the test by calling the tearDown function. With the PlacelessSetup
           mixin class, the clean up functionality is inherited implicitly. Here it has
           to be taken care of explicitly.

Example 11.3.2 Test module for running doc tests (tests/test_size_
doctest.py)

```
1   import unittest
2   from zope.testing.doctestunit import DocTestSuite
3
4   def test_suite():
5       return unittest.TestSuite((DocTestSuite('worldcookery.size'),))
6
7   if __name__ == '__main__':
8       unittest.main(defaultTest='test_suite')
```

2 and 5.   We return a test suite which we create from a *doctest suite*. The
            DocTestSuite class takes as an argument the dotted path of the module
            that is supposed to contain components that have doctests. If not given,
            the current module is assumed which is always useful when providing
            doctests external to the module of the actual component.

To run the doctest, we need to provide a test suite so that the *PyUnit*
infrastructure can work with it. Example 11.3.2 shows a listing of the test
module that creates the test suite necessary for running the doctest in the
test runner or from the command line. To run the doctest now, we simply
execute this module from the command line:

```
~/Zope3Instance$ python lib/python/worldcookery/tests/
test_size_doctest.py
.
-----------------------------------------------------------
Ran 1 test in 0.337s

OK
```

Having looked at Example 11.3.1, doctests do not seem all that unfamiliar
now. We have exercised tests with components on the interactive interpreter
shell before, only that those tests seemed to be tests for our sake, not for
the component's sake. We now know that the doctest philosophy does not
make that distinction. Whatever is documentation for us is a test for the
component.

Doctests from text files

Sometimes, component documentation is too extensive to fit into a single docstring so one would rather provide a separate text file. Using `DocFile-Suite` instead of `DocTestSuite`, it is possible to generate a test suite from a text file instead of docstrings. The structure of that file corresponds to the structure of regular docstring-based doctests. Example 11.3.3 exercises a test on the file representation adapters that were introduced in Section 10.2. If you jump back to these pages, you will see that the file-based test does exactly what we did on the interactive interpreter shell to test the adapters, including the explanations in between.

Example 11.3.3 Text file-based test for file representation adapters (`filerepresentation.txt`)

```
1   =========================================
2   File representation adapters for recipes
3   =========================================
4
5   Let us first create a recipe object through a file factory.  In order
6   to acquire the factory, we need a folder object since we registered
7   the factory as an adapter for folders.  We can throw the folder away
8   afterwards.  Even though the factory is an adapter, we cannot look it
9   up by calling the interface anymore because that will not count in the
10  name.  We need to use 'getAdapter' from the 'zapi' now:
11
12      >>> from zope.app.folder import Folder
13      >>> from zope.app.filerepresentation.interfaces import IReadFile, \
14      ...         IWriteFile, IFileFactory
15      >>> from zope.app import zapi
16      >>> folder = Folder()
17      >>> factory = zapi.getAdapter(folder, IFileFactory, ".recipe")
18
19  Now we can call the factory with some made-up data.  We expect to get
20  a recipe object back, of course, and that the recipe's description
21  equals to the data we passed to the factory.
22
23      >>> data = "Add spices to the water and bring it to boil. Then add the
        couscous"
24      >>> couscous = factory("couscous", "text/plain", data)
25      >>> from worldcookery.recipe import Recipe
26      >>> isinstance(couscous, Recipe)
27      True
28      >>> couscous.name
29      'Couscous'
30      >>> couscous.description
31      u'Add spices to the water and bring it to boil. Then add the couscous'
32
33  Now we can get a file representation for the recipe again and read its
34  data.  Note that the file representation returns a string object, not
```

```
35    a unicode object, since only the former can be written to a file stream.
36
37        >>> readfile = IReadFile(couscous)
38        >>> readfile.size()
39        67
40        >>> readfile.read()
41        'Add spices to the water and bring it to boil. Then add the couscous'
42
43    Finally, we can adapt the recipe object to a writeable file and store
44    new data on it.  The recipe will be changed accordingly, of course:
45
46        >>> writefile = IWriteFile(couscous)
47        >>> writefile.write("Couscous consists of grains made from semolina")
48        >>> couscous.description
49        u'Couscous consists of grains made from semolina'
```

Just like with the regular doctest, a file-based test needs to be turned into a test suite object so that the *PyUnit* framework can deal with it. Note that the tests in the file do not handle any form of test setup such as the necessary service initialization. This will no doubt have to be handled by the test module, too. Example 11.3.4 shows how to do it.

Example 11.3.4 Test module for running the text file-based file representation tests (tests/test_filerepresentation.py)

```
1     import unittest
2     from zope.testing.doctestunit import DocFileSuite
3     from zope.app.tests import ztapi, placelesssetup
4     from zope.app.folder.interfaces import IFolder
5     from zope.app.filerepresentation.interfaces import IReadFile, \
6         IWriteFile, IFileFactory
7
8     from worldcookery.interfaces import IRecipe
9     from worldcookery.filerepresentation import RecipeReadFile, \
10        RecipeWriteFile, RecipeFactory
11
12    def setUp(test):
13        placelesssetup.setUp(test)
14        ztapi.provideAdapter(IRecipe,  IReadFile,  RecipeReadFile)
15        ztapi.provideAdapter(IRecipe,  IWriteFile, RecipeWriteFile)
16        ztapi.provideAdapter(IFolder, IFileFactory, RecipeFactory,  '.recipe')
17
18    def test_suite():
19        return unittest.TestSuite((
20            DocFileSuite('filerepresentation.txt',
21                         package='worldcookery',
22                         setUp=setUp,
23                         tearDown=placelesssetup.tearDown),
24            ))
25
26    if __name__ == '__main__':
27        unittest.main(defaultTest='test_suite')
```

2 and   Instead of `DocTestSuite` we now use `DocFileSuite` which creates a
20 – 23.   test suite from a regular text file whose name we pass in as the first pa-
             rameter. The `package` parameter specifies the Python package in which
             the text file can be found, while the optional `setUp` and `tearDown` pa-
             rameters can be used to pass in initialization and a cleanup functions. For
             initialization, we provide our own `setUp` function while the one provided
             by `zope.app.tests.placelessetup` suffices for cleanup.

12 – 16.   The `setUp` function will be called by the test suite before the file
             test is executed. We use it to initialize the basic services by calling
             `placelesssetup`'s `setUp` function as well as for providing the adapters
             that we want to test. Once again, the `ztapi` module provides useful meth-
             ods for registering components in test contexts, such as `provideAdapter`
             here.

Summary

- Regular unit tests are unnatural to write and difficult to understand for a third person.
- *Doctests* cope with this problem by being both documentation and test for a component.
- Doctests are typically located in a component's docstring. Verbatim output of interactive interpreter sessions are used as demonstrations and test code at the same time.

11.4 Integration tests

As mentioned earlier, Zope calls functional tests what are really integration tests. Functional tests would treat Zope like a black box. "Functional tests" in Zope, though, do not simulate a browser client program and connect through the HTTP port. They only simulate the necessary objects, such as the browser request. That means, they are more like integration tests. In any case, Zope's "functional tests" are still a good way to test behaviour normally not covered by unit tests, such as all view-related actions. The reaction of a button clicked in an HTML form cannot be covered by unit tests, but by integration or functional tests.

As a simple demonstration, we shall provide an integration test for the `IBrowserLanguages` adapter we wrote in Section 10.3, as this is a component that other components rely on and it itself relies on a request envi-ronment. That means it can pretty much only be tested with an integration test. Example 11.4.1 shows the code listing of the test case, while Exam-ple 11.4.2 presents the additional configuration needed for the test setup. Integration tests are placed in a package called `ftests` ("*functional tests*") by convention.

Example 11.4.1 Integration test for the alternate IBrowserLanguages adapter (browser/ftests/test_adapter.py)

```
1   import unittest
2
3   from zope.i18n import translate
4   from zope.i18n.interfaces import ITranslationDomain
5   from zope.i18n.simpletranslationdomain import SimpleTranslationDomain
6   from zope.i18nmessageid import MessageIDFactory
7   _ = MessageIDFactory('worldcookery_test')
8
9   from zope.app.tests import ztapi
10  from zope.app.tests.functional import BrowserTestCase
11  from zope.app.publisher.browser import BrowserView
12
13  class TestView(BrowserView):
14
15      def __call__(self):
16          msg = _(u'msg', u"This is a message")
17          return translate(msg, context=self.request)
18
19  class LanguageAdapterTestCase(BrowserTestCase):
20
21      def setUp(self):
22          super(LanguageAdapterTestCase, self).setUp()
23          messages = {('es', u'msg'): u"Eso es un mensaje",
24                      ('de', u'msg'): u"Dies ist eine Nachricht"}
25          domain = SimpleTranslationDomain('worldcookery_test', messages)
26          ztapi.provideUtility(ITranslationDomain, domain,
     'worldcookery_test')
27
28      def tearDown(self):
29          ztapi.unprovideUtility(ITranslationDomain, 'worldcookery_test')
30          super(LanguageAdapterTestCase, self).tearDown()
31
32      def test_default(self):
33          response = self.publish('/@@testview')
34          self.assertEqual(response.getBody(), u"This is a message")
35
36      def test_http_header(self):
37          response = self.publish('/@@testview',
38                                  env={"HTTP_ACCEPT_LANGUAGE": 'de'})
39          self.assertEqual(response.getBody(), u"Dies ist eine Nachricht")
40
41      def test_browser_form(self):
42          response = self.publish('/@@testview', form={"ZopeLanguage": 'es'})
43          self.assertEqual(response.getBody(), u"Eso es un mensaje")
44
45      def test_form_overrides_header(self):
46          response = self.publish('/@@testview', form={"ZopeLanguage": 'es'},
47                                  env={"HTTP_ACCEPT_LANGUAGE": 'de'})
48          self.assertEqual(response.getBody(), u"Eso es un mensaje")
49
```

```
50   def test_suite():
51       suite = unittest.TestSuite()
52       suite.addTest(unittest.makeSuite(LanguageAdapterTestCase))
53       return suite
54
55   if __name__ == '__main__':
56       unittest.main()
```

13 – 17.   In order to test the effects of the adapter, we need a simple view that returns a short, predictable message id, such as the one we see here.

10 and 19.   Zope's "functional" test cases inherit from BrowserTestCase, meaning a browser request environment is simulated. It is provided by the zope.app.tests.functional package.

21–30.   For the test setup, we need to provide some translations of the message that the above view is going to return and register them in a translation domain object as a utility. Of course, we must not forget to first call the inherited setUp method so that not only the basic services are initialized, but, as we are in an integration tests, all Zope 3 components including third party ones like ours are configured. It is also recommended to undo any registrations of test components in the tearDown method so that subsequently executed tests are not potentially affected.

33, 37 – 38,   In a unit test, we would test the adapter directly. In this integration test,
42, and   we simulate a browser request by calling the publish method which
46 – 47.   is inherited from BrowserTestCase. It takes the relative URL of the page to be virtually published as well as the following optional keyword parameters:

basic can be a string holding fictitous authentication information, e.g. "mgr:mgrpw" as defined in etc/ftesting.zcml in your Zope instance.

form can be a dictionary holding simulated data from an HTML form, in other words, simulated HTTP GET or POST parameters.

env can be a dictionary holding additional HTTP headers. Here, the HTTP_ACCEPT_LANGUAGE header is obviously of interest to us since it simulates the preferred language of the user's operating system or browser preferences.

Example 11.4.2 Configuration file for integration test bootstrapping (browser/ftests/configure.zcml)

```
1   <configure
2       xmlns="http://namespaces.zope.org/zope"
3       xmlns:browser="http://namespaces.zope.org/browser"
4       >
5
```

```
6     <browser:page
7         name="testview"
8         for="zope.app.folder.interfaces.IRootFolder"
9         class=".test_adapter.TestView"
10        attribute="__call__"
11        permission="zope.Public"
12        />
13
14   </configure>
```

Example 11.4.3 Overrides configuration file for integration tests (etc/ overrides_ftesting.zcml)

```
1    <configure xmlns="http://namespaces.zope.org/zope"
2               xmlns:browser="http://namespaces.zope.org/browser">
3
4      <!-- Provide local overrides of standard configurations -->
5      <!-- Copy this file to your instance's etc directory -->
6
7      <browser:defaultSkin name="WorldCookery" />
8
9      <adapter
10         for="zope.publisher.interfaces.browser.IBrowserRequest"
11         provides="zope.i18n.interfaces.IUserPreferredLanguages"
12         factory="worldcookery.browser.adapter.BrowserFormLanguages"
13         />
14
15     <include package="worldcookery.browser.ftests" />
16
17   </configure>
```

In order for the custom adapter as well as the test configuration to be loaded, we also need to provide an etc/overrides_ftesting.zcml file, the integration test equivalent of etc/overrides.zcml. Its listing is shown in Example 11.4.3.

The test case is executed like any other test case before. Again, you have to make sure that the Zope 3 libraries are in your PYTHONPATH environment variable. Also do not forget to place the etc/overrides_ftesting.zcml file. Then, simply run the test module:

```
~/Zope3Instance$ python lib/python/worldcookery/browser/
ftests/test_adapter.py
....
----------------------------------------------------------
Ran 4 tests in 4.662s

OK
```

Functional doctests

Regular integration tests are tedious to write because they need to simulate browser request or other types of user interaction. Doing that from a Python program is not only difficult, it also requires some insights into the way Zope's publishing works.

To cope with that problem, Zope allows us to write integration tests as doctests ("functional doctests"). These are very explicit with respect to the browser emulation because they are essentially literal recordings of HTTP sessions (request and response output).

Of course, it is very unlikely that one writes down a whole HTTP session down in a file (though it is of course possible). Instead, we can rely on a much simpler way of creating functional doctests. The Python program *tcpwatch*[2] can interact as an intermediary between a web browser and a web server and save the server/client communication of a whole HTTP session to log files. The dochttp program which comes with Zope can convert these log files into a doctest text file.

To create a functional doctest by "recording" an HTTP session, do the following:

1. Create a temporary directory where tcpwatch can write the log files to, for example /tmp/tcpwatch or C:\temp\tcpwatch on Windows. Then start the tcpwatch program with appropriate parameters:

   ```
   ~/tcpwatch$ python tcpwatch.py -L 9080:8080 -s
   -r /tmp/tcpwatch
   Forwarding :9080 -> :8080
   Recording to directory /tmp/tcpwatch/.
   ```

   This will let tcpwatch listen on port 9080 and forward all requests to port 8080 which it is assumed that your Zope instance is listening to. In case it is listening to a different port or that port 9080 is already taken for something else you will have to adjust the command line.
   On Windows, the command is essentially the same except for the different paths:

   ```
   C:\tcpwatch> \Python23\python tcpwatch.py
   -L 9080:8080 -s -r C:\temp\tcpwatch
   Forwarding :9080 -> :8080
   Recording to directory C:\temp\tcpwatch\.
   ```

---

[2] Shane   Hathaway's   website   <http://hathawaymix.org/Software/ TCPWatch> or Zope CVS repository <http://cvs.zope.org/Packages/ tcpwatch/>

2. In case your tests involve components that are security protected (all management and editing views generally are), it is recommended to create a manager principal with the login name mgr and password mgrpw. This account is setup by the functional test setup machinery and only available during tests. However, since we are trying to make a test from a regular HTTP session recording, we need to simulate things like user authentication.

To configure the manager test principal, add the following lines to your instance's etc/prinicipals.zcml file:

```
<principal
    id="zope.test_manager"
    title="Functional Test Manager"
    login="mgr"
    password="mgrpw"
    />
```

3. Now open the pages you want to test in a web browser. Be careful to tcpwatch's port and not Zope's port directly; otherwise the session will not be recorded. When asked for authentication, login with the mgr account. Everything you do with your browser now will be recorded. You therefore should try to pay attention not to open too many pages that are not related to the test, even though these unnecessary steps can be deleted later.

When you have completed testing the application through the browser, quit tcpwatch by hitting **Ctrl–C**.

4. The temporary directory that was used to store tcpwatch's recordings in should now contain several files, one for each request and one for each response that was made. The dochttp.py Python script can now be used to convert these files into a doctest file:

```
~/Zope3Instance$ python /usr/local/ZopeX3-3.x.y/lib/
python/zope/app/tests/dochttp.py /tmp/tcpwatch > lib/
python/.../test.txt
```

On Windows, you need to adjust the command to the different installation and logging directories:

```
C:\Zope3Instance> \Python23\python C:\Python23\Lib\
site-packages\zope\app\tests\dochttp.py C:\temp\
tcpwatch > lib\python\...\test.txt
```

5. As one of the last steps, edit the generated doctest file. Add your test specific comments and get rid of request/response pairs that unrelevant

to the test. Finally, create a test module that instantiates a test suite so that the test is executable.

As an example for a functional doctest, the integration test for the IBrowser-Languages adapter was converted to a doctest. It was created in the above described manner using tcpwatch and then edited to include a few explaining comments. It not only can now serve as another test for the component, it is also a very clear piece of documentation of the component for anyone familiar with the HTTP protocol. Example 11.4.4 lists the doctest file whereas Example 11.4.5 shows the module for the test suite instantiation and set-up methods.

Example 11.4.4 Functional doctest for the IBrowserLanguages adapter (browser/adapter.txt)

```
1   ================================================
2   Form variable-based browser language adapter
3   ================================================
4
5   The ``IUserPreferredLanguages`` adapter provided by the ``adapter.py``
6   module allows the preferred language to be specified in a request form
7   variable in addition to the HTTP headers.
8
9   Without any language specification, the default translation (English)
10  is returned:
11
12      >>> print http(r"""
13      ... GET /@@testview HTTP/1.1
14      ... """)
15      HTTP/1.1 200 Ok
16      Content-Length: 17
17      Content-Type: text/plain;charset=utf-8
18      <BLANKLINE>
19      This is a message
20
21  When the `Accept-Language` HTTP header is provided, the adapter works
22  like the default one:
23
24      >>> print http(r"""
25      ... GET /@@testview HTTP/1.1
26      ... Accept-Language: de
27      ... """)
28      HTTP/1.1 200 Ok
29      Content-Length: 23
30      Content-Type: text/plain;charset=utf-8
31      <BLANKLINE>
32      Dies ist eine Nachricht
33
34  The innovation is that when a request variable, e.g. from a GET form,
35  is provided, it influences the target translation language, too:
36
```

```
41   >>> print http(r"""
42   ... GET /@@testview?ZopeLanguage=es HTTP/1.1
43   ... """)
44   HTTP/1.1 200 Ok
45   Content-Length: 17
46   Content-Type: text/plain;charset=utf-8
47   <BLANKLINE>
48   Eso es un mensaje
49
50   Note that the request variable takes precedence over any HTTP header:
51
52   >>> print http(r"""
53   ... GET /@@testview?ZopeLanguage=es HTTP/1.1
54   ... Accept-Language: de
55   ... """)
56   HTTP/1.1 200 Ok
57   Content-Length: 17
58   Content-Type: text/plain;charset=utf-8
59   <BLANKLINE>
60   Eso es un mensaje
```

12, 24, 37, and 48.
The http function is the key to functional doctests. It simulates a browser request and is the equivalent of the publish method of regular functional test cases. It is always available as a global function in doctests without having to be imported. It returns a response object that, when printed, outputs the body of Zope's response to the fictitious browser.

18, 31, 43, and 55.
In an HTTP response, a blank line is used to mark the boundary between the response header and body. However when occurring in a doctest, a blank line would be misinterpreted as a boundary between two paragraphs in the text file. The doctest interpreter lets us use a special marker, <BLANKLINE>, to match blank lines in test output therefore.

You may run the functional doctest like the traditional one we wrote before that. The same requirements apply with regard to test configuration (overrides_ftesting.zcml).

Summary

- In Zope 3, integration tests are incorrectly called "functional tests"
- Integration tests test whether a component integrates correctly with others by simulating user behaviour.
- Classic integration test cases inherit from BrowserTestCase which most importantly provides the publish method for simulating the publishing of a browser request.
- Functional doctests provide a way to spell out integration tests as doctests; they can easily be generated from a HTTP browser session recorded by *tcpwatch*.

Example 11.4.5 Test module for running the functional doctest (`browser/`
`ftests/test_adapter_doctest.py`)

```
1   import unittest
2
3   from zope.i18n import translate
4   from zope.i18n.interfaces import ITranslationDomain
5   from zope.i18n.simpletranslationdomain import SimpleTranslationDomain
6   from zope.i18nmessageid import MessageIDFactory
7   _ = MessageIDFactory('worldcookery_test')
8
9   from zope.app.tests import ztapi
10  from zope.app.tests.functional import FunctionalDocFileSuite
11
12  def setUp(test):
13      messages = {('es', u'msg'): u"Eso es un mensaje",
14                  ('de', u'msg'): u"Dies ist eine Nachricht"}
15      domain = SimpleTranslationDomain('worldcookery_test', messages)
16      ztapi.provideUtility(ITranslationDomain, domain, 'worldcookery_test')
17
18  def tearDown(test):
19      ztapi.unprovideUtility(ITranslationDomain, 'worldcookery_test')
20
21  def test_suite():
22      return FunctionalDocFileSuite('adapter.txt',
23                                    package='worldcookery.browser',
24                                    setUp=setUp, tearDown=tearDown)
25
26  if __name__ == '__main__':
27      unittest.main(defaultTest='test_suite')
```

12 – 19.   The `setUp` and `tearDown` functions are nearly identical to their corresponding methods in the regular test case.

10 and   In total analogy to `DocFileSuite`, `FunctionalDocFileSuite` makes
22 – 24.   a functional doctest out of a text file. Both test suite constructors are
identical in other respects, for example parameters.

To make test execution easier, Zope comes with a test runner script that finds
tests automatically. It is covered in the next section.

11.5 Running tests

In this chapter we have already written four test cases, all residing in different
modules. More tests will come as we extend the application. Calling each
test individually would take quite some time and when dealing with a large
number of test cases, one might also easily forget to run a few. To solve this
problem, Zope is equipped with a *test runner*, a program that automatically
finds test suites in source code packages and runs them. It can be found in a
Zope instance under `bin/test`.

When looking for tests to run, the test runner searches for `tests.py`
modules or for modules below a `tests` pacakges. Within each of those mod-

ules, it executes the test_suite function to obtain a TestSuite object
(or a derivative, in case of doctests). It then uses the test suite to execute
the tests. When running integration tests, ftests.py modules or modules
in an ftests package are searched for.

The test runner offers a variety of options for running tests, such as different report facilities and which types of test to include in a test run. Options
can either be specified as command line arguments or in a configuration file
called test.config located in the current directory. Command line arguments take precedence over configuration file settings.

Program synopsis

```
bin/test [options] [module filter] [test filter...]
```

Parameters

Test filtering

-a level, --at-level level runs the tests at the given level. All tests
    at a level above the specified one are not run. Level 0 runs all tests, the
    default is level 1. Configuration file setting: LEVEL.
    The level of a test is determined by an optional level attribute on the
    TestCase derivative class.

--all runs all tests. This is a shortcut for -a 0.

-s directory, --dir directory searches for tests only in the specified
    directory. This is useful for limiting the search scope of the test runner,
    thus limiting the number of tests to be run. This option can be specified
    more than once. Configuration file setting: TEST_DIRS.

-f, --skip-unit runs only integration tests ("functional tests"), not unit
    tests. Corresponding configuration file settings are RUN_UNIT and
    RUN_FUNCTIONAL.

-u, --skip-functional runs only the unit tests, not "functional tests".
    Corresponding configuration file settings are RUN_UNIT and
    RUN_FUNCTIONAL.

--test filter, --module filter Filter test names or module names,
    respectively. *filter* is a case-sensitive regular expression. Addtionally to
    standard regular expression syntax, a leading exclamation mark (*!*)
    negates the expression. When used with --test, *filter* is applied to the
    (method) name of the test. When used with --module, *filter* is applied to

the test files' path. Both options can be specified more than once and used together. Configuration file settings: TEST_FILTERS, MODULE_FILTERS.

Output

-p, --progress shows the running progress in percent. Configuration file setting: PROGRESS.

-v, --verbose switches to verbose output. With one -v, a dot is printed for each test. With -vv the name of each test is printed. If no -v is specified at all, no output is given while running the tests, except when errors occur. Configuration file setting: VERBOSE.
The behaviour changes slightly when specified together with -p. With -p and -v, the percent indicator and the test name is printed. With -p and -vv, the test name is not truncated to fit into 80 columns.

-U, --gui invokes the *PyUnit* graphical user interface (GUI) instead of outputting to the command line. The GUI finds tests on its own and ignores the test filters as well as the debug (-d), verbose (-v) and progress (-p) options. Configuration file setting: GUI.

-M, --minimal-gui starts the GUI minimized. Double-clicking on the progress bar will start the test run.

Execution modes

-d, --debug runs the tests in a debugging environment. In a normal test environment, exceptions are caught and presented as tracebacks at the end of the test run. In the debugging environment, they are not caught. Configuration file setting: DEBUG.

-D, --debug-inplace runs the test in a debugging environment and loads the Python Debugger (pdb) when an exception occurs. Configuration file setting: DEBUGGER.

-k, --keepbytecode prevents the test runner from deleting stale bytecode before running tests. Configuration file setting: KEEP_STALE_BYTECODE.

-L, --loop runs the selected tests in a loop. This is very useful for detecting memory leakages in components. Configuration file setting: LOOP.

-N n, --repeat n repeats the selected tests *n* times.

Profiling

-P, --profile runs the tests with the Python Profiler and displays the top
    50 statistics, sorted by cumulative time and number of calls.

-t, --top-fifty times the individual tests and prints a list of the top 50,
    sorted from longest to shortest time needed. Configuration file setting:
    TIMETESTS.

--times n, --times outfile times the tests. With an integer argu-
    ment, a list of the top *n* tests is printed, sorted from longest to shortest
    time needed. A non-integer argument specifies a file to which timing in-
    formation is written. Configuration file setting: TIMESFN.

Examples

The following command runs all tests, both unit and functional, in modules
whose name contain worldcookery. This essentially means, run all tests in
the worldcookery package.

```
~/Zope3Instance$ bin/test -v worldcookery
Running UNIT tests at level 1
Running UNIT tests from ~/Zope3Instance/lib/python
....
-----------------------------------------------------------
Ran 4 tests in 0.400s

OK
Running FUNCTIONAL tests at level 1
Running FUNCTIONAL tests from ~/Zope3Instance/lib/python
Parsing ~/Zope3Instance/etc/ftesting.zcml
....
-----------------------------------------------------------
Ran 5 tests in 4.934s

OK
```

In the following command, only unit tests are invoked and the output is at the
highest verbosity. Notice the different types of tests (docfile, doctest, regular
unit test):

```
~/Zope3Instance$ bin/test -u -vv worldcookery
Running UNIT tests at level 1
Running UNIT tests from  ~/Zope3Instance/lib/python
```

```
~/Zope3Instance/lib/python/worldcookery/
filerepresentation.txt ... ok
RecipeSize (worldcookery.size) ... ok
test_size_for_display (worldcookery.tests.test_size
.RecipeSizeTestCase) ... ok
test_size_for_sorting (worldcookery.tests.test_size
.RecipeSizeTestCase) ... ok

----------------------------------------------------------
Ran 4 tests in 0.596s

OK
```

The following command narrows the test search down to unit tests in the
worldcookery package whose names contain "size" or "Size". Of course,
we expect the two unit test and the doc test to be executed. As the output
the percentage of total tests run shall be printed:

```
~/Zope3Instance$ bin/test -u -p worldcookery [Ss]ize
Running UNIT tests from ~/Zope3Instance/lib/python
  3/3 (100.0%)
----------------------------------------------------------
Ran 3 tests in 0.639s

OK
```

Summary

- Running tests individually from their modules can be tiresome when a
  large number of tests are involved
- Zope's test runner automatically finds tests and executes them, making
  automatic testing very easy.
- Various options control the amount and type of tests that are found, the
  way they are run and the way output is presented.

12

Views

In Chapter 7 we have added through-the-web adding, editing, and displaying functionality to recipes by defining appropriate browser views. That was relatively easy to do because the adding and editing views are auto-generated and the displaying is handled by a Page Template which is more HTML than anything else.

In this chapter, we will explore view components a bit more, after having learned about adapters. Their theory plays an important role in the understanding of views. We will see that more complex views cannot and should not be handled by Page Templates or at least not solely by them. We will learn how to enhance Page Template-based views with additional logic from Python, how to implement browser and non-browser views purely in Python, and how to write views for other HTTP protocols.

12.1 Enhanced browser pages

We can now easily display recipes as HTML using Page Templates. ZPTs provide a great way to XML markup dynamic, but they are limited in their functionality. This is very much intended, since they are purely meant to cover presentational responsibilities. If Page Templates would expose the same functionality as the Python environment, one would be tempted to mix application logic and presentation. After all, separating the two is what the Component Architecture is really all about.

You will, however, sometimes find yourself in the position where you need additional logic in presentation that cannot be covered with only what Page Templates provide. A typical use case for additional logic is when other components need to be acquired so that they can perform some extra computation on the data that is to be presented. A supplementary Python class which will be mixed into the component representing the browser page is the solution here.

Rendering plain text

The description field of recipes is usually plain text. Any HTML that a user would enter would be escaped by the Page Template anyway. However, any plain text formatting, such as empty lines for starting paragraphs, is ignored when inserted into the HTML. Browsers do not interpret this formatting.

Zope has support for rendering different types of plain text to HTML. Among fancier renderers for StructuredText [17] and reStructuredText [22], it can also render simple plain text to HTML. This support for text rendering can be found in the zope.app.renderer package.

To render a portion of text to HTML, we have to tell the renderer machinery what type of text we are dealing with. For doing so, three factories that create accordingly marked unicode objects are provided:

- zope.source.plaintext for regular plain text,
- zope.source.stx for StructuredText,
- and zope.source.rest for reStructuredText.

When a text is successfully marked using either one of these factories, a rendering view can render it to HTML. Example 12.1.1 demonstrates this by treating the description field of recipes as a plain text source. The method defined in that class now just has to be called by the view Page Template (recipeview.pt). The simple change that is necessary for that is described in Example 12.1.2.

Example 12.1.1 Supplementary view class for additional view logic (browser/recipe.py)

```
1   from zope.app import zapi
2
3   class RecipeView(object):
4
5       def renderDescription(self):
6           plaintext = zapi.createObject(None, 'zope.source.plaintext',
7                                          self.context.description)
8           view = zapi.getView(plaintext, '', self.request)
9           return view.render()
```

3. This class could not be simplier (it is an example, after all), but yet it is necessary because most zapi functionality cannot be accessed from Page Templates – for a good reason. If it were available, Page Templates would be stuffed will all sorts of logic that would make them not only unreadable but hard to maintain and exchange.

5–9. This method will be called later from the Page Template. As introduced in Chapter 5, the zapi.createObject function creates new objects by invoking factories. Here, we use the plain text factory to convert the recipe's description attribute into a marked source text for which we can one line later get a view that will render us the HTML.

Example 12.1.2 Recipe view template using the view class's rendering functionality (`browser/recipeview.pt`)

```
1   <html xmlns="http://www.w3.org/1999/xhtml"
2         xmlns:tal="http://xml.zope.org/namespaces/tal"
3         xmlns:metal="http://xml.zope.org/namespaces/metal"
4         xmlns:i18n="http://xml.zope.org/namespaces/i18n"
5         metal:use-macro="context/@@standard_macros/page"
6         i18n:domain="worldcookery">
7   <head>
8     <title metal:fill-slot="title"
9            tal:content="context/name/title">recipe name goes here</title>
10  </head>
11  <body>
12  <div metal:fill-slot="body">
13
14    <h2 tal:content="context/name/title">recipe name goes here</h2>
15
16    <table>
17      <tbody>
18
19        ...
20
21      </tbody>
22    </table>
23
24    <p tal:content="structure view/renderDescription">
25      Longer description goes here.
26    </p>
27
28  </div>
29  </body>
30  </html>
```

24 – 26. To access the supplementary class's method, we use the global `view` variable in the top-level ZPT namespace. The TALES expression will automatically call the method and we end up with the rendered HTML. Thus, it is important not to forget to use the `structure` modifier in the TALES expression, otherwise the resulting HTML would be escaped by ZPT.

Example 12.1.3 Defining a supplementary view class for a browser page (`browser/configure.zcml`)

```
1   ...
2   <browser:page
3       for="worldcookery.interfaces.IRecipe"
4       name="index.html"
5       template="recipeview.pt"
6       class=".recipe.RecipeView"
7       permission="zope.View"
8       />
9   ...
```

6. A browser page that consists of a template and a supplementary view class is configured using the `browser:page` directive carrying both the *template* and *class* parameter. Here we specify the dotted name of the class defined in Example 12.1.1.

Last but not least we need to hook the supplementary view class up to the view Page Template. Example 12.1.3 shows what we need to do with the template's configuration directive. To finally test the effects of the change, enter formatted text, for example text containing several new-lines, into the description field of a recipe and see what happens when you display it.

Summary

- Application logic in Page Templates should be limited to a minimal amount.
- Supplementary Python classes can aid Page Templates when more complex logic is needed than Page Templates can or should handle.
- Zope provides rendering functionality for a few different types of plain text in the `zope.app.renderer` package.

12.2 Complex views implemented in Python

By now you have probably noticed what Steve Alexander meant when he defined Zope as a platform that "manages complexity in gluing software components together". Since we wrote the `Recipe` class in Chapter 5, we have not changed it a bit, but look where we are now thanks to adapters! You might ask, only adapters? What about the browser views?

It was already mentioned earlier that views are essentially adapters because they are just a way of looking at an object differently, providing additional functionality outside of it. Of course, they are not regular adapters like the ones we wrote in Chapter 10. Aside from having names most of the time, views not only have to take the object that is to be presented into account, but also the request – a browser view should obviously be a different adapter than an FTP view, for example. An adapter that adapts multiple objects and can optionally have a name is called a *multi-adapter*.

Since views are adapters, they must provide an interface. All views that are supposed to be published, for example to a web browser through HTTP, must provide `IBrowserPublisher`. The browser pages we defined in Chapter 7 were automatically turned into components providing that interface.

A view providing PDF rendering functionality

In a first example, we shall write a view component that is not a browser view nor meant to be published. Its nature is very much adapter-like. The only real difference to an adapter is that the view constructor takes two arguments, the object to be presented and the request. The functionality that is supposed to be provided is representation as PDF data. PDF is a very popular format for presentation of read-only data and useful for providing printable output of a website's contents. The simple interface that describes PDF data, IPDFPresentation is shown in Example 12.2.1.

Example 12.2.1 Interface for PDF representation (pdf/interfaces.py)

```
1   from zope.interface import Interface
2   from zope.schema import Bytes
3   from zope.i18nmessageid import MessageIDFactory
4   _ = MessageIDFactory('worldcookery')
5
6   class IPDFPresentation(Interface):
7       """Present objects as PDF data
8       """
9
10      data = Bytes(
11          title=_(u"Data"),
12          description=_(u"PDF data as raw bytes string."),
13          required=True
14          )
```

We can now write a view for recipes that provides IPDFPresentation. Formally, we are writing a multi-adapter for IRecipe and IRequest. For the actual PDF generation, we will use the *ReportLab* library, a third-party package that allows the creation of PDF files from Python code, as well as *PIL/Imaging*, a third-party package that allows image manipulation from Python code and is used by ReportLab. See sidebar 12.2 for installation instructions.

Installing necessary third-party libraries

The *ReportLab* library is a third-party library for creating PDF files from Python, while the *PIL/Imaging* library is a third-party library for image manipulation from Python. Both are freely available as open source software under BSD-style licenses. You maybe obtain source packages or Windows binaries from the ReportLab Open Source website[a] and the PythonWare website[b], respectively.

---
[a] ReportLab Open Source website <http://www.reportlab.org>
[b] PythonWare   website   <http://www.pythonware.com/products/pil/>

Installing from source (Unix)

The source installation of ReportLab follows the standard *distutils* procedure as known from most other Python libraries. Extract the source archive in an arbitrary directory and run the following commands:

```
reportlab-1_xx/reportlab$ python setup.py build
reportlab-1_xx/reportlab$ python setup.py install
```

This will first compile the extension modules and then install it in the Python's `site-packages` directory so that it is available for import. Note that you will most likely need administrator rights to issue the second command. Alternatively, you can install the library into your home directory or another place where you have write permissions to. Issue `python setup.py install --help` for further information.

The installation of PIL/Imaging is almost identical. Only here you will first have to compile the `libImaging` library manually. To do that enter the following commands after extracting the source archive:

```
Imaging-1.x.y$ cd libImaging
Imaging-1.x.y/libImaging$ ./configure
Imaging-1.x.y/libImaging$ make
```

When that has successfully completed, run the standard *distutils* procedure like with ReportLab above:

```
Imaging-1.x.y/libImaging$ cd ..
Imaging-1.x.y$ python setup.py build
Imaging-1.x.y$ python setup.py install
```

Windows

The installation of Imaging/PIL is nearly identical to the one of Zope X3 itself on Windows. The binary PIL download contains an automatic installer which will detect a valid Python installation and install itself into its library path automatically.

Installing the ReportLab package requires a bit more manual interaction. You will have to download both the source archive as well as the Windows binary archive which only contains the binary shared libraries. Extract the source archive and copy the `reportlab` directory to your Python's `site-packages` directory, e.g. `C:\Python23\Lib\site-packages`. Then extract the archive containing the binary shared libraries. The files contained should have the file extension `pyd`. Copy them to your Python's `DLL` directory, e.g. `C:\Python23\DLL`. ReportLab is now installed.

Because PDF generation is a rather complex task, a base class as shown in Example 12.2.2 takes care of a few basic initialization steps which could be reused when providing PDF views for other content types, too.

Example 12.2.2 Base class for the generation of *World Cookery* PDF documents (`pdf/__init__.py`)

```
1   import os.path
2   from reportlab.pdfbase import pdfmetrics
3   from reportlab.pdfbase.ttfonts import TTFont
4   from reportlab.platypus import Image
5   from reportlab.lib import styles, units, pagesizes
6
7   class WorldCookeryPDF(object):
8       """Base class for all WorldCookery PDF documents
9       """
10
11      def __init__(self):
12          fonts = {'LuxiSans': 'luxisr.ttf',
13                   'LuxiSansOblique': 'luxisri.ttf',
14                   'LuxiSansBold': 'luxisb.ttf',
15                   'LuxiSansBoldOblique': 'luxisbi.ttf'}
16          for name, file in fonts.items():
17              filename = os.path.join(os.path.dirname(__file__), file)
18              pdfmetrics.registerFont(TTFont(name, filename))
19
20          self.stylesheet = styles.getSampleStyleSheet()
21          self.stylesheet['Normal'].fontName = 'LuxiSans'
22          self.stylesheet['title'].fontName = 'LuxiSansBold'
23          self.stylesheet['h1'].fontName = 'LuxiSansBold'
24          self.stylesheet['h2'].fontName = 'LuxiSansBold'
25          self.stylesheet['h3'].fontName = 'LuxiSansBoldOblique'
26          self.pagesize = pagesizes.A4
27
28          logofile = os.path.join(os.path.dirname(__file__),'worldcookery.png')
29          self.logo = Image(logofile, 2060.0*units.inch/600,651*units.inch/600)
```

12 – 18.   Zope 3 uses unicode strings everywhere to support internationalization
properly. The standard PDF fonts as required by the specification do
not support unicode. The ReportLab library however supports unicode
in conjunction with TrueType fonts. So, in order to allow unicode in our
PDF document, we register such a TrueType font including its bold and
italic variants[a]

28 – 29.   This creates an image object of the World Cookery logo which is most
likely to be used in all World Cookery PDF doucments so it makes sense
to define it here in a central place.

---

[a] The *Luxi Sans* font used here is part of a freely distributable set of fonts copy-
righted by Bigelow & Holmes Inc. Please refer to `pdf/COPRYGIHT.BH` in the
example package for more information.

Example 12.2.3 shows the listing of the actual view providing a PDF
representation of recipes. As you can easily see, the request is only needed
for translation. If translation was not involved, this could also have been a
simple adapter. Since the view does not need the request directly, it does
not need to make any assumptions about the type of the request, either.
That means, this view works with *any* type of request (including FTP, for
example).

Since ReportLab is not a part of Zope itself, the library's functionality
cannot be explained here in detail. The examples in this chapter are as simple as possible to merely demonstrate the principle of non-HTML, Python-
implemented views. For a complete reference, please refer to the *ReportLab
User Guide* [16] and the *ReportLab API Reference* [15].

The configuration of views is very analogous to the configuration of
adapters. Example 12.2.5 shows how to do it. Since we chose to put all PDF-
related components in the `worldcookery.pdf` subpackage, do not forget
to include its configuration in `configure.zcml`:

```
<include package=".pdf" />
```

Apart from demonstrating the implementation of a Python-implemented
view component, Example 12.2.2 and Example 12.2.3 also show how easily
one can use third-party libraries within Zope components. This allows you
to take advantage of the numerous open source Python libraries in your
Zope application. The Python website has a catalog of most of the freely
available packages known as the *Python Package Index*[1]. If you are looking
for a certain toolset outside of Zope's traditional focus you might find useful
libraries there.

---

[1] Python Package Index `<http://www.python.org/pypi>`

Example 12.2.3 All-purpose view that provides PDF representation of recipes (pdf/recipe.py)

```
1   from cStringIO import StringIO
2   from reportlab.platypus import SimpleDocTemplate, Paragraph
3
4   from zope.interface import implements
5   from zope.i18n import translate
6   from zope.i18nmessageid import MessageIDFactory
7
8   from worldcookery.pdf import WorldCookeryPDF
9   from worldcookery.pdf.interfaces import IPDFPresentation
10  _ = MessageIDFactory('worldcookery')
11
12  class RecipePDF(WorldCookeryPDF):
13      implements(IPDFPresentation)
14
15      def __init__(self, context, request):
16          self.context = context
17          self.request = request
18          super(RecipePDF, self).__init__()
19
20          # prepare strings (translate, encode in utf-8)
21          def transcode(msg):
22              """Translate and encode in UTF-8"""
23              return translate(msg, context=request).encode('utf-8')
24
25          title = ('<para spaceBefore="20" spaceAfter="40">%s</para>'
26                       % context.name.encode('utf-8'))
27          description = ('<para spaceBefore="15">%s</para>'
28                           % context.description.encode('utf-8'))
29          ingr = [ingr.encode('utf-8') for ingr in context.ingredients]
30          tools = [tool.encode('utf-8') for tool in context.tools]
31          time_to_cook = _(u'${time_to_cook} mins')
32          time_to_cook.mapping['time_to_cook'] = context.time_to_cook
33          time_to_cook = transcode(time_to_cook)
34
35          # create the document structure
36          style = self.stylesheet
37          doc_structure = [
38              self.logo,
39              Paragraph(title, style['title']),
40              Paragraph(transcode(_(u"Name of the dish:")), style['h3']),
41              Paragraph(context.name.encode('utf-8'), style['Normal']),
42              Paragraph(transcode(_(u"Ingredients:")), style['h3']),
43              Paragraph(', '.join(ingr), style['Normal']),
44              Paragraph(transcode(_(u"Needed kitchen tools:")), style['h3']),
45              Paragraph(', '.join(tools), style['Normal']),
46              Paragraph(transcode(_(u"Time needed for preparation:")),
    style['h3']),
47              Paragraph(time_to_cook, style['Normal']),
48              Paragraph(description,  style['Normal'])
49          ]
```

```
51    # build the PDF document
52    stream = StringIO()
53    doc = SimpleDocTemplate(stream, pagesize=self.pagesize)
54    doc.build(doc_structure)
55    self.data = stream.getvalue()
```

8, 12,   We inherit from the base class defined in Example 12.2.2, not forgetting
and 18. to call its initialization method.

21–23.   Message ids used for translation need to be translated before inserted into
         the PDF document. Also, ReportLab does not work directly with unicode
         objects but accepts only UTF-8 which is why we have to encode all unicode
         objects in UTF-8 beforehand.

Example 12.2.4 Browser view for recipes that provides a PDF file for download (pdf/browser.py)

```
1     from zope.app import zapi
2     from zope.app.publisher.browser import BrowserView
3
4     from worldcookery.pdf.interfaces import IPDFPresentation
5
6     class PDFView(BrowserView):
7
8         def __call__(self):
9             pdf = zapi.getViewProviding(self.context, IPDFPresentation,
10                                         self.request)
11            filename = zapi.name(self.context) + '.pdf'
12            response = self.request.response
13            response.setHeader('Content-Disposition',
14                               'attachment; filename=%s' % filename)
15            response.setHeader('Content-Type', 'application/pdf')
16            response.setHeader('Content-Length', len(pdf.data))
17            response.write(pdf.data)
```

2 and 6. For Python-implemented browser views, the zope.app.publisher.
          browser package provides a simple yet useful base class BrowserView.

8.   It is recommended that browser views implement the __call__ method,
          as this is the method that is preferably called by the publisher when
          the view is published to the browser. When a browser view class provides
          more than one page, it is acceptable to use arbitrary method names. Keep
          in mind that that changes the view's configuration (see explanation of
          Example 12.2.5).

9–10.   For obvious reasons we want to delegate the PDF generation work off to
          the view we wrote earlier. Since it is a view providing an interface, we will
          look it up with zapi.getViewProviding instead of zapi.getView.

12–16.   This browser page is not returning regular HTML. It is returning binary
          data of a special content type. Additionally, we would like to enforce a
          filename (the object name of the recipe) in case the user wants to save the
          PDF on disk. All this is done by setting appropriate HTTP headers on
          the response object. The response is stored as an attribute on the request
          object.

17.   When the PDF view is acquired and the response is prepared for PDF
       output, we can write the data provided by the view to the client. The
       response object provides the appropriate `write` method for this.

A browser page for retrieving a recipe's PDF data

Like an adapter, a view providing an interface is a component that is useful
programmatically. It is not useful to a user visiting the *World Cookery* website
– yet. In order to allow users to get a presentation of a recipe as a PDF file, we
will have to write a browser page that returns the data. This is obviously far
too much logic to be handled in a Page Template and it even does not involve
the generation of HTML. That means this example will demonstrate how to
write browser pages completely in Python. Since we want to involve the
previously written view, it will also show us how to acquire a view providing
an interface.

Example 12.2.4 shows the browser view for retrieving PDF data, Example
12.2.5 also shows how to configure it. As you can see, the configuration is not
that much different than from browser pages implemented in Page Templates.

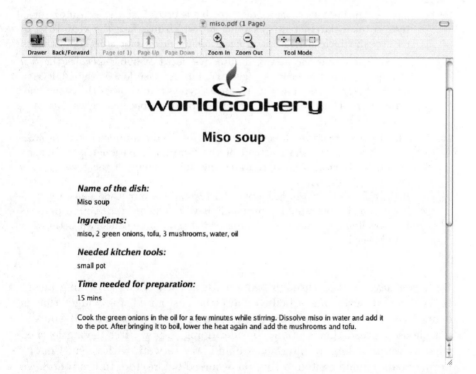

Fig. 12.1. A PDF viewer showing a PDF document generated by the World Cookery application.

Example 12.2.5 Configuring the PDF browser page (pdf/configure. zcml)

```
1   <configure
2       xmlns="http://namespaces.zope.org/zope"
3       xmlns:browser="http://namespaces.zope.org/browser"
4       >
5
6     <view
7           for="worldcookery.interfaces.IRecipe"
8           provides=".interfaces.IPDFPresentation"
9           type="zope.publisher.interfaces.IRequest"
10          factory=".recipe.RecipePDF"
11          />
12
13    <browser:page
14          for="worldcookery.interfaces.IRecipe"
15          name="pdf"
16          class=".browser.PDFView"
17          permission="zope.View"
18          />
19
20    </configure>
```

6–11.   For configuring views, the view directive is used. Like the adapter direc-
        tive, it takes parameters specifying *for* which interface the view is to be
        registered, which interface it *provides*, and a *factory* for creating instances.

9.   A parameter that the adapter directive does not know specifies the *type*
        of request that the view is registered for. As mentioned, the PDF view
        does not rely on any particular request type, it only needs the request for
        translation. Thus, we register it for the most unspecific request interface,
        IRequest.

16.   The browser:page directive is used for Python-implemented browser
        views, too, except that instead of the template parameter the class
        parameter is now used. It contains the dotted name of the browser view
        class.
        If the class as shown in Example 12.2.4 would use a method name different
        from __call__, we would additionally have to add an attribute parame-
        ter, specifying the name of the method that is to be called when the view
        is published.

If you have worked through Section 7.4 already, views providing an interface should have rung a bell, because the custom editing widget that is
defined there is a view providing the IInputWidget interface. If you did
not choose to read that section, consider doing so now after having learned
what views providing an interface are and how to work with them. Finally,
browser pages implemented in Python occurred before, too. In Chapter 8, we
implemented the standard_macros view in Python.

Summary

- Views are *multi-adapters*, optionally named; they adapt a context object and a request object to provide view functionality in return.
- Views should be implemented in Python when complex tasks are to be solved, such as facilitating components from (third-party) Python libraries.
- Python-implemented views are implemented like adapters except that, apart from the context object, the constructor now also takes a request object.
- Like all-purpose views, browser pages can be implemented in Python as well; they are configured with the same configuration directive as views written with Page Templates. Unless otherwise specified in configuration, their __call__ method is called when published to a browser.

12.3 Browser menus

Menus are a concept known from graphical user interfaces (GUIs). They offer the user to choose items from a list of options; their selection typically causes an action to be carried out, a dialog window or new file to be opened.

Zope has a feature called *browser menus*. Like regular menus, they are context-sensitive lists of options that a user can choose from, only that these options are other browser pages that one can open. Browser menus do not have to look like menus known from regular GUI applications. Their look is determined by how they are rendered in HTML and how that HTML is styled using stylesheets.

Zope makes use of browser menus in various places. The ZMI itself frequently presents us with three browser menus: the tabs for different ZMI object management screens (zmi_views), general management screens as listed in the blue bar (zmi_actions), and the list of content objects that are addable to a folder (add_content). The entries in these menus point to other browser pages, in most of the above cases management screens. As you can see, all of these menus are presented differently in ZMI, even though they are all browser menus.

A custom menu offers alternatives

As an example for a custom browser menu we shall provide a menu that lists alternative views for an object. In the case of recipes we want it to list the PDF view we wrote above as an alternative view.

First, we need to define our own browser menu which we will call alternate_views. This, of course, is done in ZCML (see Example 12.3.1). We will also have to modify the configuration of the PDF browser page so that it is registered with this menu (see Example 12.3.2).

Example 12.3.1 Defining a browser menu (`browser/configure.zcml`)

```
1      ...
2     <browser:menu
3         id="alternate_views"
4         title="Menu containing a list of alternative views for an obj
5         />
6      ...
```

2–5.   Browser menus are defined with the `browser:menu` directive. They are later looked up by their *id*. The *title* parameter merely exists for documentation purposes.

Example 12.3.2 Adding the PDF browser page to the browser menu (`pdf/configure.zcml`)

```
1    <configure
2        xmlns="http://namespaces.zope.org/zope"
3        xmlns:browser="http://namespaces.zope.org/browser"
4        >
5
6      <view
7          for="worldcookery.interfaces.IRecipe"
8          provides=".interfaces.IPDFPresentation"
9          type="zope.publisher.interfaces.IRequest"
10         factory=".recipe.RecipePDF"
11         />
12
13     <browser:page
14         for="worldcookery.interfaces.IRecipe"
15         name="pdf"
16         class=".browser.PDFView"
17         permission="zope.View"
18         menu="alternate_views" title="PDF"
19         />
20
21   </configure>
```

8.   Adding browser pages to browser menus is no news for us. We have done so previously with the adding and editing forms as well as the preview page in Chapter 7.

Now we will have adjust the view Page Template for recipes to present us with a list of alternative views as they are registered in the menu. However, menus and their entries are managed by the *Browser Menu Service*. Since services cannot be acquired from Page Templates, we need to extend the supplementary Python class to acquire the Browser Menu Service for us, query for the menu entries and provide the data in a form so that the Page Template can process it in the easiest way. Remember, we want to do as little logic as possible in Page Templates. Example 12.3.3 shows the supplementary

Example 12.3.3 Looking up browser menus in the supplementary view class (`browser/recipe.py`)

```
1   from zope.app import zapi, servicenames
2
3   class RecipeView(object):
4
5       def renderDescription(self):
6           plaintext = zapi.createObject(None, 'zope.source.plaintext',
7                                       self.context.description)
8           view = zapi.getView(plaintext, '', self.request)
9           return view.render()
10
11      def alternateViews(self):
12          menu_service = zapi.getService(servicenames.BrowserMenu)
13          menu_id = 'alternate_views'
14          return menu_service.getMenu(menu_id, self.context, self.request)
```

12. Here we are actually acquiring a service on our own for the first time. Before, we never had to get in touch with services because the Component Architecture provides convenience functions which are exposed in the zapi. As you can see, a service itself is acquired using a zapi function, getService. Service names by which services are acquired are simple strings. To avoid mistakes like typos, they are defined as string constants in zope.component.servicenames (core Component Architecture) and zope.app.servicenames (Zope application server), respectively.

Example 12.3.4 Recipe view template offering alternate views (`browser/recipeview.pt`)

```
1   <html xmlns="http://www.w3.org/1999/xhtml"
2         xmlns:tal="http://xml.zope.org/namespaces/tal"
3         xmlns:metal="http://xml.zope.org/namespaces/metal"
4         xmlns:i18n="http://xml.zope.org/namespaces/i18n"
5         metal:use-macro="context/@@standard_macros/page"
6         i18n:domain="worldcookery">
7   <head>
8     <title metal:fill-slot="title"
9            tal:content="context/name/title">recipe name goes here</title>
10  </head>
11  <body>
12  <div metal:fill-slot="body">
13
14      ...
15
16    <div class="message">
17    <h4 i18n:translate="">Also viewable as:</h4>
18
19    <ul>
20      <li tal:repeat="item view/alternateViews">
```

```
21        <a href=""
22           tal:attributes="href string:${context/@@absolute_url}/
   ${item/action}"
23           tal:content="item/title">alternate view</a>
24     </li>
25   </ul>
26   </div>
27
28 </div>
29 </body>
30 </html>
```

20. Again we use the global view variable in the top-level ZPT namespace to call the supplementary class's method we defined in Example 12.3.3. The method returns a browser menu object which supports iteration. Looping over the menu will return the menu entries one-by-one.

view class, Example 12.3.4 shows the modified version of the view template for recipes.

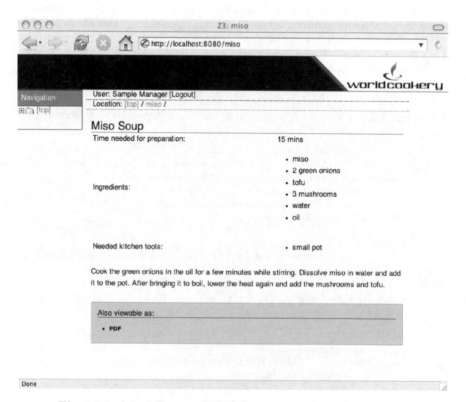

Fig. 12.2. A browser menu offering alternative views for a recipe.

When we now display a recipe, we are offered a PDF document as an alternative form of viewing a recipe (see Figure 12.2). As an optional exercise, write yet another view for displaying recipes using either Page Templates or Python classes. Register the view with our `alternate_views` menu.

Summary

- Browser menus provide lists of browser pages based on context, permission and other filter options.
- Browser pages can be registered for a browser menu in their configuration.
- Browser menus are managed by the Browser Menu Service, one of the few services of Zope that one has to get in touch with oneself using `zapi.getService`.

12.4 Other HTTP protocols

The HTTP protocol is not only used for browser communication in the web. There is the *Distributed Authoring and Versioning* protocol, commonly called *DAV* or *WebDAV* [12]. It enhances the set of HTTP's methods such as GET and POST with a number of a methods allowing content editing and versioning. This makes it the number one alternative to FTP in web publishing environments.

Then there is also XML-RPC [20], a remote procedure protocol based on HTTP and XML. Its almost simplistic approach to remote procedures makes it easily implementable in any kind of environment with any kind of programming language, provided XML and HTTP libraries are available. Zope has support for both of these HTTP subprotocols built in. It is a just a matter of wiring your components up to it.

Before we can start though, we must understand how Zope decides whether an incoming HTTP connection is to be treated as a browser request, an XML-RPC call or a WebDAV request:

- If the request method is GET or POST, a browser request is instantiated.
- If the request method is POST and the content type is `text/xml`, an XML-RPC request is created.
- In all other cases, a regular HTTP/WebDAV request is created.

12.4.1 WebDAV

In Zope WebDAV is treated like HTTP because it is essentially HTTP with extra methods. WebDAV requests are therefore represented as regular HTTP requests. Views for WebDAV and HTTP views are implemented the same way.

In contrast to browser views whose names are exposed in the URL to which the client browser either sends a GET or POST request, HTTP views are named after the HTTP method they are supposed to handle. Therefore, when a DAV client issues a PROPFIND request on an object, the Zope publisher will look up a view for this object called PROPFIND.

DAV support in Zope X3.0 is still in its early stages. As of this release, the zope.app.http and zope.app.dav packages provide views for the following HTTP methods:

OPTIONS This view gives information about which HTTP methods are allowed on an object by checking if the necessary views can be looked up.

PUT This view uses the file representation adapter for IWriteFile or, in case a new object is uploaded, for IFileFactory to save incoming data. We already implemented file representation adapters in Chapter 10, so recipes will automatically support this view.

DELETE This is a view on containers, for example folders, allowing contained objects to be deleted. To do that, is uses an file representation adapter for IWriteDirectory. Containers and their file representation adapters will be covered in Chapter 14.

MKCOL This is also a view containers and can be used to create sub-containers (in DAV lingo, collections). It uses the file representation adapters IWriteDirectory IDirectoryFactory to create and store a new container. Containers and their file representation adapters will be covered in Chapter 14.

PROPFIND This view returns metadata associated with an object to a DAV client using annotation adapters. Metadata using annotations will be covered in Chapter 13.

Summary

- In Zope 3, WebDAV requests are identical to HTTP requests.
- HTTP/WebDAV views are looked up differently. Instead of looking up a named page like with browser views, a view with the name of the request method is looked up.
- It is uncommon to write HTTP/WebDAV views yourself. Zope provides a number of views for HTTP methods that make use of adapters, where per-component customization is needed.

12.4.2 XML-RPC

XML-RPC allows us to remote control a Zope application. Client implementations for this protocol exist for many programming languages, allowing simple data exchange between heterogenous environments. For this to work properly, XML-RPC is limited to the following data types:

- boolean (in Python `bool`),
- integer (in Python `int`),
- double (in Python `float`),
- string (in Python `str`, `unicode`),
- array (in Python `list`, `tuple`),
- struct (in Python `dict`),
- date and time (in Python `xmlrpclib.DateTime`),
- binary data (in Python `xmlrpclib.Binary`).

Zope makes the implementation of XML-RPC views very easy. Our goal is obviously to be able to retrieve and change information about recipes. For this we need to write two views which we conveniently combine in one view class as shown in Example 12.4.1. As it is probably obvious to you by now, we need some configuration, too. See Example 12.4.2. Note that we are again using a subpackage (`worldcookery.xmlrpc`) for XML-RPC-specific components, just like we put browser components in the `worldcookery.browser` subpackage. Therefore, do not forget to include the following line in `configure.zcml`:

```
<include package=".xmlrpc" />
```

A Python client

To test these views, we need an XML-RPC client that communicates with them. Fortunately Python's standard library includes a module for XML-RPC communication, `xmlrpclib`, that allows us to easily write a client program in Python. Example 12.4.3 shows the listing of a small Python program that can be used to retrieve and display the information of a recipe via XML-RPC. To do so now, issue the following command on your command line:

`.../worldcookery/xmlrpc/demo$` **`./displayrecipe.py`**
`http://localhost:8080/miso`

or if you are on Windows:

`...worldcookery\xmlrpc\demo>` **`\Python23\python`**
`displayrecipe.py http://localhost:8080/miso`

Example 12.4.1 XML-RPC view class for retrieving/editing information of recipes (xmlrpc/recipe.py)

```
1   from zope.schema import getFields
2   from zope.app.publisher.xmlrpc import XMLRPCView
3   from worldcookery.interfaces import IRecipe
4
5   def to_unicode(string):
6       if isinstance(string, unicode):
7           return string
8       return string.decode('utf-8')
9
10  class RecipeView(XMLRPCView):
11
12      def info(self):
13          items = [(field, getattr(self.context, field))
14                      for field in getFields(IRecipe)]
15          return dict(items)
16
17      def edit(self, info):
18          context = self.context
19          context.name = to_unicode(info['name'])
20          context.ingredients = \
21              [to_unicode(ingr) for ingr in info['ingredients']]
22          context.tools = [to_unicode(tool) for tool in info['tools']]
23          context.time_to_cook = info['time_to_cook']
24          context.description = to_unicode(info['description'])
25
26          return "Object updated successfully"
```

2 and 10. Just like `zope.app.publisher.browser` provides a base class for browser views (`BrowserView`), a base class for XML-RPC views is also provided.

13 – 15. Since we have to wrap the information contained in a recipe in XML-RPC-compatible datatypes, we simply ask the `IRecipe` schema for its fields, get the data from the object's attributes according to those fields, and return it in a dictionary, a datatype that XML-RPC can handle.

5 – 8. When saving data back on the recipe object, we need to make sure that we assign unicode objects, not just regular strings. Otherwise we would invalidate the schema. XML-RPC itself only knows the string data type. `xmlrpclib` converts strings that contain non-ASCII characters to unicode objects automatically. This function takes care of pure ASCII strings, thus always ensuring a unicode object.

26. At the end of every XML-RPC method, we must not forget to always return some value compatible with XML-RPC data types. By default, if a Python method or function does not have a `return` statement, it returns None. XML-RPC does not support such a null value and a lacking `return` statement might lead to a failure[a].

---

[a] `xmlrpclib` actually *does* support the serialization of null values (None). However, as this is not part of the XML-RPC specification, it is most likely not supported by other XML-RPC implementations.

Example 12.4.2 Configuration of XML-RPC views (`xmlrpc/configure.zcml`)

```
1   <configure
2       xmlns="http://namespaces.zope.org/zope"
3       xmlns:xmlrpc="http://namespaces.zope.org/xmlrpc"
4       >
5
6     <xmlrpc:view
7         for="worldcookery.interfaces.IRecipe"
8         class=".recipe.RecipeView"
9         methods="info"
10        permission="zope.View"
11        />
12
13    <xmlrpc:view
14        for="worldcookery.interfaces.IRecipe"
15        class=".recipe.RecipeView"
16        methods="edit"
17        permission="zope.ManageContent"
18        />
19
20  </configure>
```

9 and 16.   XML-RPC views are configured with `xmlrpc:view` which works similar to `browser:page`. The difference lies in the `methods` parameter which specifies a list of method names of the view class. For each name in that list, an XML-RPC view will be registered under that name. Since we want different permissions for the `info` and `edit` views, we have to use the `xmlrpc:view` directive twice.

XML-RPC is called a *remote* procedure protocol for a good reason. It means you are not limited to a locally running server when issuing procedure calls.

The example client program presented here is obviously very limited. It does not check whether the given URL is well-formed, does not catch any exceptions occurring when connecting to the remote server or when issuing the remote procedure call. It also does not handle authentication. Furthermore and most importantly, it does call the second view we configured, the `edit` XML-RPC method. Do not worry about not being able to test it, though. There exists a functional doctest in the `xmlrpc/README.txt` file which exercises both the `info` and `edit` methods. Only it's sheer length prevents this file from being printed here as a listing.

As an optional exercise, you may write a small application that retrieves a recipe's data, lets you edit it (e.g. in a file using a regular text editor program) and saves the data back to the recipe.

Example 12.4.3 Retrieving a recipe's information via XML-RPC in a Python program (xmlrpc/demo/displayrecipe.py)

```python
1   #! /usr/bin/env python
2   """%(script)s -- retrieves and displays information about a recipe
    via XML-RPC
3
4   Usage: python %(script)s URL-of-a-recipe-object
5   """
6   import sys
7   import xmlrpclib
8
9   def heading1(string):
10      return "=" * len(string) + "\n" + string + "\n" + "=" * len(string)
11
12  def heading2(string):
13      return string + "\n" + "-" * len(string)
14
15  def itemizedlist(list):
16      bulletpoints = ["* " + item.encode('utf-8') for item in list]
17      return '\n'.join(bulletpoints)
18
19  def main():
20      if len(sys.argv) < 2:
21          print >>sys.stderr, __doc__ % {'script': sys.argv[0]}
22          sys.exit(1)
23
24      recipe_url = sys.argv[1]
25      server = xmlrpclib.Server(recipe_url)
26      info = server.info()
27
28      print heading1(info['name'].encode('utf-8'))
29      print
30      print "Time needed for preparation: %s mins" % info['time_to_cook']
31      print
32      print heading2("Ingredients:")
33      print
34      print itemizedlist(info['ingredients'])
35      print
36      print heading2("Needed kitchen tools:")
37      print
38      print itemizedlist(info['tools'])
39      print
40      print info['description'].encode('utf-8')
41
42  if __name__ == "__main__":
43      main()
```

7. XML-RPC support is provided by the xmlrpclib module. It is part of Python's standard library and does not have to be downloaded.

25. A server providing XML-RPC functionality is represented using the xmlrpclib.Server class.

26. A remote procedure is simply invoked as if it were a method on the server object. Here we obtain a recipe's data in a dictionary (sent as an XML-RPC "struct" over the wire). Note that xmlrpclib converts strings with non-ASCII strings into unicode objects, so before outputting to the console we need to encode all strings, preferrably in UTF-8.

A Java client

It was mentioned earlier that XML-RPC allows client-server communication in a heterogenous environment. Many other web solutions are based on languages like Java, Perl or PHP. All of these have support for XML-RPC, too, which means you can exchange data between systems written in these languages and Zope very easily. For a demonstration, consider the Java program DisplayRecipe as shown in Example 12.4.4. It uses the XML-RPC library from the Apache project which is free of charge and freely distributable under the Apache Software License [1]. A compiled package can be obtained from its website[2].

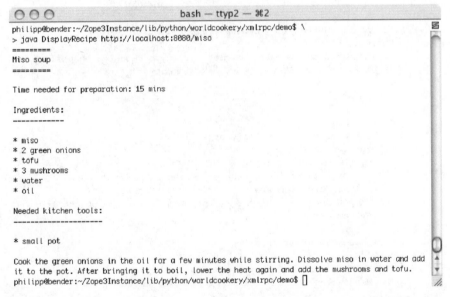

Fig. 12.3. Java client program retrieving recipe data from the Zope server via XML-RPC.

In order to run the program now, you need a Java 2 Runtime Environment (J2RE) which can be downloaded for many operating system from Sun's

---

[2] Apache XmlRpc package website <http://ws.apache.org/xmlrpc/>

Example 12.4.4 Retrieving a recipe's information via XML-RPC in a Python script (`xmlrpc/demo/DisplayRecipe.java`)

```
1   import java.util.Vector;
2   import java.util.Hashtable;
3   import java.util.Enumeration;
4   import org.apache.xmlrpc.XmlRpcClient;
5   import org.apache.xmlrpc.XmlRpcException;
6
7   public class DisplayRecipe {
8
9       private static String heading1(String string) {
10          String s = "";
11          for(int i=0; i<string.length(); i++) { s += "="; }
12          s += "\n" + string + "\n";
13          for(int i=0; i<string.length(); i++) { s += "="; }
14          return s;
15      }
16
17      private static String heading2(String string) {
18          String s = string + "\n";
19          for(int i=0; i<string.length(); i++) { s += "-"; }
20          return s += "\n";
21      }
22
23      private static String itemizedlist(Vector list) {
24          String s = "";
25          for(Enumeration enum=list.elements(); enum.hasMoreElements();) {
26              s += "* " + (String) enum.nextElement() + "\n";
27          }
28          return s;
29      }
30
31      public static void main(String[] args) {
32          if(args.length < 1) {
33              System.err.println(
34                  "DisplayRecipe -- retrieves and displays " +
35                  "information about a recipe via XML-RPC\n\n" +
36                  "Usage: java DisplayRecipe URL-of-a-recipe-object");
37              System.exit(1);
38          }
39          String server_url = args[0];
40          try {
41              XmlRpcClient server = new XmlRpcClient(server_url);
42              Hashtable result = (Hashtable) server.execute("info",
    new Vector());
43                  String name = (String) result.get("name");
44                  Vector ingredients = (Vector) result.get("ingredients");
45                  Vector tools = (Vector) result.get("tools");
46                  Integer time_to_cook = (Integer) result.get("time_to_cook");
47                  String description = (String) result.get("description");
48
49                  System.out.println(heading1(name));
50                  System.out.println();
```

```
51        System.out.println("Time needed for preparation: " +
52                          time_to_cook.toString() + " mins");
53      System.out.println();
54      System.out.println(heading2("Ingredients:"));
55      System.out.println(itemizedlist(ingredients));
56      System.out.println(heading2("Needed kitchen tools:"));
57      System.out.println(itemizedlist(tools));
58      System.out.println(description);
59    } catch (XmlRpcException exception) {
60      System.err.println("JavaClient: XML-RPC Fault #" +
61                        Integer.toString(exception.code) + ": " +
62                        exception.toString());
63    } catch (Exception exception) {
64      System.err.println("JavaClient: " + exception.toString());
65    }
66  }
67 }
```

4–5.   XML-RPC support is provided by a third-party library from the Apache project.

41–42.   The XmlRpcClient class represents a connection to the server. Its execute takes two parameters:

- The name of the remote prodecure to be called.
- A Vector object containing parameters to be passed to the remote procedure.

42–47.   All values returned from the remote procedure call have to be casted to Java objects. As you can see, XML-RPC's structs end up as Hashtables, arrays as Vectors.

59–65.   Because the execute method might throw the XmlRpcException, Java requires us to catch it here explicitly.

Java website [3]. In order for the Java Virtual Machine to find the XmlRpc library, we have to set the CLASSPATH environment variable (it corresponds to Python's PYTHONPATH variable):

$ **export CLASSPATH=$CLASSPATH:/path/to/xmlrpc-x.y.jar**

or if you are on Windows:

C:\> **set CLASSPATH=$CLASSPATH;C:\path\to\xmlrpc-x.y.jar**

Assuming that the Java Virtual Machine (the java program) is in your PATH environment variable, enter the following command on the commandline:

---

[3] Sun Java website <http://java.com>

```
.../worldcookery/xmlrpc/demo$ java DisplayRecipe
http://localhost:8080/miso
```

The command is the same on Unix and on Windows. When issued, the ouput should be identical to the output of the Python program.

Summary

- XML-RPC is a simplistic protocol for remote procedure calls.
- It is based on HTTP and uses XML for the data exchange.
- XML-RPC is limited to the most basic data types, thus allowing the data exchange between heterogenous environments.
- Zope has built-in support for XML-RPC views; Python comes with a library for building XML-RPC clients.

13

Metadata

An important aspect of many web applications, especially content management systems (CMS), is not only the storage of primary data. Extra or secondary data associated with objects, generally called *metadata*, plays an increasingly important role. Common examples of metadata include:

- information about the creator, author, or editor of a document,
- time and date of the creation or last modification of an object,
- state of a document in an organizational workflow.

Of course, Zope as a system which is state of the art knows how to handle metadata very well and supports important standards out-of-the-box. We will see how to use them in this chapter.

13.1 Annotations

Our recipe class knows how to store information about recipes. It does not know how to store metadata and we would really like to keep it that way. After all, metadata is just data that is *associated* with primary data; it is not part of it.

In order to allow us to store metadata without modifying our recipe component, Zope has come up with a system called annotation. As this is again functionality that the original component does not provide, you can bet that adapters are involved.

In annotations, we must distinguish the following two terms:

annotatable When an object promises to be *annotatable* it means that it implements IAnnotatable or a subinterface of that. This interface does not promise any additional functionality expressed in methods or attributes. It is an implied contract, a *marker interface*. The implied contract is that it is possible to get an *annotations* adapter for any annotatable object.

annotations When an object is annotatable, it is possible to get an annotations adapter for it. This adapter, also referred to as just annotations, extends the object with metadata capabilities. Storing data on the adapter means storing metadata on the object.

Now just the question remains where metadata is stored? Obviously, the annotations adapter has to take care of that. It would be no other component's responsibility. Since there are different ways of storing metadata, some of them appropriate for persistent objects, some of them not, there can be no general annotations adapter.

However, Zope would not be Zope if it did not provide a built-in solution already. Most objects in Zope are persisted in the ZODB. Its persistency machinery automatically stores objects and their attributes in the database. The *attribute annotations* adapter makes use of this by storing an object's annotations in an __annotations__ attribute on the object. Objects can decide whether they want to allow that by implementing IAttribute-Annotatable, a subinterface of IAnnotatable. The adapter is registered for IAttributeAnnotatable.

Trying out annotations

For a demonstration, consider the following interactive interpreter session. After initializing Zope, we create a bare recipe object and try to adapt it. It obviously fails because it is not marked annotatable.

```
>>> from zope.app.debug import Debugger
>>> debugger = Debugger(db="var/Data.fs",
...                      config_file="etc/site.zcml")
>>>
>>> class Recipe(object):
...     pass
...
>>> meatloaf = Recipe()
>>> from zope.app.annotation.interfaces import \
...     IAnnotations
>>> annotations = IAnnotations(meatloaf)
Traceback (most recent call last):
...
TypeError: ('Could not adapt', <__main__.Recipe object
at 0x35c4f0>,
            <InterfaceClass zope.app.annotation
.interfaces.IAnnotations>)
```

However, we can instantly make it annotatable by directly providing IAttributeAnnotatable on it. This marks it as annotatable and allows us to adapt it to IAnnotations:

```
>>> from zope.interface import directlyProvides
>>> from zope.app.annotation.interfaces import \
...       IAttributeAnnotatable
>>> directlyProvides(meatloaf, IAttributeAnnotatable)
>>> annotations = IAnnotations(meatloaf)
```

The annotations adapter behaves like a standard mapping object, such as a dictionary. Since there are different types of metadata, it is not recommended to directly store data in this mapping. The convention is to store an additional mapping under a key, usually the name of the software's Python package, and to store that metadata in that second mapping. World Cookery-specific metadata, for example, would be the cook who first invented the dish:

```
>>> annotations['worldcookery'] = {}
>>> annotations['worldcookery']['cook'] = 'Philipp von
Weitershausen'
```

Similarly, Dublin Core metadata is stored using the zope.app.dublin-core.ZopeDublinCore key, rating meta-data with the worldcookery.rating key (more on those later). This way different metadata will not conflict.

When we provided IAttributeAnnotatable on the recipe object, we not only made it annotatable; we also explicitly allowed annotations to be stored on the object as an attribute. The following lines reveal that this has indeed happened:

```
>>> meatloaf.__annotations__
<BTrees._OOBTree.OOBTree object at 0x28a3a50>
>>> dict(meatloaf.__annotations__)
{'worldcookery': {'cook': 'Philipp von Weitershausen'}}
```

For objects persisted in the ZODB, attribute annotations are a care-free and easy solution, because they are persisted with the object automatically. There are circumstances, however, when it is not good to use attribute annotations, for example when content objects are generated from data coming from the file-system or an SQL database. Then, attribute annotation data would not be stored automatically which is why you would have to handle annotations differently in those cases.

In any case, it should not matter to the components storing metadata. All they care about is getting an annotations adapter to store metadata in. Where it is stored does not matter to them, really.

Annotations per class

Now we obviously would like to allow annotations on all recipe objects, so having the class implement IAttributeAnnotatable sounds like a reasonable thing to do. However, it is not common to add such a statement to the Python code directly. The Recipe class as a content object only cares to implement those interfaces that require implementation, such as IRecipe.

IAttributeAnnotatable, however, is a marker interface promising an abstract contract. Whether or not this promise should be given is more of a configuration issue than an implementation issue. Therefore, the implementation of IAttributeAnnotatable is generally expressed in a class's configuration, as shown by Example 13.1.1.

Example 13.1.1 Making recipes annotatable through attribute annotations (configure.zcml)

```
1     ...
2     <content class=".recipe.Recipe">
3       <factory
4           id="worldcookery.Recipe"
5           title="Create a new recipe"
6           description="This factory instantiates new recipes"
7           />
8       <implements
9           interface="zope.app.annotation.interfaces.IAttributeAnnotatable"
10          />
11      <require
12          permission="zope.View"
13          interface=".interfaces.IRecipe"
14          />
15      <require
16          permission="zope.ManageContent"
17          set_schema=".interfaces.IRecipe"
18          />
19    </content>
20    ...
```

8–10. Classes can be made to implement interfaces additionally to what they already implement from their source code using the implements subdirective of the content directive. This directive only makes sense for marker interfaces because otherwise classes could promise to implement certain interfaces which in fact they do not. IAttributeAnnotatable is by far the number one interface that this directive is used for.

Summary

- As it is not part of an object's primary data, metadata should be managed and possibly stored separately from the content objects it is associated with.
- Zope 3 uses annotation adapters as metadata storage; an annotation adapter manages all metadata associated with a particular object.
- For persistent objects, attribute annotations is the preferred way to handle annotations. On objects marked as attribute-annotatable the annotations adapter stores metadata in a hidden attribute on the object, thus letting it to be persisted with the object.
- Different software packages should use different annotation keys to distinguish their metadata and avoid conflicts and ambiguities.

13.2 The Dublin Core

A definite standard in the field of metadata is the *Dublin Core* [4], [11]. It defines a set of information that is generally found useful in document-oriented systems. The following terms for resources, as the standard calls documents and other items whose metadata is of interest, are defined by the Dublin Core:

Title provides a human-readable and meaningful name for the resource. Most of the time, even in Zope, documents are referred to by their filename or name within their container which is not always meaningful to a person, unlike the contents of this propery is supposed to be.

Creator states a person or organization responsible for the content of the resource.

Subject contains a list of keywords thematically describing the contents of the resource.

Description is usally a short abstract of what the resource depicts.

Publisher states a person or organization responsible for making the resource available.

Contributor lists possible contributors to the contents of the resource.

Date can be one or more dates representing an important event in the resource's life-cycle. Most of the time, a creation date and modification dates are recorded.

Type gives information about what kind of information the resource contains. This may include general categories or even genres.

Format informs readers and editors about the data format that the information is stored and presented in. This would most typically be a MIME type identifier.

Identifier gives a unique and unambigious reference to the resource. This can be anything within a system of unique identifiers, such as an ISBN number, a URI, or even an IP address or telephone number.

Source is a list of resources from which the current resource was derived from.

Language states the language the resource's text is written and presented in.

Relation can contain a list of identifiers with which the resource stands in relation with. Which type of relation is meant is arbitrary and up to the application to fill with a meaning.

Coverage defines the scope of the resource.

Rights gives information about intellectual rights, copyrights, etc. regarding the resource.

All Dublin Core elements support multiple values. This obviously only makes sense for a few of them, such as *Subject*, *Contributor*, and *Rights*. Others properties, such as *Date* and *Relation*, only make sense when treated with qualifiers that tell the application which date and what kind of a relation are meant. Zope supports the Dublin Core standard to its full extent, but the general interfaces are designed for every-day use-cases, thus simplifying the unnecessary complexity.

Zope's support for Dublin Core resides in the `zope.app.dublincore` package. At the heart of this package operates the `ZopeDublinCore` adapter, an adapter for annotatable objects that allows one to work with Dublin Core properties without having to go through annotations, even though the properties are stored in annotations, of course. Key interfaces are `IZopeDublinCore` for property read access and `IWriteZopeDublinCore` for write access, respectively.

Trying it out in the interpreter shell

Again we want to demonstrate how the Dublin Core adapter works with an example from the interactive interpreter shell:

```
>>> from zope.app.debug import Debugger
>>> debugger = Debugger()
>>>
>>> class Recipe(object):
...      pass
...
>>> fried_chicken = Recipe()
```

Since the object is not annotatable, we cannot adapt it to the Dublin Core
interface.

```
>>> from zope.app.dublincore.interfaces import \
...      IWriteZopeDublinCore
>>> dc = IWriteZopeDublinCore(fried_chicken)
Traceback (most recent call last):
...
TypeError: ('Could not adapt', <__main__.Recipe object
at 0x227fc30>,
              <InterfaceClass zope.app.dublincore
.interfaces.IWriteZopeDublinCore>)
```

However, after marking it attribute-annotatable, the adaption works. We can
successfully assign Dublin Core metadata, more importantly without going
through annotations:

```
>>> from zope.interface import directlyProvides
>>> from zope.app.annotation.interfaces import \
...      IAttributeAnnotatable
>>> directlyProvides(fried_chicken,
...                    IAttributeAnnotatable)
>>> dc = IWriteZopeDublinCore(fried_chicken)
>>> dc.title = u'Fried chicken'
```

Of course, the metadata still ends up in the annotations as the following look
behinds the scenes reveals:

```
>>> dict(fried_chicken.__annotations__)
{'zope.app.dublincore.ZopeDublinCore':
 <zope.app.dublincore.annotatableadapter
.ZDCAnnotationData object at 0x29036b0>}
```

We see that the Dublin Core adapter in fact stores its data under the
`zope.app.dublincore.ZopeDublinCore` annotation key. How and in
what format is secondary. We will not have to worry about ever having to
work with this manually.

Metadata automation

Zope does a lot more for us when our objects are annotatable than just
providing the Dublin Core adapter. As you may have noticed, recipes now
have a new management tab, *Metadata* (see Figure 13.1). It allows content
editors to edit the most basic metadata, namely title and description.

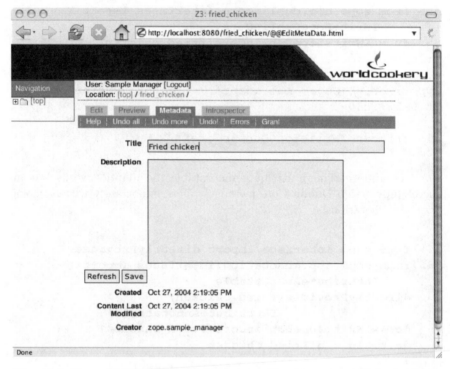

Fig. 13.1. Zope provides a form for all annotatable objects in which basic Dublin
Core metadata can be edited.

The *Metadata* ZMI view also reveals automatically computed metadata:

- creation date,
- date of last modification,
- and the user name of the creator.

If you add a new recipe to a folder, you will see that these values has automatically been computed and annotated to the object. We will learn in

Chapter 15 how this works, for now it is just important to know that Zope does this.

As a defacto industry standard, Dublin Core is not only used within a document or resource management system. It also comes into action when data is interchanged. The WebDAV protocol, for example, allows a client program to query object metadata using the PROPFIND method. Zope's central view implementation for PROPFIND builds upon annotations and annotation-related adapters such as Dublin Core, thus allowing client programs to query Dublin Core and other metadata directly though WebDAV.

Permissions

Viewing and changing Dublin Core properties is protected by special permissions:

zope.app.dublincore.view is required from all principals when accessing Dublin Core metadata. Like zope.View, it is granted to anonymous by default.

zope.app.dublincore.change is required for changing Dublin Core properties.

An example in Page Templates

Since Zope's Dublin Core solution is very integrated, most of the times one has to work with the Dublin Core is in presentation components, such as Page Templates. Therefore, before we use the Dublin Core adapter in Python component, a simple example should demonstrate how to access Dublin Core metadata in ZPT.

In order not to overcomplicate things, we will simply extend the Page Template responsible for displaying recipes, recipeview.pt, so that it prints a small line at the bottom of the page stating when the recipe was created and when it was last modified. The changes that need to be applied to the template are shown in Example 13.2.1.

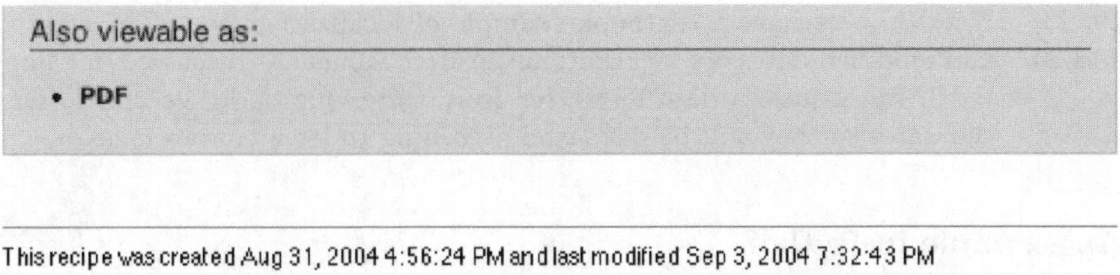

Also viewable as:

• **PDF**

This recipe was created Aug 31, 2004 4:56:24 PM and last modified Sep 3, 2004 7:32:43 PM

Fig. 13.2. Showing created and last modified dates at the bottom of the page.

Example 13.2.1 Accessing Dublin Core metadata from Page Templates (`browser/recipeview.pt`)

```
1   <html xmlns="http://www.w3.org/1999/xhtml"
2         xmlns:tal="http://xml.zope.org/namespaces/tal"
3         xmlns:metal="http://xml.zope.org/namespaces/metal"
4         xmlns:i18n="http://xml.zope.org/namespaces/i18n"
5         metal:use-macro="context/@@standard_macros/page"
6         i18n:domain="worldcookery">
7   <head>
8     <title metal:fill-slot="title"
9            tal:content="context/name/title">recipe name goes here</title>
10  </head>
11  <body>
12  <div metal:fill-slot="body">
13
14      ...
15
16      <div style="font-size: 75%; margin-top: 24pt; border-top: 1px
    solid #116692;">
17      <p tal:define="created context/zope:created;
18                     modified context/zope:modified;
19                     formatter python:request.locale.dates.getFormatter
    ('dateTime')"
20         i18n:translate="">
21        This recipe was created
22        <span i18n:name="created_date"
23              tal:replace="python:formatter.format(created)" />
24        and last modified
25        <span i18n:name="modified_date"
26              tal:replace="python:formatter.format(modified)" />
27      </p>
28      </div>
29
30  </div>
31  </body>
32  </html>
```

17–18.   Apart from traversal to attributes or dictionary keys, ZPT's path expressions can make use of *namespace adapters*. These are special traversing adapters for the TALES expressions that allow accessing additional information, such as metadata. The `zope` namespace adapter provides access to the most basic set of Dublin Core metadata, such as *Title*, *Created Date*, and *Modified Date*. The latter two are accessed here.

19, 23,   Note that we have a textbook example of localization here. The created
and 26.   and modified dates are localization-sensitive values. As discussed in Chapter 9, we acquire a date formatter from the request's locale and format the dates so they will be displayed according to local conventions.

An example in Python

As an example for working with the Dublin Core adapter from Python, let us a extend the XML-RPC view class from the previous chapter to provide another method for Dublin Core metadata retrieval. Example 13.2.2 shows the modified XML-RPC view class whereas Example 13.2.3 displays the little change necessary in order to configure the additional view method.

Since we already wrote an XML-RPC client in Chapter 12, consider it an optional exercise to write one for the new view method. The functional

Example 13.2.2 Enhanced XML-RPC view class providing a view method for metadata retrieval (xmlrpc/recipe.py)

```
1   import time
2   import xmlrpclib
3   from zope.schema import getFields
4   from zope.app.publisher.xmlrpc import XMLRPCView
5   from zope.app.dublincore.interfaces import IZopeDublinCore
6   from worldcookery.interfaces import IRecipe
7
8   def to_unicode(string):
9       if isinstance(string, unicode):
10          return string
11      return string.decode('utf-8')
12
13  class RecipeView(XMLRPCView):
14
15      def info(self):
16          items = [(field, getattr(self.context, field))
17                      for field in getFields(IRecipe)]
18          return dict(items)
19
20      def dublincore_info(self):
21          dc = IZopeDublinCore(self.context)
22          items = [(field, getattr(dc, field))
23                      for field in getFields(IZopeDublinCore)]
24          info = dict(items)
25          for name in ('effective', 'created', 'expires', 'modified'):
26              if info[name]:
27                  epochtime = time.mktime(info[name].timetuple())
28                  info[name] = xmlrpclib.DateTime(epochtime)
29              else:
30                  info[name] = ''
31          return info
32
33      def edit(self, info):
34          context = self.context
35          context.name = to_unicode(info['name'])
36          context.ingredients = \
37              [to_unicode(ingr) for ingr in info['ingredients']]
38          context.tools = [to_unicode(tool) for tool in info['tools']]
39          context.time_to_cook = info['time_to_cook']
40          context.description = to_unicode(info['description'])
41
42          return "Object updated successfully"
```

20 – 24.   After adapting the recipe object to IZopeDublinCore, we use the same
trick as in the info method to populate a dictionary with values from
the instance attributes, this time from the adapter.

25 – 30.   As specified by the IZopeDublinCore interface, the date values are
stored as datetime objects, a data type that xmlrpclib cannot serialize[a]. To ensure proper data exchange between Zope and the XML-RPC
client, we have to convert datetime objects into xmlrpclib.DateTime
objects. Values that are None are converted to empty strings.

---

[a] Even though XML-RPC and even xmlrpclib support a combined date and
time datatype, the serializer does not support instances of the datetime class
which was added only recently in Python 2.3.

Example 13.2.3 Adding another XML-RPC view method to the configuration (xmlrpc/configure.zcml)

```
1   <configure
2       xmlns="http://namespaces.zope.org/zope"
3       xmlns:xmlrpc="http://namespaces.zope.org/xmlrpc"
4       >
5
6     <xmlrpc:view
7         for="worldcookery.interfaces.IRecipe"
8         class=".recipe.RecipeView"
9         methods="info dublincore_info"
10        permission="zope.View"
11        />
12
13    <xmlrpc:view
14        for="worldcookery.interfaces.IRecipe"
15        class=".recipe.RecipeView"
16        methods="edit"
17        permission="zope.ManageContent"
18        />
19
20  </configure>
```

9. By adding the dublincore_info method to this list it will be registered as
an XML-RPC view, protected with the zope.View permission like the info
method.

doctest in xmlrpc/README.txt was updated, so the functionality of the
view is ensured either way.

Summary

• The Dublin Core specification describes a set of metadata commonly associated with resources in document management systems.
• Zope's Dublin Core support lies mainly in an adapter provided by the
zope.app.dublincore package.

Since it is metadata, the adapter stores Dublin Core information in annotations.

- Zope also provides automated metadata updating facilities that are triggered when objects are added and/or modified.
- In Page Templates, the zope TALES namespace adapter provides access to basic Dublin Core fields.

Flashback

In Zope 2, the Content Management Framework (CMF) first introduced Dublin Core support, mainly through a set of interfaces. CMF content classes can choose to implement these to signal to the rest of application that they supported Dublin Core methods. This is by far the most prominant usage of interfaces in a Zope application prior to Zope 3.

The CMF also provides an implementation of these interfaces, Default-DublinCoreImpl, that content classes can inherit from to gain Dublin Core functionality. The obvious difference to Zope 3 here is, again, that extra functionality like handling metadata, especially a certain kind like Dublin Core, is constrained to external components like adapters. This makes it much more flexible, since the an adapter can easily be exchanged – a base class cannot.

Finally, Zope 3 absolutely surpasses the CMF's metadata model by offering a totally generic solution: annotations. They not only allow us to associate information useful to humans but also application-relevant data, such as workflow states, revision control status, etc.

13.3 Custom metadata

More than often it is necessary to store custom metadata. Experience shows that advanced and complex applications always require at least one or two fields more than the Dublin Core standard provides. All that is not tragic, we can simply write a custom adapter to store the custom metadata in annotations.

As a simple example for such a component, consider an online rating system through which visitors of the *World Cookery* website can rate recipes according to how good they found the dish or the recipe description. Again, the rating information is not part of the actual recipe data schema; since it clearly is metadata, it belongs in annotations.

Interfaces

First, we will have to define two interfaces (see Example 13.3.1). IRatable is a marker interface identifying objects that can be rated. It extends the IAnnotatable marker interface to express the dependency on annotations.

The second interface, IRating, describes the actual rating API. It allows to gather rating information and to perform a ratings. An adapter for ratable objects will provide this interface.

Example 13.3.1 Interfaces for the simple rating system (interfaces.py)

```
1    ...
2
3    from zope.schema import Float
4    from zope.app.annotation.interfaces import IAnnotatable
5
6    class IRatable(IAnnotatable):
7        """Marker interface that promises that an implementing object maybe
8        rated using ``IRating`` annotations.
9        """
10
11   class IRating(Interface):
12       """Give and query rating about objects, such as recipes.
13       """
14
15       def rate(rating):
16           """Rate the current object with `rating`, a floating point number
17           between 0 and 1.
18           """
19
20       averageRating = Float(
21           title=_(u"Average rating"),
22           description=_(u"The average rating of the current object"),
23           required=True
24           )
25
26       numberOfRatings = Int(
27           title=_(u"Number of ratings"),
28           description=_(u"The number of times the current has been rated"),
29           required=True
30           )
```

An adapter

In analogy to the IZopeDublinCore adapter, we now provide the IRating adapter for ratable objects. Of course, it will store all rating information in the ratable object's annotations, thus providing a frontend to this particular type of metadata through the IRating interface. Example 13.3.2 shows the source code.

For configuration, we will not only have to configure the adapter, but we will also have to make the Recipe class ratable so that the adapter works on it. Example 13.3.3 shows how configure.zcml needs to be enhanced.

As usual, we can now test the adapter on the command line. Consider a recipe:

Example 13.3.2 Adapter providing rating functionality based on annotations (rating.py)

```
1   from persistent.dict import PersistentDict
2   from persistent.list import PersistentList
3   from zope.interface import implements
4   from zope.app.annotation.interfaces import IAnnotations
5   from worldcookery.interfaces import IRating
6
7   KEY = "worldcookery.rating"
8
9   class Rating(object):
10      implements(IRating)
11
12      def __init__(self, context):
13          self.context = context
14          annotations = IAnnotations(context)
15          mapping = annotations.get(KEY)
16          if mapping is None:
17              blank = {'average': 0.0, 'ratings': PersistentList()}
18              mapping = annotations[KEY] = PersistentDict(blank)
19          self.mapping = mapping
20
21      def rate(self, rating):
22          ratings = self.mapping['ratings']
23          ratings.append(float(rating))
24          self.mapping['average'] = sum(ratings)/len(ratings)
25
26      def averageRating(self):
27          return self.mapping['average']
28      averageRating = property(averageRating)
29
30      def numberOfRatings(self):
31          return len(self.mapping['ratings'])
32      numberOfRatings = property(numberOfRatings)
```

7.   As mentioned earlier in this chapter, annotations are stored under a certain key so that different sets of metadata do not conflict. The constant here defines the key used for storing rating information

14–15.   Like the Dublin Core adapter, we read and write to and from annotations, so get yet another adapter, the annotations adapter. From it we acquire a mapping object for storing rating data in. The IAnnotations interface requires the annotations adapter to behave like a mapping object itself.

17–18.   In case the mapping object cannot be acquired, it means that this adapter is invoked on this particular object instance for the first time. We thus provide a default mapping with a zero average and an empty list. Since the annotations are likely to be persisted, we have to be careful that we comply with the rules of persistency. To be safe, we use PersistentDict and PersistentList instead of their non-persistent flavours.

Example 13.3.3 Configuring the rating adapter and making recipes ratable
(`configure.zcml`)

```
 1    ...
 2
 3    <content class=".recipe.Recipe">
 4      <factory
 5          id="worldcookery.Recipe"
 6          title="Create a new recipe"
 7          description="This factory instantiates new recipes"
 8          />
 9      <implements
10          interface="zope.app.annotation.interfaces.IAttributeAnnotatable
11                         .interfaces.IRatable"
12          />
13      <require
14          permission="zope.View"
15          interface=".interfaces.IRecipe"
16          />
17      <require
18          permission="zope.ManageContent"
19          set_schema=".interfaces.IRecipe"
20          />
21    </content>
22
23    ...
24
25    <adapter
26        for=".interfaces.IRatable"
27        provides=".interfaces.IRating"
28        factory=".rating.Rating"
29        trusted="true"
30        />
31
32    <content class=".rating.Rating">
33      <require
34          permission="zope.View"
35          attributes="averageRating numberOfRatings rate"
36          />
37    </content>
38
39    ...
```

9–12.   We want recipes to be ratable, we therefore add `IRatable` to the list of
         additional interfaces the `Recipe` class should implement.

29.   Like all other components invoked through user-interaction, adapters have
         to respect security-protected methods and attributes. That is usually not
         a problem because the object's attributes that the adapter works with
         should have security declarations that requires a permission from the user.
         The problem is that this mechanism does not work with attribute anno-
         tations because the `__annotations__` attribute is hardly ever configured
         with security declarations. After all, the classes are not supposed to know
         about it.

The solution here is to mark this adapter as *trusted*. This will prevent any security checks when the adapter accesses attributes on the object; it will have free access.

32 – 37.   Since the IRatable adapter is a trusted adapter, another component could freely use it and modify recipe objects without security checkins, even if it is only some secondary metadata. To prevent that, we ensure that the adapter implementation, the Rating class, has proper security declarations. This will prevent anyone not having the right permission to abuse the trusted adapter.

```
>>> from zope.app.debug import Debugger
>>> debugger = Debugger(db="var/Data.fs",
...                     config_file="etc/site.zcml")
>>>
>>> class Recipe(object):
...     pass
...
>>> hamburgers = Recipe()
```

In order to mark it ratable, it also needs to be annotatable, for example attribute-annotatable:

```
>>> from zope.app.annotation.interfaces import \
...     IAttributeAnnotatable
>>> from worldcookery.interfaces import IRatable
>>> from zope.interface import directlyProvides
>>> directlyProvides(hamburgers, IAttributeAnnotatable,
...     IRatable)
```

Now we can rate the object using the IRating adapter:

```
>>> from worldcookery.interfaces import IRating
>>> rating = IRating(hamburgers)
>>> rating.rate(1)    # I don't like hamburgers
>>> rating.rate(9)    # I like hamburgers
```

Of course, the adapter also tells about the average rating and number of ratings that have been issued yet:

```
>>> rating.averageRating
5.0
>>> rating.numberOfRatings
2
```

Of course, this small intepreter session makes a nice doctest if slightly modified. Example 13.3.4 shows the listing of a docfile test, serving as a test and documentation for the rating system at the same time. Example 13.3.5 contains the mandatory test suite and initialization routines as known from Chapter 11.

Example 13.3.4 Docfile test for the rating adapter (`rating.txt`)

```
 1   ==============
 2   Rating objects
 3   ==============
 4
 5   The rating system allows users to rate objects on a continuous scale
 6   (a discrete scale can be enforced by a view).  We distinguish
 7   *ratable* objects which have to annotatable and implement ''IRatable'
 8   on one hand and the ''IRating'' adapter for ratable objects which the
 9   rating of the latter on the other hand.
10
11   Consider a simple object, e.g. a recipe:
12
13      >>> from worldcookery.recipe import Recipe
14      >>> hamburgers = Recipe()
15
16   In order to mark it ratable, it also needs to annotatable, for example
17   attribute-annotatable:
18
19      >>> from zope.app.annotation.interfaces import IAttributeAnnotatable
20      >>> from worldcookery.interfaces import IRatable
21      >>> from zope.interface import directlyProvides
22      >>> directlyProvides(hamburgers, IAttributeAnnotatable, IRatable)
23
24   Now we can rate the object using the ''IRating'' adapter:
25
26      >>> from worldcookery.interfaces import IRating
27      >>> rating = IRating(hamburgers)
28      >>> rating.rate(1)    # this person does not like hamburgers
29      >>> rating.rate(9)    # this person seem to like them
30
31   Of course, the adapter also tells about the average rating and number
32   of ratings that have been issued yet:
33
34      >>> rating.averageRating
35      5.0
36      >>> rating.numberOfRatings
37      2
```

Example 13.3.5 Test suite and initialization routines for the rating docfile test (tests/test_rating.py)

```
1   import unittest
2   from zope.testing.doctestunit import DocFileSuite
3   from zope.app.tests import ztapi, placelesssetup
4   from zope.app.annotation.interfaces import IAnnotations
5   from zope.app.annotation.interfaces import IAttributeAnnotatable
6   from zope.app.annotation.attribute import AttributeAnnotations
7
8   from worldcookery.interfaces import IRatable, IRating
9   from worldcookery.rating import Rating
10
11  def setUp(test):
12      placelesssetup.setUp(test)
13      ztapi.provideAdapter(IAttributeAnnotatable, IAnnotations,
14                           AttributeAnnotations)
15      ztapi.provideAdapter(IRatable, IRating, Rating)
16
17  def test_suite():
18      return unittest.TestSuite((
19          DocFileSuite('rating.txt',
20                       package='worldcookery',
21                       setUp=setUp,
22                       tearDown=placelesssetup.tearDown),
23          ))
24
25  if __name__ == '__main__':
26      unittest.main(defaultTest='test_suite')
```

Browser views

Like with the Dublin Core, an adapter will do no good for the user. A visitor of the *World Cookery* wants to rate objects through a web browser. That means we have to provide browser views for the rating system.

To make things easier for us and the users, we extend the view Page Template for recipes again, this time with a simplistic form for rating (Example 13.3.6). The ZPT obviously will not be able to handle this all by itself since the object needs to be adapted in order to display the average rating and number of votes so far. We will also have to provide a view that acts as the form handler and invokes the IRating adapter when the user submits a rating. Its source code is listed in Example 13.3.7, along with its configuration in Example 13.3.8.

Example 13.3.6 Rating enhancements to the recipe view Page Template
(browser/recipeview.pt)

```
1   <html xmlns="http://www.w3.org/1999/xhtml"
2         xmlns:tal="http://xml.zope.org/namespaces/tal"
3         xmlns:metal="http://xml.zope.org/namespaces/metal"
4         xmlns:i18n="http://xml.zope.org/namespaces/i18n"
5         metal:use-macro="context/@@standard_macros/page"
6         i18n:domain="worldcookery">
7   <head>
8     <title metal:fill-slot="title"
9            tal:content="context/name/title">recipe name goes here</title>
10  </head>
11  <body>
12  <div metal:fill-slot="body">
13
14     ...
15
16     <div>
17     <h4 i18n:translate="heading-ratings">Ratings</h4>
18
19     <p i18n:translate=""
20        tal:define="rating view/rating;
21                    average rating/averageRating;
22                      votes rating/numberOfRatings;
23                  formatter python:request.locale.numbers.getFormatter('decimal')">
24      This recipe has received an average rating of
25      <strong tal:content="python:formatter.format(average, '###0.0')"
26              i18n:name="rating">0.0</strong>
27      (<strong i18n:name="votes" tal:content="votes">12</strong> votes).
28     </p>
29
30     <form action="@@rate.html" method="post">
31       <p><span i18n:translate="">Rate this recipe:</span>
32       <tal:loop tal:repeat="rating view/ratingChoices">
33         <input type="radio" name="rating:float"
34                tal:attributes="value rating;
35                                id string:rating-${repeat/rating/number}"
36                />
37         <label tal:attributes="for string:rating-${repeat/rating/number}"
38                tal:content="rating">rating</label> 
39       </tal:loop>
40       <input type="submit" value="Rate" i18n:attributes="value rate-button" />
41       </p>
42     </form>
43     </div>
44
45     ...
46
47  </div>
48  </body>
49  </html>
```

20, 32, and 30. From the supplementary view class instance (shown in Example 13.3.7) we acquire the rating adapter instance and a list of possible ratings. The form handler, @@rate.html, is also provided by it.

23 and 25. Here we have an another example of localization. The average rating is obviously a floating point number, which is localization-sensitive too. Again, we acquire a number formatter from the request's locale to format the number according to a pattern. Here, it makes sense to round to the first digit after the dot.

Example 13.3.7 View class enhanced with rating functionality (browser/recipe.py)

```
1   from zope.app import zapi, servicenames
2   from zope.app.publisher.browser import BrowserView
3   from worldcookery.interfaces import IRating
4
5   class RecipeView(BrowserView):
6
7       def renderDescription(self):
8           plaintext = zapi.createObject(None, 'zope.source.plaintext',
9                                         self.context.description)
10          view = zapi.getView(plaintext, '', self.request)
11          return view.render()
12
13      def alternateViews(self):
14          menu_service = zapi.getService(servicenames.BrowserMenu)
15          menu_id = 'alternate_views'
16          return menu_service.getMenu(menu_id, self.context, self.request)
17
18      def rating(self):
19          return IRating(self.context)
20
21      def rate(self, rating):
22          IRating(self.context).rate(rating)
23          self.request.response.redirect('.')
24
25      ratingChoices = (1, 2, 3, 4, 5)
```

2 and 5.   Since RecipeView also acts as a browser view class now, we should to subclass BrowserView.

21 – 23.   The rate method acts is the form handler and will be invoked when the user rates an object. As expected, it uses the IRating adapter to do the actual rating. In Example 13.3.8, this method is configured as a browser page for recipe objects called @@rate.html.

Example 13.3.8 Configuration for rating browser view (`browser/recipe.py`)

```
1     ...
2     <browser:page
3         for="worldcookery.interfaces.IRecipe"
4         name="rate.html"
5         class=".recipe.RecipeView"
6         attribute="rate"
7         permission="zope.View"
8         />
9     ...
```

amount of soup and add it. Finally, add the scallion. Shut off the heat after a few minutes.

Ratings

This recipe has received an average rating of **2.7** (**14** votes).

Rate this recipe: ⌒ 1 ⌒ 2 ⌒ 3 ⊙ 4 ⌒ 5 | Rate |

Also viewable as:

• **PDF**

This recipe was created Aug 31, 2004 4:56:24 PM and last modified Sep 3, 2004 7:43:04 PM

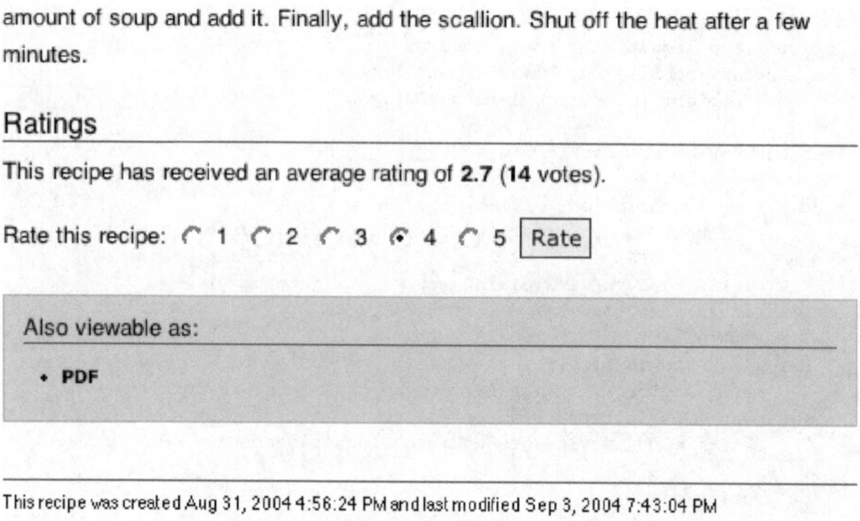

Fig. 13.3. A recipe inviting the viewer to rate it.

Summary

- Sometimes, custom metadata outside of the already supported Dublin Core needs to be associated with objects.
- It is recommended to abstract custom metadata – including the functionality to change it – in an interface, such as `IRating` in the example.
- Instead of directly reading and writing annotated data, an adapter for the abstract metadata interface takes care of storing the annotated data, like the `IRating` adapter does in the example.

14

Containers

When we created recipes through the web interfaces, we added them to folders. Folders are special content components because they contain other content components. They are *content containers*. Containment is an important concept in Zope and containers are important components. They occur everywhere, not only where content components are involved.

After introducing the basic concepts and interfaces, this chapter will go on explaining common applications of containers, such as containment constraints and sites. With this chapter we will complete the key concepts of the Zope application server.

14.1 Containers, containment, and location

Containers group objects and allow them to be looked up by name, exactly like Python dictionaries. In fact, a dictionary is the simplest container imaginable. The only constraint with containers is that the key by which objects are looked up has to be a string or unicode object, whereas dictionaries accept any hashable object as key. Most of the time, though, simple dictionaries do not suffice. A container for persistent objects, for example, should most probably be persistent itself.

The whole container API is described in the `IContainer` interface which is a combination of the `IReadContainer` and `IWriteContainer` interfaces, all provided by the `zope.app.container.interfaces` module. As the names say it, `IReadContainer` describes methods for read access whereas `IWriteContainer` contains the API for write access. This distinction makes security configuration very easy.

Location

Objects that are contained in a container normally have no idea that they are contained. Most of the time, they themselves do not even need to know.

However, components operating on the object might need to know whether an object is contained, and if, the container it is contained in and by which name it is known to the container. A commonly used component of this kind is the absolute_url or IAbsoluteURL view. It needs to know the name of the object it is supposed to compute the URL for as well as the names of all parent objects in order to compute the full URL.

The Zope framework that allows such parent relations is the *location* framework provided by the zope.app.location package. The ILocation interface is the piece that ties everything together. If a component provides ILocation, it promises to provide the following attributes:

- __parent__ (its container),
- __name__ (its name in the container).

If these attributes are not None, then the object is *locatable*, meaning it is part of a hierarchy and can be found via traversal through this hierarchy.

For a demonstration we will use the interactive interpreter shell as usual. A simplistic object will serve as a locatable object. A class exactly like this is provided by the zope.app.location package as a potential base class. We will define it here ourselves for demonstration purposes, though:

```
>>> from zope.app.location.interfaces import ILocation
>>> from zope.interface import implements
>>>
>>> class Location(object):
...         implements(ILocation)
...         __name__ = __parent__ = None
...
```

Instances of this class are potentially locatable. They are not, of course, as long as the name and parent attributes are None. As an example we create three instances of which one is always the parent object of the next one, like grandfather, father, and son. The locate function can be used to wire the location information into potentially locatable objects. It is a shorter spelling of assigning the __name__ and __parent__ attributes:

```
>>> son = Location()
>>> father = Location()
>>> grandfather = Location()
>>>
>>> from zope.app.location import locate
>>> locate(son, father, name=u"son")
>>> locate(father, grandfather, name=u"father")
>>> grandfather.__name__ = u"grandfather"
```

Note that the parent of a locatable object does not necessarily have to be container. Locatability makes no assumptions about the parent object. As you can see from the example, the syntax of the locate function is

```
locate(object, parent, name=None)
```

The *name* parameter is optional.

A function of locatability is a walkable hierarchy of object ancestors. An object's parent can have a parent itself and so forth. The LocationIterator makes this sequence of parents iterable, for example in a simple loop:

```
>>> from zope.app.location import LocationIterator
>>> for obj in LocationIterator(son):
...         print obj.__name__
...
son
father
grandfather
```

Since the grandfather object was not assigned a parent, the iteration stops there.

Containment

Containment is just another aspect of locatability. It is locatability from a container's point of view. Locatability by itself expresses mere parent-child relationships. Containment adds the notion of being contained in a Zope container.

Whether or not an object is contained is expressed through the IContained interface which is provided by the zope.app.container package. This is a marker interface that extends ILocation. Any contained object is therefore locatable.

Imagine a simple container such as SampleContainer from the zope.app.container.sample module. We can easily store potentially locatable objects on it by using standard dictionary syntax. This time we will resort to the simple Location class as it is provided by zope.app.location to save typing:

```
>>> from zope.app.container.sample import SampleContainer
>>> from zope.app.location import Location
>>> gazpacho = SampleContainer()
>>> container[u'gazpacho'] = gazpacho = Location()
```

Now we would also like to express the containment relation between this object and its container. That includes making the container the parent of this object. To do that we have to use the `contained` function instead of `locate`:

```
>>> contained(gazpacho, container, name=u'gazpacho')
<zope.app.location.location.Location object at
0x134ff90>
```

As you can see, the syntax of the `contained` function is exactly like the one of `locate`.

Now, the objects are located in the container, as a quick test verifies:

```
>>> gazpacho.__parent__ is container
True
>>> gazpacho.__name__
u'gazpacho'
```

Not only that, they are also marked as *contained* now, meaning they now provide `IContained`:

```
>>> from zope.app.container.interfaces import IContained
>>> IContained.providedBy(gazpacho)
True
```

Last but not least it should be mentioned that adding the object to the container and making it contained can be combined in one step by using the `setitem` function:

```
>>> chorizo = Location()
>>> from zope.app.container.contained import setitem
>>> setitem(container, container.__setitem__,
...          u'chorizo', chorizo)
>>> IContained.providedBy(chorizo)
True
>>> chorizo.__parent__ is container
True
>>> chorizo.__name__
u'chorizo'
>>> container[u'chorizo'] is chorizo
True
```

The syntax of the setitem function differs from one of locate and contained:

```
setitem(container, setitem_method, name, object)
```

What happens with non-locatable objects?

So far we have only added locatable objects to containers. They can easily be made contained because they already have __name__ and __parent__ attributes. Setting these attributes and marking them with IContained is just a formality.

Not all objects are locatable, though. As a matter of fact the majority is not locatable, including instances of our Recipe class. The containment machinery cannot assign the __name__ and __parent__ attributes by force either. It might simply not be allowed by the class and result in an AttributeError.

Zope's answer to this problem are *contained proxies*. Like security proxies, they wrap an object almost transparently. While security proxies protect the wrapped object against unallowed access, contained proxies add containment functionality to non-locatable objects. In other words, they make it look like the object had __name__ and __parent__ attributes without actually modifying it.

The containment machinery will make use of contained proxies transparently. That means it finds out automatically when an object needs to be wrapped in one and when not. As we have seen above, it does not wrap objects that are already locatable. Let us repeat the above experiment with an object that is *not* locatable such as a regular recipe object:

```
>>> from worldcookery.recipe import Recipe
>>> paella = Recipe()
>>> setitem(container, container.__setitem__, u'paella',
paella)
```

At first, the contained object looks like a regular recipe object. But a closer look reveals that it now has __name__ and __parent__ attributes. The type function discovers the real nature of this object – a proxy wrapping a recipe object:

```
>>> container[u'paella']
<worldcookery.recipe.Recipe object at 0x795b30>
>>> container[u'paella'].__name__
u'paella'
>>> container[u'paella'].__parent__ is container
```

```
True
>>> type(container[u'paella'])
<class 'zope.app.container.contained.ContainedProxy'>
```

As we expect, the original object has not been modified. It does not have the containment-relevant attributes that the proxied one had:

```
>>> paella.__name__
Traceback (most recent call last):
...
AttributeError: 'Recipe' object has no attribute
'__name__'
>>> paella.__parent__
Traceback (most recent call last):
...
AttributeError: 'Recipe' object has no attribute
'__parent__'
```

Summary

- The relationship between an object and its parent in an object hierarchy can be expressed through the location machinery by providing ILocation.
- Containment is locatability in the context of containers; it is expressed through IContained.
- When located in a container, locatable objects are marked as contained; non-locatable objects are proxied so that they comply with the containment machinery.

Flashback

Containers are called *object managers* in Zope 2. Their API differs from the widely used mapping API, even though they do not provide additional functionality. In Zope 3, any mapping object can potentially be a container, even a dictionary.

Zope 2 does not have a system of containment per se. It does have a mighty, powerful and quite intriguing acquisition system which can wrap objects that are acquired so that they gain acquisition information. In other words, if an object is acquired from its containing object manager, then this object manager is its acquisitional parent. However, if the object is acquired from a different object over several hierarchy levels, then whichever object is last in the traversal chain becomes the acquisitional parent. To summarize, the acquisitional parent is dynamic and depends on the acquisition context. Containment relations are not expressed explicitly.

Zope 3 content objects do not have to have identifiers (IDs). The `IRecipe` schema does not include any declaration of an identifier, nor does the recipe implementation provide such information. Whether or not objects have identifiers or names is a containment issue, not an issue of the object. That is why the Zope 2 *ID* that objects absolutely have to provide in order to function within a Zope object manager is completely abolished. Objects *can* have names in Zope 3, but those are assigned and managed by the container without any implications on the object itself (unless the object explicitly wants to be involved by providing `ILocation`).

14.2 Constraints and preconditions

Apart from general containment relations as they were introduced before, it also often necessary to implement constraints on what a container can contain and in which type of container an object may be contained in.

In the previous section, we have seen that containment relations are not taken care of by the containers themselves. It is an extra machinery that does this. That guarantees light-weight implementations of the containers and objects. Containment constraints are not part of an implementation either. As with any type of constraint they are expressed in interfaces.

In Example 14.2.1, we define two new interfaces. `IRecipeContainer` describes the interface of a container that only holds recipe objects, while `IRecipeContained` extends the already known `IContained` interface with a constraint for the parent object.

Container implementation

As mentioned before, containers are simple mapping objects. Implementing their API is trivial. A simple container implementation that one can derive from is `SampleContainer` or, if persistency is needed, `BTreeContainer`. The general content container `Folder` is an option when containment constraints are not the primary goal of the component in question.

Example 14.2.2 shows the trivial implementation of `IRecipeContainer`. Containment-relevant statements were made in the interface which only leaves us with the usual security declarations in `configure.zcml` (shown in Example 14.2.3).

Testing the container

As usual we shall take the time to test the component on the interpreter shell. It will also help us understand how constraints and preconditions are checked. We instantiate our recipe folder:

Example 14.2.1 Containment constraints expressed in interfaces
(`interfaces.py`)

```
1    ...
2
3    from zope.schema import Field
4    from zope.app.container.interfaces import IContainer, IContained
5    from zope.app.container.constraints import ContainerTypesConstraint
6    from zope.app.container.constraints import ItemTypePrecondition
7
8    class IRecipeContainer(IContainer):
9
10       def __setitem__(name, object):
11           """Add a recipe"""
12
13       __setitem__.precondition = ItemTypePrecondition(IRecipe)
14
15   class IRecipeContained(IContained):
16
17       __parent__ = Field(
18           constraint = ContainerTypesConstraint(IRecipeContainer)
19           )
```

10–13.   This interface extends `IContainer` unmodified except that it redefines
         the `__setitem__` method (which is called when an object is stored in the
         container) with a precondition.
         Preconditions are small components that verify to-be-contained objects
         (items) before they are added to containers based on the container they're
         added to, their supposed name inside the object and the object it-
         self. `ItemTypePrecondition` is a precondition component that decides
         based on whether the object in question provides one of a set of required
         interfaces. The precondition in this case will only allow objects providing
         `IRecipe`, namely recipes.

17–19.   This custom derivative of the `IContained` interface redefines
         the `__parent__` field with a custom constraint. In analogy to
         `ItemTypePrecondition`, the `ContainerTypesConstraint` only al-
         lows objects providing this interface to be added to containers providing
         `IRecipeContainer`, namely recipe folders.

```
>>> from worldcookery.folder import RecipeFolder
>>> folder = RecipeFolder()
```

The `checkObject` function can now check constraints and preconditions.
As we expect, an error is raised trying to check an object that does not
provide `IRecipe`:

```
>>> from zope.app.container.constraints import checkObject
>>> tortillas = object()
```

```
>>> checkObject(folder, u'tortillas', tortillas)
Traceback (most recent call last):
...
zope.app.container.interfaces.InvalidItemType:
(<worldcookery.folder.RecipeFolder object at 0x367130>,
 <object object at 0x354448>,
 (<InterfaceClass worldcookery.interfaces.IRecipe>,))
```

Example 14.2.2 Simple container implementation for recipes (`folder.py`)

```
1  from zope.interface import implements
2  from zope.app.container.btree import BTreeContainer
3  from worldcookery.interfaces import IRecipeContainer
4
5  class RecipeFolder(BTreeContainer):
6      implements(IRecipeContainer)
```

Example 14.2.3 Mandatory security declarations for the recipe folder (`configure.zcml`)

```
1   ...
2   <content class=".folder.RecipeFolder">
3     <implements
4         interface="zope.app.annotation.interfaces.IAttributeAnnotatable"
5         />
6     <require
7         permission="zope.View"
8         interface="zope.app.container.interfaces.IReadContainer"
9         />
10    <require
11        permission="zope.ManageContent"
12        interface="zope.app.container.interfaces.IWriteContainer"
13        />
14  </content>
15    ...
```

8 and 12. Now we see that two interfaces, one that contains method definitions relevant for read access and one with write access, pays off for security declarations. Instead of listing the relevant attributes we simply refer to the interfaces.

When we now take an object providing `IRecipe`, `checkObject` will execute without any error because the precondition is fulfilled:

```
>>> from zope.interface import implements
>>> from worldcookery.interfaces import IRecipe
>>> class Recipe(object):
...         implements(IRecipe)
```

```
. . .
>>> sangria = Recipe()
>>> checkObject(folder, u'sangria', sangria)
>>>
```

Similarly we can test the constraint for recipes. A plain recipe object that does not provide IRecipeContained allows itself to be added to any container, for example a sample container:

```
>>> from zope.app.container.sample import \
...       SampleContainer
>>> container = SampleContainer()
>>> checkObject(container, u'sangria', sangria)
>>>
```

When we now introduce the constraint on the __parent__ field by providing IRecipeContained directly on the object, checkObject will report an invalid container:

```
>>> from zope.interface import directlyProvides
>>> from worldcookery.interfaces import \
...       IRecipeContained
>>> directlyProvides(sangria, IRecipeContained)
>>> checkObject(container, u'sangria', sangria)
Traceback (most recent call last):
. . .
zope.app.container.interfaces.InvalidContainerType:
(<zope.app.container.sample.SampleContainer object at
0x142ff10>,
 (<InterfaceClass worldcookery.interfaces
.IRecipeContainer>,))
```

As usual, this interpreter session was added as a docfile test (folder.txt). Listing this file again here would only be redundant.

Enforcing containment constraints

To enforce the container type constraint on recipe objects used within Zope, we let the Recipe class implement IRecipeContained. Because the IContained, the interface that IRecipeContained is derived from, requires objects to provide __name__ and __parent__ attributes, we have to modify the Recipe class for the first time since Chapter 6. Example 14.2.4 shows the trivial change that lets Recipe provide these attributes by default.

Example 14.2.4 Enforcing the container type constraints on the Recipe class (recipe.py)

```
1   from persistent import Persistent
2   from zope.interface import implements
3   from worldcookery.interfaces import IRecipe, IRecipeContained
4
5   class Recipe(Persistent):
6       implements(IRecipe, IRecipeContained)
7
8       __name__ = __parent__ = None
9
10      name = u''
11      ingredients = []
12      tools = []
13      time_to_cook = 0
14      description = u''
```

Browser configuration

As with recipes we also need to provide some browser-relevant configuration so that we can use the recipe folder immediately in the ZMI. Example 14.2.5 declares an entry in the browser *Add* menu for it and configures container-typical browser views. The latter are conveniently configured with one directive that registers the following views:

- The contents page (@@contents.html) which is the first management screen of folders and other containers. Apart from a detailed object listing it provides copy and paste functionality, among others.
- The index view (@@index.html) which either redirects to an object inside the container called index.html or, if that does not exist, displays a list of contained objects similar to the contents page.
- The adding view (+) that is responsible for producing add forms (such as the ones registered with browser:addform), checking item preconditions and container constraints (using checkObject like shown above) as well as adding created objects to the container.

Last but not least, we extend the *WorldCookery* skin with an icon for recipe folders (Example 14.2.6).

When you now go the Zope Management Interface, you will see that you cannot add *Recipe* objects to regular folders anymore. Instead you have to create a recipe folder in which you may add recipes.

Example 14.2.5 Browser configuration for the recipe folder (`browser/configure.zcml`)

```
1      ...
2      <browser:addMenuItem
3          title="Recipe Folder"
4          class="worldcookery.folder.RecipeFolder"
5          permission="zope.ManageContent"
6          />
7
8      <browser:containerViews
9          for="worldcookery.interfaces.IRecipeContainer"
10         contents="zope.ManageContent"
11         index="zope.View"
12         add="zope.ManageContent"
13         />
14     ...
```

8 – 13. This directive defines the common browser views necessary to make containers work in the ZMI in one statement. We are only required to give the permissions for the different views it registers.

Example 14.2.6 Configuring an icon for the recipe folder in the *WorldCookery* skin (`browser/skin/configure.zcml`)

```
1      ...
2      <browser:icon
3          name="zmi_icon"
4          for="worldcookery.interfaces.IRecipeContainer"
5          file="folder_icon.png"
6          layer="worldcookery"
7          />
8      ...
```

Summary

- The container machinery allows to specify constraints on which type of object maybe added to containers and to which container an object may be added to.
- As with any type of constraint these are specified in interfaces.
- Item type preconditions constrain the type of objects that may be added to a container by interface while container type constraints specify the type of containers than an object may be contained in.
- Container implementations are trivial and can rely on common base classes most of the time.
- Security declarations, browser menu configuration, and browser icons are configured like with any other content object; common container views can be registered with a combined directive.

14.3 Names of contained objects

Not in all cases it is acceptable to allow arbitrary names for objects inside containers. Zope allows containers to influence names of contained objects in either one of two ways:

- The object name is entered by the user and post-validated. This is the default.
- The object name is computed and cannot be influenced by the user.

In both cases it is usually not the container itself that pre-computes or post-validates names. It is an adapter that adapts containers to the INameChooser interface. This interface describes two methods, checkName and choose-Name, which are called according to the either one of the above described cases.

Whether a container chooses names or not

How does Zope decide whether a container pre-computes names or not? The answer is simple: It assumes that all regular containers allow arbitrary names and that a mere validation of the name entered by the user is sufficient, unless a name was not entered by the user.

Now if the container provides IContainerNamesContainer, a marker interface derived from IContainer, then it is assumed that it wants to choose its own names. In this case, the add form does not include an input field for the object name and the container adding view calls the chooseName method of the INameChooser adapter. The adapter is also consulted when objects are moved and renamed.

Choosing names

In our worldcookery application, we have a redundancy of names already. Recipes have a name attribute which is documented in the IRecipe schema and as contained objects they have names inside the container. Why not synchronize these names and make recipe's names automatically their names inside the container?

In order to let recipes' container names be synchronized with their name attribute we need to do two things: First, we need to provide a custom INameChooser adapter that computes a recipe's container name from its actual name. Example 14.3.1 shows how to implement this adapter.

Secondly, we need to declare RecipeFolder as an IContainerNames-Container. This is best done in ZCML (Example 14.3.2) since we are dealing with a marker interface. In the same listing we also register the INameChooser adapter.

Example 14.3.1 Recipe folder with name chooser adapter (`folder.py`)

```
1   from zope.interface import implements
2   from zope.i18nmessageid import MessageIDFactory
3   _ = MessageIDFactory('worldcookery')
4
5   from zope.app.container.btree import BTreeContainer
6   from zope.app.container.contained import NameChooser
7   from zope.app.exception.interfaces import UserError
8
9   from worldcookery.interfaces import IRecipeContainer
10
11  class RecipeFolder(BTreeContainer):
12      implements(IRecipeContainer)
13
14  class RecipeNameChooser(NameChooser):
15
16      def checkName(self, name, object):
17          if name != object.name:
18              raise UserError(_(u"Given name and recipe name do not match!"))
19          return super(RecipeNameChooser, self).checkName(name, object)
20
21      def chooseName(self, name, object):
22          name = object.name
23          self.checkName(name, object)
24          return name
```

6, 14, and 19.   A default name chooser adapter for standard IContainers is already provided by the zope.app.container.contained module. It makes sense to subclass it here because it already implements checks for invalid characters in containers and non-emptiness. That is why we delegate to its checkName method after performing a check agains the recipe's name.

7 and 18.   The INameChooser interface requires us to raise UserError if the validation of a name fails. User errors (and other exceptions providing IUserError) are displayed to the user (as opposed to system errors). That is why we have to mark the error message as an i18n message id to allow translation.

Tests

No component shall be left untested, especially when it is one that can be tested so easily from the interpreter shell. To keep things simple we instantiate the INameChooser adapter manually. This way we do not have to load site configuration:

```
>>> from worldcookery.folder import RecipeFolder, \
...     RecipeNameChooser
>>> folder = RecipeFolder()
>>> chooser = RecipeNameChooser(folder)
```

Example 14.3.2 Enabling the name chooser adapter (`configure.zcml`)

```
1    ...
2    <content class=".folder.RecipeFolder">
3      <implements
4          interface="zope.app.annotation.interfaces.IAttributeAnnotatable
5                     zope.app.container.interfaces.IContainerNamesContainer"
6          />
7      <require
8          permission="zope.View"
9          interface="zope.app.container.interfaces.IReadContainer"
10         />
11     <require
12         permission="zope.ManageContent"
13         interface="zope.app.container.interfaces.IWriteContainer"
14         />
15   </content>
16
17   <adapter
18       for=".interfaces.IRecipeContainer"
19       provides="zope.app.container.interfaces.INameChooser"
20       factory=".folder.RecipeNameChooser"
21       />
22   ...
```

5. Like `IAttributeAnnotatable`, `IContainerNamesContainer` is a marker interface and therefore best set in ZCML. Whether or not the `INameChooser` adapter is enabled is a configuration issue anyway.

18. `INameChooser` adapters are adapters for containers. Since this adapter is specific to recipes, we register it only for `IRecipeContainer`.

A blank recipe object has an empty name (this is the class default), which is not acceptable for a container name:

```
>>> from worldcookery.recipe import Recipe
>>> tapas = Recipe()
>>> tapas.name
u''
>>> chooser.chooseName(u'', tapas)
Traceback (most recent call last):
...
zope.app.exception.interfaces.UserError:
An empty name was provided. Names cannot be empty.
```

When we now provide a name that is acceptable for container names (the restrictions for container names are minimal), we see that the name chooser adapter chooses a name for us (the recipe's name). When checking a name, it expectedly accepts the recipe's name while rejecting anything else with a user error:

```
>>> tapas.name = u"Tapas"
>>> chooser.chooseName(u'', tapas)
u'Tapas'
>>> chooser.checkName(tapas.name, tapas)
True
>>> chooser.checkName(u'Tasty tapas', tapas)
Traceback (most recent call last):
...
zope.app.exception.interfaces.UserError:
Given name and recipe name do not match!
```

As mentioned, the restrictions on container names are minimal. An important one is that it may not be empty. Apart from that, characters critical to traversal (+, @, and /) may not occur either:

```
>>> tapas.name = u'Tapas with/without olives'
>>> chooser.checkName(tapas.name, tapas)
Traceback (most recent call last):
...
zope.app.exception.interfaces.UserError:
Names cannot begin with '+' or '@' or contain '/'
```

This test can also be found in the recipe folder docfile test (folder.txt).

Setting values at the right time

Before we can test the INameChooser adapter in action, we have to adjust a minor detail in the configuration of automatically generated add forms for recipes. Normally, a recipe object is generated, added to the container, and then populated with values entered through the add form.

This process order would be most unfortunate for the INameChooser adapter because all it ever would be presented with were brand-new recipe objects whose name attribute had not yet been set. To have the form machinery set this attribute before adding the object to the container, we have to tweak the configuration of the add form in browser/configure.zcml. Example 14.3.3 shows how.

When we now restart Zope to add a recipe to a recipe folder, we will not be asked for the object name anymore. The INameChooser adapter will choose the name from the recipe name.

Example 14.3.3 Tweaking the add form to set the name attribute early (browser/configure.zcml)

```
 1    ...
 2    <browser:addform
 3        schema="worldcookery.interfaces.IRecipe"
 4        content_factory="worldcookery.recipe.Recipe"
 5        label="[label-add-recipe] Add Recipe"
 6        name="AddRecipe.html"
 7        permission="zope.ManageContent"
 8        set_before_add="name"
 9        >
10      <widget field="ingredients" class=".widget.DynamicSequenceWidget" />
11      <widget field="tools" class=".widget.DynamicSequenceWidget" />
12    </browser:addform>
13    ...
```

8. This attribute causes the add form view to set a given set of attributes *before* adding the object to the container. By specifying the name attribute here, we ensure that the INameChooser adapter is always dealing with recipe objects whose name attributes are already set.

In case you are wondering whether unicode with mixed case and possibly contained spaces and other non-alphanumeric characters is such a good idea for container names, do not worry. Unicode is very much allowed in URLs and is encoded using UTF-8. Unlike other systems, Zope has always valued human-readable URLs very highly, which is why you will rarely see Zope applications with URLs that are composed of numbers and other cryptic, human-unfriendly characters.

Summary

- Container names can be influenced through either post-validation of a user-provided name or pre-computation of a name without user influence.
- Names are validated and/or computed by an INameChooser adapter for the container.
- Container names can hold any unicode characters except those relevant to traversal (+, @, and /); names may not be empty.

14.4 File representation

In Chapter 10 where we initially covered file representation adapters, we did not have a custom container for recipes. Before, recipes were added to regular folders, now they can only be contained in `IRecipeContainers`. That means we have to at least adjust the configuration of the recipe file factory which until now was registered for `IFolder`.

File representation adapters for containers are fortunately quite easy. Of course, containers are represented as directories, not as files most of the time. The corresponding file representation interfaces `IReadDirectory` and `IWriteDirectory` extend `IReadContainer` and `IWriteContainer`, respectively, unchanged. In other words, a container is usually its own file representation adapter, unless it is supposed to do something additional to delegate between file representations and the container. That we do not consider necessary here and therefore save ourselves the work of defining file representation adapters.

One item on the list remains, though. As much as there exists a file factory that creates objects when files are uploaded there exists a directory factory that creates sub-containers in containers when a directory is created over WebDAV or FTP. In our case, recipe folders may not contain any other object than recipe objects; that implies that they cannot contain subfolders, which means we should disallow the creation of subcontainers.

Example 14.4.1 shows a simple directory factory that raises an error when invoked. The necessary configuration including the change to the registration of the recipe file factory is listed in Example 14.4.2. The doctest that was provided in Chapter 11 was also updated and can be read for documentation purposes in Example 14.4.3, along with its test module in Example 14.4.4.

Example 14.4.1 Directory factory disallowing subcontainers in recipe folders (`filerepresentation.py`)

```
1   ...
2
3   from zope.app.filerepresentation.interfaces import IDirectoryFactory
4   from zope.app.exception.interfaces import UserError
5
6   class RecipeDirectoryFactory(object):
7       implements(IDirectoryFactory)
8
9       def __init__(self, context):
10          self.context = context
11
12      def __call__(self, name):
13          raise UserError(u"Cannot create subfolders in recipe folders.")
```

Example 14.4.2 (Re-)configuring file and directory factories for recipe folders (`configure.zcml`)

```
 1    ...
 2    <adapter
 3        for=".interfaces.IRecipeContainer"
 4        provides="zope.app.filerepresentation.interfaces.IFileFactory"
 5        factory=".filerepresentation.RecipeFactory"
 6        permission="zope.ManageContent"
 7        />
 8
 9    <adapter
10        for=".interfaces.IRecipeContainer"
11        provides="zope.app.filerepresentation.interfaces.IDirectoryFactory"
12        factory=".filerepresentation.RecipeDirectoryFactory"
13        permission="zope.ManageContent"
14        />
15    ...
```

3 and 10. Notice that we configure both factories for `IRecipeContainer` now.

7. Now that recipes are the only objects allowed inside `IRecipeNameContainer`, we can safely assume to be the only file factory registered for this container. That means we do not have to register it as a named adapter (where the name was the file extension) anymore. The name parameter is missing from the directive.

Example 14.4.3 Doctest for file representation adpaters of the new recipe folder (`filerepresentation.txt`)

```
 1    =========================================
 2    File representation adapters for recipes
 3    =========================================
 4
 5    Let us first create a recipe object through a file factory.  In order
 6    to acquire the factory, we need a folder object since we registered
 7    the factory as an adapter for folders.  We can throw the folder away
 8    afterwards.
 9
10        >>> from worldcookery.folder import RecipeFolder
11        >>> from zope.app.filerepresentation.interfaces import IReadFile, \
12        ...         IWriteFile, IFileFactory
13        >>> folder = RecipeFolder()
14        >>> factory = IFileFactory(folder)
15
16    Now we can call the factory with some made-up data.  We expect to get
17    a recipe object back, of course, and that the recipe's description
18    equals to the data we passed to the factory.
19
20        >>> data = "Add spices to the water and bring it to boil. Then add the
        couscous"
21        >>> couscous = factory("couscous", "text/plain", data)
```

```
22    >>> from worldcookery.recipe import Recipe
23    >>> isinstance(couscous, Recipe)
24    True
25    >>> couscous.name
26    'Couscous'
27    >>> couscous.description
28    u'Add spices to the water and bring it to boil. Then add the couscous'
29
```

```
30    Now we can get a file representation for the recipe again and read its
31    data.  Note that the file representation returns a string object, not
32    a unicode object, since only the former can be written to a file stream.
33
```

```
34    >>> readfile = IReadFile(couscous)
35    >>> readfile.size()
36    67
37    >>> readfile.read()
38    'Add spices to the water and bring it to boil. Then add the couscous'
39
```

```
40    Finally, we can adapt the recipe object to a writeable file and store
41    new data on it.  The recipe will be changed accordingly, of course:
42
```

```
43    >>> writefile = IWriteFile(couscous)
44    >>> writefile.write("Couscous consists of grains made from semolina")
45    >>> couscous.description
46    u'Couscous consists of grains made from semolina'
47
```

```
48    Note that it is not possible to create subfolders in a recipe folder.
49    Doing so raises a ``UserError':
50
```

```
51    >>> from zope.app.filerepresentation.interfaces import IDirectoryFactory
52    >>> factory = IDirectoryFactory(folder)
53    >>> factory(u"subfolder")
54    Traceback (most recent call last):
55    ...
56    UserError: Cannot create subfolders in recipe folders.
```

Example 14.4.4 Test suite for file representation adpaters of the new recipe folder (tests/test_filerepresentation.py)

```
1    import unittest
2    from zope.testing.doctestunit import DocFileSuite
3    from zope.app.tests import ztapi, placelesssetup
4    from zope.app.filerepresentation.interfaces import IReadFile, \
5        IWriteFile, IFileFactory, IDirectoryFactory
6
7    from worldcookery.interfaces import IRecipe, IRecipeContainer
8    from worldcookery.filerepresentation import RecipeReadFile, \
9        RecipeWriteFile, RecipeFactory, RecipeDirectoryFactory
```

```
10   def setUp(test):
11       placelesssetup.setUp(test)
12       ztapi.provideAdapter(IRecipe, IReadFile, RecipeReadFile)
13       ztapi.provideAdapter(IRecipe, IWriteFile, RecipeWriteFile)
14       ztapi.provideAdapter(IRecipeContainer, IFileFactory, RecipeFactory)
15       ztapi.provideAdapter(IRecipeContainer, IDirectoryFactory,
16                            RecipeDirectoryFactory)
17
18   def test_suite():
19       return unittest.TestSuite((
20           DocFileSuite('filerepresentation.txt',
21                        package='worldcookery',
22                        setUp=setUp,
23                        tearDown=placelesssetup.tearDown),
24           ))
25
26   if __name__ == '__main__':
27       unittest.main(defaultTest='test_suite')
```

Summary

- The file representation interfaces for directories are identical to the corresponding container interfaces; a container can therefore be its own filerepresentation adapter.
- Directory factories create sub-containers when a directory is created through WebDAV or FTP.

Part III

Expert

15

Events

All the things one should know to be called a professional Zope developer have now been covered. Our example application has grown from a mere content object to a respectable piece of software. For the last few chapters we shall now look at fairly advanced subjects that will make you as the reader a true Zope expert.

One of these subjects are *events*. In many applications, it is necessary to trigger certain operations in particular circumstances. Zope provides a flexible and efficient event system that makes the implementation of such event-triggered components as well as the triggering itself very easy.

15.1 Introduction

Describing the Zope event system is quite simple: components can inform other components that something has happened by sending events. *What* has happened is determined by the type of event that is sent. Components that react upon events are called *event subscribers*.

Event types are, of course, described through interfaces. Event subscribers subscribe to certain event interfaces, not to event objects themselves. When an event is sent out, subscribers to the interfaces the event object provides will be invoked. That also works if the event implements a more specific one than the subscriber subscribed to.

An example

To understand how the event system works we will use the trusty interpreter shell again. As an example event consider the circumstance that a meal has been cooked, which means that the cooking has now been finished. The event that would be sent out in such a case is described by the simple interface we now define:

```
>>> from zope.interface import Interface, Attribute
>>> class IDinnerIsDone(Interface):
...        recipe = Attribute("Recipe")
...
>>>
```

The recipe attribute will hold the recipe that was cooked for dinner.
An implementation of this interface is of course quite simple:

```
>>> from zope.interface import implements
>>> class DinnerIsDone(object):
...        implements(IDinnerIsDone)
...        def __init__(self, recipe):
...            self.recipe = recipe
...
>>>
```

Now we need a subscriber that is called whenever this event occurs. Subscribers can be any callable object; usually they are simple functions. As
their only argument they take the event object. Our subscriber tells the fam-
ily that dinner is ready and informs them of the meal that is served:

```
>>> def tellFamily(event):
...        print "Dinner is ready! We're having a" \
...              "delicious %s!" % event.recipe.name
...
>>>
```

To register the subscriber, the adapter service[1] needs to be set up. As we
know from doctests, PlacelessSetup takes care of basic service setup for
tests. The ztapi module then conveniently provides a function for registering
event subscribers:

```
>>> from zope.app.tests.placelesssetup import setUp
>>> setUp()
>>> from zope.app.tests import ztapi
>>> ztapi.handle([IDinnerIsDone], tellFamily)
```

---

[1] Because they subscribe to interfaces and are managed by the adapter service,
subscribers are also sometimes called subscription adapters.

Now we are ready to receive events. Sending out events is quite simple, one simply calls the `notify` function from the `zope.event` package with the event object as parameter. It will dispatch to the adapter service which will look up all subscribers for the interfaces the event object provides and call them. When we now send out an instance of `DinnerIsDone`, we will see that the `tellFamily` subscriber is called:

```
>>> from worldcookery.recipe import Recipe
>>> cordon_bleu = Recipe()
>>> cordon_bleu.name = u"Cordon bleu"
>>>
>>> from zope.event import notify
>>> notify(DinnerIsDone(cordon_bleu))
Dinner is ready! We're having a delicious Cordon bleu!
```

Note that the event subscribers are notified synchronously. This is necessary because subscribers usually perform actions that require the presence of authentication credentials; these are only available through the security interaction (see Chapter 19) during the request processing. All this means that the active Zope thread will be blocked if a subscriber is doing some time-consuming data processing. It is important, therefore, not to perform such operations in subscribers.

Summary

- Zope allows components to notify other components of certain circumstances by sending events.
- Events are identified by their interfaces; they can carry as much information needed to describe the event.
- Event subscribers subscribe to event interfaces; they are usually simple callables that take the event object as an argument.
- Event notification is *synchronous*!

15.2 Object events

A commonly used set of events includes the *object events*. These are events that can be triggered when certain operations are performed on a particular object, such as creation and modification. Table 15.1 gives an overview over the types of events that Zope sends out, including the object events.

Table 15.1. Events sent out by Zope

Interface	Defined in module	Description
IObjectEvent	zope.app.event. interfaces	Indicates that something has happened to an object. More detailed specification by subinterfaces.
IObjectCreatedEvent	zope.app.event. interfaces	Sent when an object has been created.
IObjectCopiedEvent	zope.app.event. interfaces	Indicates that an object has been copied.
IObjectModifiedEvent	zope.app.event. interfaces	Triggered when an object has been modified.
IObjectAnnotations-ModifiedEvent	zope.app.event. interfaces	Triggered when an object's annotations have been modified.
IObjectContent-ModifiedEvent	zope.app.event. interfaces	Triggered when an object's content has been modified.
IObjectMovedEvent	zope.app. container. interfaces	Indicates that an object has been moved to a different container.
IObjectAddedEvent	zope.app. container. interfaces	Sent when an object has been added to a container.
IObjectRemovedEvent	zope.app. container. interfaces	Indicates that an object has been removed from a container.
IDatabaseOpenedEvent	zope.app. appsetup. appsetup	Indicates that a ZODB instance has been opened.
IProcessStartingEvent	zope.app. appsetup. appsetup	Triggered when the Zope process is starting up.
IBeforeTraverseEvent	zope.app. publication. interfaces	Triggered before each traversal step.
IEndRequestEvent	zope.app. publication. interfaces	Indicates the end of a request.
IMailEvent	zope.app.mail. interfaces	Generic mail event.
IMailSentEvent	zope.app.mail. interfaces	Sent when an email has been sent successfully.
IMailErrorEvent	zope.app.mail. interfaces	Indicates that an email cannot be delivered.

Zope acts and reacts

We have not yet dealt with any events in our sample application, yet they are being sent. The automatically generated add and edit forms, for example, send out IObjectAddedEvent and IObjectModifiedEvent events. Similarly, when an object's Dublin Core metadata is changed through the

Metadata ZMI form, an `IObjectAnnotationsModifiedEvent` event is sent.

The `setitem` function from the previous chapter sends out `IObject-AddedEvent` or `IObjectMovedEvent`, respectively, depending on whether an object is newly added to a container or whether it is moved from another container. Accordingly, the copy/paste/move machinery from `zope.app.copypastemove` sends `IObjectCopiedEvent` when an object is cloned.

Zope does not only send out events; some components have subscribed to certain events. For example, the Dublin Core machinery has a subscriber to the `IObjectCreatedEvent` and `IObjectModifiedEvent` events that updates the Creator, Creation Date, and Modification Date Dublin Core properties of the object.

Sending object events

Our applications needs to be made ready for events. The changes in this section are cosmetic rather than functional. It is still a good practice the usage of object events, not only because they are the most common type of events, but also because they are a powerful way to add dynamic elements to an application without substantially modifying existing components.

As a first exercise, we will send out object events. This is as trivial as it was in the interpreter example in the last section. The component that we will extend to send out an object event is the ratings adapter from Chapter 13. It does not yet send out `IObjectAnnotationsModifiedEvent` even though it should. The trivial enhancement that is necessary to do this is shown in Example 15.2.1.

Testing whether an event is sent out could be done with a custom subscriber and a check whether the custom subscriber was invoked. While that is straight-forward, it complicates tests unnecessarily. The event machinery fortunately provides a way to retrieve all events that have been sent especially for tests which makes testing event-based components quite easy. See the last paragraph in Example 15.2.2 for how it is done.

Subscribing to object events

As mentioned in the introduction, subscribers are usually simple callables, such as functions. That makes it almost trivial to implement them and lets the developer focus on the actual task they are supposed to cover.

It is of course usually not very practical being subscribed to an object event by itself, for example `IObjectModifiedEvent`. Such a subscriber would be called whenever *any* object is modified. Apart from being a burden on the application's performance, it is not even necessary most of the time. Usually one would like to subscribe to object events that are sent out for specific content types. That is why most object event subscribers are subscribed

Example 15.2.1 Sending out an object event in the ratings adapter (rating.py)

```
1   from persistent.dict import PersistentDict
2   from persistent.list import PersistentList
3
4   from zope.interface import implements
5   from zope.event import notify
6   from zope.app.annotation.interfaces import IAnnotations
7   from zope.app.event.objectevent import ObjectAnnotationsModifiedEvent
8
9   from worldcookery.interfaces import IRating
10
11  KEY = "worldcookery.rating"
12
13  class Rating(object):
14      implements(IRating)
15
16      def __init__(self, context):
17          self.context = context
18          annotations = IAnnotations(context)
19          mapping = annotations.get(KEY)
20          if mapping is None:
21              blank = {'average': 0.0, 'ratings': PersistentList()}
22              mapping = annotations[KEY] = PersistentDict(blank)
23          self.mapping = mapping
24
25      def rate(self, rating):
26          ratings = self.mapping['ratings']
27          ratings.append(float(rating))
28          self.mapping['average'] = sum(ratings)/len(ratings)
29          notify(ObjectAnnotationsModifiedEvent(self.context))
30
31      def averageRating(self):
32          return self.mapping['average']
33      averageRating = property(averageRating)
34
35      def numberOfRatings(self):
36          return len(self.mapping['ratings'])
37      numberOfRatings = property(numberOfRatings)
```

7 and 29.	The zope.app.event.objectevent module provides implementations for all object event interfaces. They are instantiated with the object in question as parameter.

for the event type interfaces in combination with the content type interface that the object provides.

In an example of ours, we want to register a subscriber to IObjectModifiedEvent to update the modified object's Dublin Core metadata. The idea is to synchronize the Title property of Dublin Core and the recipe's name; currently we have a redundancy in these properties and there is no

Example 15.2.2 Testing whether object events are being sent (rating. txt)

```
1    ==============
2    Rating objects
3    ==============
4
5    The rating system allows users to rate objects on a continuous scale
6    (a discrete scale can be enforced by a view).  We distinguish
7    *ratable* objects which have to annotatable and implement ''IRatable'
8    on one hand and the ''IRating'' adapter for ratable objects which the
9    rating of the latter on the other hand.
10
11   Consider a simple object, e.g. a recipe:
12
13     >>> from worldcookery.recipe import Recipe
14     >>> hamburgers = Recipe()
15
16   In order to mark it ratable, it also needs to annotatable, for example
17   attribute-annotatable:
18
19     >>> from zope.app.annotation.interfaces import IAttributeAnnotatable
20     >>> from worldcookery.interfaces import IRatable
21     >>> from zope.interface import directlyProvides
22     >>> directlyProvides(hamburgers, IAttributeAnnotatable, IRatable)
23
24   Now we can rate the object using the ''IRating'' adapter:
25
26     >>> from worldcookery.interfaces import IRating
27     >>> rating = IRating(hamburgers)
28     >>> rating.rate(1)    # this person does not like hamburgers
29     >>> rating.rate(9)    # this person seem to like them
30
31   Of course, the adapter also tells about the average rating and number
32   of ratings that have been issued yet:
33
34     >>> rating.averageRating
35     5.0
36     >>> rating.numberOfRatings
37     2
38
39   Since the adapter uses annotations to store rating information and
40   rating an object causes its annotations to be modified, we expect that
41   an ''IObjectAnnotationsModifiedEvent'' event is sent:
42
43     >>> from zope.app.event.tests.placelesssetup import getEvents
44     >>> from zope.app.event.interfaces import IObjectAnnotationsModifiedEvent
45     >>> events = getEvents(IObjectAnnotationsModifiedEvent)
46     >>> len(events)
47     2
48     >>> for event in events:
49     ...     print event.object is hamburgers
50     ...
51   True
52   True
```

43 and 45. getEvent returns a list of events that were sent out. The query can be narrowed down by providing the event type interface.

reason why these should not contain the same information. The subscriber that is does this is ridiculously short in its implementation; just two lines are necessary (Example 15.2.3).

The doctest for the subscriber and the corresponding test suite module (Example 15.2.4 take up much more lines than the actual implementation, though. It also took substantially longer to write. While it might seem irritating, sometimes even frustrating for the developer to spend more code and time on automated testing, it is an investment that will pay off when a bug in the application has be to chased down, and any software developer knows: software is *never* bugfree.

Last but not least we need to configure the subscriber. This is done via the subscriber ZCML directive as shown in Example 15.2.5. Note that we only want to subscribe to object modified events for recipe objects which is why the subscriber is registered for the combination of IRecipe objects and IObjectModifiedEvent events.

Summary

- Object events are sent out to notify subscribers when something has happened to an object.
- Object event subscribers are usually registered for the event type and the type of the object that the event is sent for.
- Zope's automation frameworks such as the form and container machineries send out appropriate events that one can subscribe to.

Flashback

In Zope 2, objects themselves can be notified when something has happened with them, such as creation or cloning. As always in Zope 2, they need to provide certain methods which are called in the corresponding circumstances:

- manage_afterAdd (after being added to an object manager, equivalent to IObjectAddedEvent),
- manage_beforeDelete (before being deleted, roughly equivalent to IObjectRemovedEvent),
- manage_afterClone (after being cloned, equivalent to IObject-CopiedEvent).

Of course, using the event machinery for such notifications is much more flexible than requiring the object itself to provide certain methods. That way, existing applications can be extended with external dynamic components quite easily.

Example 15.2.3 A subscriber that updates a recipe's Dublin Core Title property (dublincore.py)

```
 1   from zope.app.dublincore.interfaces import IWriteZopeDublinCore
 2
 3   def updateRecipeDCTitle(recipe, event):
 4       """Update a recipe's Dublin Core Title property with its name
 5
 6       Before we can start we need to register the subscriber:
 7
 8           >>> from zope.app.event.interfaces import IObjectModifiedEvent
 9           >>> from worldcookery.interfaces import IRecipe
10           >>> from zope.app.tests import ztapi
11           >>> ztapi.handle([IRecipe, IObjectModifiedEvent],
     updateRecipeDCTitle)
12
13       Now consider a simple recipe object with a name:
14
15           >>> from worldcookery.recipe import Recipe
16           >>> noodles = Recipe()
17           >>> noodles.name = u"Noodles"
18
19       In order for Dublin Core to work we need it to be annotatable:
20
21           >>> from zope.interface import directlyProvides
22           >>> from zope.app.annotation.interfaces import IAttributeAnnotatable
23           >>> directlyProvides(noodles, IAttributeAnnotatable)
24
25       It does not have a title yet:
26
27           >>> dc = IWriteZopeDublinCore(noodles)
28           >>> dc.title
29           u''
30
31       Now we send out the event and, voila!, the title has been set:
32
33           >>> from zope.event import notify
34           >>> from zope.app.event.objectevent import ObjectModifiedEvent
35           >>> notify(ObjectModifiedEvent(noodles))
36           >>> dc = IWriteZopeDublinCore(noodles)
37           >>> dc.title
38           u'Noodles'
39       """
40       dc = IWriteZopeDublinCore(recipe)
41       dc.title = recipe.name
```

3. Object event subscribers take two arguments, the object that the event is being sent for and the event object itself. They are also registered as subscribers for the combination of those two interfaces (content type, event type). See Example 15.2.5.

Example 15.2.4 Test suite setup for the object event subscriber doctest (tests/test_dublincore.py)

```
1   import unittest
2   from zope.testing.doctestunit import DocTestSuite
3   from zope.app.tests import ztapi
4   from zope.app.tests.placelesssetup import setUp, tearDown
5
6   def updateRecipeDCTitleSetUp(test):
7       setUp(test)
8       from zope.app.annotation.interfaces import IAttributeAnnotatable
9       from zope.app.annotation.interfaces import IAnnotations
10      from zope.app.annotation.attribute import AttributeAnnotations
11      ztapi.provideAdapter(IAttributeAnnotatable, IAnnotations,
12                               AttributeAnnotations)
13
14      from zope.app.dublincore.interfaces import IWriteZopeDublinCore
15      from zope.app.dublincore.annotatableadapter import
    ZDCAnnotatableAdapter
16      ztapi.provideAdapter(IAttributeAnnotatable, IWriteZopeDublinCore,
17                               ZDCAnnotatableAdapter)
18
19  def test_suite():
20      return unittest.TestSuite((
21          DocTestSuite('worldcookery.dublincore',
22                       setUp=updateRecipeDCTitleSetUp, tearDown=tearDown),
23          ))
24
25  if __name__ == '__main__':
26      unittest.main(defaultTest='test_suite')
```

6 – 17. Apart from the usual PlacelessSetup that is necessary for events, we also have to register the annotations adapter so that the Dublin Core adapter that is used in the doctest works.

Example 15.2.5 Configuring an object event subscriber (configure. zcml)

```
1   ...
2       <subscriber
3           for=".interfaces.IRecipe
4                   zope.app.event.interfaces.IObjectModifiedEvent"
5           factory=".dublincore.updateRecipeDCTitle"
6           />
7   ...
```

15.3 Sending emails for event notification

As a more advanced use case of object events we will now cover email notification. This will not only get us more comfortable with events in general, as a by-product we will also learn about the email machinery of Zope. Email notification is a very typical use case of object events because it actually involves notifying real users and not just other components that are part of an application.

In our example application, we will allow users to subscribe to certain recipes with their email address. This information will be stored in the recipe's annotations. The interface that describes how to access to this annotation data and the adapter providing this interface are shown in Example 15.3.1 and Example 15.3.2, respectively. Because we are creating the email-specific components in a subpackage to the worldcookery package, do not forget to include into the main configure.zcml file the following line:

```
<include package=".mail" />
```

Example 15.3.1 Interface for managing email subscriptions to objects (mail/interfaces.py)

```
1   from zope.interface import Interface
2   from zope.schema import Tuple, TextLine
3   from zope.i18nmessageid import MessageIDFactory
4   _ = MessageIDFactory('worldcookery')
5
6   class IMailSubscriptions(Interface):
7
8       subscribers = Tuple(
9           title=_(u"Subscribers"),
10          description=_(u"Email addresses of subscribers"),
11          value_type=TextLine(title=_(u"Subscriber")),
12          readonly=True
13          )
14
15      def subscribe(email):
16          """Subscribe an email address to the notifications"""
17
18      def unsubscribe(email):
19          """Unsubscribe an email address"""
```

The email subscription adapter is quite similar to the rating adapter we wrote in Chapter 12. Like the rating adapter, we configure it as a trusted adapter and provide security settings for the adapter class, as shown in Example 15.3.3.

Now we can write subscribers that send out emails when object events are invoked for recipes. The mail framework that comes with Zope uses queued delivery by default. That means emails are not directly sent out synchronously when the send method is called. Rather, a *maildir* [6] directory is used to the store messages temporarily. Later when the Zope transaction is committed, the mails are sent out. This avoids race conditions in threaded environments like the Zope web server.

Example 15.3.4 contains the callables that subscribe to the different events. Note that this example only creates emails with English text for simplicity's sake. An internationalized example would for example have to take the preferences of the email subscribers into account, thus requiring a more complicated set of data to be stored in annotations. The recipe contents, though, can obviously still be in any language; in fact, the emails are sent out in UTF-8, thus compatible with any language in the unicode specification.

Example 15.3.2 Adapter that keeps email subscriptions to an object in its annotations (mail/annotations.py)

```
1   from persistent.list import PersistentList
2   from zope.interface import implements
3   from zope.event import notify
4   from zope.app.annotation.interfaces import IAnnotations
5   from zope.app.event.objectevent import ObjectAnnotationsModifiedEvent
6
7   from worldcookery.mail.interfaces import IMailSubscriptions
8
9   KEY = "worldcookery.subscriptions"
10
11  class MailSubscriptionAnnotations(object):
12      implements(IMailSubscriptions)
13
14      def __init__(self, context):
15          self.context = context
16          annotations = IAnnotations(context)
17          emails = annotations.get(KEY)
18          if emails is None:
19              emails = annotations[KEY] = PersistentList()
20          self.emails = emails
21
22      def subscribers(self):
23          return tuple(self.emails)
24      subscribers = property(subscribers)
25
26      def subscribe(self, email):
27          if email not in self.emails:
28              self.emails.append(email)
29              notify(ObjectAnnotationsModifiedEvent(self.context))
30
31      def unsubscribe(self, email):
32          if email in self.emails:
33              self.emails.remove(email)
34              notify(ObjectAnnotationsModifiedEvent(self.context))
```

Example 15.3.3 Configuring the email subscription adapter (`mail/configure.zcml`)

```
1   <configure
2       xmlns="http://namespaces.zope.org/zope"
3       >
4
5     <adapter
6         for="zope.app.annotation.interfaces.IAnnotatable"
7         provides=".interfaces.IMailSubscriptions"
8         factory=".annotations.MailSubscriptionAnnotations"
9         trusted="true"
10        />
11
12    <content class=".annotations.MailSubscriptionAnnotations">
13      <require
14          permission="zope.View"
15          interface=".interfaces.IMailSubscriptions"
16          />
17    </content>
18
19   </configure>
```

Example 15.3.4 Object event subscribers for recipes that send out notification emails (`mail/recipe.py`)

```
1   import email.Charset
2   email.Charset.add_charset('utf-8', email.Charset.SHORTEST, None, None)
3
4   from datetime import datetime
5   from email.MIMEText import MIMEText
6   from zope.app import zapi
7   from zope.app.mail.interfaces import IMailDelivery
8   from worldcookery.mail.interfaces import IMailSubscriptions
9
10  def notifyAdded(recipe, event):
11      return emailNotifications(recipe, "added")
12
13  def notifyModified(recipe, event):
14      return emailNotifications(recipe, "modified")
15
16  def notifyRemoved(recipe, event):
17      return emailNotifications(recipe, "removed")
18
19  def _messageBody(recipe):
20      body = u"""Name: %(name)s
21
22  Time to cook: %(time_to_cook)s
23
24  Ingredients:
25  %(ingredients)s
26
```

```
27   Necessary Kitchen Tools:
28   %(tools)s
29
30   %(description)s"""
31       return body % {
32           'name': recipe.name,
33           'time_to_cook': recipe.time_to_cook,
34           'ingredients': '\n'.join([u'- ' + ingr for ingr in recipe
     .ingredients]),
35           'tools': '\n'.join([u'- ' + tool for tool in recipe.tools]),
36           'description': recipe.description
37           }
38
39   def emailNotifications(recipe, action):
40       subscriptions = IMailSubscriptions(recipe, None)
41       if subscriptions is None or not subscriptions.subscribers:
42           return
43       subject = "'%(name)s' was %(action)s" % {'name': recipe.name,
     'action': action}
44       message = MIMEText(_messageBody(recipe).encode('utf-8'), 'plain',
     'utf-8')
45       message['Subject'] = subject
46       message['From'] = 'notify@worldcookery.com'
47       message['To'] = ', '.join(subscriptions.subscribers)
48       message['Date'] = datetime.now().strftime('%a, %d %b %Y %H:%M:%S %z')
49       mailer = zapi.getUtility(IMailDelivery, 'worldcookery-delivery')
50       mailer.send("notify@worldcookery.com", subscriptions.subscribers,
51                       message.as_string())
```

1–2.   We use components provided by the email package from Python's standard library to generate MIME messages. A small glitch in this package lets messages encoded in UTF-8 normally be re-encoded in base64. The second line here overrides this so that messages encoded in UTF-8 are sent out in their original encoding.

5 and   To create an email document according to the email specification [14]
44–48. [13] and the MIME standard [10] we use Python's MIMEText class. It represents text email messages and instantiated with the message body as an encoded string, the text minor type (plain, html, etc.), and the encoding used. It also allows us to conveniently set MIME headers using a regular mapping API. At last, the as_string method can be used to retrieve the text representation of MIMEText objects.

10–17. The subscriber functions for the three object events we choose to subscribe to simply delegate the work to the emailNotifications function.

7 and   Email delivery is handled by named utilities providing IMailDelivery.
49–51. It is generally a good idea to configure a mail delivery for each package. Here we use the utility named worldcookery-delivery which is configured in Example 15.3.5. Delivery utilities have a send method which takes the *from* and *to* addresses as well as the message text as arguments.

Example 15.3.5 Configuring email event subscribers and mail sender utilities (mail/configure.zcml)

```
1   <configure
2       xmlns="http://namespaces.zope.org/zope"
3       xmlns:mail="http://namespaces.zope.org/mail"
4       >
5
6     ...
7
8     <mail:smtpMailer
9         name="worldcookery-mailer"
10        hostname="localhost"
11        port="25"
12        />
13
14    <mail:queuedDelivery
15        name="worldcookery-delivery"
16        permission="zope.SendMail"
17        queuePath="mail-queue"
18        mailer="worldcookery-mailer"
19        />
20
21    <subscriber
22        for="worldcookery.interfaces.IRecipe
23              zope.app.container.interfaces.IObjectAddedEvent"
24        factory=".recipe.notifyAdded"
25        />
26
27    <subscriber
28        for="worldcookery.interfaces.IRecipe
29              zope.app.event.interfaces.IObjectModifiedEvent"
30        factory=".recipe.notifyModified"
31        />
32
33    <subscriber
34        for="worldcookery.interfaces.IRecipe
35              zope.app.container.interfaces.IObjectRemovedEvent"
36        factory=".recipe.notifyRemoved"
37        />
38
39  </configure>
```

3. Configuration directives regarding the mail framework are available under the http://namespace.zope.org/mail namespace, typically bound to the mail prefix.

8–12. Configuring mail delivery utilities in Zope takes two configuration directives, one for the delivery utility itself (see below) and one for the mailer utility which actually takes care of the mail transport. This could theoretically happen through any protocol but SMTP is the obvious standard. Zope provides a utility for SMTP transport; the one that is configured here assumes that a mail server is running on the same server that the Zope application is running.

14 – 19.   This directive configures a utility providing IMailDelivery that queues emails that are to be sent during a transaction and synchronizes the sending with the underlying transaction mechanism when the transaction is committed. It is named worldcookery-delivery and using the above configured mail transport utility (worldcookery-mailer). The queuePath argument specifies a file-system path for the *maildir* directory that shall contain the queued emails.

Testing

Instead of going through an interactive interpreter session now we will just write a doctest. I am sure that by now you should be comfortable enough with the interpreter to do your own tests with components.

In the test setup we need to provide the necessary components that the subscription adapter and the event subscriber functions expect. That includes the IAnnotations adapter, the subscriptions adpater itself, and also a mail delivery utility of which we simply provide a dummy implementation that prints the email message to the shell. That makes it easy for us writing the doctest and for others reading it as a piece of documentation. The test setup is shown in Example 15.3.7, the actual doctest text file is listed in Example 15.3.6.

Example 15.3.6 Doctest for the mail subscription machinery (mail/ emailsubscriptions.txt)

```
1   ===================
2   Email subscriptions
3   ===================
4
5   Using the event subscribers in this package, Zope can send out
6   notification emails when an object has changed, for example for a
7   recipe:
8
9       >>> from worldcookery.recipe import Recipe
10      >>> cordon_bleu = Recipe()
11      >>> cordon_bleu.name = u'Cordon bleu'
12      >>> cordon_bleu.time_to_cook = 45
13      >>> cordon_bleu.ingredients = [u'Ham', u'Cheese', 'Filet']
14      >>> cordon_bleu.tools = [u'Tooth picks']
15      >>> cordon_bleu.description = u'Hmm, cordon bleu!'
16
17  The recipients of such noficiation emails are stored in annotations.
18  We therefore have to make the object attribute annotatable:
19
20      >>> from zope.interface import directlyProvides
21      >>> from zope.app.annotation.interfaces import IAttributeAnnotatable
22      >>> directlyProvides(cordon_bleu, IAttributeAnnotatable)
23
```

24   Without any subscribers, there will be no email sent, though:
25
26   >>> from zope.event import notify
27   >>> from zope.app.event.objectevent import ObjectModifiedEvent
28   >>> notify(ObjectModifiedEvent(cordon_bleu))
29
30   We first have to subscribe to the object (upon which a notification
31   email is already sent):
32
33   >>> from worldcookery.mail.interfaces import IMailSubscriptions
34   >>> subscriptions = IMailSubscriptions(cordon_bleu)
35   >>> subscriptions.subscribe('chicken@worldcookery.com')
36   Content-Type: ...
37   ...
38
39   When we now send out an object modified event, the email subscriber
40   will send out an email that looks like this:
41
42   >>> notify(ObjectModifiedEvent(cordon_bleu))
43   Content-Type: text/plain; charset="utf-8"
44   MIME-Version: 1.0
45   Content-Transfer-Encoding: 7bit
46   Subject: 'Cordon bleu' was modified
47   From: notify@worldcookery.com
48   To: chicken@worldcookery.com
49   Date: ...
50   <BLANKLINE>
51   Name: Cordon bleu
52   <BLANKLINE>
53   Time to cook: 45
54   <BLANKLINE>
55   Ingredients:
56   - Ham
57   - Cheese
58   - Filet
59   <BLANKLINE>
60   Necessary Kitchen Tools:
61   - Tooth picks
62   <BLANKLINE>
63   Hmm, cordon bleu!

Browser views

Last but not least we need to implement a browser form that lets users sign up
for email notification. With our experience in Page Templates and Python-
implemented browser views this should be simple task. Note that for now
we will not take care of security. Anybody with the permission to view the
subscription page can subscribe to an object with any email address; anybody
can also unsubscribe any email address.

Example 15.3.7 Test suite for the mail subscription tests (`mail/tests.py`)

```
1   import unittest
2   from zope.interface import implements
3   from zope.testing.doctest import ELLIPSIS
4   from zope.testing.doctestunit import DocFileSuite
5   from zope.app.tests import ztapi, placelesssetup
6   from zope.app.mail.interfaces import IMailDelivery
7
8   class DummyMailDelivery(object):
9       implements(IMailDelivery)
10      def send(self, fromaddr, toaddr, msg):
11          print msg
12
13  def setUp(test):
14      placelesssetup.setUp(test)
15      from zope.app.annotation.interfaces import IAnnotations
16      from zope.app.annotation.interfaces import IAttributeAnnotatable
17      from zope.app.annotation.attribute import AttributeAnnotations
18      ztapi.provideAdapter(IAttributeAnnotatable, IAnnotations,
19                           AttributeAnnotations)
20
21      from worldcookery.mail.interfaces import IMailSubscriptions
22      from worldcookery.mail.annotations import MailSubscriptionAnnotations
23      ztapi.provideAdapter(IAttributeAnnotatable, IMailSubscriptions,
24                           MailSubscriptionAnnotations)
25
26      ztapi.provideUtility(IMailDelivery, DummyMailDelivery(),
27                           'worldcookery-delivery')
28
29      from zope.app.event.interfaces import IObjectModifiedEvent
30      from worldcookery.interfaces import IRecipe
31      from worldcookery.mail.recipe import notifyModified
32      ztapi.handle((IRecipe, IObjectModifiedEvent), notifyModified)
33
34  def test_suite():
35      return unittest.TestSuite((
36          DocFileSuite('emailsubscriptions.txt',
37                       setUp=setUp,
38                       tearDown=placelesssetup.tearDown,
39                       optionflags=ELLIPSIS),
40          ))
41
42  if __name__ == '__main__':
43      unittest.main(defaultTest='test_suite')
```

8–11 and   As a mail delivery utility we register a dummy implementation that
26–27.   simply prints the message text to the console.

3 and 39.   Doctests allow several options to be set by using binary flags. The
            ELLIPSIS flag tells the doctest parser to interpret a set of triple dots
            (...) as an ellipsis. This is frequently needed in functional doctests
            when large HTTP return messages are to be shortened in the test; here
            we use them to ellide the time and date of the created email message
            (see line 30 of the doctest).

Example 15.3.8 Page Template with email subscription form (mail/subscribe.pt)

```
1  <html xmlns="http://www.w3.org/1999/xhtml"
2        xmlns:tal="http://xml.zope.org/namespaces/tal"
3        xmlns:metal="http://xml.zope.org/namespaces/metal"
4        xmlns:i18n="http://xml.zope.org/namespaces/i18n"
5        metal:use-macro="context/@@standard_macros/page"
6        i18n:domain="worldcookery">
7  <head>
8    <title metal:fill-slot="title" i18n:translate="">
9      Subscribe to
10     <tal:var i18n:name="obj_title" tal:replace="context/zope:title">
11       obj_title
12     </tal:var>
13   </title>
14 </head>
15 <body>
16 <div metal:fill-slot="body">
17
18   <h2 i18n:translate="">
19     Subscribe to
20     <em i18n:name="obj_title" tal:replace="context/zope:title">
   obj_title</em>
21   </h2>
22
23   <p i18n:translate="">
24     Using this form you can change the status of your email
25     subscription to
26     <em i18n:name="obj_title" tal:content="context/zope:title">
   obj_title</em>.
27     Enter your email address in the field below and click the
28     <em>Subscribe</em> button to subscribe; to unsubscribe, click the
29     <em>Unsubscribe</em> button.
30   </p>
31
32   <form action="" method="post"
33         tal:attributes="action context/@@absolute_url">
34     <p>
35       <label for="email" i18n:translate="">Email address:</label>
36       <input id="email" name="email" type="text" />
37     </p>
38     <p>
39       <input type="submit" name="@@subscribe:method" value="Subscribe"
40              i18n:attributes="value button-subscribe" />
41       <input type="submit" name="@@unsubscribe:method" value="Unsubscribe"
42              i18n:attributes="value button-unsubscribe" />
43     </p>
44   </form>
45
46 </div>
47 </body>
48 </html>
```

33, 39,   Each button shall invoke a different view. Like Zope 2's ZPublisher,
and 41.   Zope 3's publishing machinery allows to mark form names as names of
           views that shall be invoked by appending :method. The actual action
           of the form has to be the URL of the object whose views shall be in-
           voked. This is totally transparent to the views. In this example, the *Sub-
           scribe* button invokes the @@subscribe view, the *Unsubscribe* button the
           @@unsubscribe view.

The HTML form for email subscription (Example 15.3.8) simply contains
a text input box that lets users enter an email address. Two buttons, *Subscribe*
and *Unsubscribe* lead to views that handle subscription and unsubscription,
respectively.

Example 15.3.9 Browser view for subscribing/unsubscribing email addresses to an object (mail/browser.py)

```
1   from zope.app.publisher.browser import BrowserView
2   from worldcookery.mail.interfaces import IMailSubscriptions
3
4   class MailSubscriptionView(BrowserView):
5
6       def subscribe(self, email):
7           subscriptions = IMailSubscriptions(self.context)
8           subscriptions.subscribe(email)
9           self.request.response.redirect('.')
10
11      def unsubscribe(self, email):
12          subscriptions = IMailSubscriptions(self.context)
13          subscriptions.unsubscribe(email)
14          self.request.response.redirect('.')
```

Going beyond the examples

If you want to experiment more with email notifications and how components
work together, try to combine the PDF generation and the mail framework.
Why not send out generated PDFs as attachments? Or if that is too heavy
for you on the network bandwidth or the user's mailboxes, HTML emails
generated by Page Templates could jazz the simple text email up, too. Maybe
implement both and let the user choose between plain text, HTML and PDF?

Example 15.3.10 Combined browser page configuration (mail/configure.zcml)

```
1   <configure
2       xmlns="http://namespaces.zope.org/zope"
3       xmlns:mail="http://namespaces.zope.org/mail"
4       xmlns:browser="http://namespaces.zope.org/browser"
5       >
6
7   ...
8
9     <browser:pages
10        for="worldcookery.interfaces.IRecipe"
11        class=".browser.MailSubscriptionView"
12        permission="zope.ManageContent"
13        >
14      <browser:page
15          name="subscribe"
16          attribute="subscribe"
17          />
18      <browser:page
19          name="unsubscribe"
20          attribute="unsubscribe"
21          />
22      <browser:page
23          name="subscribe.html"
24          template="subscribe.pt"
25          menu="alternate_views" title="Mail subscriptions"
26          />
27    </browser:pages>
28
29  </configure>
```

9–27.   When several browser pages are to be registered for one interface with a common permission and possibly using the same supplementary class, the browser:pages directive allows one to group browser:page directives and thus avoid repitition.

25.   We add the email subscription form page to the menu of alternate views. That way a link to it will show up when displaying recipes.

Summary

- Zope has a framework for sending out emails. Object events are a typical use case for notification via emails.
- The email framework differentiates between mail delivery utilities which accept emails from an application and mail transport utilities which take care of the actual email transportation.
- It is recommended to use the queued delivery method which queues all emails that are to be delivered in a transaction and synchronizes the delivery with the commit of the transaction.

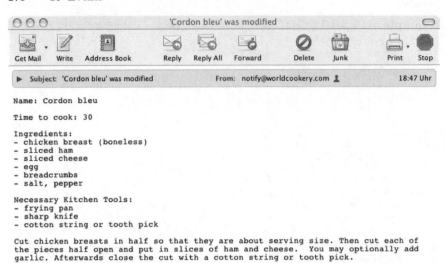

Name: Cordon bleu

Time to cook: 30

Ingredients:
- chicken breast (boneless)
- sliced ham
- sliced cheese
- egg
- breadcrumbs
- salt, pepper

Necessary Kitchen Tools:
- frying pan
- sharp knife
- cotton string or tooth pick

Cut chicken breasts in half so that they are about serving size. Then cut each of the pieces half open and put in slices of ham and cheese. You may optionally add garlic. Afterwards close the cut with a cotton string or tooth pick.

Now brush the breasts with the beaten egg and coat them with the breadcrumbs. Heat oil or butter in a frying pan and fry breasts until golden brown and crisp.

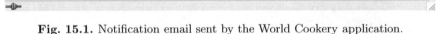

Fig. 15.1. Notification email sent by the World Cookery application.

16

Vocabularies

In Chapter 4, we introduced a variant of interfaces that allow easy data modelling: schemas. Schemas are composed of fields which describe constraints on certain data value, such as the type, the length, size or range of the value stored. All fields also support a `constraint` keyword parameter in order to allow you to specify totally custom constraints.

While all this is not only flexible but also quite convenient, it is missing a particular but quite common problem: a limited value set. In many cases, an object's attribute or some other value described by a schema has to be taken from a set of acceptable values. These sets of values, whether static or dynamically built, are called *vocabularies* and are the subject of this chapter.

Note

Vocabularies have been deprecated for upcoming versions of Zope 3 and will be replaced by a similar system called *sources*.

16.1 Simple choices

Before we dive into the admittedly complex world of vocabularies, let us cover some simple cases of limited value sets. In schemas, those are expressed through the `Choice` field. Imagine the following simple interface typed in at the interactive interpreter shell:

```
>>> from zope.interface import Interface
>>> from zope.schema import Choice
>>> class IYouCanChoose(Interface):
...     value = Choice(
```

```
...           title=u"A value",
...           values=[1, 2, 3, "four", (5,6,7)]
...       )
...
```

Through the values parameter, we have given the Choice field a set of allowed values for the field. Note that they do not have to be of the same type at all. Here we mix integers, strings and tuples.

When we now validate, we expect the validation to pass for items contained in the above list:

```
>>> IYouCanChoose['value'].validate(1)
>>> IYouCanChoose['value'].validate('four')
>>> IYouCanChoose['value'].validate((5,6,7))
```

In case a value is not found in the list of allowed values, a ConstraintNot-Satisfied error is raised:

```
>>> IYouCanChoose['value'].validate(4)
Traceback (most recent call last):
...
zope.schema._bootstrapinterfaces.ConstraintNotSatisfied:
4
```

Of course, it is not very practical to specify a list of allowed values right in the schema definition. Often, such a list is dynamically computed, or at least it should be configurable without the editing of code, which brings us back to vocabularies. They will be introduced in the next section.

Summary

- In many applications, an object's attribute value needs to be in a list of valid values in order to be acceptable.
- Zope formalizes such lists in vocabularies.
- The limited value set constraint is expressed through the Choice field which can either accept a list of acceptable values or a vocabulary name.

16.2 Theory and applications of vocabularies

A vocabulary describes a set of values usually implied by a value constraint. Apart from the values itself, which can be objects of any type, vocabularies keep extra information to allow them being used in user interfaces. In vocabulary jargon, we distinguish the following terms:

Value is the name for an object that is part of the vocabulary. In our example, a unicode string containing the name of a kitchen tool would be a value.

Term is an abstract object that represents values inside the vocabulary. This layer of abstraction is necessary because arbitrary, not even consistently-typed objects can be part of the same vocabulary. Terms are described by the ITerm interface.

Token is an ASCII-only string giving a term a unique identifer. The relation between terms and tokens has to be a one-to-one function. Tokens are necessary to uniquely identify terms in encoding-sensitive environments such as browser views and the filesystem. Terms that have tokens provide the ITokenizedTerm interface which extends ITerm. Vocabularies inidicate that they support tokenized terms by providing IVocabularyTokenized apart from IVocabulary.

Title gives terms a name for presentation purposes. This is an optional feature, but useful when a list of terms are to be displayed in a user interface. Tokens are usually too cryptic to serve this purpose, nor do they support translation. Titles are therefore typically message ids. Terms that have a title indicate this by providing ITitledTokenizedTerm.

A vocabulary itself has to provide IBaseVocabulary at a minimum. This interface promises that one can use the in operator to check whether a value is part of the vocabulary and that one can get a term object for a value.

Iterability

In most cases, one would also expect a vocabulary to be able to list all of its terms. Vocabularies that provide this functionality indicate this by providing the IIterableVocabulary, allowing other components to iterate over a list of terms. The general IVocabulary interface is a combination of IBaseVocabulary and IIterableVocabulary.

There are cases, however, where iterability does *not* make sense. The vocabulary concept only knows terms and their containment in a vocabulary. It does not require a vocabulary to include a finite number of values. For example, a vocabulary can describe all real numbers between 0 and 2. This vocabulary could not list all of its terms, but it can very easily decide whether a value is part of it or not. In other words, this vocabulary would provide IBaseVocabulary, but not IIterableVocabulary.

Simple vocabularies

Both ITerm and IVocabulary are interfaces that are easy to implement. The requirements on vocabularies and their terms are very light from the Zope side. The difficult part about implementing vocabularies is the modelling of real data or relationships.

For simple use cases where a list of values is already available, Simple-Vocabulary from the zope.schema.vocabulary module can be used as a vocabulary implementation. It can easily be tried out on the interpreter shell. When a sequence of values is already available, using the fromValues class method can be used to create a vocabulary from it, for example from a list of numbers:

```
>>> numbers = range(10)
>>> from zope.schema.vocabulary import SimpleVocabulary
>>> vocab = SimpleVocabulary.fromValues(numbers)
```

One of the minimum requirements of vocabularies is that they allow a containment check using the in operator. As expected, the integer 1 is contained in the vocabulary, 10 is not.

```
>>> 1 in vocab
True
>>> 10 in vocab
False
```

Since they are created from an iterable sequence, simple vocabularies are always iterable. Elements of the iteration are the term objects:

```
>>> from zope.schema.interfaces import \
...        IIterableVocabulary
>>> IIterableVocabulary.providedBy(vocab)
True
>>> for term in vocab:
...        print term.value,
...
0 1 2 3 4 5 6 7 8 9
```

Terms of SimpleVocabulary possess tokens which are computed by converting values to strings. Titles are not available.

```
>>> one = vocab.getTerm(1)
```

```
>>> one.value
1
>>> from zope.schema.interfaces import ITokenizedTerm
>>> ITokenizedTerm.providedBy(one)
True
>>> one.token
'1'
>>> from zope.schema.interfaces import \
...         ITitledTokenizedTerm
>>> ITitledTokenizedTerm.providedBy(one)
False
```

It is generally not a good idea to trust `SimpleVocabulary` with generating tokens. First, not everything converts to a string uniquely, if at all. Second, a string object can still contain non-ASCII characters which are not allowed in tokens. Therefore, it is better to either provide the tokens yourself or a custom and fail-safe routine that produces unique ASCII tokens.

A `SimpleVocabulary` instance with custom tokens can be instantiated using the `fromItems` class method. It accepts nested sequences like a dictionary's `items` method generates:

```
>>> numbers = {
...         'zero': 0,
...         'one': 1,
...         'two': 2,
...         'three': 3,
...         'four': 4,
...         'five': 5,
...         'six': 6,
...         'seven': 7,
...         'eight': 8,
...         'nine': 9
... }
>>> vocab = SimpleVocabulary.fromItems(numbers.items())
>>> 1 in vocab
True
>>> 10 in vocab
False
>>> one = vocab.getTerm(1)
>>> one.token
'one'
```

Of course, vocabulary terms can be re-identified by their given token, as long
as the vocabulary implements IVocabularyTokenized. Of course, this is
the case with SimpleVocabulary:

```
>>> from zope.schema.interfaces import \
...      IVocabularyTokenized
>>> IVocabularyTokenized.providedBy(vocab)
True
>>> two = vocab.getTermByToken('two')
>>> two.value
2
```

Utility vocabularies

Zope itself makes use of vocabularies in a few places, for example when a
site administrator chooses a permission by which a component is protected
through the ZMI. Here it is obviously desired to only list valid permissions
and to double-check the submitted form values whether they are allowed. In
short, a vocabulary is used.

As discussed before, small software components, like permissions and factories, are registered as named utilities with the utility service. Their type is
identified by the interface they provide. This way, a generic utility vocabulary can be used to query named utilities of a certain type. Using the right
interfaces, the utility vocabulary can be used to query permissions, factories, interfacees, content types, and more. See Table 16.1 for a list of utility
vocabularies provided by Zope.

As an example, consider the permissions vocabulary. After having loaded
the configuration, we can acquire a factory for the vocabulary from the utility
service. As you can see, vocabulary factories themselves are named utilities.
The permissions vocabulary is registered under the name Permissions:

```
>>> from zope.app.debug import Debugger
>>> debugger = Debugger(db="var/Data.fs",
...                       config_file="etc/site.zcml")
>>>
>>> from zope.app import zapi
>>> from zope.app.schema.vocabulary import \
...      IVocabularyFactory
>>> permissions_factory = zapi.getUtility(
...      IVocabularyFactory, u"Permissions")
```

Table 16.1. Default vocabularies for certain types of named utilities and other components

Name	Values	Tokens	Package
Cache Names	IDs of cache utilities providing ICache.	Same as values	zope.app. cache
Interfaces	All registered interfaces (providing IInterface).	Dotted name of the interfaces	zope.app. component
Content Types	Content type interfaces (providing IContentType).	Dotted name of the interfaces	zope.app. content
Object Interfaces	Interfaces that the current context object provides.	Dotted name of the interfaces	zope.app. interface
SourceTypes	Factory name of a text source factory.	Same as the value	zope.app. content
Permissions	Permission objects providing IPermission.	Permission ids	zope.app. security
Permission Ids	IDs of permission objects	Same as value	zope.app. security
Connection Names	Names of database connection utilities providing IZopeDatabaseAdapter.	Same as value	zope.app. sqlscript

We can now instantiate the vocabulary, passing None as context. A quick check verifies that we are indeed dealing with a utility vocabulary. As a final demonstration, we can iterate over the vocabulary's terms to see that the terms' tokens are the permission ids while the values are, of course, the permission objects themselves:

```
>>> permissions = permissions_factory(None)
>>> permissions
<zope.app.utility.vocabulary.UtilityVocabulary object at
0x2883950>
>>> for term in permissions:
...     print term.token, term.value
...
zope.AddImages <zope.app.security.permission.Permission
object at 0x2ca1d30>
zope.AddSQLScripts <zope.app.security.permission
.Permission object at 0x2ca1b50>
zope.ManageApplication <zope.app.security.permission
.Permission object at 0x2ca1c90>
...
```

Summary

- Vocabularies deal with abstractions of the actual values called *terms*; each term can be represented uniquely by a *token*.
- Simple vocabularies are best implemented using `SimpleVocabulary` from the schema package.
- Zope itself provides and uses a number of vocabularies, most importantly *utility vocabularies* which represent utilities registered with the utility service.

16.3 Using vocabularies

In actual applications, vocabularies recruit their values from a few typical places. If you are building an application for component management (for example like the ZMI), you would probably use utility vocabularies a lot. It is also quite common to store sets of allowed valued for a certain field in the annotations of the object or one of its containers. That is not only quite easy and practical too, it also expresses the tight relation between the vocabulary as metacontent or metadata and the actual content.[1]

In the *World Cookery* example application, we will use a different approach. We suppose that the list of kitchen tools that can be added to a recipe shall recruit its values from a vocabulary. The values in this vocabulary shall be defined site-wide, thus not dependent on the location of the recipe within the site. Therefore, we are going to use a utility that provides the vocabulary values; where these come from is only a question of which utility we wire in. This allows us to easily provide a different implementation of the utility. In the next chapter, we will then even see how to do this customization based on a site-based configuration within one Zope instance.

Making the schema ready for vocabularies

First, we change the `IRecipe` schema so that values for the `tools` field are taken from a vocabulary. As we have learned in the beginning of this chapter, this is done using the `Choice` field. Only this time, we do not give it a defined set of values but a vocabulary name. Example 16.3.1 shows the modified `IRecipe` schema.

---

[1] As an optional exercise, try to re-implement the vocabulary that is introduced in this section as an annotations-based one. Store the annotations on the object containing the recipe and provide a browser view for editing the vocabulary items.

Example 16.3.1 Recipe schema with a Choice field (interfaces.py)

```
1   from zope.interface import Interface
2   from zope.schema import List, Text, TextLine, Int, Choice
3   from zope.i18nmessageid import MessageIDFactory
4   _ = MessageIDFactory('worldcookery')
5
6   class IRecipe(Interface):
7       """Store information about a recipe.
8       """
9
10      name = TextLine(
11          title=_(u"Name"),
12          description=_(u"Name of the dish"),
13          required = True
14          )
15
16      ingredients = List(
17          title=_(u"Ingredients"),
18          description=_(u"List of ingredients necessary for this recipe."),
19          required=True,
20          value_type=TextLine(title=_(u"Ingredient"))
21          )
22
23      tools = List(
24          title=_(u"Tools"),
25          description=_(u"List of necessary kitchen tools"),
26          required=False,
27          value_type=Choice(title=_(u"Tool"), vocabulary="Kitchen Tools"),
28          unique=True
29          )
30
31      time_to_cook = Int(
32          title=_(u"Time to cook"),
33          description=_(u"Necessary time for preparing the meal described, "
34                        "in minutes."),
35          required=True
36          )
37
38      description = Text(
39          title=_(u"Description"),
40          description=_(u"Description of the recipe"),
41          required=True
42          )
```

27 – 28. Since we still want to allow the selection of multiple kitchen tools, we keep the List field; only the values *inside* the list shall come from the vocabulary. To ensure that no value occurs twice in the list, we pass the unique parameter as True.

Now we have to provide the vocabulary to which we refer in the schema. As stated earlier, we want the vocabulary to retrieve the actual values from a utility, which is why we have to provide such a utility, too. The interface that the utility provides can be as simple as `IKitchenTools` shown in Example 16.3.2.

Example 16.3.2 Interface for the kitchen tools utility (`interfaces.py`)

```
1    ...
2
3    from zope.schema import Iterable
4
5    class IKitchenTools(Interface):
6
7        kitchen_tools = Iterable(
8            title=_(u"Kitchen tools"),
9            description=_(u"A list of valid kitchen tools"),
10           )
```

Providing the vocabulary and a utility implementation

As an implementation for this utility, we will provide one that reads values from a UTF-8 encoded text file, `kitchentools.dat`, in which the acceptable kitchen tools are listed line by line. Note that this is just a very primitive sample implementation. As always, you can provide your own `IKitchenTools` utility that provides values from a different data source. In the next chapter, for example, we will do so ourselves.

As for the vocabulary itself, we can rely on existing infrastructure. In the previous section, we saw how to create vocabularies from a set of existing values by using `SimpleVocabulary`. This approach fits here, too. See Example 16.3.3 for the utility implementation and the vocabulary factory.

Example 16.3.3 Implementation of the kitchen tool utility and the vocabulary factory (`kitchentools.py`)

```
1    import os.path
2    from zope.interface import implements
3    from zope.schema.vocabulary import SimpleVocabulary
4    from zope.app import zapi
5    from worldcookery.interfaces import IKitchenTools
6
7    class KitchenToolsFromFile(object):
8        """Kitchen tools utility that reads data from a file
9        """
10       implements(IKitchenTools)
11
12       def kitchen_tools(self):
13           file_name = os.path.join(os.path.dirname(__file__),
         "kitchentools.dat")
```

```
14        for line in file(file_name):
15            if line.strip():
16                yield line.strip().decode('utf-8')
17    kitchen_tools = property(kitchen_tools)
18
19 def kitchenToolVocabulary(context):
20    utility = zapi.getUtility(IKitchenTools)
21    return SimpleVocabulary.fromValues(utility.kitchen_tools)
```

13. The utility reads its data from a file called `kitchentools.dat` in the same directory that the `kitchentools.py` module is located in.

14. In Python, file objects are iterators which allow one to easily iterate over the lines within the file (only in the case of text files, of course). This also works platform independently.

16. Instead of loading the whole file into memory at once, we return items only one by one using the `yield` keyword. That way this method will not return a list but an iterable generator object, thus still fulfilling the `IKitchenTools` interface which requires a simple iterable. Before items are yielded, they are stripped of whitespace and decoded from UTF-8, the encoding that the file is supposed to be encoded in.

Configuration

As always after we have implemented components, we need to configure them. You already know how to configure components; configuring vocabularies is what is new here. Example 16.3.4 shows how that is done.

Before we can try out our vocabulary-based content type in the browser using add and edit forms, we must not forget to disable the custom widget we applied to the `tools` field (see Example 16.3.5). Zope provides a special widget for `Choice` fields and for `Choice` fields within sequences (`List` and `Tuple` fields). It presents us with a list of items in the vocabulary that we can choose from. In our case, we can select multiple items from the list (in

Example 16.3.4 Configuring the vocabulary and the related utility (`configure.zcml`)

```
1    ...
2    <utility
3        provides=".interfaces.IKitchenTools"
4        factory=".kitchentools.KitchenToolsFromFile"
5        />
6
7    <vocabulary
8        name="Kitchen Tools"
9        factory=".kitchentools.kitchenToolVocabulary"
10       />
11   ...
```

some web browsers, you need to press down the **Ctrl** key in order to be able to select multiple items from the list).

Example 16.3.5 Updated browser form configuration (browser/configure.zcml)

```
1    ...
2    <browser:addform
3        schema="worldcookery.interfaces.IRecipe"
4        content_factory="worldcookery.recipe.Recipe"
5        label="[label-add-recipe] Add Recipe"
6        name="AddRecipe.html"
7        permission="zope.ManageContent"
8        set_before_add="name"
9        >
10       <widget field="ingredients" class=".widget.DynamicSequenceWidget" />
11   </browser:addform>
12
13   <browser:editform
14       schema="worldcookery.interfaces.IRecipe"
15       label="[label-edit] Edit"
16       name="edit.html"
17       menu="zmi_views" title="[label-edit] Edit"
18       permission="zope.ManageContent"
19       >
20       <widget field="ingredients" class=".widget.DynamicSequenceWidget" />
21   </browser:editform>
22   ...
```

Summary

- Vocabularies are configured using the vocabulary ZCML directive.
- Zope provides special widgets for Choice fields that make custom widgets unnecessary, unless one is dealing with special vocabularies, such as infinitely sized ones.

17

Sites

In many content management applications, hierarchical structures play an important role for organizing content. Structures like these can easily be modelled in Zope using the location and containment concepts we covered in Chapter 14. In some cases, however, it is not only content that has to conform to a certain structure. More than often, different software policies are needed for different locations, too. Zope allows us to model such policies using *sites*, the topic of this chapter.

Note that the primary focus of Zope X3 still is filesystem-based development. Configuration, registration and modification of local software components is not the primary target of development for now; it is still being developed and improved for upcoming versions.

17.1 Introduction

A Zope instance is typically used to serve one particular web application. Of course, one instance can serve different web sites that offer the same application, possibly in different variants (for example using different skins, different user databases, etc.). Our *World Cookery* website, for instance, could offer English recipes at http://worldcookery.com while German recipes are published under the subsite http://worldcookery.com/de/, http://www.de.worldcookery.com or even http://www.world-cookery.de.

A part of a Zope instance that contains such a subsite is simply called a *site*. Any object can be a site as long as it provides ISite, but it makes most sense when containers are sites. The most typical example is Zope's Folder content type. Folders are *possible sites* (they provide IPossibleSite) which means they can be turned into sites. The root folder of a ZODB instance is always a site. Sites can be nested.

Global vs. local

All components we have written so far were global ones. They were always registered with a global service, be it the adapter service, the utility service, or the presentation service. Global components are always available everywhere.

Local components, on the other hand, are components that are defined at a particular place – a site. They are only available within a site, which includes subobjects, of course. Local definitions of components can shadow global ones, thus allowing customization of component definitions at a site level. In the case of nested sites, component lookup cascades from the most local site up to the root folder site and ends with the global services.

Services themselves are managed by a *service service*. The global service service manages global services; it itself is always available everywhere and ensure that its global services are as well. Local services, on the other hand, are managed by a local service service; because these only ever occur in sites, local service services are called *site managers*.

Creating a site from a folder

The easiest way to create a site is to create a folder and turn it into a site. To do that, go to the ZMI and select *Folder* from the *Add* menu. Give the folder a name, for example worldcookery_site, then click on it to see its contents. The blue actions menu should now contain a *Make a site* entry. Clicking on this will turn the current folder into a site. You should then be shown the *Common Site Management Tasks* page of the newly created site manager.

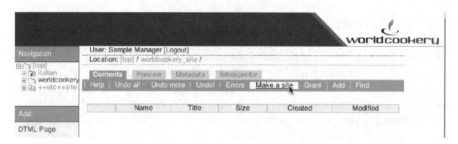

Fig. 17.1. Regular folders can easily be turned into a site using this link.

Turning folders into sites creates a site manager, the local service service that is necessary to manage local services which in turn manage local components. As you can see from the URL of the site management page, the name of site managers of folder-based sites is ++etc++site. It can be accessed through a URL much like it were a subfolder.

Something else happens to a folder when it is turned into a site. As a regular folder, it only provides IPossibleSite, indicating that it can be turned into a site at any time. After we have turned the folder into a site, it now provides ISite. You can verify this by going to the *Introspector* tab. The entry *Interfaces from Object* shoud list ISite (see Figure 17.2).

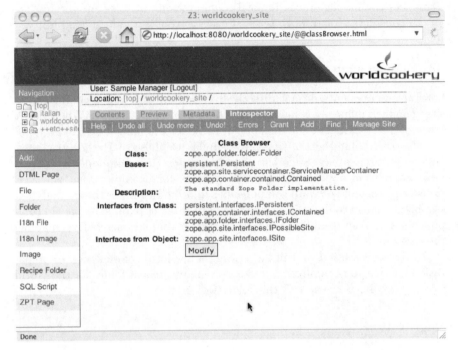

Fig. 17.2. A folder that was turned into a site now provides ISite.

A folder's site manager offers several management pages accessible through ZMI tabs:

Tasks (default) provides a general overview. Here you have direct links to tool, service and utility management as well as creation of site management folders.

Services gives you an overview over available services and where they are being acquired from. For a newly created site, most services will be acquired from the global service service. Other services, such as Error-Logging, PrincipalAnnotation, and Utilities are acquired from the parent site manager located in the root folder.

Interface Browse lets you browse through interfaces and view their fields and methods. This management screen was introduced in Chapter 5.

Software lists the contents of the site manager. Apart from being service services, site managers are containers and contain site management folders.
More on that below.

Tools lets you manage tools. In local configurations, utilities and services are
all considered local tools. In most cases, a tool is a named local utlity.

Site-management folders

Software components do not directly live inside a site manager. Instead, a
site manager manages a number of *site-management folders*. When newly
created, a site manager contains one of these folders named default.

The idea behind site managers is similar to those of Python packages.
Different libraries have different namespaces for their components. This is
also useful from a deployment point of view, for example when new versions of persistent software components are to be installed. Having different
site-management folders allows one to install these in parallel to the old components and then disabling the registration of the old ones before enabling
the new ones.

In the next section we will be creating a few local components. In preparation for this you can already create a site management folder for the World
Cookery application and call this folder worldcookery.

Registrations

As mentioned before, site management folders allow different versions of the
same components to co-exist peacefully. Obviously, you can always only look
up one of them at most. To solve this problem, site managers and their site
management folders keep *registrations*.

When adding a local component to a site management folder, it is not
automatically registered. Like a global component that first has to be configured through ZCML, a local component needs to be registered first before
it becomes active. A special component, the *registration manager*, manages
these registrations. This registration manager also allows concurrent registrations of two versions of the same component. It keeps them in a registration
stack and only the most recent registration is the one that counts for component lookup. If the registration or the even the component is removed, the
next active registration in the stack is promoted. In the next section, we will
exercise concurrent registrations at the example of local utilities.

Summary

- Sites allow the customization of global software components by using local, persistent components.

- Any object can be a site; usually, regular Zope folders are turned into sites; the root folder of a ZODB instance always is a site.
- Local services are managed in a site manager, the local equivalent of a service serviced; local components are located inside site management folders.
- Concurrent component registrations are stacked within a site management folder's registration manager.

Flashback

The CMF was among the first Zope-based frameworks that introduced the concept of a *site*. A CMF Site object or a derivative always has to be the root of a CMF-based application. Persistent CMF components, *CMF Tools*, can only be added within such a site. In that respect, Zope 3 sites take a lot after the CMF. The difference is that Zope 3 also knows global components. In fact, global configuration plays a much stronger role in Zope 3 than it does in the CMF. The general experience is that this is not only easier on development (global components do not require extensive browser views for their configuration), but also for deployment.

Another major difference is that sites can be anywhere in the location hierarchy in Zope 3, that includes being nested in other sites. The local components, successors to CMF Tools, do not live in the same namespace with content objects. Instead, if a folder turns out to be a site, application components live in separate site management folderes below the site manager.

Finally, site management folders and their registration managers are a great improvement over Zope 2 and the CMF regarding deployment. Not only is content separated from application component space; components can also be instantiated before they are actually activated, something that is completely unknown in earlier versions of Zope. The generic registration process through registration managers also makes work-around solutions like the *QuickInstaller* tool for CMF unnecessary.

17.2 Local utilities

Local utilities are the most common type of local component because utilities, especially named utilities, are widely used throughout Zope. Thus, a lot of software behaviour can be influenced by registering local utilities. Good example for local flavours of named utilities we already know are *roles* and *translation domains*.

Local utilities are also easy to create. It is not much harder than writing a persistent content component. After all, utilities are meant to be small, useful components and Zope already aids us a lot in user interface matters, such as browser menus and generated forms.

For a demonstration let us simply implement a local utility. A good candidate for a local utility is the kitchen tools utility from last chapter. By offering a local flavour of this utility, site administrators can customize the allowed values for the `Kitchen Tools` vocabularies without having to edit the `kitchentools.dat` file. More importantly, different policies can be implemented for different parts in the application by using different sites with different instances of the local utility. One reason to do this might be a subsite that contains recipes in a different language, like it was suggested in the introduction. In this case, the kitchen tool names obviously need to be translated, too.

Writing a local utility

When we now implement the local utility, we obviously want to take advantage of automatic form generation like we do with content components. The `IKitchenTools` interface which describes the utility interface is not entirely sufficient for that because it merely declares the `kitchen_tools` field as an `Iterable`; it does not specify an exact type, thus it cannot be represented by a widget.

Example 17.2.1 shows the `ILocalKitchenTools` interface which extends `IKitchenTools` and declares the `kitchen_tools` field as a `List`. This has two implications: first, every utility that provides `ILocalKitchen-Tools` also provides `IKitchenTools` by interface inheritance. Secondly, a definite type information for the iterable attribute has been given so that a widget can easily be looked up.

Example 17.2.1 Interface for a local version of the kitchen tools utility (`interfaces.py`)

```
1   ...
2
3   from zope.app.registration.interfaces import IRegisterable
4
5   class ILocalKitchenTools(IKitchenTools, IRegisterable):
6
7       kitchen_tools = List(
8           title=_(u"Kitchen tools"),
9           description=_(u"A list of valid kitchen tools"),
10          value_type=TextLine(title=_(u"Kitchen tool")))
11          )
```

3 and 5.   We extend `IRegisterable` to indicate that items providing this interface may be registered in a local registration manager.

7 – 11.   We redefine the `kitchen_tools` field by using a concrete type constraint (`List`) instead of a mere functionality constraint (`Iterable`). Also, we do not forget to specify the `value_type` of the items contained in the list so that the widget can validate properly.

ILocalKitchenTools also inherits from the IRegisterable interface. This interface is meant to be assigned to all components that are to be registered in a site management folder's registration manager. IRegisterable implicates:

- IContained, meaning that any IRegisterable object needs to provide __parent__ and __name__ attributes.
- a container types constraint on __parent__ allowing the object only to be placed in IRegisterableContainer providing objects. Site management folders are IRegisterableContainers.
- IAnnotatable, meaning that registerable objects need to be annotatable. Note that this still does not say which kind of annotation the registerable class supports. You will still have to let it implement IAttributeAnnotatable to support attribute annotations, for example.

The implementation of ILocalKitchenTools is just as easy to produce as the persistent version of the IRecipe implementation. Example 17.2.2 shows the enhanced kitchentools.py module. Note that in some cases, it is even possible to have just one implementation for a global and a local utility. The fact that the global utility would be registerable and persistent does not bother the global utility service.

As for the basic configuration, we only have to configure it like a regular content component; see Example 17.2.3. The configuration directives that actually allow us to manage the local utility using the web interface are obviously browser-specific directives.

Browser configuration and registration

Since local utilities are managed through the browser management interface, the configuration directives that actually let us use them are browser-specific. Again, the analogy to content object works well because with the recipe content type we were not able to do much either until we configured the entry in the browser *Add* menu and the automated add and edit forms. Not much else we have to do now as Example 17.2.4 shows.

We are now ready to add a local utility. Go to the site management folder named worldcookery which you created earlier. Before we add a local utility, we must add a local utility service! Therefore, select *Utility Service* from the *Add* menu and provide an arbitrary name, for example utilities. You will then be shown the *Registration* tab of the newly created object.

When created, a local component is not (or at least not automatically) registered with the registration manager. In order to enable the utility service, click on the *Register* button and submit the following form. When you go back to the *Registration* tab, it should report that the object is now active (Figure 17.3).

Example   17.2.2   Local   kitchen   tools   utility   implementation
(`kitchentools.py`)

```
1   import os.path
2   from persistent import Persistent
3   from zope.interface import implements
4   from zope.schema.vocabulary import SimpleVocabulary
5   from zope.app import zapi
6   from zope.app.container.contained import Contained
7   from worldcookery.interfaces import IKitchenTools, ILocalKitchenTools
8
9   class KitchenToolsFromFile(object):
10      """Kitchen tools utility that reads data from a file
11      """
12      implements(IKitchenTools)
13
14      def kitchen_tools(self):
15          file_name = os.path.join(os.path.dirname(__file__),
    "kitchentools.dat")
16          for line in file(file_name):
17              if line.strip():
18                  yield line.strip().decode('utf-8')
19      kitchen_tools = property(kitchen_tools)
20
21  class LocalKitchenTools(Persistent, Contained):
22      """Local, persistent kitchen tools utility
23      """
24      implements(ILocalKitchenTools)
25
26      kitchen_tools = []
27
28  def kitchenToolVocabulary(context):
29      utility = zapi.getUtility(IKitchenTools)
30      return SimpleVocabulary.fromValues(utility.kitchen_tools)
```

2 and 21.   Local components obviously have to be persistent because they need to
be stored within the ZODB.

6 and 21.   Since the `IRegisterable` interface extends `IContained`, we need
to provide the `__parent__` and `__name__` attributes, or simply use the
`Contained` mixin,

26.   No further machinery is required on part of the local utility other than
to fulfill the `ILocalKitchenTools` interface. We do that here by providing an empty list as a default for the `kitchen_tools` attribute.

Now we are ready to add our local utility. Go back to the site management
folder and select *Kitchen tools* from the *Add* menu. Give this object also an
arbitrary name, for example `kitchentools`. Note that this name is not the
name the utility will be registered under. The kitchen tools utility is an unnamed utility! After having entered a name for the object, you will be shown
the *Registration* page of the utility just like it happened for the utility service.
To register the component, click on the *Register* button. The following form in

Example 17.2.3 Basic configuration of a local utility class (`configure.` `zcml`)

```
1    ...
2    <content class=".kitchentools.LocalKitchenTools">
3      <implements
4          interface="zope.app.utility.interfaces.ILocalUtility
5                     zope.app.annotation.interfaces.IAttributeAnnotatable"
6          />
7      <require
8          permission="zope.Public"
9          interface=".interfaces.IKitchenTools"
10         />
11     <require
12         permission="zope.ManageContent"
13         set_schema=".interfaces.ILocalKitchenTools"
14         />
15   </content>
16   ...
```

4.   `ILocalUtility` is a marker interface for `IRegisterable` components.
        It marks registerable components as local utilities. As with other marker
        interfaces, we apply it in configuration, because the usage whether a com-
        ponent is used a utility or something different should be determined by
        configuration, both with global and local components.

5.   `IRegisterable` requires local components to be annotatable by extending
        `IAnnotatable` itself. It does not specify which kind of annotation support
        should apply which is why we explictly have to mark `LocalKitchenTools`
        as attribute annotatable.

7 – 14. The security configuration for the local utility looks just like the one of any
        other schema-based content type. Note that this analogy only works so well
        in this case because the kitchen tools utility does not really do much; it
        really looks a lot like content. The difference is that it is content that drives
        the application.

a way is the local equivalent of the `utility` directive we know from ZCML.
We have to specify the interface the utility provides, the permission that is
needed to use it and, if desired, a name for the instance. As stated just now,
the kitchen tools utility is an unnamed utility, we therefore do not provide a
name. As for the interface, be sure to select the `IKitchenTools` entry from
the list since that is what the vocabulary will be trying to look the utility up
under. Finally, select an appropriate permission, such as `zope.Public` or
`zope.View`. Note that just the utility lookup is governed by this permission,
not the modification of the utility.

Finally, after having registered the local utility, you can freely edit it using
the automatically generated edit form we configured. Of course, you could
have first edited the kitchen tools list and then registered it or viceversa.
Once you have supplied a number of acceptable kitchen tools, go back to the
folder that we turned into a site earlier, the `worldcookery_site` folder.

Example 17.2.4 Browser configuration for a local utility (browser/configure.zcml)

```
1      ...
2      <browser:tool
3          interface="worldcookery.interfaces.ILocalKitchenTools"
4          title="Kitchen tools"
5          description="This tool stores kitchen tools."
6          />
7
8      <browser:addMenuItem
9          class="worldcookery.kitchentools.LocalKitchenTools"
10         title="Kitchen tools"
11         permission="zope.ManageContent"
12         />
13
14     <browser:editform
15         schema="worldcookery.interfaces.ILocalKitchenTools"
16         label="[label-edit] Edit"
17         name="edit.html"
18         menu="zmi_views" title="[label-edit] Edit"
19         permission="zope.ManageContent"
20         fields="kitchen_tools"
21         >
22       <widget field="kitchen_tools" class=".widget.DynamicSequenceWidget" />
23     </browser:editform>
24     ...
```

2 – 6.   The browser:tool directive configures a local component as a *browser tool*. This is not strictly necessary for the configuration of a local utility, but it provides aids in the user interface.

8 – 12.   As with any content component, too, this entry takes care of adding the local utility implementation to the *Add* menu. Of course, it is not possible to add local utilities to regular folders. The container type constraint that comes with IRegisterable forbids that. It allows local components to only be added to registrable containers such as site management folders.

22.   Since we are dealing with a List field that contains TextLines, we can apply our custom widget here, just like with the recipe form configuration. This, of course, is just as optional as it is for the recipe content type.

When you add a recipe in there now, you will realize that the add form now presents you with the list of kitchen tools from the local utility, not from the global one, where in places outside the site the global one is still active. The best part is, it is totally transparent to the vocabulary! For all it knows, it is still looking up an IKitchenTools utility.

A close-up on registrations

As mentioned in the introduction, registrations are managed by *registration managers*. Every site management folder has one called Registration-

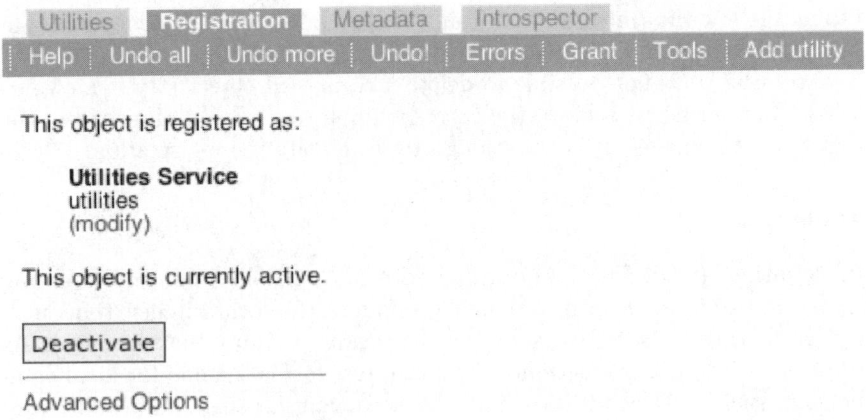

Utilities | **Registration** | Metadata | Introspector
Help | Undo all | Undo more | Undo! | Errors | Grant | Tools | Add utility

This object is registered as:

Utilities Service
utilities
(modify)

This object is currently active.

| Deactivate |

Advanced Options

Fig. 17.3. A registered local utility service.

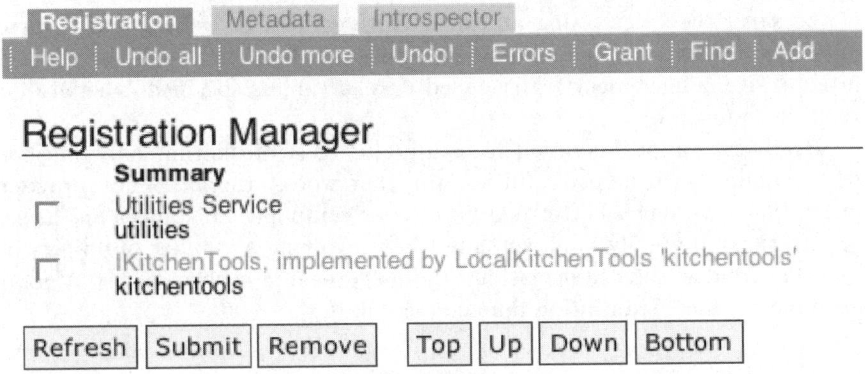

Registration | Metadata | Introspector
Help | Undo all | Undo more | Undo! | Errors | Grant | Find | Add

Registration Manager

Summary

☐ Utilities Service
utilities

☐ IKitchenTools, implemented by LocalKitchenTools 'kitchentools'
kitchentools

| Refresh | Submit | Remove | | Top | Up | Down | Bottom |

Fig. 17.4. Registration manager containing two registration objects.

Manager. Registration managers are actually containers and the registrations themselves are objects. They are kept in an order, the registration stack, so that concurring registrations do not cause ambigious component lookup.

An object can have two states regarding registrations, unregistered or registered, depending on whether a registration object is present. Registration objects themselves can be active or inactive. For example, this way it is possible to deactivate an existing registration without deleting it in order to reactivate it later more easily.

Registrations can, of course, be modified after they have been created. For example, if you wanted to change the permission by which the kitchen tools utility is protected, you would have to go to the utility's *Registration* tab and follow the *(modify)* link. You will then be shown the same form that was presented to you when you added the registration.[1]

Note that it is not possible to delete a registered object (try it for yourself!). One must first remove the corresponding registration object from the registration manager. It is not enough to deactivate the registration.

Tools

In addition to declaring `LocalKitchenTools` a class implementing `ILocalUtility`, we can optionally configure the local kitchen tools utility as a *browser tool* (Example 17.2.4 already contains the directive). As mentioned in the introduction to this chapter, *tool* is a name for local components such as local utilities that can be managed using the browser user interface below the site manager. As of version Zope X3.0, registering a type of component as a browser tool only makes it appear in the *Tools* page of a site manager and registers several managing views for listing tool instances of the same type, activating and deactivating them as well as adding new ones. Components created through these pages will automatically be created inside a site management folder called `tools` (unless specified otherwise in their configuration).

Registering a local component as a tool is most of the time only efficient when dealing with named utilities. In other words, the simplified browser pages that give much better overviews over component instances and their registrations are really only worth it when involving a number of objects of the same kind so their information can be aggregated in these pages. A good example are local translation domains or roles.

Summary

- Local utilities are, apart from services, the most common form of local component, especially named utilities such as roles and translation domains.
- A local utility is often only a persistent re-implementation of an existing global implementation; sometimes even one implementation can be used for both purposes.
- All local components are *registerables*, which implies they that they are contained in site management folders and annotatable.
- Registrations influence component look up for a certain local component; if active and topmost, the corresponding component will be looked up; registrations are managed by registration managers.
- By configuring a local component as a *tool*, Zope generates a couple of extra administrative screens that provide a better overview over existing components and their registrations.

---

[1] As you can imagine, these forms are also auto-generated add and edit forms.

17.3 Virtual hosting

Up to here we have covered the features of software policy customization that sites provide for an application from the inside. Though not strictly related to sites nor local component configuration, virtual hosting is also an aspect of placeful software customization. Unlike local components, though, it does not influence the software itself. It usually is just an aspect of deployment.

Why virtual hosting?

Virtual hosting is called *virtual* because it applies when one server machine and the software running on it pretend to be more than just one machine by responding to many different names differently. This practice is quite common for web sites when offering subsites out of the same server. As the initial example at the beginning of the chapter mentioned, `worldcookery.com` could have a subsite for German users under `de.worldcookery.com` or `worldcookery.de`. With our experience from this chapter and the ones before, we know that Zope can easily handle those two sites out of one instance. They could simply be two sites with custom language policies, or one could be a subsite of the other, thus acquiring useful configuration from the other without duplicating it.

Virtual hosting is often done with just one IP address. Web servers can still figure out which website the incoming request means because most HTTP clients send the hostname of which they request the website in the *Host* HTTP header. Zope, however, does not interpret this header. It does not support virtual hosting by itself. For that, a third party webserver software, such as the Apache webserver, has to be used to act in front of Zope. The most common form of such a set up usually is:

- The Zope HTTP server is configured to only listen on `localhost` on a high port such as 8080. That means it can be run under a non-priviledged user account which increases the security of the Zope sandbox. Only binding it to `localhost` ensures that noone from the outside gains access to Zope directly.
- A third party webserver software, such as the Apache webserver, is used to server the HTTP port 80. It delegates incoming requests to the Zope server on port 8080. Optionally, the URL can be rewritten to gain or lose path segments. That way, the root of the Zope hierarchy does not necessarily have to match the root of the served pages' hierarchy.

Such a system is very flexible and presents itself with advantages that even apply to applications which are only single-hosted. Consider the following ones:

- One can exclude certain areas of a website not to be served by Zope but by the regular webserver, for example for serving a download area's large file archives directly from the file system instead of the ZODB.

- Unlike Zope, many webservers support SSL nowadays. By using such a software in front of Zope, one can easily serve a Zope application in an encrypted form out of a webserver software that has been geared towards these security-related matters.
- When delegating pages to Zope, it is quite possible to enable a caching mechanism in between the webserver and Zope. That way, a performance-expensive Zope application can be sped up tremendously when certain pages are cached.

As said these points also apply to applications that do not require virtual hosting because they need to be served under several host names. Experience has shown that it is usually recommended to use the virtual hosting approach for production systems, even if only one host name is involved. Development setups obviously are still better off with a bare Zope.

Rewriting URLs

Zope generates a lot of URLs from object paths. The most convenient way to do that is the `absolute_url` view which we too have used more than once. The problem is that when Zope is hidden behind a dedicated webserver software that manages virtual hosting, Zope only ever receives requests on `http://localhost:8080`. It must think that somebody is always accessing it from a web browser on the local machine, while actually the webserver software is just proxying requests for remote clients.

Even though it does not support virtual hosting per se, Zope allows URL rewriting so that the URLs it generates match the URLs that a Zope website is accessed under from the outside. For example, imagine that the *World Cookery* website lives in the `worldcookery_site` folder. That means it can be accessed through the bare Zope server as `http://localhost:8080/worldcookery_site`. Of course, we would like it to appear under `http://worldcookery.com`. That means we need to tell Zope to strip of the `http://localhost:8080/worldcookery_site` part and preprend `http://worldcookery.com` instead when generating URLs.

Rewriting URLs is achieved through a traversal adapter. We already know `++view++` and `++skin++`. The one for rewriting is called `++vh++`. It is used in the following way:

```
http://host:port/path_to_site/++vh++virtual_protocol:
virtual_host:virtual_port/virtual_path/++/
```

In our case, it would be:

```
http://localhost:8080/worldcookery_site/++vh++http:
worldcookery.com:80/++/
```

This tells Zope to rewrite URLs so that they use the HTTP protocol (an alternative would be HTTPS, for example), `worldcookery.com` for the host name of the virtual host and port 80 for the virtual port. It is important to always specify the port even if it is the standard HTTP port 80. If you try the above URL in a web browser, you will see that all URLs generated by Zope now will start with `http://worldcookery.com` and that the page lacks all layouting because the stylesheets cannot be loaded from `http://worldcookery.com`.

Apache in front of Zope

The most successful webserver in the internet is the Apache HTTP server. Its advantage is that it runs on both Unix-based and Windows operating systems which is why we will describe setting up our example application in a virtual hosting environment using this software. Other webservers or webproxies have similar functionality, so any lesson learned here should be easily applicable to other systems.

In the following we assume that you have a running installation of the Apache 2 webserver. In addition, the following Apache shared modules are required to be installed:

mod_proxy and *mod_proxy_http* These modules allow the Apache webserver to act as a proxy between the user client and Zope.

mod_rewrite (optional) This module allows rewriting URLs from within Apache. This is useful when serving local pages and pages from Zope in the same virtual host.

The example listings configure the virtual host settings for the fictitious `worldcookery.com` website.

Apache allows us to configure virtual hosts by using the `<VirtualHost>` environments in its configuration file. Virtual hosts based on the *Host* HTTP header have to be enabled with the following directive:

```
NameVirtualHost *
```

Make sure it is in the main Apache configuration file.

We now have two options for configuring the proxying to Zope. The easiest way is to use the simple `ProxyPass` and `ProxyPassReverse` directives. Example 17.3.1 shows the configuration of a virtual hosting using these directives. The disadvantage here is that every request that is identified to be handled by this virtual host goes to Zope. There is no way to declare an exception, for example to serve certain files statically.

Example 17.3.1 Simple Apache 2 virtual host configuration (etc/ apache2-proxypass.conf)

```
1   <VirtualHost *>
2       ServerName worldcookery.com
3       ServerAlias worldcookery.com *.worldcookery.com
4       ServerAdmin webmaster@worldcookery.com
5       DocumentRoot "/var/www/worldcookery"
6
7       CustomLog "logs/worldcookery-access.log" combined
8       ErrorLog "logs/worldcookery-error.log"
9       LogLevel warn
10      ServerSignature On
11
12      ProxyPass / http://localhost:8080/worldcookery_site/++vh++http:
    worldcookery.com:80/++
13      ProxyPassReverse / http://localhost:8080/worldcookery_site/++vh++http:
    worldcookery.com:80/++
14  </VirtualHost>
```

12–13. `ProxyPass` und `ProxyPassReverse` tell Apache to forward incoming requests to the following URL and to send the response that came out of that URL back to the original client. As a URL, we use the one that rewrites URLs according to the virtual host used; it is the same one that we tested in a webbrowser earlier.

The other possibility is to use the advanced mod_rewrite module. It allows URL rewriting within Apache based on regular expression matches. That allows us, for example, to serve certain URLs from the file system whereas the rest is patched through to Zope. It would also allow us to combine several Zope instances under one virtual host. An example configuration file using the rewrite functionality is shown in Example 17.3.2.

To enable these settings in Apache, you can either copy and paste them into the webserver's configuration file, usually `httpd.conf` or `apache2. conf`, or you can copy one of the files to the Apache configuration directory and use the following statement to have it included:

```
Include "/etc/apache2/apache2-proxypass.conf"
```

Or, if you prefer using the mod_rewrite approach:

```
Include "/etc/apache2/apache2-rewrite.conf"
```

Example 17.3.2 Advanced Apache 2 virtual host configuration (etc/apache2-rewrite.conf)

```
1   <VirtualHost *>
2       ServerName worldcookery.com
3       ServerAlias worldcookery.com *.worldcookery.com
4       ServerAdmin webmaster@worldcookery.com
5       DocumentRoot "/var/www/worldcookery"
6
7       CustomLog "logs/worldcookery-access.log" combined
8       ErrorLog "logs/worldcookery-error.log"
9       LogLevel warn
10      ServerSignature On
11
12      RewriteEngine On
13      RewriteRule ^/files/(.*) - [L]
14      RewriteRule ^/(.*) \
15          http://localhost:8080/worldcookery_site/++vh++http:%{SERVER_NAME}:
        80/++/$1 [P,L]
16  </VirtualHost>
```

13.   This rewrite rule tells Zope to serve all URLs that begin with /files/ to serve locally from the file system. This could be useful for a download area where large files can be downloaded from that would bloat the ZODB instance otherwise.

14 – 15. This rewrite rule enables the proxy function for all other URLs so that content is pulled from the Zope instance. Again we specify the URL that takes care of rewriting.

Testing

You can easily test whether the virtual host setup works. Make sure your Zope instance is running under the port specified (usually 8080) and the Apache 2 server is also running. Now you need to make the operating system think that your local machine is actually worldcookery.com. This can be done most easily in the hosts file. On Unix-like operating systems, this file resides in the /etc directory. On recent Windows versions, it can be found under C:\Windows\system32\drivers\etc. Add the following line to the file using a simple text editor:

```
127.0.0.1    worldcookery.com
```

Now you should be able to open the URL http://worldcookery.com in a normal web browser and see your Zope instance served via Apache.

Summary

*   Virtual hosting allows one server to respond to requests that are issued for different host names.

- Zope itself does not support virtual hosting but it supports URL rewriting so that it can easily be used behind a third party webserver software.
- As a popular webserver, the Apache webserver is often installed on many systems; it provides virtual hosting capabilities and is the recommendes webserver software to be used in front of Zope.

Flashback

Zope 2 provides simple built-in virtual hosting functionality through *Virtual Host Monster* (VHM) objects. Once added to a folder, it hooks itself into object traversal and can dispatch requests to different folders based on the *Host* HTTP header. Using the VHM in this direct way is very uncommon for production systems, though. For performance as well as security reasons, most setups only use the VHM for URL rewriting and trust a third party webserver like Apache with handling incoming requests.

Since this setup has proven its performance and reliability, only the support for rewriting URLs has survived in Zope 3. Even though it is spelled out differently, the concept is the same. For example, the configuration of an Apache software serving in front of Zope 2 only has to be adjusted to the new URL rewrite spelling in order to support Zope 3. The rest can stay as it is.

18

Security

Before this book is over, this chapter shall give you a deep and thorough look into Zope's security architecture. This chapter can certainly be considered the book's climax because it comes near the end and yet it is crucial to any web application. The reasons why it has not been presented earlier are simple:

First, it was the book's intention to provide a gradual approach to building applications with Zope. Even though we did the necessary security declarations for components, we were able to build an application quickly without having to worry too much about security. It is one of the long-term lessons of this book that Zope does not force you to think too hard about security in the beginning of creating an application.

Second, security requires a great deal of understanding of how components work and how they interact. The concept of a trusted adapter, for example, can only be understood when understanding what an adapter itself is. Therefore, we could only deal with security after having gained enough experience and confidence in dealing with Zope's components.

18.1 Overview

When building a complex web application, security is a crucial factor. Different users need to be able to do different things and they should prevented from doing things they are not allowed to do. As much as the functionality of a web application differs from one to another, security requirements need to be customized as well.

Zope breaks up security into several high-level and low-level components which interact with each other. On one hand, this allows us not to mix security concerns with functionality concerns when implementing components because security is banned to its own types of components. On the other hand, we can customize security components just as any other component is customizable.

In the following section the different types of security components shall be introduced first before we dive into hands-on examples on the interpreter shell. The purpose of this section is not to improve the security of our example application in any way. Rather, it should help you as a software developer understand how security components interact which is the key to providing custom security implementations and an overall secure application.

High-level components

Zope's security system knows several high-level components which influence the way security checking is performed. They are also projections of Zope's fundamental security concepts. Some of these components are likely to be customized in applications with specific and special requirements regarding security, unlike low-level components which do not determine security behaviour as much. The following list gives detailed definitions and explanations for each security component. If not specified otherwise, the described machinery is defined in the zope.security package.

Permission Permissions protect component functionality. Usually they describe a certain action and the kind of access that is required to carry it out. Components and component lookup can be protected by permissions.

Principal Any entity that interacts with the application is called a principal. This can be an unauthenticated browser client, a user who logged in using some form of credentials, or some other entity. Principals take place in participations. They are described by the IPrincipal interface (defined in zope.app.security).

Participation Participations are the means by which principals can actually reach the system and interact with it. Any Zope request, for example, is a participation. For each principal interacting with the system there exists exactly one participation. Participations are described by the IParticipation interface.

Interaction An interaction aggregates all current participations. Most importantly, interactions are the actual components that check whether principals have a certain permission on an object. Usually, interactions begin with a request and end when the response has been sent out to the client. They are in a way for security what transactions are for storages. Interactions provide IInteraction.

Security policy Security policies are simple callables that return an interaction. By registering a custom security policy one can influence which interaction implementation is being used, thus the way security checking is performed. Usually, a security policy is a class *providing* ISecurity-

`Policy` and *implementing* `IInteraction` (classes are callables which return an instance of themselves). Simple security policies reside in `zope.security.simplepolicies`. The default one for the Zope application server can be found under `zope.app.securitypolicy`.

Low-level components

The following components operate on a low level. They make it possible to abstract security issues into more high-level components; they also allow us to work with objects in security contexts transparently. These components are generally not customized because the whole high-level definition of Zope security depends on these low-level ones not being modified.

Security proxy Any object that is exposed to security-sensitive components such as views is wrapped in a security proxy. These proxies protect the object against unauthorized access and modification. The checking whether an object access is authorized or not is delegated to checkers. Objects have to be wrapped in security proxies explicitly. In the Zope application server, the publication takes care of this during traversal. Once an object is wrapped, all objects retrieved from it through attribute access are proxied as well. Immutable objects such as strings and tuples are not wrapped since they cannot be changed.

Checker Checkers perform the security checking for security proxies. A security proxy asks the checker whether a certain action is allowed on an object. The checker can decide whether the access is authorized based on many criteria. The most common checker is the permission-based one that looks up a permission that is required for the action in question and then asks the interaction whether the current participants have that permission on the object.

Examples

To give you an idea how these components work together, let us try to mimic their interaction on the interactive interpreter shell. We start out with providing security declarations for our `Recipe` class. We normally do this in ZCML with a `require` directive. Here it is sufficient to protect an attribute, for example name, with an arbitrary permission that is not `zope.Public`:

```
>>> from worldcookery.recipe import Recipe
>>> from zope.app.security.protectclass import \
...     protectName
>>> protectName(Recipe, 'name', 'some.permission')
```

Now we play the role of the publication and "find" a recipe object. We do what we must do to protect it towards user-invoked code: we wrap it in a security proxy. That is done using `ProxyFactory`. Note that we do not provide any information *how* the object shall be protected. We have already done that (see above), it is usually done in the ZCML.

```
>>> pudding = Recipe()
>>> pudding.name = u'Pudding'
>>> from zope.security.proxy import ProxyFactory
>>> wrapped_pudding = ProxyFactory(pudding)
```

You might remember contained proxies from Chapter 14. These are a different kind of proxy but essentially behave very much like security proxies. To the outside, a wrapped object looks just like the original. Only the object's type tells the real story:

```
>>> wrapped_pudding
<worldcookery.recipe.Recipe object at 0x35cd70>
>>> type(wrapped_pudding)
<type 'zope.security._proxy._Proxy'>
```

Note that at this point any attribute that was not protected with a permission above (or in ZCML for a real application) cannot be accessed anymore. Any attempt will result in a `ForbiddenAttribute` error:

```
>>> pudding.ingredients
Traceback (most recent call last):
...
zope.security.interfaces.ForbiddenAttribute:
('ingredients', <worldcookery.recipe.Recipe object at
0x35cd70>)
```

When we now play the role of user-invoked code that has to operate on the wrapped object, for example a browser view, we realize very quickly that we forgot to start an interaction:

```
>>> wrapped_pudding.name
Traceback (most recent call last):
...
AttributeError: 'zope.thread.local' object has no
attribute 'interaction'
```

As this example well demonstrates, all user-invoked components and other components that have to deal with security-proxied objects need to be executed during an interaction. A new interaction is started using the new-Interaction function. This function executes the security policy callable which is ParanoidSecurityPolicy by default. This particular security policy implementation only ever allows participations involving the system user, a special principal for carrying out system activities. This is, of course, not to be confused with the default security policy for the Zope application server.

In order to simulate what happens when a participant does not have the authorization to access an attribute, we start an interaction with a participation that does not have any principal. For ParanoidSecurityPolicy, this participation should definitely not suffice for access:

```
>>> class InterpreterParticipation(object):
...         interaction = principal = None
...
>>> from zope.security.management import newInteraction
>>> newInteraction(InterpreterParticipation())
```

As expected, trying to access the name attribute now results in an Unauthorized error:

```
>>> wrapped_pudding.name
Traceback (most recent call last):
...
zope.security.interfaces.Unauthorized: ('name',
'some.permission')
```

Note the difference to ForbiddenAttribute which only occurs when code tries to access an attribute that it really should not accesse (no security delcarations were provided for it so it cannot be considered a public attribute). Unauthorized is raised when the privileges of the participations in the current interaction are not sufficient to access a protected attribute.

If we wanted to be authorized to access the attribute we would have to satisfy ParanoidSecurityPolicy. The way to do that is to either add a system user participation to the current interaction or to create a new interaction with that participation. If we wanted to do the latter, we are told that we first need to end the existing interaction.

```
>>> from zope.app.appsetup.appsetup import \
...         SystemConfigurationParticipation
>>> newInteraction(SystemConfigurationParticipation())
```

```
Traceback (most recent call last):
...
AssertionError: newInteraction called while another
interaction is active:
...
```

As with transactions in a database system, there can only ever be one current interaction; in case of interactions, this is a rule that applies per thread. An interaction is ended with the endInteraction function. After having called this function we can create an interaction in which the system user participates. We are authorized for any kind of access now:

```
>>> from zope.security.management import endInteraction
>>> endInteraction()
>>> newInteraction(SystemConfigurationParticipation())
>>> wrapped_pudding.name
u'Pudding'
```

Summary

- Zope's security system knows low-level and high-level components of which the former are seldomly customized, the latter are intended to be customized for complex security requirements.
- Principals (users) participate in interactions, for example through a request.
- Components that are dealt with in user-invoked code (such as views) are wrapped in security proxies to protect them from unauthorized access.
- Security proxies delegate the security checking to checkers which can decide authorization based on different circumstances, usually the privileges of the participants in an interaction.
- Interactions, which decide whether a participant in an interaction (a principal) is authorized for a certain permission, are pluggable through different security policies.

Flashback

Some of the security concepts found in Zope 3 today have evolved from their Zope 2 predecessors. For example, a high-level security component in Zope 2 is the *security manager* which is instanticated on a per-thread basis and builds the bridge between the *security context* that represents the user and the *security policy* that does the actual security checking (by default based on roles). From a transaction perspective, Zope 3 interactions are derived from Zope 2 security managers. From a security checking perspective, they are also derived from Zope 2 security policies (in Zope 3, security policies are merely factories for interactions).

The permission concept is also a very important one that has been borrowed from Zope 2, although the differences are more than subtle. Apart from the difference in identification (full title vs. dotted name), the way classes are protected with them has changed, too. Even though the notation of security declarations has changed in Zope 2 over time, the underlying implementation and the semantics were always the same. The so-called *declarative security*, the most popular and most recent notation in Zope 2, is just syntactic sugar for storing permissions directly on the class, interspersed with the code that is to be protected. That makes it impossible to change security declarations for a class without having to modify its code, a mishap that has been changed in Zope 3 thanks to ZCML.

Declarative security knows three different forms of protection for attributes of a Zope 2 class:

declarePrivate makes the attribute inaccessible from outside the object. In Zope 3, this is the default when no security declaration was made for the attribute.

declareProtected protects an attribute with a certain permission, much like it is done in Zope 3 via the require ZCML directive.

declarePublic makes an attribute publicly accessible. The Zope 3 equivalent is protecting an attribute with the zope.Public permission or using the allow ZCML directive.

18.2 Permissions

Up until now we secured components in ZCML by providing appropriate security declarations. In the last section we learned that not doing so would actually let our application fail utterly – we would get ForbiddenAttribute errors everywhere.

Even though we provided these declarations, we have not yet paid close attention to the permissions we protected the components with. Zope itself provides a few default permissions (they were already listed in Table 3.2) of which we only ever used zope.View for components that we wanted to be accessible by anonymous users and zope.ManageContent for actions that required authentication, such as editing content.

This approach is not very practical, obviously. Right now, adding and editing recipe folders requires the same permission as adding and editing recipes. In some setups, this *might* not make a difference, but often one would

Example 18.2.1 Defining fine-grained permissions for the World Cookery application (`permissions.zcml`)

```
1   <configure xmlns="http://namespaces.zope.org/zope">
2
3     <permission
4         id="worldcookery.ViewRecipes"
5         title="View recipes"
6         />
7
8     <permission
9         id="worldcookery.EditRecipes"
10        title="Edit recipes"
11        />
12
13    <permission
14        id="worldcookery.ViewRecipeFolders"
15        title="View recipe folders"
16        />
17
18    <permission
19        id="worldcookery.EditRecipeFolders"
20        title="Edit recipe folders"
21        />
22
23    <permission
24        id="worldcookery.EditKitchenTools"
25        title="Edit kitchen tools"
26        />
27
28    <permission
29        id="worldcookery.Rate"
30        title="Rate objects"
31        />
32
33    <permission
34        id="worldcookery.ViewPDF"
35        title="View PDF rendering of objects"
36        />
37
38    <permission
39        id="worldcookery.Subscribe"
40        title="Subscribe to objects via email"
41        />
42
43  </configure>
```

like to be flexible about what is allowed to whom. In other words, more fine-grained permissions should be used as much as possible. As you might remember from Chapter 3, permissions can be grouped in roles so that one does not have to grant users every single permission but only the roles that entail the permissions.

Fine-grained permissions

To allow a more flexible security control by site administrators, let us define more fine-grained permissions. Those permissions will, of course, be specific to the World Cookery application, or at least the worldcookery package; that is why we will use the worldcookery prefix in their dotted name. Example 18.2.1 lists the permission definitions.

Now that we have defined fine-grained permissions we can change the configuration of all World Cookery components so that they are protected by an appropriate one. Since the change involves no more than a simple search and replace, file listings are not provided again for brevity reasons. Note that since we defined the permissions in a separate ZCML file, it has to be included explicitly with the following statement at the top of configure.zcml:

```
<include file="permissions.zcml" />
```

By protecting World Cookery components with custom permissions, we have made the application temporarily unusable because we have not yet granted any of these permissions to a principal. We will do that in the next section.

Summary

- Fine-grained permissions allow one to be more flexible with security privileges without interfering too much with an application's configuration.
- With fine-grained permissions, site administrators can configure a system's security without knowing much of Zope internals.
- Permissions are usually grouped in roles so that they do not have to be granted individually.

18.3 Roles

In Chapter 3, roles were introduced with the hat analogy. This chapter gives us an opportunity to look behind the scenes a little further.

Roles are a mechanism to group permissions according to responsbilities. This responsibility-driven approach is often perceived as orthogonal to groups. While groups ask the question "where does a user have privileges?", roles ask the question "what kind of privileges/responsibilities does the user have?"

Roles are *not* fundamental security components in Zope (otherwise they would have been covered in Section 18.1). They are a concept from a particular security policy, the default one that comes with Zope. This security policy does not support groups; fortunately, security policies are pluggable which means that a custom one can always support groups, in combination with roles or not.

To make the World Cookery application usable again we define roles according to the typical activities of users in the application. A sensible approach would be to divide responsibilities into those who write recipes (editors) and those who read them (visitors). Example 18.3.1 defines the two roles and grants the permissions we defined earlier to them accordingly. As with `permissions.zcml`, this file also has to be included at the top of `configure.zcml`, below `permissions.zcml`.

Granting roles

Now we still have not made the application usable again, but we are a step closer. Principals that have the `zope.Manager` role (such as the user that is created when creating a Zope instance) always have any access, thus we do not need to take care of them. It is the anonymous principal that currently lacks the proper privileges. Before, it was able to view recipes because it is granted the `zope.View` permission by default. If we wanted to restore that situation, we would have to grant it the `worldcookery.Visitor` role. That is best done in an instance's `principals.zcml` file where the unauthenticated principal is defined. Example 18.3.2 shows what the `principals.zcml` file could look like.

With the anonymous users granted the `worldcookery.Visitor` role, we should be able to view recipes again without authenticating. As for editing recipes, it seems obvious that editors should not be granted manager privileges. The `zope.Manager` principal really is just a development or emergency user that should be disabled for production systems (as should any non-anonymous principal that is defined through ZCML because the password appears in plain text). In the next chapter we will learn how to manage principals and their grants properly.

Local roles and grants

As mentioned in Chapter 3, roles are named utilities. The utility name is the role identifier (the dotted name) and they provide `IRole`. It was also mentioned in the last chapter that roles can be created locally in sites – after all, they are just utilities so local roles are local utilities. Local roles are also registered as browser tools so they can be managed quite efficiently under the *Tools* administration page.

It is also possible to make local grants, meaning that a certain principal only has certain roles or that a certain role only has certain permissions in

a particular area. These grants, managed by the default security policy, are
stored in an object's annotations; that way, any annotatable object can be
the location of local grants. If the object is located in a location hierarchy,
grants from parent objects are acquired; local grants can override (and revoke)
global grants and grants from parents.

Example 18.3.1 Defining roles in the World Cookery application (`roles.
zcml`)

```
 1  <configure xmlns="http://namespaces.zope.org/zope">
 2
 3    <role
 4        id="worldcookery.Visitor"
 5        title="Visitor of the WorldCookery website"
 6        />
 7
 8    <role
 9        id="worldcookery.Editor"
10        title="An editor in the WorldCookery website"
11        />
12
13    <grant
14        permission="worldcookery.ViewRecipes"
15        role="worldcookery.Visitor"
16        />
17
18    <grant
19        permission="worldcookery.EditRecipes"
20        role="worldcookery.Editor"
21        />
22
23    <grant
24        permission="worldcookery.ViewRecipeFolders"
25        role="worldcookery.Visitor"
26        />
27
28    <grant
29        permission="worldcookery.EditRecipeFolders"
30        role="worldcookery.Editor"
31        />
32
33    <grant
34        permission="worldcookery.EditKitchenTools"
35        role="worldcookery.Editor"
36        />
37
38    <grant
39        permission="worldcookery.Rate"
40        role="worldcookery.Visitor"
41        />
42
```

```
43    <grant
44        permission="worldcookery.ViewPDF"
45        role="worldcookery.Visitor"
46        />
47
48    <grant
49        permission="worldcookery.Subscribe"
50        role="worldcookery.Visitor"
51        />
52
53    </configure>
```

3–11.   Roles are defined using the `role` directive. Like permissions, they are identified by a dotted name and should have an explanatory title.

13–51.   The `grant` directive can be used to grant permissions to roles.

Example 18.3.2 Granting the anonymous principal the visitor role (`etc/principals.zcml`)

```
1     <configure xmlns="http://namespaces.zope.org/zope">
2
3       <unauthenticatedPrincipal
4           id="zope.anybody"
5           title="Unauthenticated User"
6           />
7
8       <grant
9           role="worldcookery.Visitor"
10          principal="zope.anybody"
11          />
12
13      <principal
14          id="zope.manager"
15          title="Manager"
16          login="manager"
17          password="secret"
18          />
19
20      <grant
21          role="zope.Manager"
22          principal="zope.manager"
23          />
24
25    </configure>
```

8–11.   The `grant` directive can also be used to grant a role to a principal.

13–18.   You should adjust the login name and password of the emergency/development manager principal according to the values you provided to the `mkzopeinstance` script that first created the instance (see Chapter 2).

Local grants can be managed in the ZMI. Go to the location in which you would like to make the local grant and select *Grant* from the blue actions menu. You can then decide whether you would like to grant permissions to roles or roles to principals.

Summary

- Roles combine certain permissions necessary for an action, thus provide a way to spell out security in a responsibility-driven manner.
- Roles are a feature of Zope's default security policy, thus not required in custom security policies.
- Roles are named utilities providing `IRole`; global roles are defined using the `role` ZCML directive.
- Roles and grants can be defined locally; local roles are simply local utilities; local grants can be stored on any annotatable object (through annotations).

19

Authentication and user management

In the last chapter we saw how users (represented as principals) interact with Zope's security system. What has been missing from this was how users are actually authenticated. In other words, we have not yet discussed how users can provide their credentials and how these are verified. We will take a look in this chapter.

Like the high and low-level security is the responsiblity of several different components, authentication is also the responsibility of more than one component. At the heart of the authentication system is the authentication service. A particular implementation of this service, the *pluggable authentication service* (pluggableauth), delegates common authentication tasks to different components; most importantly, principals are looked up from principal sources which can provide user accounts to Zope from any type of source.

Note

The authentication system of Zope 3 has been improved tremendously for upcoming versions. The *Pluggable Authentication Service* (PAS), a very flexible and highly customizable authentication system for Zope 2, has been ported to Zope 3 to use the Component Architecture.

19.1 Credentials

A particular aspect of authentication is requesting credentials from the user for a certain action, followed by retrieving and extracting them as well as associating a principal with the provided login name. The component that extracts the credentials for the authentication service also takes care of challenging the user to provide credentials. This component is an adapter from the request to the ILoginPassword interface. Upon each request, the request is adapted to that interface in order to extract the user's credentials, if provided.

As we learned in the last chapter, the security machinery raises the Unauthorized exception when a certain action is not permitted. When that happens, the ILoginPassword adapter is ordered to challenge the user; if it chooses not to, the Unauthorized exception is displayed to the user by using the exception's default view.

Cookie-based authentication

If one wanted to customize the way credentials are requested and extracted, the ILoginPassword adapter and the default view to the Unauthorized exception are excellent places to start with.

In the following we shall implement an ILoginPassword adapter for browser requests that stores user authentication data in a cookie in the browser. Example 19.1.1 shows the implementation of such an adapter along with a view that permits users to log out.

Example 19.1.1 Authentication adapter using browser cookies (browser/cookieauth.py)

```
1   from zope.interface import implements
2   from zope.app import zapi
3   from zope.app.publisher.browser import BrowserView
4   from zope.app.publisher.interfaces.http import ILogout
5   from zope.app.security.basicauthadapter import BasicAuthAdapter
6
7   class CookieAuthAdapter(BasicAuthAdapter):
8
9       def __init__(self, request):
10          super(CookieAuthAdapter, self).__init__(request)
11          self.request = request
12
13      def getLogin(self):
14          request = self.request
15          username = request.form.get('zope_user', None)
16          if username is not None:
17              request.response.setCookie('zope_user', username, path='/')
18          else:
19              username = request.cookies.get('zope_user', None)
20          if username is None:
21              return super(CookieAuthAdapter, self).getLogin()
22          return username
23
24      def getPassword(self):
25          request = self.request
26          password = request.form.get('zope_pass', None)
```

```
27        if password is not None:
28            request.response.setCookie('zope_pass', password, path='/')
29        else:
30            password = request.cookies.get('zope_pass', None)
31        if password is None:
32            return super(CookieAuthAdapter, self).getPassword()
33        return password
34
35    def needLogin(self, realm):
36        pass
37
38 class CookieAuthLogout(BrowserView):
39    implements(ILogout)
40
41    def logout(self):
42        self.request.response.expireCookie('zope_user', path='/')
43        self.request.response.expireCookie('zope_pass', path='/')
44        return self.request.response.redirect('/@@loggedout.html')
```

5, 7, and 10.   We subclass BasicAuthAdapter, the adapter for generic HTTP basic authentication. That way, we inherit its functionality and HTTP clients can still provide credentials using the HTTP header information. We do not forget to also initialize our base class.

13 – 33.   We override the two extractor methods in order to look for credentials in cookies. If they have not been provided in cookies but in form values (most probably sent by the login form), we set the cookie so that the user stays logged in until logout is triggered. If credentials are neither provided in cookies nor in form values, lookup is delegated to the base class.

35 – 36.   We do not challenge the user to provide credentials explicitly because we provide a login form as a custom default view for Unauthorized. That means we should rather not do anything here.

42 – 43.   This browser view is triggered when the user chooses to log out. It expires all authentication-relevant cookies in the client's browser.

The custom adapter does not challenge the user to provide credentials. That means the Unauthorized exception will be displayed. We make sure that our custom view for this exception will show a login form. That way, whenever an unauthorized user tries to access something outside the user's privileges, that login form will be shown. Example 19.1.2 shows the Page Template defining the form.

Example 19.1.1 also defines a view for logging out which invalidates any previous cookies and thus prevents the browser from further sending credentials. Afterwards it redirects to a logout notification page whose template is shown in Example 19.1.3. This template is configured along with the ILoginPassword adapter in Example 19.1.4. Since there already exist login forms, logout views, and a view for the Unauthorized exception in the Zope core, we need to configure those in overrides.zcml in order to avoid conflicting configuration. Example 19.1.5 shows what it must look like. Do not forget to copy this new version of the file to your instance's configuration directory!

As it should happen with any browser-specific component, a functional doctest was recorded using the tcpwatch program; it is available for reference at `browser/cookieauth.txt` since it is too lengthy to be printed here like the tests of previously covered components.

Example 19.1.2 Login form for cookie-based authentication (`browser/login.pt`)

```
1   <html xmlns="http://www.w3.org/1999/xhtml"
2         xmlns:tal="http://xml.zope.org/namespaces/tal"
3         xmlns:metal="http://xml.zope.org/namespaces/metal"
4         xmlns:i18n="http://xml.zope.org/namespaces/i18n"
5         metal:use-macro="context/@@standard_macros/dialog"
6         i18n:domain="worldcookery">
7   <head>
8     <title metal:fill-slot="title" i18n:translate="">Please log in</title>
9   </head>
10  <body>
11  <div metal:fill-slot="body">
12
13    <h1 i18n:translate="">Please log in</h1>
14
15    <form action="." method="post">
16      <table>
17        <tbody>
18          <tr>
19            <td i18n:translate="">User name:</td>
20            <td><input type="text" name="zope_user" /></td>
21          </tr>
22          <tr>
23            <td i18n:translate="">Password:</td>
24            <td><input type="password" name="zope_pass" /></td>
25          </tr>
26          <tr>
27            <td></td>
28            <td><input type="submit" value="Login"
29                       i18n:attributes="login button-login" /></td>
30          </tr>
31        </tbody>
32      </table>
33    </form>
34
35    <p>
36      <span i18n:translate="">Not a member yet?</span>
37      <a href="@@signup.html" i18n:translate="">Sign up for a user
38      account now!</a>
39    </p>
40
```

```
41    </div>
42    </body>
43    </html>
```

5. Instead of the page macro we now use the `dialog` macro. Skins that support different layouts for different macros can then display the login form as a dialog-like page.

15. The form action is really arbitrary here because the `ILoginPassword` adapter is invoked on every request anyway. Thus it does not matter which page we call next; here we just let the folder index page handle be displayed.[a]

---

[a] If you wanted to improve the user experience, you could write a form action view that redirects the user back to the page that the user was trying to access when the login form was presented (the HTTP *Referer*).

Example 19.1.3 Logout notification page (`browser/loggedout.pt`)

```
1   <html xmlns="http://www.w3.org/1999/xhtml"
2         xmlns:tal="http://xml.zope.org/namespaces/tal"
3         xmlns:metal="http://xml.zope.org/namespaces/metal"
4         xmlns:i18n="http://xml.zope.org/namespaces/i18n"
5         metal:use-macro="context/@@standard_macros/dialog"
6         i18n:domain="worldcookery">
7   <head>
8     <title metal:fill-slot="title" i18n:translate="">
9       You have been logged out
10    </title>
11  </head>
12  <body>
13  <div metal:fill-slot="body">
14
15    <h1 i18n:translate="">You have been logged out</h1>
16
17    <p><a href="" tal:attributes="href string:${request/URL/0}/"
18          i18n:translate="">Back to the main page.</a></p>
19
20  </div>
21  </body>
22  </html>
```

Example 19.1.4 Configuring the cookie authentication adapter (`browser/configure.zcml`)

```
1     ...
2     <adapter
3         for="zope.publisher.interfaces.browser.IBrowserRequest"
4         provides="zope.app.security.interfaces.ILoginPassword"
5         factory=".cookieauth.CookieAuthAdapter"
6         />
7
```

```
8      <browser:page
9          for="*"
10         name="loggedout.html"
11         template="loggedout.pt"
12         permission="zope.Public"
13         />
14     ...
```

3. The BasicAuthAdapter that is provided in the Zope core is registered for all HTTP requests. Since cookies only make sense for browser clients, we register our CookieAuthAdapter just for browser requests.

12. The logout notification page should be accessible to anyone. After all, having to login again just to be told about logging out is undoubtedly confusing to the user.

Summary

- At the top of the authentication process is the extraction of credentials from the request before they are used to match a user database.
- For this task, the Zope authentication machinery adapts the request to ILoginPassword.
- Zope provides such an adapter for all HTTP-based requests; it supports HTTP Basic authentication.
- If the current principal's privileges are insufficient, the ILoginPassword adapter can be used to challenge the user to (re-)authenticate; otherwise the Unauthorized exception is displayed.

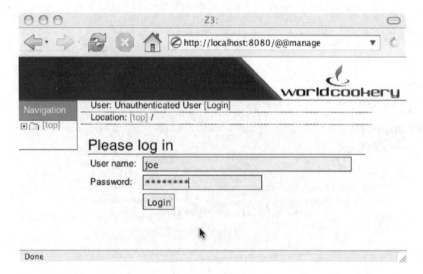

Fig. 19.1. Login form as a default view for the Unauthorized exception.

Example 19.1.5 Overriding authentication browser pages (etc/overrides.zcml)

```
1   <configure xmlns="http://namespaces.zope.org/zope"
2               xmlns:browser="http://namespaces.zope.org/browser">
3
4     <!-- Provide local overrides of standard configurations -->
5     <!-- Copy this file to your instance's etc directory -->
6
7     <browser:defaultSkin name="WorldCookery" />
8
9     <adapter
10         for="zope.publisher.interfaces.browser.IBrowserRequest"
11         provides="zope.i18n.interfaces.IUserPreferredLanguages"
12         factory="worldcookery.browser.adapter.BrowserFormLanguages"
13         />
14
15     <configure package="worldcookery.browser">
16
17       <browser:page
18           for="zope.exceptions.IUnauthorized"
19           name="index.html"
20           template="login.pt"
21           permission="zope.Public"
22           />
23
24       <browser:page
25           for="*"
26           name="login.html"
27           template="login.pt"
28           permission="zope.Public"
29           />
30
31       <browser:page
32           for="*"
33           name="logout.html"
34           class="worldcookery.browser.cookieauth.CookieAuthLogout"
35           attribute="logout"
36           permission="zope.Public"
37           allowed_interface="zope.app.publisher.interfaces.http.ILogout"
38           />
39
40     </configure>
41
42   </configure>
```

15.   In the following browser:page directives we refer to template files that are located in the worldcookery.browser package. Therefore we wrap these directives in a second configure directive that sets the right package context. That way the filenames can be resolved relative to the intended package.

19.	The default view for a component is by default index.html which is why we register the login form template as this view for the Unauthorized exception.
21 and	We must not forget to unrestrict any view concerning logging in and out.
28.	It must be possible for any user to log in and out at any time (unless you would like to restrain that).

19.2 Managing principals

As mentioned in the introduction, a very flexible implementation of a local authentication service is provided with the Pluggable Authentication Service (pluggableauth). It acts as a mediator between Zope's security system and different principal sources. A default principal source that stores principals persistently as objects in BTrees is provided with Zope.

Working with pluggableauth

A pluggableauth instance is created like any other local component. Go to a site management folder, for example the one we created in Chapter 17, select *Authentication Service* from the *Add* menu, and provide a name for the instance, for example pluggableauth. Afterwards you will be shown the usual *Registration* screen where you can register the service with the registration manager.

A pluggableauth instance itself is a container of principal sources. In the usual *Contents* page you can add principal sources to the service from the *Add* menu. By default there is only one type of principal source available, BTreePrincipalSource, which is behind the *Add Principal Source* entry. Again, you can use an arbitrary name for the principal source, such as managed_users.

As you will easily see, BTree-based principal sources are containers as well. Each contained object is a persistent principal instance. Again, the *Add* menu is the facility that lets us add the subobjects. When adding a persistent principal, you will be shown an add form like the one shown in Figure 19.2. Note that BTreePrincipalSource is a container that chooses its own names (like our RecipeFolder, see Chapter 14); the names of the principal objects inside the container are the principals' login names.

After having created the principal we can log out and log in again using the newly created account. Note, though, that the principal is only available at the site level at which you created it. Thus, if you try to log in to access an object higher in the hierarchy than the worldcookery_site folder, the new principal will not be found and your credentials cannot be matched against a user database. Also note that you will not be able to do much with the new user account since it does not have any granted roles or permissions (other than zope.Public). You can, however, make local grants for the principal as described in Chapter 18.

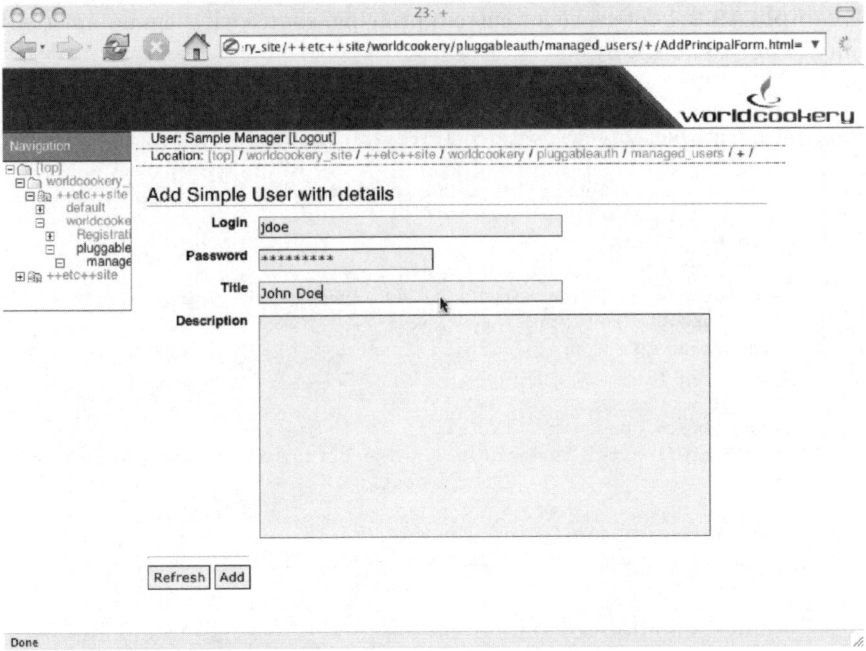

Fig. 19.2. Adding a persistent principal to a pluggableauth principal source.

A custom principal source for signup

Some internet applications, especially portals and community websites, allow visitors to sign up as users. That way, users themselves do the user management and site administrators merely have to control their behaviour rather than doing administrative tasks themselves. As we are dealing with a community-oriented application in this book, this feature is should definitely not be left out. Going into the internals of pluggableauth will also give us a better idea of how the authentication system works and how to effectively manage principals and their grants.

To support member sign up we will provide a custom principal source based on BTreePrincipalSource. It extends the functionality of its base class with two important methods, one for signing up as a new user and one for changing the principal's title and its password. Example 19.2.1 shows the interface for the custom principal source and Example 19.2.2 depicts its implementation using BTreePrincipalSource as a base class.

ISignupPrincipalSource defines a list field for the roles that should be granted to newly created principals. As the source of available roles we obviously use a vocabulary which we yet have to define. The ZCML code snippet shown in Example 19.2.3 does that as well as providing the usual security configuration for the SignupPrincipalSource class.

Example 19.2.1 Interface for custom principal source with signup functionality (`interfaces.py`)

```
1   ...
2
3   from zope.app.pluggableauth import IBTreePrincipalSource
4
5   class ISignupPrincipalSource(IBTreePrincipalSource):
6
7     signup_roles = List(
8         title=_(u"Roles for new principals"),
9         description=_(u"These roles will assigned to new principals."),
10        value_type=Choice(vocabulary="Roles"),
11        unique=True
12        )
13
14    def signUp(login, password, title):
15        """Add a principal for yourself.  The principal object is returned.
16        """
17
18    def changePasswordTitle(login, password, title):
19        """Change the principal's password and/or title.
20        """
```

Example 19.2.2 BTree-based principal source with signup functionality (`signup.py`)

```
1   from zope.interface import implements
2   from zope.app.pluggableauth import BTreePrincipalSource, SimplePrincipal
3   from worldcookery.interfaces import ISignupPrincipalSource
4
5   class SignupPrincipalSource(BTreePrincipalSource):
6       """Persistent principal source that allows users to sign up.
7       """
8       implements(ISignupPrincipalSource)
9
10      signup_roles = []
11
12      def signUp(self, login, password, title):
13          if login in self:
14              raise ValueError, "Login already exists"
15          self[login] = SimplePrincipal(login, password, title)
16          return self[login]
17
18      def changePasswordTitle(self, login, password, title):
19          if login not in self:
20              raise ValueError, ("Principal is not managed by this "
21                                 "principal source.")
22          principal = self[login]
23          principal.password = password and password or principal.password
24          principal.title = title and title or principal.title
25          return principal
```

2 and 5.   We base our custom principal source on `BTreePrincipalSource`. That way we do not have to worry about any of the actual principal source functionality. We inherit all that from it. Instead we can focus on signup part.

2 and 15.   During the signup process, an actual principal object has to be created. `SimplePrincipal` is a class that implements `IPrincipal` and is persistent, thus these simple principals can be added to our BTree-based principal source.

Example   19.2.3   Configuration   for   the   signup   principal   source (`configure.zcml`)

```
1    ...
2    <vocabulary
3        name="Roles"
4        factory="zope.app.utility.vocabulary.UtilityVocabulary"
5        interface="zope.app.securitypolicy.interfaces.IRole"
6        nameOnly="True"
7        />
8
9    <content class=".signup.SignupPrincipalSource">
10      <require
11          like_class="zope.app.pluggableauth.BTreePrincipalSource"
12          />
13      <require
14          permission="worldcookery.SignUp"
15          attributes="signUp signup_roles"
16          />
17      <require
18          permission="worldcookery.ManageSignUp"
19          set_attributes="signup_roles"
20          />
21      <require
22          permission="worldcookery.ChangePassword"
23          attributes="changePasswordTitle"
24          />
25    </content>
26    ...
```

2-7.   In `ISignupPrincipalSource` (see Example 19.2.1), we refer to the Roles vocabulary which we configure here. As you might remember from last chapter, roles are named utilities providing `IRole`. That makes it quite easy to define a vocabulary, we do not even have to write any code. We just use `UtilityVocabulary` with the right interface discriminator. Since we are only interested in role identifiers instead of the actual utility objects, we set the nameOnly flag.

11.   The `require` directive is usually used to explicitly protect one or several attributes with a certain permission. For cases of similar class configurationks, however, it also provides this shortcut of acquiring an already existing class's security declarations. That way we save ourselves from having to protect our principal source implementation against the `IPrincipalSource` interface; it would only be mindless code repetition anyway.

You probably noticed that Example 19.2.3 uses three new permissions, worldcookery.SignUp, worldcookery.ManageSignUp, and worldcookery.ChangePassword. These are permissions that we require from users in order for them to use certain functionality of the signup machinery we are creating. The permissions are defined in Example 19.2.4 and granted to their corresponding roles in Example 19.2.5. In the latter configuration file, we also defined a new role, worldcookery.Member which can be granted to principals that signed up. By granting individual permissions to members, you can then allow signed up users to take more responsibilities within the application.

Example 19.2.4 Signup-related permissions (permissions.zcml)

```
1   <configure xmlns="http://namespaces.zope.org/zope">
2
3     ...
4
5     <permission
6        id="worldcookery.SignUp"
7        title="Sign up as a user to the site"
8        />
9
10    <permission
11       id="worldcookery.ManageSignUp"
12       title="Manage user sign up"
13       />
14
15    <permission
16       id="worldcookery.ChangePassword"
17       title="Change a principal's password"
18       />
19
20  </configure>
```

Example 19.2.5 Granting signup-related permissions to roles (roles. zcml)

```
1   <configure xmlns="http://namespaces.zope.org/zope">
2
3     <role
4        id="worldcookery.Visitor"
5        title="Visitor of the WorldCookery website"
6        />
7
8     <role
9        id="worldcookery.Editor"
10       title="An editor in the WorldCookery website"
11       />
12
```

```
13    <role
14        id="worldcookery.Member"
15        title="A member of the WorldCookery website"
16        />
17
18    ...
19
20    <grant
21        permission="worldcookery.SignUp"
22        role="worldcookery.Visitor"
23        />
24
25    <grant
26        permission="worldcookery.ChangePassword"
27        role="worldcookery.Member"
28        />
29
30    </configure>
```

Browser views for signup

Now that we have a principal source that provides signup functionality, we should make a few browser views that actually let users enter and change their user information. Example 19.2.6 shows the HTML form through which users can sign up; the form for changing their information (full name and

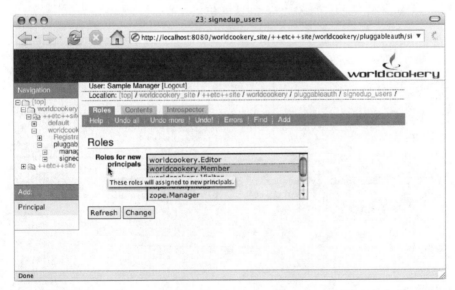

Fig. 19.3. The roles that are granted to principals upon signup can be selected in the edit form of the Signup Principal Source.

password) works analogously which is why it is not printed here. Example
19.2.7 shows the form handler view that takes care of the actual signup,
Example 19.2.8 shows the view that changes a principal's title and password
while the configuration of all of it is demonstrated in Example 19.2.9.

Example 19.2.6 Signup form (`browser/signup.pt`)

```
1   <html xmlns="http://www.w3.org/1999/xhtml"
2         xmlns:metal="http://xml.zope.org/namespaces/metal"
3         xmlns:i18n="http://xml.zope.org/namespaces/i18n"
4         metal:use-macro="context/@@standard_macros/dialog"
5         i18n:domain="worldcookery">
6   <head>
7     <title metal:fill-slot="title" i18n:translate="">Sign up</title>
8   </head>
9   <body>
10  <div metal:fill-slot="body">
11
12    <h1 i18n:translate="">Sign up</h1>
13
14    <form action="@@signup" method="post">
15      <table>
16        <tbody>
17          <tr>
18            <td i18n:translate="">Login name:</td>
19            <td><input type="text" name="login" /></td>
20          </tr>
21          <tr>
22            <td i18n:translate="">Full name:</td>
23            <td><input type="text" name="title" /></td>
24          </tr>
25          <tr>
26            <td i18n:translate="">Password:</td>
27            <td><input type="password" name="password" /></td>
28          </tr>
29          <tr>
30            <td i18n:translate="">Confirm password:</td>
31            <td><input type="password" name="confirmation" /></td>
32          </tr>
33          <tr>
34            <td></td>
35            <td><input type="submit" value="Sign up"
36                       i18n:attributes="value button-signup" /></td>
37          </tr>
38        </tbody>
39      </table>
40    </form>
41
42  </div>
43  </body>
44  </html>
```

Example 19.2.7 Signup browser view (`browser/signup.py`)

```
1  from zope.i18nmessageid import MessageIDFactory
2  from zope.security.proxy import removeSecurityProxy
3
4  from zope.app import zapi
5  from zope.app.publisher.browser import BrowserView
6  from zope.app.exception.interfaces import UserError
7  from zope.app.pluggableauth.interfaces import
   IPluggableAuthenticationService
8  from zope.app.securitypolicy.interfaces import IPrincipalRoleManager
9  _ = MessageIDFactory('worldcookery')
10
11 from worldcookery.interfaces import ISignupPrincipalSource
12
13 class SignUpView(BrowserView):
14
15     def _getPrincipalSource(self):
16         pluggableauth = zapi.getService(zapi.servicenames.Authentication,
17                                         context=self.context)
18         if not IPluggableAuthenticationService.providedBy(pluggableauth):
19             raise LookupError, "Signup requires a pluggableauth instance."
20         for principal_source in pluggableauth.values():
21             if ISignupPrincipalSource.providedBy(principal_source):
22                 return principal_source
23         raise TypeError, "Signup requires a SignupPrincipalSource."
24
25     def signUp(self, login, title, password, confirmation):
26         if confirmation != password:
27             raise UserError(_(u"Password and confirmation didn't match"))
28         principal_source = self._getPrincipalSource()
29         if login in principal_source:
30             raise UserError(_(u"This login has already been chosen."))
31
32         try:
33             principal = principal_source.signUp(login, password, title)
34         except ValueError:
35             raise UserError(_("There already exists a principal with this "
36                               "login. Please choose a different one."))
37
38         role_manager = IPrincipalRoleManager(self.context)
39         role_manager = removeSecurityProxy(role_manager)
40         for role in principal_source.signup_roles:
41             role_manager.assignRoleToPrincipal(role, principal.id)
42         self.request.response.redirect("@@welcome.html")
```

6, 27, 30, and 35.   Wherever the current action has to be aborted because of an error, we raise `UserError` because only this exception type (and deriving ones) will be shown to the user (as opposed to any other exception which simply generates a *System error* display). Also, `UserError` allows to pass a message id as the error message so that it will be translated.

15 – 23. The signup view is meant to be a view for regular content-space components (it probably makes most sense to register it for a site, as shown in Example 19.2.9). That in turn means that we have to acquire the principal source that we want to add principals to manually. We do that by first acquiring an authentication service, making sure that we really got a pluggableauth instance. Then we iterate over the principal sources in the pluggableauth service and just use the first signup principal source that we find.

38 – 41. Here we grant the requested roles to newly created principals. We do that by adapting the context (the place where users are signing up) to IPrincipalRoleManager. This adapter manages local grants of roles to principals. Since it is a trusted adapter, it itself will be security-proxied. The principal currently participating in the interaction is most probably the unauthenticated user (after all, why would anyone else sign up for an account?) which most probably does not have any role-granting privileges. Therefore, we have to ignore all security checking at this point and remove the security proxies manually using the removeSecurityProxy function. Note that you should only do this if you really know what you are doing.

Example 19.2.8 Browser view for changing a principal's name and password (browser/password.py)

```
1   from zope.i18nmessageid import MessageIDFactory
2   from zope.exceptions import Unauthorized
3   from zope.app.exception.interfaces import UserError
4   _ = MessageIDFactory('worldcookery')
5
6   from worldcookery.browser.signup import SignUpView
7
8   class PasswordView(SignUpView):
9
10      def changePasswordTitle(self, title, password=None, confirmation=None):
11          if confirmation != password:
12              raise UserError(_(u"Password and confirmation didn't match"))
13
14          principal_source = self._getPrincipalSource()
15          login = self.request.principal.login
16          if login not in principal_source:
17              raise UserError(_(u"Can only change the title and password "
18                                "of signed up users."))
19
20          principal_source.changePasswordTitle(login, password, title)
21          self.request.response.redirect(".")
```

6, 8,   We inherit from the SignUpView so that we can use the existing method
and 14.   for looking up the Signup Principal Source.

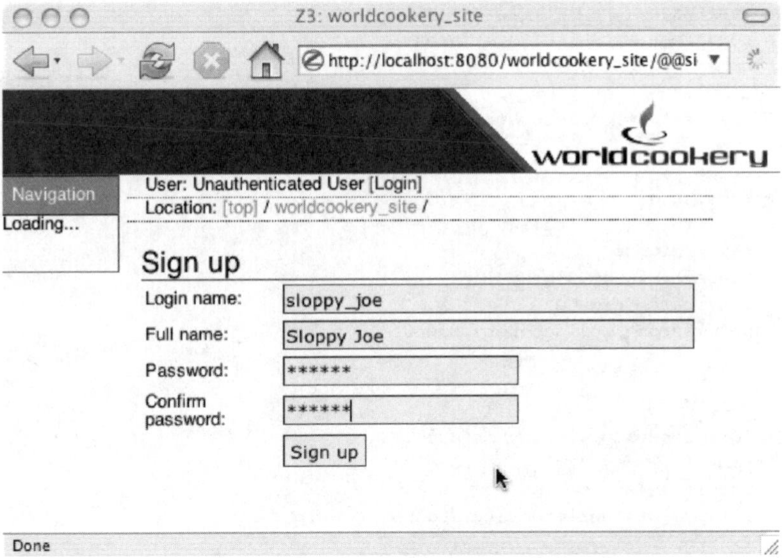

Fig. 19.4. User signing up as a member of the World Cookery website.

Our application is now ready for people who would like to participate as a member of the website. The elementary actions that one needs to be able to do (sign up and change one's own password) is supported. Similar to what we did with the cookie authentication adapter in the previous section, a functional test was recorded using tcpwatch and is available for reference at browser/signup.txt.

Example 19.2.9 Browser configuration for signup views (browser/configure.zcml)

```
1     ...
2     <browser:addMenuItem
3         title="Sign-up Principal Source"
4         class="worldcookery.signup.SignupPrincipalSource"
5         permission="worldcookery.ManageSignUp"
6         />
7
8     <browser:editform
9         schema="worldcookery.interfaces.ISignupPrincipalSource"
10        label="[label-roles] Roles"
11        name="roles.html"
12        menu="zmi_views" title="[label-roles] Roles"
13        permission="worldcookery.ManageSignUp"
14        fields="signup_roles"
15        />
16
```

```
17    <browser:page
18        for="zope.app.site.interfaces.ISite"
19        name="signup.html"
20        template="signup.pt"
21        permission="worldcookery.SignUp"
22        />
23
24    <browser:page
25        for="zope.app.site.interfaces.ISite"
26        name="signup"
27        class=".signup.SignUpView"
28        attribute="signUp"
29        permission="worldcookery.SignUp"
30        />
31
32    <browser:page
33        for="zope.app.site.interfaces.ISite"
34        name="welcome.html"
35        template="welcome.pt"
36        permission="worldcookery.SignUp"
37        />
38
39    <browser:page
40        for="zope.app.site.interfaces.ISite"
41        name="changePassword.html"
42        template="password.pt"
43        permission="worldcookery.ChangePassword"
44        />
45
46    <browser:page
47        for="zope.app.site.interfaces.ISite"
48        name="changePassword"
49        class=".password.PasswordView"
50        attribute="changePasswordTitle"
51        permission="worldcookery.ChangePassword"
52        />
53    ...
```

18, 25,   The signup views and templates are held pretty neutral as to which type
33, 40,   of component they are registered for. It makes most sense, though, to
and 47.   enable signup functionality at a site level. First, local services (such as
pluggableauth) can only be defined at site level which is why a site is
needed anyway. Second, users usually sign up for a whole website or a
at least subsite where they can use an application that is customized
(possibly with local components in a site manager) for their needs. Chapter
17 mentioned that sites are exactly meant for that purpose. We therefore
reigster all signup-related views for ISite.

Connecting third party user databases via pluggableauth

The reasonably small example of a custom principal source with signup functionality demonstrates the power and pluggability of pluggableauth quite

well. There are many in-depth scenarios and edge cases that cannot be covered here, unfortunately. One direction that you might want to explore into is connecting a third party user database such as LDAP or another directory service to Zope. As long as it supports access through a Python API, any user database can be connected using a custom principal source component. Principal sources do not have to fulfill much other than being persistent classes (and the IPrincipalSource interface, of course).

On a last note it should be mentioned that the signup principal source implementation from above cheats in several ways, mostly for reasons of space. The most obvious and apparent cheat is that it mixes an authentication component (the principal source) with roles which are a concept of a certain security policy. That will make it impossible to use the principal source component without Zope's default policy, at least not without modifying it. If one is not aiming at this much pluggability, the provided solution is of course quite sufficient.

Summary

- User authentication is handled by an *authentication service*.
- A local (persistent) version of an authentication that supports different user database plugins is provided with the pluggableauth service.
- A pluggableauth instance can be added to site management folders like any other local component.
- A pluggableauth instance works like a container with its principal sources as contained objects; they also need to be persistent but can acquire their user data from any possible source, including external systems.

Flashback

In Zope 2, users are managed by *user folders*. These are containers that live inside regular content space folders and always have to be named acl_users. Zope's default user folder implementation stores users in the ZODB, but there exist many third party implementations that support other user databases. However, the actual user folder interface is scarcely documented. That has led to confusion and incompatabilities in the past. The interface continues to be undocumented, but a few pluggable user folder implementations have established themselves as quasi-standards, such as GRUF (Group User Folder), XUF (eXtensible User Folder), and PAS (Pluggable Authentication Service).

The advantages of the Zope 3 authentication system compared to Zope 2 are quite obvious. One can always implement a custom authentication service or, to save oneself from reinventing the wheel, use the pluggableauth service and custom principal sources. All those components are very well documented in interfaces.

Local authentication services are managed in site managers and thus benefit from the local component management infrastructure, as opposed to Zope 2 user folders being based in content space. Pluggableauth also brings the advantage that more than one (possibly external) user database can be used at the same site level because it is possible to add an unlimited amount of principal sources to a pluggableauth instance. In Zope 2 it is only possible to add one acl_users object per folder.

19.3 Principal metadata

As a final topic in this chapter we will look at associating additional data with principals, something that fits more into the category *user management* than *authentication*.

It is often required to know more about a principal than just its login name and title. Most principals represent real people with names, phone numbers, email addresses, etc. In short, there are many cases for associating metadata with principals.

The Principal Annotation Service

Of course, when we hear metadata mentioned, we immediately should think of annotations. The problem with principals is, though, that they are not necessarily stored in the ZODB. They can be globally defined in ZCML or come from a pluggableauth principal source or any other authentication service implementation. Since not all external user database systems support additional user metadata, especially arbitrary metadata, we often want to store principal metadata in the ZODB, even though the principal itself might not be a persistent object at all. This functionality is provided by the *Principal Annotation Service*.

The Principal Annotation Service is basically a local service that functions as a container for annotations objects (objects providing IAnnotations). The service can only occur in a local form since it obviously has to be persistent itself in order to store the annotation data. By default, an empty ZODB instance already contains an instance of the Principal Annotation Service in the site manager of the root folder. For most setups one such instance should be sufficient. After all, principal IDs (by which principals are identified for annotations) are globally unique. In any case, creating an instance of the service in a custom site is just as easy as adding any type of local component.

A short example of user metadata

As a short example of principal annotations, consider some very basic user information as described by IUserInfo in Example 19.3.1. This interface contains three fields: first name, last name, and email address. For the latter field, an additional constraint in form of a regular expression is given so that values entered for the email address actually have to be in the form of an email address. This saves us from having to write a special email field.

Example 19.3.1 Interface describing a simple user information (`interfaces.py`)

```
1   ...
2
3   import re
4   pattern = re.compile('^[0-9a-zA-Z_&.%+-]+@'
5                        '([0-9a-zA-Z]([0-9a-zA-Z-]*[0-9a-zA-Z])?\.)+'
6                        '[a-zA-Z]{2,6}$')
7
8   class IUserInfo(Interface):
9
10      first = TextLine(
11          title=_(u"First name"),
12          required=True
13          )
14
15      last = TextLine(
16          title=_(u"Last name"),
17          required=True
18          )
19
20      email = TextLine(
21          title=_(u"Email address"),
22          required=False,
23          constraint=pattern.match
24          )
```

Now we write an adapter for principals that provides our `IUserInfo`. This adapter works pretty much like any other annotation-based adapter we have written so far, except that it does not adapt its context to `IAnnotations`. Instead it invokes the Principal Annotation Service and acquires an annotations object from it. Example 19.3.2 shows the adapter implementation.

Example 19.3.2 User information adapter for principal objects (`userinfo.py`)

```
1   from persistent.dict import PersistentDict
2   from zope.interface import implements
3   from zope.app import zapi
4   from worldcookery.interfaces import IUserInfo
5
6   KEY = "worldcookery.userinfo"
7
```

```
8    def getterAndSetter(key):
9        def getter(self):
10           return self.mapping[key]
11       def setter(self, obj):
12           self.mapping[key] = obj
13       return getter, setter
14
15   class UserInfo(object):
16       implements(IUserInfo)
17
18       def __init__(self, context):
19           self.context = context
20           service = zapi.getService(zapi.servicenames.PrincipalAnnotation)
21           annotations = service.getAnnotations(context)
22           mapping = annotations.get(KEY)
23           if mapping is None:
24               blank = {'first': u'', 'last': u'', 'email': u''}
25               mapping = annotations[KEY] = PersistentDict(blank)
26           self.mapping = mapping
27
28       first = property(*getterAndSetter('first'))
29       last = property(*getterAndSetter('last'))
30       email = property(*getterAndSetter('email'))
```

20 – 21.   This adapter looks like pretty much like any other annotations-based
adapter we have written so far. The only difference is the way the
IAnnotations object is acquired. Usually we just adapted the context
object to that interface. In this case, however, we acquire it from the
Principal Annotation service.

Testing

As usual we can give the adapter a quick test drive on the interactive interpreter shell. Before we can start, though, we need to set up the Principal
Annotation Service. The first step is to define the service type:

```
>>> from zope.app import zapi
>>> from zope.app.principalannotation.interfaces \
...        import IPrincipalAnnotationService
>>> service_service = zapi.getGlobalServices()
>>> service_service.defineService(
...        zapi.servicenames.PrincipalAnnotation,
...        IPrincipalAnnotationService)
```

The second step is to register the service. The Principal Annotation Service
is a local service because it needs to store data in the ZODB. Therefore we
need set up a site and create a service instance within its site manager:

```
>>> from zope.app.tests import setup
>>> from zope.app.principalannotation import \
...         PrincipalAnnotationService
>>> site = setup.placefulSetUp(site=True)
>>> service = setup.addService(site.getSiteManager(),
...         zapi.servicenames.PrincipalAnnotation,
...         PrincipalAnnotationService())
```

Now we can start. As a principal object, we simply use a dummy imple-mentation; all it really needs is an ID so that the service can uniquely identify it:

```
>>> class DummyPrincipal:
...         id = "sloopy_joe"
>>> sloppy_joe = DummyPrincipal()
```

With this principal object we invoke the IUserInfo adapter and store some user metadata on it:

```
>>> from worldcookery.userinfo import UserInfo
>>> info = UserInfo(sloppy_joe)
>>> info.first = u"Sloppy"
>>> info.last = u"Joe"
>>> info.email = u"sloppyjoe@usafood.com"
```

Not surprisingly, retrieving the information works just as well:

```
>>> info.first, info.last, info.email
(u'Sloppy', u'Joe', u'sloppyjoe@usafood.com')
```

The service instance has stored our data in the IAnnotations object:

```
>>> service.hasAnnotations(sloppy_joe)
True
>>> annotations = service.getAnnotations(sloppy_joe)
>>> items = list(
...         annotations['worldcookery.userinfo'].items())
>>> items.sort()
>>> tuple(items)
(('email', u'sloppyjoe@usafood.com'), ('first',
u'Sloppy'), ('last', u'Joe'))
```

Like many other interpreter sessions, this one was also added as a doctest and can be found at `userinfo.txt` for reference.

Now that we have assured the adapter works, there is not much left to do other than configuring it in ZCML. Like other annotations-based adapters, we configure this one also as a trusted adapter so that we can make security declarations about the adapter class itself. See Example 19.3.3.

Example 19.3.3 Configuring the principal annotations adapter (`configure.zcml`)

```
1   ...
2   <adapter
3       for="zope.app.security.interfaces.IPrincipal"
4       provides=".interfaces.IUserInfo"
5       factory=".userinfo.UserInfo"
6       trusted="true"
7       />
8
9   <content class=".userinfo.UserInfo">
10    <require
11        permission="worldcookery.ManageUserInfo"
12        interface=".interfaces.IUserInfo"
13        set_schema=".interfaces.IUserInfo"
14        />
15   </content>
16   ...
```

Browser configuration

In order to configure an automatically generated form for editing user information on any kind of principal, we just add the following directive to the browser configuration file (`browser/configure.zcml`):

```
<browser:editform
    for="zope.app.security.interfaces.IPrincipal"
    schema="worldcookery.interfaces.IUserInfo"
    label="User information"
    name="userinfo.html"
    menu="zmi_views" title="User information"
    permission="worldcookery.ManageUserInfo"
    />
```

Note that here we register the form *for* IPrincipal because those are the objects that the view should be registered for. However, the *schema* that principals are supposed to be edited by is a different one; it is our IUserInfo schema. What happens is that the form machinery adapts objects to the specified schema before updating the data with values from the form. Most of the time that is not necessary because the object that is to be edited already provides the schema. For example, our recipe objects provide IRecipe which is also the basis for the generated form.

In this case, of course, we want principals to be adapted to IUserInfo because we want our annotation adapter to be used.

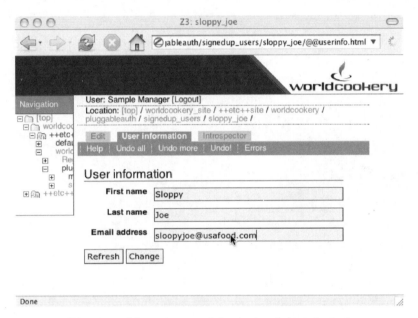

Fig. 19.5. Managing user information for a principal.

Doing more with user metadata

The example presented in this chapter can only be considered a short introduction to managing user metadata. We have not even started talking about possible uses cases of the data that we can now store in principal annotations.

One can make a lot of use of a principal's email address, for example for sending an email when the password has been forgotten. Or in Chapter 15, we wrote a small email notification framework with subscription capabilities. This framework could be modified so that authenticated principals do not have to enter their email address; instead it would be taken from their annotations. Finally, the sign up forms that were developed in this chapter could be extended with the fields from IUserInfo so that users signing up already provide their metadata along with the login information.

Summary

- It is often desirable to associate additional (meta)data with principals.
- Principal objects do not have to be persistent since they can come from any sort of user database, for example by means of a principal source.
- The Principal Annotation Service allows one to store principal metadata as annotations in the ZODB, even though the principal object itself might not be a ZODB-persistent object.

Part IV

Appendices

1

ZAPI Reference

The `zope.app.zapi` package combines essential Zope functionality in the form of easy-to-use functions from different packages. This includes basic functions like the ones from the Component Architecture (`zope.component` package) as well as Zope application server specific ones, such as functions from the traversing and location machinery.

Using `zapi` not only shortens the list of long imports in Zope code. It also usually makes code easier to read.

ZAPI conventions

Many `zapi` functions follow certain conventions. You will find them easier to use when you know the conventions. The following list gives an overview:

- Many functions that acquire adapters, views or other types of components are named *getComponent*. When look up fails, these will usually raise `ComponentLookupError`. To the majority of those functions, a *queryComponent* pendant exists that performs the same task but accepts a *default* parameter (which defaults to None). When the lookup fails, this function will not raise an error but return the default value.
- Most functions from `zope.component` accept a *context* parameter. It allows the caller to influence in which the component lookup shall be carried out. When provided, the context value will be adapted to `IServiceService` and the corresponding service will be retrieved from the resulting service service.
  Within an application running atop the Zope application server, it is usually not necessary to specify this context. The nearest service service will be set during traversal, meaning when traversal encounters sites, it will remember the most local site manager and use that for service lookup.
- Some components can occur in named flavours, such as named utilities, named adapters, named views, etc. Their unnamed flavours are always registered with an *empty string* for their name, not (as one might think)

with None. Therefore, the *name* argument on the corresponding lookup methods usually defaults to u' ', meaning it will by default acquire un-named components.

absoluteURL

Computes an absolute URL of an object.

Synopsis

absoluteURL (*object*, *request*)

Origin

zope.app.traversing

Description

absoluteURL computes an absolute URL of the given *object* in the context of the *request*. A TypeError is raised if the URL cannot be computed, for example because of unsufficient location information.

Examples

A call to absoluteURL,

```
>>> zapi.absoluteURL(obj, request)
```

is equivalent to the following view lookup:

```
>>> str(zapi.getViewProviding(obj, IAbsoluteURL,
...                                  request))
```

See also

getPath

canonicalPath

Returns a canonical absolute path for a given path or object.

Synopsis

canonicalPath (*path_or_object*)

Origin

zope.app.traversing

Description

If passed an object, canonicalPath will return its absolute physical path,
exactly like getPath. If passed a string or unicode object, it will treat it as
an object path with / separators and return a normalized version, meaning
it will resolve . and .. segments.

Examples

When passed an object, canonicalPath works just like getPath (see
getPath example):

```
>>> zapi.canonicalPath(son)
u'/father/son'
```

When passed a string or unicode object, it normalizes the path:

```
>>> zapi.canonicalPath('/foo/.././bar')
u'/bar'
```

See also

getPath, joinPath

createObject

Creates an object using a factory.

Synopsis

createObject (*context, name, *args, **kw,*)

Origin

zope.component

Description

createObject invokes a factory named *name* to create a new object. It
passes **args* and ***kw* to the factory.

context can be used to make the underlying service lookup context-
dependent. This parameter being at the beginning of the parameter list might
suggest that it is more important here than in all other Component Architecture functions. The actual reason is that it cannot be an optional one after
all other arguments because of the variable parameter length (**args* and
**kw) of the function. As always, *context* seldomly makes sense in regular
Zope web applications. One can safely pass None for it.

Examples

A call to createObject,

```
>>> zapi.createObject('Recipe')
```

can always be written as an explicit factory lookup:

```
>>> zapi.getUtility(IFactory, 'Recipe')()
```

See also

getFactoriesFor, getFactoryInterfaces

getAdapter, queryAdapter

Acquires a named adapter for a given object.

Synopsis

getAdapter (*object*, *interface*, *name*, *context=None*)
queryAdapter (*object*, *interface*, *name*, *default=None*,
context=None)

Origin

zope.component

Description

getAdapter looks up a named adapter for *object* providing *interface*.
Note that regular (unnamed) adapters should be acquired by calling the
interface directly.

   context can be used to make the underlying service lookup context-
dependent.

   If the adapter is not found, ComponentLookupError is raised. query-
Adapter works like getAdapter except that it accepts a *default* param-
eter whose value is returned when the adapter lookup fails. This defaults to
None.

Examples

In Zope, for example, named adapters that are not multi-adapters are used
for path traversal. The following retrieves the adapter that is responsible for
++acquire++ traversal:

>>> **zapi.getAdapter(obj, IPathAdapter, 'acquire')**

See also

getMultiAdapter

getAdapterInContext, queryAdapterInContext

Acquires an unnamed adapter for a given object.

Synopsis

getAdapterInContext (*object, interface, context*)
queryAdapterInContext (*object, interface, context default=*
None,)

Origin

zope.component

Description

getAdapterInContext looks up an unnamed adapter for *object* providing *interface* in the context of *context*. Note that regular adapter lookup that does not require a certain context should be done by calling the interface directly.

Like the adapter look up through interface calling, getAdapterInContext first checks whether *object* has a __conforms__ method. If it has, the adapter look up will not be performed and instead this method will be called with *interface* as parameter and its return value is returned.

If the adapter is not found, ComponentLookupError is raised. queryAdapterInContext works like getAdapterInContext except that it accepts a *default* parameter whose value is returned when the adapter lookup fails. This defaults to None.

Examples

In regular Zope web applications, getAdapterInContext has no application since local component look up is influenced during traversal and not by adapting a context to IServiceService.

See also

getAdapter

getAllUtilitiesRegisteredFor

Returns all utilities registered for an interface.

Synopsis

getAllUtilitiesRegisteredFor (*interface*, *context=None*)

Origin

zope.component

Description

getAllUtilitiesRegisteredFor finds and returns *all* utilities that are
registered for *interface*. This includes utilities that are registered for more
specific interfaces than *interface* and named utilities that override other
named utilities. In short, getAllUtilitiesRegisteredFor returns all
utilities, whether they have been overridden or not. The returned value is an
iterable.

Examples

getAllUtilitiesRegisteredFor has its application mainly when utilities are used like event subscribers, for example when catalog index utilities have to be invoked upon an object event. Since this functionality is not
present in Zope X3.0, it is not being used.

See also

getUtilitiesFor

getDefaultViewName, queryDefaultViewName

Returns the name of the default view for a given object.

Synopsis

getDefaultViewName (*object*, *request*, *context=None*)
queryDefaultViewName (*object*, *request*, *default=None*,
context=None)

Origin

zope.component

Description

getDefaultViewName returns the name of the default view for *object* and the request type of *request*. The request must provide IPresentationRequest. Within the Zope application server, this is usually index. html for browser requests but can be changed individually for different interfaces through ZCML.

context can be used to make the underlying service lookup context-dependent.

If a default view name cannot be found, NotFoundError is raised. queryDefaultViewName works like getDefaultViewName except that it accepts a *default* parameter whose value is returned when the lookup fails. This defaults to None.

Examples

The default view name for objects in the context of a browser request usually is index.html:

```
>>> zapi.getDefaultViewName(obj, request)
u'index.html'
```

See also

defaultView and browser:defaultView ZCML directives

getFactoriesFor

Returns factories that can make objects that provide a certain interface.

Synopsis

getFactoriesFor (*interface*, *context=None*)

Origin

zope.component

Description

getFactoriesFor returns all factories that instantiate objects of a certain kind. In other words, objects created with these factories will always provide *interface*. The returned value is an iterable wherein each item is a (name, factory) tuple.

context can be used to make the underlying service lookup context-dependent.

Examples

You might remember from Chapter 12 that Zope has a small framework for rendering formatted text as HTML. Renderers are implemented as views for certain source types which can be created using appropriate factories. All source types have the base interface ISource. The following example retrieves all factories that create ISource objects:

```
>>> from zope.app.renderer import ISource
>>> from pprint import pprint
>>> pprint(list(zapi.getFactoriesFor(ISource)))
[(u'zope.source.rest', <zope.app.renderer.SourceFactory
object at 0x2cf6250>),
 (u'zope.source.plaintext',
  <zope.app.renderer.SourceFactory object at 0x2ca8e50>),
  (u'zope.source.stx', <zope.app.renderer.SourceFactory
object at 0x2cb3710>)]
```

See also

createObject, getFactoryInterfaces

getFactoryInterfaces

Returns interfaces that will be provided by objects created by a factory.

Synopsis

getFactoryInterfaces (*name, context=None*)

Origin

zope.component

Description

getFactoryInterfaces returns an iterable of interfaces that will be provided by those objects that are created with a certain factory. The method is quite obsolete since factories are regular utilities and provide that information themselves.

getFactoryInterfaces is not to be confused with getFactoriesFor. Basically, the former returns what instances created by a certain factory will provide while the latter returns those factories that create instances providing a certain interface.

Examples

A call to getFactoryInterfaces,

```
>>> zapi.getFactoryInterfaces('Recipe')
```

can and should always be written as an explicit retrieval of the factory utility:

```
>>> zapi.getUtility(IFactory, 'Recipe').getInterfaces()
```

See also

createObject, getFactoriesFor

getGlobalService

Looks up a global service.

Synopsis

```
getGlobalService ( name )
```

Origin

```
zope.component
```

Description

getGlobalService looks up a service with the *global* service manager (also known as the service service). All other rules and remarks of getService apply.

Examples

Using getGlobalService,

```
>>> zapi.getGlobalService(zapi.servicenames.Utilities)
```

is equivalent to but shorter than acquiring the global service manager and getting the service from it:

```
>>> service_service = zapi.getGlobalServices()
>>> service_service.getService(
...      zapi.servicenames.Utilities)
```

See also

getGlobalServices, getService, servicenames

getGlobalServices

Returns the global service service.

Synopsis

getGlobalServices()

Origin

zope.component

Description

getGlobalServices returns the global service manager, also known as
the service service, regardless of which local service manager might be active
due to traversal.

Examples

getGlobalServices can be used whenever a global service is to be retrieved explicitly. This is used during ZCML processing, for example, where
all components are to be registered as global components.

For example, retrieving the global utilities service explicitly,

```
>>> service_service = zapi.getGlobalServices()
>>> service_service.getService(
...         zapi.servicenames.Utilities)
```

is equivalent to using getGlobalService:

```
>>> zapi.getGlobalService(zapi.servicenames.Utilities)
```

See also

getGlobalService, getService, getServices, servicenames

getMultiAdapter, queryMultiAdapter

Acquires a multi-adapter for given combination of objects.

Synopsis

getMultiAdapter (*objects, interface, name=u' '*, *context=None*)
queryMultiAdapter (*objects, interface, name=u' '*,
default=None, context=None)

Origin

zope.component

Description

getMultiAdapter adapts a combination of objects given in the *object*
tuple to *interface*. An optional *name* can be given to look up a named
multi-adapter. Unnamed adapters have an empty name.

   context can be used to make the underlying service lookup context-
dependent.

   If no adapter is found, ComponentLookupError is raised. query-
MultiAdapter works like getMultiAdapter except that it accepts
a *default* parameter whose value is returned when the adapter lookup
fails. This defaults to None.

Examples

Views can be understood as named multi-adapters since they adapt both
an object and a request to some presentation interface, e.g. IBrowserPub-
lisher or IInputWidget. In fact, views are implemented that way in
Zope X3.1. In this version, the line

```
>>> zapi.getView(object, u'index.html', request)
```

could be equivalently written as:

```
>>> zapi.getMultiAdapter((object, request), Interface,
...                       name=u'index.html')
```

Equally, multi-views are simply multi-adapters with more than two objects being adapted. In Zope X3.1, the example from getMultiView,

```
>>> zapi.getMultiView((field, field.vocabulary),
...                        request, IInputWidget)
```

can be equivalently written in the following form:

```
>>> zapi.getMultiAdapter((field, field.vocabulary,
...                        request), IInputWidget)
```

See also

getMultiView

getMultiView, queryMultiView

Acquires a multi-view for given combination of objects.

Synopsis

getMultiView (*objects*, *request*, *name=u''*, *providing= Interface*, *context=None*)
queryMultiView (*objects*, *request*, *name=u''*, *providing= Interface*, *default=None*, *context=None*)

Origin

`zope.component`

Description

`getMultiView` looks up a multi-view for a combination of objects given in the *object* tuple. Only views of the request type of *request* will be looked up. The request must provide `IPresentationRequest`.

The look up can optionally also take into account an interface that the view must provide (*provides* parameter) and/or a name that it was registered under (*name* parameter).

context can be used to make the underlying service lookup context-dependent.

If no view is found, `ComponentLookupError` is raised. `queryMultiView` works like `getMultiView` except that it accepts a *default* parameter whose value is returned when the view lookup fails. This defaults to None.

Examples

Look up an input widget for a `Choice` field in combination with its vocabulary:

```
>>> zapi.getMultiView((field, field.vocabulary),
...                       request, IInputWidget)
```

See also

`getView`, `getMultiAdapter`

getName, name

Returns the name of an object.

Synopsis

getName (*object*)
name (*object*)

Origin

zope.app.traversing

Description

getName returns the name of an object. It does so by adapting the object to
IPhysicallyLocatable. This adaption works out-of-the-box with objects
providing ILocation or objects that are location proxied. If no adapter can
be found, TypeError is raised.

name is an alias for getName.

Examples

getName can only retrieve the name of objects that can be adapted to
IPhysicallyLocatable:

```
>>> from zope.app.location import Location
>>> obj = Location()
>>> obj.__name__ = u"location"
>>> zapi.getName(obj)
u'location'
```

The failing adaption raises a TypeError otherwise:

```
>>> obj = object()
>>> zapi.getName(obj)
Traceback (most recent call last):
...
TypeError: ('Could not adapt', <object object at
0x3544a0>,
            <InterfaceClass zope.app.traversing
.interfaces.IPhysicallyLocatable>)
```

See also

getPath

getParent

Returns an object's parent.

Synopsis

getParent (*object*)

Origin

zope.app.traversing

Description

getParent returns the parent of *object* that is located in an object hierarchy, in other words, it can be adapted to IPhysicallyLocatable. In case *object* is the root object of the hierarchy, None is returned. If *object* cannot be adapted to IPhysicallyLocatable, TypeError is raised.

For objects using Zope's location machinery (providing ILocation or IContained, either themselves or by proxy), getParent will simply return the __parent__ attribute.

Examples

For locatable objects in regular Zope web applications, a call to getParent,

```
>>> zapi.getParent(obj)
```

is equivalent to simply working with the __parent__ attribute:

```
>>> obj.__parent__
```

See also

getParents, getRoot

getParents

Returns an object's parents.

Synopsis

getParents (*object*)

Origin

zope.app.traversing

Description

getParents returns a list of *object*'s parent objects. *object* needs to be located in an object hierarchy, in other words, it must be adapted to IPhysicallyLocatable. In case *object* is the root object of the hierarchy, an empty list is returned. If *object* cannot be adapted to IPhysicallyLocatable or if the location hierarchy does not go all the way up to the root object (an object providing IContainmentRoot), TypeError is raised.

Examples

Imagine three objects in a location hierarchy with grandfather mimicking the root object:

```
>>> from zope.interface import directlyProvides
>>> from zope.app.location import Location, locate
>>> from zope.app.traversing.interfaces import \
...     IContainmentRoot
>>> son = Location()
>>> father = Location()
>>> grandfather = Location()
>>>
>>> locate(son, father, name=u"son")
>>> locate(father, grandfather, name=u"father")
>>> directlyProvides(grandfather, IContainmentRoot)
>>>
>>> zapi.getParents(son) == [father, grandfather]
True
```

See also

getParent, getRoot

getPath

Returns the physical path of an object.

Synopsis

getPath (*object*)

Origin

zope.app.traversing

Description

getPath returns the physical path of an object. It does so by adapting the object to IPhysicallyLocatable. This adaption works out-of-the-box with objects providing ILocation or objects that are location proxied. If no adapter can be found or the location hierarchy does not go all the way up to the root object (an object providing IContainmentRoot), TypeError is raised.

Examples

Imagine three objects in a location hierarchy with grandfather mimicking the root object:

```
>>> from zope.interface import directlyProvides
>>> from zope.app.location import Location, locate
>>> from zope.app.traversing.interfaces import \
...     IContainmentRoot
>>> son = Location()
>>> father = Location()
>>> grandfather = Location()
>>>
>>> locate(son, father, name=u"son")
>>> locate(father, grandfather, name=u"father")
>>> directlyProvides(grandfather, IContainmentRoot)
>>>
>>> zapi.getPath(son)
u'/father/son'
```

See also

absoluteURL, canonicalPath, joinPath, getName

getResource, queryResource

Acquires a named resource for a given request.

Synopsis

getResource (*name*, *request*, *providing=Interface*,
context=None)
queryResource (*name*, *request*, *default=None*,
providing=Interface, *context=None*)

Origin

zope.component

Description

getResource looks up a named resource for the request type of *request*.
The request must provide IPresentationRequest. If the *providing*
parameter is specified, only resources providing that interface will be found.

 context can be used to make the underlying service lookup context-
dependent.

 If the resource is not found, ComponentLookupError is raised. query-
Resource works like getResource except that it accepts a *default* pa-
rameter whose value is returned when the view lookup fails. This defaults to
None.

Examples

```
>>> zapi.getResource(u'worldcookery.css', request)
```

getRoot

Returns the root object in a location hierarchy.

Synopsis

getRoot (*object*)

Origin

zope.app.traversing

Description

When an object is located in an object hierarchy, in other words, when it can be adapted to IPhysicallyLocatable, getRoot traverses back to the parent of the hierarchy (the object providing IContainmentRoot and returns this object. If the object cannot be adapted or or the location hierarchy does not go all the way up to the root object, TypeError is raised.

For objects contained in Zope containers within regular Zope web applications, getRoot will return the root folder of the ZODB instance the objects are stored in.

Examples

Imagine three objects in a location hierarchy with grandfather mimicking the root object:

```
>>> from zope.interface import directlyProvides
>>> from zope.app.location import Location, locate
>>> from zope.app.traversing.interfaces import \
...        IContainmentRoot
>>> son = Location()
>>> father = Location()
>>> grandfather = Location()
>>>
>>> locate(son, father, name=u"son")
>>> locate(father, grandfather, name=u"father")
>>> directlyProvides(grandfather, IContainmentRoot)
>>>
>>> zapi.getRoot(son) is grandfather
True
```

See also

getParents

getService

Looks up a service.

Synopsis

getService (*name*, *context=None*)

Origin

zope.component

Description

getService looks up a service with the current service manager (also known as service service). If the *context* parameter is used, then that value will be adapted to IServiceService and used as service manager. Fallback is always the global service manager.

Unlike other components which are registered and looked up by interface, services are looked up by well-defined names (which represent interfaces, though). It is good practice to use the service name constants from the servicenames submodule instead of using a string literal.

There exists *no* queryService function. Services are always available everywhere. If an application fails because a service lookup fails, there is either something wrong with the application or the service setup. One can always assume that services are present.

Examples

It is good practice to use service name constants from servicenames,

```
>>> zapi.getService(zapi.servicenames.Utilities)
```

which is equivalent but more elegant than using string literals:

```
>>> zapi.getService("Utilities")
```

See also

getGlobalService, getGlobalServices, getServiceDefinitions, getServices, servicenames

getServiceDefinitions

Returns a mapping of service type definitions.

Synopsis

getServiceDefinitions (*context=None*)

Origin

zope.component

Description

Even though service functionality is described by an interface, services are registered and looked up by well-defined names. The Component Architecture keeps the mapping between service names and the interface that describes the service functionality in the *service definitions* which are returned by getServiceDefinitions as a list of item tuples as known from dictionaries.

Examples

Without any service setup, there is only the global service service available:

```
>>> zapi.getServiceDefinitions()
[('Services', <InterfaceClass zope.component.interfaces
.IServiceService>)]
```

If we, however, set up some services, for example through PlaclessSetup, the mapping will be populated:

```
>>> from zope.app.tests.placelesssetup import setUp
>>> setUp()
>>> from pprint import pprint
>>> pprint(zapi.getServiceDefinitions())
[('Services', <InterfaceClass zope.component.interfaces
.IServiceService>),
 ('Presentation',
  <InterfaceClass zope.component.interfaces
.IPresentationService>),
 ('Adapters', <InterfaceClass zope.component.interfaces
.IAdapterService>),
 ('Utilities', <InterfaceClass zope.component
.interfaces.IUtilityService>)]
```

See also

serviceType ZCML directive

getServices

Returns the global service service.

Synopsis

getServices (*context=None*)

Origin

zope.component

Description

getServices returns the current service manager, also known as the service service. Usually it is an application-defined policy that determines which service manager is the current one. Fallback is always the global service manager.

To manually influence which service manager should be returned, one can pass a value for the optional *context* parameter. This will then be adapted to IServiceService and the adapter will be returned.

Examples

getServices can be used whenever a global service is to be retrieved explicitly. This is used during ZCML processing, for example, where all components are to be registered as global components.

Usually, retrieving the service manager explicitly,

```
>>> service_service = zapi.getServices()
>>> service_service.getService(
...        zapi.servicenames.Utilities)
```

is pointless because one can simply look up the service directly:

```
>>> zapi.getService(zapi.servicenames.Utilities)
```

Thus, getService is often used when programmatically changing service registration and the like. This obviously only makes sense for test setups and ZCML directive handlers. In regular applications, ZCML configuration should be used to register services.

See also

getGlobalService, getGlobalServices, getService, servicenames

getUtilitiesFor

Returns named utilities for a given interface.

Synopsis

getUtilitiesFor (*interface, context=None*)

Origin

zope.component

Description

getUtilitiesFor returns an iterable of named utilities registered for a certain *interface*. Elements in the iteration are (name, utility) pairs.

getUtilitiesFor differs from getAllUtilitiesRegisteredFor in subtle ways. First, getUtilitiesFor only finds utilities that were registered for exactly the interface that is passed as a parameter to the function. Second, a utility that was overridden by another utility in both interface and name does not appear in the iteration returned by getUtilitiesFor. It returns one utility per name and interface. Last, getAllUtilities-RegisteredFor only returns utility instances, no names, since it is only interested in their subscription status, not by which name they were registered.

Examples

getUtilitiesFor obviously makes only sense for named utilities, not for singletons. Common named utilities are roles as defined by the default Zope security policy:

```
>>> from zope.app.securitypolicy.interfaces import IRole
>>> from pprint import pprint
>>> pprint(list(zapi.getUtilitiesFor(IRole)))
[(u'zope.Manager', <zope.app.securitypolicy.role.Role
object at 0x30ffc50>),
 (u'zope.Member', <zope.app.securitypolicy.role.Role
object at 0x30ffe90>),
 (u'zope.Anonymous', <zope.app.securitypolicy.role.Role
object at 0x30f9190>)]
```

See also

getAllUtilitiesRegisteredFor, getUtility

getUtility, queryUtility

Looks up a utility.

Synopsis

getUtility (*interface, name='', context=None*)
queryUtility (*interface, name='', default=None*
context=None)

Origin

zope.component

Description

getUtility acquires a utility providing *interface*. An optional *name*
can be given when a named utility should be looked up. *context* can be
used to make the underlying service lookup context-dependent.

If a utility cannot be found, ComponentLookupError is raised. query-
Utility works like getUtility except that it accepts a *default* param-
eter whose value is returned when the view lookup fails. This defaults to
None.

Examples

Look up a regular (singleton) utility:

```
>>> zapi.getUtility(IKitchenTools)
```

Look up a named utility:

```
>>> zapi.getUtility(IPermission,
...                 name='worldcookery.EditRecipes')
```

See also

getAllUtilitiesRegisteredFor, getUtilitiesFor

getView, queryView

Acquires a named view for a given object.

Synopsis

```
getView ( object, name, request, providing=Interface,
context=None )
queryView ( object, name, request, default=None,
providing=Interface, context=None )
```

Origin

```
zope.component
```

Description

getView looks up a named view for *object* for the request type of *request*. The request must provide IPresentationRequest.

If the *providing* parameter is specified, only views providing that interface will be found. *context* can be used to make the underlying service lookup context-dependent.

If the view is not found, ComponentLookupError is raised. queryView works like getView except that it accepts a *default* parameter whose value is returned when the view lookup fails. This defaults to None.

Examples

Look up a regular view, e.g. a browser page:

```
>>> zapi.getView(obj, u'index.html', request)
```

Using the default functionality of queryView:

```
>>> zapi.queryView(obj, u'index.html', request,
...                 default=fallback_view)
```

Look up a view providing an interface, e.g. the absolute URL view:

```
>>> zapi.queryView(obj, u'', request,
...                 providing=IAbsoluteURL)
```

See also

```
getViewProviding
```

getViewProviding, queryViewProviding

Acquires an unnamed view providing an interface.

Synopsis

```
getView ( object, providing, request, context=None )
queryView ( object, providing, request, default=None,
context=None )
```

Origin

```
zope.component
```

Description

getViewProviding looks up an unnamed view for *object* for the request type of *request*. Only views providing the interface *providing* will be found. The request must provide IPresentationRequest. *context* can be used to make the underlying service lookup context-dependent.

If the view is not found, ComponentLookupError is raised. query-ViewProviding works like getViewProviding except that it accepts a *default* parameter whose value is returned when the view lookup fails. This defaults to None.

Examples

A typical example for a view providing an interface are widgets:

```
>>> zapi.getViewProviding(field, IInputWidget, request)
```

Any call to getViewProviding can also be exchanged for one to getView. For example, the one above could be equivalently written as:

```
>>> zapi.getView(field, u'', request,
...                 providing=IInputWidget)
```

Notice how an empty string is passed for the *name*.

See also

```
getView
```

isinstance

Checks whether an object object is an instance of a class.

Synopsis

isinstance (*object*, *cls*,)

Origin

zope.security

Description

Like the isinstance function that is built into Python, zapi.isinstance checks whether *object* is an instance of a class *cls* and returns either True or False. The difference to the built-in version is that this also works when *object* is security proxied.

Examples

isinstance works like its built-in pendant when dealing with regular objects, e.g. an integer:

```
>>> zapi.isinstance(2, int)
True
```

In case an object is security proxied, the built-in isinstance function fails. zapi.isinstance returns the expected value:

```
>>> from worldcookery.recipe import Recipe
>>> pudding = Recipe()
>>> from zope.security.proxy import ProxyFactory
>>> wrapped_pudding = ProxyFactory(pudding)
>>> wrapped_pudding
<worldcookery.recipe.Recipe object at 0x35cd70>
>>> type(wrapped_pudding)
<type 'zope.security._proxy._Proxy'>
>>> __builtins__.isinstance(wrapped_pudding, Recipe)
False
>>> zapi.isinstance(wrapped_pudding, Recipe)
True
```

See also

__builtins__.isinstance

joinPath

Joins path segments or parts of paths.

Synopsis

joinPath (*path*, **args*)

Origin

zope.app.traversing

Description

Join two or more path segments or parts of paths together to one path. *path* should not end in / (unless it is the root element itself). Path segments that are to be added should not start or end with / either. They may, however, contain . and .. to indicate the current or parent location relative to the previous segment. Overall, its behaviour is very similar to the one of os.path.join from the Python standard library.

Examples

Join multiple path segments:

```
>>> zapi.joinPath('/foo', '..', './bar')
u'/bar'
```

See also

canonicalPath, getPath

queryType

Returns the nearest type interface for an object.

Synopsis

queryType (*object*)

Origin

zope.app.interface

Description

Often, interfaces are used to express types. Then these interfaces provide
an additional type interface. For example, content type interfaces provide
IContentType. For a given object *object*, queryType returns the nearest provided interface of a certain type. None is returned if the object does
not provide an interface of the given type.

Examples

The most prominent example of interface types are content types. Without a
designated content type interface, recipes object do not have a content type:

```
>>> from zope.app.content.interfaces import IContentType
>>> from worldcookery.interfaces import IRecipe
>>> from worldcookery.recipe import Recipe
>>> zapi.queryType(Recipe(), IContentType)
```

If we turn IRecipe into a content type (meaning, IRecipe will now provide
IContentType), a recipe's content type will now be IRecipe:

```
>>> from zope.interface import directlyProvides
>>> directlyProvides(IRecipe, IContentType)
>>> zapi.queryType(Recipe(), IContentType)
<InterfaceClass worldcookery.interfaces.IRecipe>
```

Another application of interface types are browser tools, where tool interfaces provide IToolType.

See also

Chapter 5

servicenames

Service name constants.

Origin

`zope.app`

Description

Unlike other components, services are looked up by well-defined names.
`servicenames` provides access to constants containing these service names.
It is considered good practice to use these constants instead of the string literals themselves.

The stock Zope X3.0 knows the following service names:

- `Adapters`
- `Authentication`
- `BrowserMenu` (the browser menu service has been removed from Zope X3.1 in favour of an adapter-based implementation)
- `ErrorLogging`
- `Presentation` (the presentation service has been removed from Zope X3.1 as views are implemented as multi-adapters).
- `PrincipalAnnotation`
- `Services`
- `Utilities`

Examples

Using `servicename` constants,

```
>>> zapi.getService(zapi.servicenames.Utilities)
```

is equivalent to but more elegant than using string literals:

```
>>> zapi.getService("Utilities")
```

See also

`getService`

subscribers

Retrieves subscribers for a given set of objects.

Synopsis

`subscribers ( required, provided, context=None )`

Origin

`zope.component`

Description

`subscribers` retrieves all subscribers for a given set of *objects* that provide the interface specified as *provided*

Subscribers are managed within the adapter service. They are sometimes also called subscription adapters because they adapt a set of objects (which can also be a single object) to an interface. The difference with regular adapters is that there can only ever be one adapter that adapts an object to an interface, whereas there can many subscribers at the same time.

context can be used to make the underlying service lookup context-dependent.

Examples

Subscribers are mostly used for the event system. An event subscriber is basically a subscription adapter that subscribes to one interface or a combination of interfaces (e.g. for object events) and provides None. Therefore, the typical way of invoking event subscribers,

```
>>> from zope.event import noitfy
>>> notify(event)
```

can in regular Zope 3 web applications also be written as:

```
>>> for subscriber in zapi.subscribers((event,), None):
>>>         pass
```

See also

`subscriber` ZCML directive

traverse

Traverses path relative to an object.

Synopsis

traverse (*object*, *path*, *default=None*, *request=None*)

Origin

zope.app.traversing

Description

traverse traverses a path with path segments separated by / relative to the object *object*. *path* is a string or unicode object containing the path. *request* should be passed when invoking from presentation code. traverse will then also take traversal *views* into account instead of just traversal *adapters*. If a *default* value is given, it will be returned when the path cannot be traversed. Otherwise, NotFoundError will be raised.

Examples

Traversing a regular object path:

```
>>> zapi.traverse(folder, u'recipes/italian/tiramisu')
```

Traverse and take presentation-specific traversal adapters into account, such as ++skin++, @@, etc.:

```
>>> zapi.traverse(site,
...      u'++skin++WorldCookery/@@index.html', request)
```

See also

traverseName

traverseName

Traverses a single step relative to an object.

Synopsis

traverseName (*object*, *name*, *default=None*, *traversable=None*, *request=None*)

Origin

zope.app.traversing

Description

traverseName traverses a single step relative to the object *object*. *name* is a string or unicode object containing the name of the step to be traversed. One can optionally pass an object providing ITraversable for the *traversable* parameter which will be used to carry out the actual traversal. Otherwise the object will be adapted to ITraversable.

request should be passed when invoking from presentation code. traverseName will then also take traversal *views* into account instead of just traversal *adapters*. If a *default* value is given, it will be returned when the path cannot be traverseNamed. Otherwise, NotFoundError will be raised.

Examples

Traversing a regular object path:

```
>>> zapi.traverseName(folder, u'subfolder')
```

Traverse and take presentation-specific traversal adapters into account, such as ++skin++, @@, etc.:

```
>>> zapi.traverseName(obj, u'@@index.html', request)
```

See also

traverse

UserError

Exception for error messages that should be displayed to users.

Synopsis

```
UserError ( *args )
```

Origin

```
zope.app.exceptions
```

Description

By default, Zope will display exceptions that were not intended to be displayed to the user as simple *system errors*. UserError is an exception that can be raised whenever the current course of the application has been disturbed so that the transaction should be aborted, but the error message should still be shown to the user. Typical use cases are invalid input values provided in forms or other user-invoked errors.

Examples

Since the messages passed to user errors are displayed to the user, one should always mark them as i18n messages:

```
>>> from zope.i18nmessageid import MessageIDFactory
>>> _ = MessageIDFactory('worldcookery')
>>> raise zapi.UserError(
...        _(u"You provided an invalid value."))
```

ztapi

Like the `zapi` module combines the most common Zope APIs and helper functions in one module, the `ztapi` module of the `zope.app.tests` package combines in one module different functionality typically needed in test scenarios. Since it can therefore be seen as the test equivalent of `zapi`, is being explained here briefly.

`browserResource(`*name*, *factory*, *layer='default'*, *providing=*
  Interface`)` defines a browser resource named *name*. The resource component has to be specified with the *factory* parameter.

`browserView(`*for_*, *name*, *factory*, *layer='default'*, *providing=*
  Interface registers a named browser view for the interface *for_*. It will be named *name*. Pass the view factory (usually the view class) as the *factory* parameter.

`browserViewProviding(`*for_*, *factory*, *providing*, *layer=*
  'default'`)` registers an unnamed browser view providing an interface (*providing*). Otherwise it works like `browservView`.

`handle(`*required*, *handler*`)` registers an event handler *handler* for a set of event interfaces, *required*. Note that you *must* pass a sequence for the *required* parameter, even if you only are subscribing to a single event interface.

`provideAdapter(`*required*, *provided*, *factory*, *name=''*, *with=()*`)`
  defines an optionally named adapter for *required* providing *provided*. *factory* is the adapter factory which is usually the adapter class itself. The adapter can optionally be named in which case you need to pass a non-empty string for *name*. If *with* is provided (it should be a list or tuple), it is appended to the list of required interfaces for the adapter.

`provideNamespaceHandler(`*name*, *handler*`)` registers a new traversal namespace handler so that traversal namespaces in the form of ++*name*++ are possible. *handler* is the actual handler component.

`provideUtility(`*provided*, *component*, *name=''*`)` defines a *component* as a utility providing the interface *provided*. If you pass a non-empty string for *name*, the utility will be a named utility.

`provideView(`*for_*, *type*, *providing*, *name*, *factory*, *layer=*
  "default"`)` registers a view for the interface *for_*. *type* is an interface of a request and specifies for which kind of request the view is being

registered for. *providing* states which interface the view will provide. If you do not want the view to provide anything special, use `Interface` here. If you do not want the view to be named, pass an empty string for *name*. *factory* is the view factory which is usually a view class.

setDefaultViewName(*for_*, *name*, *layer*=`'default'`) sets the *name* of the default view for the interface *for_*.

subscribe(*required*, *provided*, *factory*) adds a subscriber/subscription adapter that provides *provided* for the set of interfaces *required*. Note that *required* needs to be a sequence of interfaces, even if it only contains one element. *factory* is the subscriber factory, often only a single function that is called upon look up (e.g. for events).

unprovideUtility(*provided*, *name*=`''`) deletes the registration of a utility that provides *provided* and is optionally named *name*.

ZCML Reference

Every component that is used within Zope 3 has to be configured through ZCML. This reference gives an overview over nearly all directives available in Zope X3.0. It explains their parameters in detail and gives examples for each one, usually ones from the book's example application.

Namespaces

Most Zope directives are part of a certain namespace. Only three special directives are available in all namespace, `configure`, `include` and `includeOverrides`. Even though it is arbitrary from an XML point of view, it is a convention to use the namespace prefixed as listed in Table 2.1.

Table 2.1. ZCML namespaces and their conventional namespace prefix

Namespace URL	Prefix
`http://namespaces.zope.org/zope`	`zope` (often also chosen as the main namespace)
`http://namespaces.zope.org/browser`	`browser`
`http://namespaces.zope.org/i18n`	`i18n`
`http://namespaces.zope.org/mail`	`mail`
`http://namespaces.zope.org/xmlrpc`	`xmlrpc`

These standard prefixes are also used in the alphabetical order of this reference. Therefore, if you are looking for the `view` directive from the `http://namespaces.zope.org/zope` namespace, search for `zope:view`.

ZCML conventions

A lot of ZCML directives look and work in similar ways. That is because a lot of components in Zope 3 are managed in similar ways, for example views are often treated as multi-adapters. The following list mentions a few common conventions shared among these directives:

- Some parameters allow more than one value being passed. A prominent example is the *for* parameter of *:view and zope:adapter which takes one or more interfaces. Another one is *layers* of the browser: skin directive which accepts a list of layer names. Individual items in such a list only have to be separated by at least one whitespace character. Any whitespace in between and around the items will be stripped. Thus, the following two directives are equivalent as far as the ZCML machinery is concerned:

```
<browser:skin
    name="WorldCookery"
    layers="worldcookery rotterdam default"
    />

<browser:skin
    name="WorldCookery"
    layers="worldcookery
            rotterdam
            default"
    />
```

- A few components that are registered by an identifier (for example named utilities such as roles) require that their identifier is a dotted name. A dotted name is composed of several name elements dots as delimiters. A typical example for a dotted name is the way Python refers to modules and subpackages in packages (worldcookery.recipe). Dotted names are not only used to refer to Python objects, they are also used to uniquely identify registered components. It is a common convention to use as a first element of such a dotted name the name of the Python package the component is being registered in. For example, the *visitor* role in the worldcookery application has the identifier worldcookery.Visitor.
- Menu items (whether configured stand-alone or within the view configuration) as well as permissions, principals and roles are configured with a title and description. The title of a menu item will usually be shown as the corresponding entry in the menu, the description is often optionally available as a tooltip. With permissions, principals and the like, the title is used as a presentable name (as opposed to the ID which is used as an internal identifier), the description is shown when more information is requested by the user, for example through a mouse tooltip.

On-line documentation

Note that this reference leaves out certain directives that are used very rarely. For a complete and up-to-date version of the ZCML reference, please refer to Zope's built-in *apidoc* tool. This is a small application running inside every Zope instance; it provides an overview over nearly all registered components, including their interfaces. This also includes a list of all available ZCML directives. The *apidoc* tool is available through a special traversing adapter, ++apidoc++. Unless you have altered the port configuration of your Zope instance, you should be able to view it by pointing your browser to http://localhost:8080/++apidoc++.

browser:addMenuItem

Defines an entry in the *Add* menu of containers.

Parameters

class A class to be used as a factory for creating new objects. You need to specify either this parameter or a *factory*.

factory The ID of a factory that should be used to create new objects. You need to specify either this parameter or a *class*.

title The text to be displayed for the menu item. This parameter is required.

description An optional description of the menu entry that is displayed together with the item or when the user requests more assistance.

filter An optional TALES condition that will be evaluated upon display of the menu. If the expression evaluates to a false value, the item is not displayed. The expression has access to the variables:
- context, the object the menu is being displayed for,
- request, the browser request,
- nothing

permission The permission that is required in order to display the menu entry. This parameter is optional because it can usually be inferred by the system; the underlying components are all protected by permissions. However, doing so may be expensive performance-wise.

view The name of a custom add view that is to be displayed when the entry from the menu is selected. This parameter is optional.

Examples

The following is a typical specimen of the browser:addMenuItem directive: a simple title, a class, a permission and the name of the add form (which is usually generated by browser:addform):

```
<browser:addMenuItem
    title="[label-recipe] Recipe"
    class="worldcookery.recipe.Recipe"
```

```
permission="zope.ManageContent"
view="AddRecipe.html"
/>
```

See also

browser:menu, browser:menuItem, browser:menuItems

browser:addform

Defines an automatically generated add form.

Parameters

for The interface the add form applies to. Unlike with regular pages and
forms, this value does not specify the interface of the object that is being
edited since the object has yet to be created. Instead, add forms are (like
all adding pages) registered by default for IAdding, the interface of the
adding view (usually +).

schema The schema from which the form is generated. This parameter is
required.

content_factory An object that is called to create the object that is to
be added. This factory is not used if a *class* was specified that has a
createAndAdd method which will then be called instead. In that case
the parameter is optional.

name The name of the browser page that is generated. This can be a traditional name ending in .html; it is quite common, too, to use a dotted
name, such as with factories. This parameter is required.

label A label to be used as the heading for the form. This parameter is
optional.

permission The permission needed to invoke the add form. This parameter
is required.

fields The fields that are to be displayed in the add form and the order in
which to display them. If this parameter is not specified, all schema fields
will be displayed in the order they are specified in the schema itself.

layer The layer the add form is registered for. This parameter is optional
and defaults to default.

class An optional class that can provide custom widget definitions and/or
methods to be used by the custom template (*template* parameter). The
class specified is used as a mix-in class. As a result, it does not need to
subclass any special classes, such as BrowserView.

template An alternate Page Template file that is to be used for the form
rendering. This parameter is optional.

menu Many browser pages are included in menus. It is convenient to name the menu in the directive defining the page, rather than having to use a separate menuItem directive. This parameter is optional.

title The label of the entry in the browser menu that was specified in the *menu* parameter. This parameter is optional.

description An optional description of the menu entry. It is may be displayed together with the menu item or when the user requests more assistance.

arguments A list of field names to supply as positional arguments to the factory (see *content_factory*). This parameter is optional.

keyword_arguments A list of field names to supply as keyword arguments to the factory (see *content_factory*). This parameter is optional.

set_after_add A list of fields to be assigned to the newly created object after it is added. This parameter is optional.

set_before_add A list of fields to be assigned to the newly created object before it is added. This parameter is optional.

Subdirectives

widget

Register custom widgets for the add form.

Parameters

field The name of the field for which a different widget shall be used.

class The class that will create the widget.

Examples

A regular add form with two customized widgets. The name will be set *before* the object is added to the container while the others will be set afterwards:

```
<browser:addform
    schema="worldcookery.interfaces.IRecipe"
    content_factory="worldcookery.recipe.Recipe"
    label="[label-add-recipe] Add Recipe"
    name="AddRecipe.html"
    permission="zope.ManageContent"
    set_before_add="name"
    >
  <widget field="ingredients"
          class=".widget.DynamicSequenceWidget" />
  <widget field="tools"
          class=".widget.DynamicSequenceWidget" />
</browser:addform>
```

See also

browser:editform, browser:schemadisplay

browser:containerViews

Define several standard container views for a container implementation.

Parameters

for The interface for which the container views are to be registered. This parameter is required.

add The permission by which the adding view (+) will be protected. If not specified, no adding view will be registered.

contents The permission by which the contents page (contents.html) will be protected. If not specified, the contents page will not be registered.

index The permission by which the index page (index.html) will be protected. If not specified, the index view will not be registered.

Examples

```
<browser:containerViews
     for="worldcookery.interfaces.IRecipeContainer"
     contents="worldcookery.EditRecipeFolders"
     index="worldcookery.ViewRecipeFolders"
     add="worldcookery.EditRecipeFolders"
     />
```

See also

browser:page

browser:defaultSkin

Sets the default browser skin.

Parameters

name Name of the default skin.

Examples

This directive is usually used in `overrides.zcml` because the `zope.app` package already defines a default skin. In the example application, we used the following line to change the default skin:

```
<browser:defaultSkin name="WorldCookery" />
```

See also

`browser:skin`

browser:defaultView

Defines the name of a browser view that should be used when no explicit view name is supplied.

Parameters

for Specifies the interface for which the default view name should be set. This parameter is required.

name Name that refers to a view that should be presented by default (if no view name is supplied explicitly). This parameter is required.

Examples

The zope.app package defines the default view for all objects as index. html. You can always make more specific definitions, for example the default view of all recipes could be changed to always the PDF view:

```
<browser:defaultView
    for="worldcookery.interfaces.IRecipe"
    name="pdf"
    />
```

See also

zope:defaultView, zapi.getDefaultViewName

browser:editform

Defines an automatically generated edit form.

Parameters

for The interface the generated form applies to. Usually this interface is the same as the *schema* from which the form is to be generated. In this case this parameter is optional.

schema The schema from which the form is generated. If the value specified with *for* parameter is different from this, the editable object needs to provide the schema or be adaptable to it.

name The name of the generated browser page. The form will be accessible under that name. This parameter is required.

label A label to be used as the heading for the form. This parameter is optional.

permission The permission needed to use the edit form. This parameter is required.

fields The fields that are to be displayed in the edit form and the order in which to display them. If this is not specified, all schema fields will be displayed in the order they are specified in the schema itself.

layer The layer the edit form is registered for. This parameter is optional and defaults to default.

class An optional class that can provide custom widget definitions and/or methods to be used by a custom template (*template* parameter). The class specified is used as a mix-in class. As a result, it does not need to subclass any special classes, such as BrowserView.

template An alternate Page Template file that is to be used for the form rendering. This parameter is optional.

menu Many browser pages are included in menus. It is convenient to name the menu in directive defining the page directive, rather than having to use a separate menuItem directive. This parameter is optional.

title The label of the entry in the browser menu that was specified in the *menu* parameter. This parameter is optional.

Subdirectives

Same as browser:addform.

Examples

An edit form with customized widgets:

```
<browser:editform
    schema="worldcookery.interfaces.IRecipe"
    label="Edit"
    name="edit.html"
    menu="zmi_views" title="Edit"
    permission="zope.ManageContent"
    >
  <widget field="ingredients"
          class=".widget.DynamicSequenceWidget" />
  <widget field="tools"
          class=".widget.DynamicSequenceWidget" />
</browser:editform>
```

See also

browser:addform, browser:schemadisplay

browser:icon

Defines an icon for an interface.

Parameters

for The interface that the icon applies to. This parameter is required.

name Name of the icon. This name shows up in URLs, for example. This parameter is required.

resource The name of a resource containing the icon. You need to specify a value for either this parameter or the *file* parameter.

file A file containing the icon. You need to specify a value for either this parameter or the *resource* parameter.

title A descriptive title of the resource. This can, for example, be used in the image's alt tag. This parameter is optional.

layer The layer that the icon is registered for. This parameter is optional and defaults to default.

Examples

From the example application:

```
<browser:icon
    name="zmi_icon"
    for="worldcookery.interfaces.IRecipe"
    file="recipe_icon.png"
    layer="worldcookery"
    />
```

See also

browser:resource

browser:layer

Defines a browser layer.

Parameters

name The name of the layer.

Examples

Layer names are typicall all lower case (as opposed to skin names which are camel case by convention):

```
<browser:layer name="worldcookery" />
```

See also

`browser:skin`

browser:menu

Defines a browser menu.

Parameters

id Identifier of the browser menus. This parameter is required and must be a dotted name.

title A descriptive title for documentation purposes. This parameter is required.

Examples

From the example application:

```
<browser:menu
    id="alternate_views"
    title="Menu containing a list of alternative views
for an object"
    />
```

See also

browser:addMenuItem, browser:menuItem, browser:menuItems

browser:menuItem

Define a menu item.

Parameters

menu The name of the menu that the entry is to be defined for. This parameter is required.

for The interface the menu item is to be defined for. The entry will only be shown in the context of objects providing this interface. If not provided, the menu entry will be available for all objects.

action Part of a URL relative to the object the menu is being displayed for. This parameter is required.

title The text to be displayed for the menu item. This parameter is required.

description An optional description of the menu entry that is displayed together with the item or when the user requests more assistance.

filter An optional TALES condition that will be evaluated upon display of the menu. If the expression evaluates to a false value, the item is not displayed. The expression has access to the variables:
- `context`, the object the menu is being displayed for,
- `request`, the browser request,
- `nothing`

permission The permission that is required in order to display the menu entry. This parameter is optional because it can usually be inferred by the system; the underlying components are all protected by permissions. However, doing so may be expensive performance-wise.

Examples

A `browser:addMenuItem` directive,

```
<browser:addMenuItem
    title="[label-recipe] Recipe"
    class="worldcookery.recipe.Recipe"
    permission="zope.ManageContent"
```

```
        view="AddRecipe.html"
        />
```

can also be written as a regular browser:menuItem directive:

```
<browser:menuItem
    menu="zope.app.container.add"
    for="zope.app.container.interfaces.IAdding"
    action="AddRecipe.html"
    title="[label-recipe] Recipe"
    permission="zope.ManageContent"
    />
```

See also

browser:addMenuItem, browser:menu, browser:menuItems

browser:menuItems

Define a number of browser menu items for the same menu and interface.

Parameters

menu The name of the menu that the entries are to be defined for. This parameter is required.

for The interface the menu items are defined for. The entries will only be shown in the context of objects providing this interface. If not provided, the menu entries will be available for all objects.

Subdirectives

menuItem

Define a menu item within a group of menu items.

Parameters

action Part of a URL relative to the object the menu is being displayed for. This parameter is required.

title The text to be displayed for the menu item. This parameter is required.

description An optional description of the menu entry that is displayed together with the item or when the user requests more assistance.

filter An optional TALES condition that will be evaluated upon display of the menu. If the expression evaluates to a false value, the item is not displayed. The expression has access to the variables:
- context, the object the menu is being displayed for,
- request, the browser request,
- nothing

permission The permission that is required in order to display the menu entry. This parameter is optional because it can usually be inferred by the system; the underlying components are all protected by permissions. However, doing so may be expensive performance-wise.

Examples

The browser:menuItems directive is very convenient when several menu items have to be registered for the same menu and possibly the same object interface:

```
<browser:menuItems
    menu="alternate_views"
    for="worldcookery.interfaces.IRecipe"
    >
  <menuItem
      action="pdf"
      title="PDF"
      />
  <menuItem
      action="subscribe.html"
      title="Mail subscriptions"
      />
</browser:menuItems>
```

See also

browser:addMenuItem, browser:menu, browser:menuItem

browser:page

Registers a browser page (view for browsers).

Parameters

for The interface the page is registered for. This parameter is required.

name The name under which the browser page will be available. This value usually ends in .html. This parameter is required.

template Name of a Page Template file that is used to render the page. Page Template files typically end in .pt or .html. If you do not specify this parameter you need to specify at least a *class* that is responsible for the view generation.

class A class that either provides additional methods used by a Page Template (when used in combination with *template*) or that provides the view component alltogether. In the latter case the class must either provide a __call__ method or you must specify a different method/callable attribute with the *attribute* parameter. This parameter is optional when used with the *template* parameter.

attribute A callable attribute (e.g. method) of a view class (*class* parameter) that is to be called when the view is published. This parameter is cannot be used at the same time as the *template* parameter. It is optional and defaults to __call__.

layer The layer the browser page is registered for. This parameter is optional and defaults to default.

permission The permission needed to use the browser page. This parameter is required.

menu Many browser pages are included in menus. It is convenient to name the menu in directive defining the page directive, rather than having to use a separate menuItem directive. This parameter is optional.

title The label of the entry in the browser menu that was specified in the *menu* parameter. This parameter is optional.

allowed_attributes A list of attributes that the *permission* should also apply to. By default, *permission* only applies to viewing views, not accessing additional attributes of the view component. This parameter is optional.

allowed_interface An interface that specifies a list of attributes that *permission* should also apply to. This parameter has the same effect of *allowed_attributes*. This parameter is optional.

Examples

Page Template-based browser page with a supplementary view class:

```
<browser:page
    for="worldcookery.interfaces.IRecipe"
    name="index.html"
    template="recipeview.pt"
    class=".recipe.RecipeView"
    permission="zope.View"
    />
```

Browser page implemented as a Python class:

```
<browser:page
    for="zope.app.site.interfaces.ISite"
    name="signup"
    class=".signup.SignUpView"
    attribute="signUp"
    permission="worldcookery.SignUp"
    />
```

See also

browser:pages, browser:view, zope:view

browser:pages

Define a number of browser pages that share common configuration parameters.

Parameters

for The interface the pages are registered for. This parameter is required.

class A class that either provides additional methods used by a Page Template (when used in combination with *template*) or that provides the view component alltogether. In the latter case you must specify different methods/callable attributes in the individual pages (page subdirective) with the *attribute* parameter. This parameter is optional.

layer The layer the browser pages are registered for. This parameter is optional and defaults to default.

permission The permission needed to use the browser pages. This parameter is required.

allowed_attributes A list of attributes that the *permission* should also apply to. By default, *permission* only applies to viewing views, not accessing additional attributes of the view component. This parameter is optional.

allowed_interface An interface that specifies a list of attributes that *permission* should also apply to. This parameter has the same effect of *allowed_attributes*. This parameter is optional.

Subdirectives

page

Register a single page within the group of pages to be registered.

Parameters

name The name under which the browser page will be available. This value usually ends in .html. This parameter is required.

template Name of a Page Template file that is used to render the page. Page Template files typically end in .pt or .html. If you do not specify this parameter you need to specify at least a *class* that is responsible for the view generation.

attribute A callable attribute (e.g. method) of a view class (*class* parameter of the superdirective) that is to be called when the view is published. This parameter is cannot be used at the same time as the *template* parameter.

menu Many browser pages are included in menus. It is convenient to name the menu in directive defining the page directive, rather than having to use a separate menuItem directive. This parameter is optional.

title The label of the entry in the browser menu that was specified in the *menu* parameter. This parameter is optional.

Examples

This directive from the example application configures three browser pages for the same interface (IRecipe), using the same view class (MailSubscriptionView) and the same permission:

```
<browser:pages
    for="worldcookery.interfaces.IRecipe"
    class=".browser.MailSubscriptionView"
    permission="worldcookery.Subscribe"
    >
  <browser:page
      name="subscribe"
      attribute="subscribe"
      />
  <browser:page
      name="unsubscribe"
      attribute="unsubscribe"
      />
  <browser:page
      name="subscribe.html"
      template="subscribe.pt"
      menu="alternate_views" title="Mail
subscriptions"
      />
  </browser:pages>
```

See also

browser:page, browser:view, zope:view

browser:resource

Defines a browser resource.

Parameters

name The name under which the resource will be available. Resource URLs are of the form *site*/@@/*name* where *site* is the URL of the nearest site and *name* the value of this parameter. Sites are used for base URLs of resources so that their URLs do not change depending on the context and caches can do their work effectively. This parameter is required.

file The name of a file containing the resource data. This parameter, *image* and *template* are exclusive to each other. When this parameter is given, a regular file resource is created.

image The name of an image file containing the resource data. If this parameter is used, an image resource rather than a regular file resource is created.

template The name of a Page Template file. If this parameter is given instead of *file* and *image*, a Page Template resource will be created. Page Template resources work like regular view Page Templates except that they do not have access to a context.

layer The layer the browser resource is registered for. This parameter is optional and defaults to default.

permission The permission needed to use the browser resource. This parameter is required.

Examples

From the example application:

```
<browser:resource
    name="worldcookery.css"
    file="worldcookery.css"
    layer="worldcookery"
    />
```

See also

zope:resource, zapi.getResource

browser:schemadisplay

Defines an automatically generated display view.

Parameters

for The interface the generated view applies to. Usually this interface is the same as the *schema* from which the page is to be generated. In this case this parameter is optional.

schema The schema from which the page is generated. If the value specified with *for* parameter is different from this, the object that is to be displayed needs to provide the schema or be adaptable to it.

name The name of the generated browser page. It will be accessible under that name in URLs. This parameter is required.

label A label to be used as the heading for the page. This parameter is optional.

permission The permission needed to use the view. This parameter is required.

fields The fields that are to be displayed and the order in which to display them. If this is not specified, all schema fields will be displayed in the order they are specified in the schema itself.

layer The layer the page is registered for. This parameter is optional and defaults to default.

class An optional class that can provide custom widget definitions and/or methods to be used by a custom template (*template* parameter). The class specified is used as a mix-in class. As a result, it does not need to subclass any special classes, such as BrowserView.

template An alternate Page Template file that is to be used for the page rendering. This parameter is optional.

menu Many browser pages are included in menus. It is convenient to name the menu in directive defining the page directive, rather than having to use a separate menuItem directive. This parameter is optional.

title The label of the entry in the browser menu that was specified in the *menu* parameter. This parameter is optional.

Examples

Instead of writing our own view Page Template in the example application, we could have used the following directive and have Zope generate a display page for us:

```
<browser:schemadisplay
    schema="worldcookery.interfaces.IRecipe"
    label="View recipe"
    name="index.html"
    menu="zmi_views" title="View"
    permission="zope.ManageContent"
    />
```

See also

browser:addform, browser:editform

browser:skin

Defines a browser skin.

Parameters

name The name of the skin. This parameter is required.

layers A list of layer names that the skin is composed of. The order in
which these layers are defined here determines the order of the lookup.
Usually one of the layers has the same name as the skin; the last layer
should be `default` to guarantee fallback to the very basic views. This
parameter is required.

Examples

A skin based on three layers, with `worldcookery` being the topmost layer:

```
<browser:skin
    name="WorldCookery"
    layers="worldcookery rotterdam default"
    />
```

See also

`browser:layer`

browser:tool

Registers a utility-based browser tool.

Parameters

interface Interface that characterizes the tool. For utility-based browser tools, this should be the interface by which utilities are looked up or a derived one. This parameter is required.

title The title of the tool. This is the name that will appear in the management interface. This parameter is optional and defaults to None.

description Narrative description of the tool. This parameter is optional and defaults to None.

folder Name of the site management folder that the tool should be installed in. This parameter is optional and defaults to tools.

Examples

From the example application:

```
<browser:tool
    interface="worldcookery.interfaces
.ILocalKitchenTools"
    title="Kitchen tools"
    description="This tool stores kitchen tools."
    />
```

See also

Chapter 17

browser:view

Defines a browser view with subpages.

Parameters

for The interface the view is registered for. This can also be a list of interfaces in which case a multi-view is registered. This parameter is required.

name The name under which the browser view will be available. It will be the base URL for the individual pages, e.g. `object/@@name/page` where `object` is the object that view is acquired for, *name* is the value of this parameter and `page` is the name of a subpage registered with the `page` subdirective.

class A class that either provides additional methods used by a Page Template (when used in combination with *template*) or that provides the view component alltogether. In the latter case you must specify different methods/callable attributes in the indiviual pages (`page` subdirective) with the *attribute* parameter. This parameter is optional.

layer The layer the browser view is registered for. This parameter is optional and defaults to `default`.

provides The interface the view provides. This can be used if this view should allow other views for itself. This parameter is optional and defaults to `Interface`.

permission The permission needed to use the browser pages. This parameter is required.

menu Many browser pages are included in menus. It is convenient to name the menu in directive defining the page directive, rather than having to use a separate `menuItem` directive. This parameter is optional.

title The label of the entry in the browser menu that was specified in the *menu* parameter. This parameter is optional.

allowed_attributes A list of attributes that the *permission* should also apply to. By default, *permission* only applies to viewing views, not accessing additional attributes of the view component. This parameter is optional.

allowed_interface An interface that specifies a list of attributes that *permission* should also apply to. This parameter has the same effect of *allowed_attributes*. This parameter is optional.

Subdirectives

This directive has a page subdirective that is equal to the one of browser: pages. It defines the individual subpages.

defaultPage

Define which subpage should be displayed by default if no subpage is specified explicitly in the URL.

Parameters

name The name of the subpage that should be displayed by default if no subpage is specified explicitly in the URL. If this directive is not specified, the first subpage defined will be the default one. This parameter is required.

Examples

Since subpages are quite uncommon, the browser:view directive is rarely used with subdirectives. A more common usage is to register a Python-based view component that is *not* a publishable browser page, for example (from the Zope sources at zope.app.renderer):

```
<browser:view
    name=""
    for=".plaintext.IPlainTextSource"
    class=".plaintext.PlainTextToHTMLRenderer"
    permission="zope.Public" />
```

See also

browser:page, browser:pages

configure

Grouping directive that starts a new configuration context, usually used as document element for ZCML files.

Parameters

i18n_domain Sets the i18n domain on the configuration context. This information is used for contained directives when strings are turned into translation messages. These will be attributed with the i18n domain that is acquired from the configuration context. An i18n domain should be a short identifier, usually chosen on a per-project or per-package basis. This parameter is optional and can be acquired from configuration contexts higher in hierarchy.

package Dotted name of a Python package which the contained directives are in context of. All contained directives that expect relative file paths for their parameters will evaluate these relative to the package's context. This parameter is optional and is usually set when a ZCML file is included by package.

Examples

By wrapping certain directives in a configure directive with a different package context, one can reuse files (e.g. Page Templates) from other packages in custom configuration. A typical use case is the *Preview* page for content types where the preview.pt template is located in the zope.app. preview package:

```
<configure package="zope.app.preview">
  <browser:page
      for="worldcookery.interfaces.IRecipe"
      name="preview.html"
      template="preview.pt"
      permission="zope.ManageContent"
      menu="zmi_views" title="Preview"
      />
</configure>
```

See also

include, includeOverrides

i18n:registerTranslations

Register i18n message catalogs.

Parameters

directory Directory containing gettext translation files. The conventions is to use `locales` for this value. The i18n machinery expects a standard gettext directory layout inside this directory, i.e. `locales/`*lang*`/LC_MESSAGES/`*domain*`.mo` where *lang* is the language of the individual translation file and *domain* its domain. This parameter is required.

Examples

You will see this directive being used the following way most of the time:

```
<i18n:registerTranslations directory="locales" />
```

See also

Chapter 9

include

Includes another ZCML file.

Parameters

file The name of a configuration file to be included, relative to the directive containing the file the directive is being used in. This parameter is
optional when the *package* parameter is given; in this case it defaults
to configure.zcml. It cannot be used at the same as the *files* parameter.

files The names of multiple configuration files to be included, expressed
as a file-name pattern, relative to the directive containing the file the
directive is being used in. The pattern can include the following elements:
- * matches zero or more characters
- ? matches a single character
- [*sequence*] matches any character in *sequence*.
- [!*sequence*] matches any character that is not in *sequence*.
The file names are included in alphanumerically sorted order, where sorting is without regard to case. This parameter is optional and cannot be
used at the same as the *file* parameter.

package Dotted name of a package from which files are included. If no *file*
parameter is given, the configure.zcml file from that package will be
included. This parameter will also set the package in the included file's
configuration context. This parameter is optional when either the *file*
or *files* parameter is given.

Examples

Include a package's configure.zcml:

```
<include package="worldcookery" />
```

Include a specific file from a package:

```
<include package="worldcookery" file="meta.zcml" />
```

Include a bunch of files using a file pattern; the following directive is used
in an instance's etc/site.zcml to include all ZCML snippets in etc/
package-includes/:

```
<include files="package-includes/*-meta.zcml" />
<include files="package-includes/*-configure.zcml" />
```

See also

configure, includeOverrides

includeOverrides

Include a file with overriding directives.

Parameters

includeOverrides accepts the same parameters as the include directive.

Examples

The following line is used in an instance's etc/site.zcml to include overrides.zcml:

```
<includeOverrides file="overrides.zcml" />
```

See also

include

mail:directDelivery

Registers a global utility for direct mail delivery (as opposed to queued delivery).

Parameters

name Specifies the name of the delivery utility. This parameter is optional and defaults to Mail.

mailer Specifies the name of the mail sending utility that is to be used for the actual delivery. This parameter is required.

permission Defines the permission needed to use this utility. This parameter is required.

Examples

Typically, a delivery utility is configured together with a mailer utility, e.g. an SMTP mailer:

```
<mail:smtpMailer
    name="smtp-mailer"
    hostname="localhost"
    port="25"
    />

<mail:directDelivery
    name="direct-delivery"
    mailer="smtp"
    permission="zope.Public"
    />
```

See also

mail:queuedDelivery, mail:sendmailMailer, mail:smtpMailer

mail:queuedDelivery

Registers a global utility for queued mail delivery.

Parameters

name Specifies the name of the delivery utility. This parameter is optional
and defaults to `Mail`.

mailer Specifies the name of the mail sending utility that is to be used for
the actual delivery. This parameter is required.

permission Defines the permission needed to use this utility. This parameter is required.

queuePath Specifies a path relative to the configuration file where the delivery utility can store its mail queue. Mails are stored in the *Maildir* format. This parameter is required.

Examples

Typically, a delivery utility is configured together with a mailer utility. The
following example is taken from the example application:

```
<mail:smtpMailer
    name="worldcookery-mailer"
    hostname="localhost"
    port="25"
    />

<mail:queuedDelivery
    name="worldcookery-delivery"
    permission="zope.SendMail"
    queuePath="mail-queue"
    mailer="worldcookery-mailer"
    />
```

See also

mail:directDelivery, mail:sendmailMailer, mail:smtpMailer

mail:sendmailMailer

Registers a mailer utility that sends mail by invoking a command line program, such as *sendmail*.

Parameters

name Name by which the mailer utility is registered. This parameter is required.

command The command template that is used for sending out mail. The template may contain %(from)s and %(to)s placeholders for the sender and recipient addresses. This parameter is optional and defaults to:

```
/usr/lib/sendmail -oem -oi -f %(from)s %(to)s
```

Examples

```
<mail:sendmailMailer
     name="sendmail-mailer"
     command="/usr/sbin/sendmail -oem -oi -f %(from)s
%(to)s"
     />
```

See also

mail:directDelivery, mail:queuedDelivery, mail:smtpMailer

mail:smtpMailer

Registers a mailer utility that sends mail by connecting to an SMTP server.

Parameters

name Name by which the mailer utility is registered. This parameter is required.

hostname Hostname of the SMTP server that mails are supposed to be sent to. This parameter is optional and defaults to `localhost`.

port Port of the SMTP server. This parameter is optional and defaults to `25`.

username A username with which the utility will try to authenticate itself with the SMTP server. This parameter is optional.

password The password for the user that was specified with the *username* parameter for SMTP authentication. This parameter is optional.

Examples

See examples of `mail:directDelivery` and `mail:queuedDelivery`.

See also

`mail:directDelivery`, `mail:queuedDelivery`, `mail:sendmailMailer`

xmlrpc:view

Registers one or more XML-RPC views.

Parameters

for The interface the XML-RPC views are registered for. This parameter is required.

class A view class that provides the methods that can be called via RPC. This parameter is required.

methods A list of methods (or attributes) of the view class (*class* parameter) that are to be published via XML-RPC. This parameter is required unless the *interface* parameter is given instead.

interface An interface that specifies a list of methods (or attributes) of the view class that are to be published. Otherwise works like *methods*. This parameter is required if *methods* is not given.

name Optional name of the XML-RPC view. Normally, the names of the methods and attributes specified via *methods* or *interface* are registered directly as XML-RPC views on the object; in other words, they would be accessible via object/*methodname*. If this parameter is given, however, they will be available as subviews of this view, i.e. though object/*name*/*methodname* where *name* is the value given in this parameter. In this case the view class (*class* parameter) should implement IPublishTraverse from the zope.publisher package.

permission The permission needed to use the views. This applies to both the case of methods being registered as individual views as well as the case of one view with subviews (*name* parameter). This parameter is optional; if it is not given, security protection should be ensured otherwise, e.g. through security declarations for the view class (*class* parameter).

Examples

The following directive taken from the example application registers two XML-RPC view methods for IRecipe objects as direct XML-RPC views (no *name* parameter given). This is the common way of registering XML-RPC views:

```
<xmlrpc:view
    for="worldcookery.interfaces.IRecipe"
    class=".recipe.RecipeView"
    methods="info dublincore_info"
    permission="zope.View"
    />
```

See also

zope:view

zope:adapter

Registers an adapter.

Parameters

for One or more interfaces that the adapter is registered for. If more than one interface is specified, a multi-adapter is registered. This parameter is required.

provides The interface that the adapter provides, in other words, the interface that the adapter adapts to. This parameter is required.

factory One or more callables that act as adapter factories. Usually only one factory is allowed for this value (most of the time the class that provides the adapter implementation). In case only one value is specified for *for*, one can pass several factories. When the adapter is to be instanciated for an object obj, the factories will be called in the following order: factory1(factory2(factory3(obj))) (when factory1 factory2 factory3 have been specified in that order. This parameter is required.

name Optional name of the adapter. If specified, the adapter will be registered as a *named* adapter. This parameter is optional and defaults to an empty string (unnamed adapter).

permission An optional permission that is required to use the adapter. If not given, the adapter will always be available.

trusted Make the adapter a trusted adapter. Regular (untrusted) adapters are given a security proxied object; in return, the adapter itself does not have any security protection (since the original object is already protected). With trusted adapters it is the other way around. They work with bare objects that have no security protection; in return, the adapters themselves are security proxied and thus need security declarations. This parameter is optional and defaults to False.

Examples

A typical adapter is the size adapter for content objects. It is an unnamed, untrusted and very simple adapter:

```
<adapter
    for=".interfaces.IRecipe"
    provides="zope.app.size.interfaces.ISized"
    factory=".size.RecipeSize"
    />
```

One application of named adapters are file factories in the context of file representation. The name is the extension of the object that is to be created:

```
<adapter
    for="zope.app.folder.interfaces.IFolder"
    provides="zope.app.filerepresentation.interfaces
.IFileFactory"
    name=".recipe"
    factory=".filerepresentation.RecipeFactory"
    permission="zope.ManageContent"
    />
```

In annotation-based components, custom adapters usually provide a nice interface to data stored in annotations. When annotation data is retrieved from the object (e.g. through attribute annotations), the data will be security proxied and most likely to be inaccessible to the adapter. That is why these adapters are made trusted ones; to ensure protection towards the data, security declarations are given for the adapter class itself. Consider an example from the example application:

```
<adapter
    for=".interfaces.IRatable"
    provides=".interfaces.IRating"
    factory=".rating.Rating"
    trusted="true"
    />

<content class=".rating.Rating">
  <require
      permission="zope.View"
      attributes="averageRating numberOfRatings rate"
      />
</content>
```

See also

`zapi.getAdapter`, `zapi.getAdapterInContext`, Chapter 10 (regular and named adapters), Chapter 13 (trusted adapters)

zope:content, zope:class

Configures a (content) class.

Parameters

class The class that is to be configured. This parameter is required.

zope:class is an alias for zope:content.

Subdirectives

allow

Declares an attribute of the class to be publicly available.

Parameters

attributes The attributes that are to be allowed. You need to specify either this parameter or *interface*.

interface An interface that specifies the names of attributes which are to be allowed. You need to specify either this parameter or *attributes*.

factory

Configure a factory from class.

Parameters

id Identifier of the factory. This needs to be a dotted name, usually starting with the name of the current package. This parameter is optional and defaults to the dotted name of the class.

title Short title that characterizes the factory. The value provided here can be used as a title for a menu entry or in some other part of a user interface. This parameter is optional.

description Longer narrative description of what this factory does. This parameter is optional.

implements

Declares that the class given implements additional interfaces.

Parameters

interface One or more interfaces that the class should implement in addition to what it already implements through declarations in Python code. These usually are marker interface that tell Zope how the class should be used in certain circumstances. This parameter is required.

require

Protect methods and attributes of the class with a permission.

Parameters

attributes A list of attributes (this includes methods) that are to be protected with the prermission (*permission* parameter). This parameter is optional, but you need to specify at least one of the *attributes*, *interface*, *set_attributes*, *set_schema* and *like_class* parameters.

interface An interface that defines a methods and attributes that are to be protected with *permission*. It otherwise works like the *attributes* parameter. This parameter is optional.

set_attributes A list of attributes whose modification shall be protected by *permission*. This parameter is optional.

set_schema A schema that specifies through fields a number of attributes whose modification shall be protected by *permission*. It otherwise works like the *set_attributes* parameter. This parameter is optional.

like_class Dotted name of a class whose security declarations should apply to the current class as well. This parameter is optional.

permission The permission that the specified attributes are to be protected with. This parameter is required.

Examples

The following ZCML snippet is a typical example of a content class being configured. It registers a factory from class, marks the class as attribute annotatable (by letting it implement an additional marker interface), and protects its attributes for read and write access:

```
<content class=".recipe.Recipe">
  <factory
      id="worldcookery.Recipe"
      title="Create a new recipe"
      description="This factory instantiates new
recipes"
      />
  <implements
      interface="zope.app.annotation.interfaces
.IAttributeAnnotatable"
      />
  <require
      permission="zope.View"
      interface=".interfaces.IRecipe"
      />
  <require
      permission="zope.ManageContent"
      set_schema=".interfaces.IRecipe"
      />
</content>
```

Allowing an attribute with the `allow` subdirective,

```
<content class="someclass">
  <allow attributes="someattribute" />
</content>
```

is equivalent to protecting it with `zope.Public`:

```
<content class="someclass">
  <require
      permission="zope.Public"
      attributes="someattribute"
      />
</content>
```

See also

`zope:factory`, `zope:module`

zope:defaultView

Defines the name of a view that should be used when no explicit view name is supplied.

Parameters

for Specifies the interface for which the default view name should be set. This parameter is required.

type Interface that specifies the request type to which this default view setting applies. This parameter is required.

name Name that refers to a view that should be presented by default (if no view name is supplied explicitly). This parameter is required.

Examples

Defining a default view name is usually only necessary for browser requests, since HTTP and FTP views are looked up by different metrics. The following ZCML directive defines a default view for browser requests:

```
<defaultView
    for="worldcookery.interfaces.IRecipe"
    type="zope.publisher.interfaces.browser
.IBrowserRequest"
    name="pdf"
    />
```

Of course, one could have simply used the `browser:defaultView` directive instead:

```
<browser:defaultView
    for="worldcookery.interfaces.IRecipe"
    name="pdf"
    />
```

See also

`browser:defaultView`

zope:factory

Defines a factory.

Parameters

id Identifier of the factory. This needs to be a dotted name, usually starting with the name of the current package. This parameter is required.

component The factory component. This should be a callable object that provides IFactory. Note that this is usually an instance, *not* a class.

title Short title that characterizes the factory. The value provided here can be used as a title for a menu entry or in some other part of a user interface. This parameter is optional.

description Longer narrative description of what this factory does. This parameter is optional.

Examples

Most factories are defined from a class using the zope:content directive. Only sometimes it is useful to define a custom directive. An example from the example application:

```
<factory
    component=".recipe.RecipeFactory"
    id="worldcookery.RecipeWithInitialValues"
    title="Create a new recipe with initial values"
    description="This factory instantiates new recipes
with initial values"
    />
```

See also

zope:content, Chapter 5

zope:grant

Grants permissions to roles and principals and roles to principals.

Parameters

permission Specifies the permission to be granted to either a role (*role* parameter) or principal (*principal* parameter). This parameter is optional if only roles are to be granted to principals.

role Specifies the role that is to be granted to a principal or that the permission is to be granted to. This parameter is optional if only permissions are to be granted to principals.

principal Specifies a prinicipal that a role or a permission is to be granted to. This parameter is optional if only permissions are to be granted to roles.

Examples

Grant a permission to a role:

```
<grant
    permission="worldcookery.ViewRecipes"
    role="worldcookery.Visitor"
    />
```

Grant a role to a principal:

```
<grant
    role="worldcookery.Visitor"
    principal="zope.anybody"
    />
```

See also

zope:grantAll, zope:permission, zope:role, Chapter 18

zope:grantAll

Grants *all* permissions to a role and/or prinicipal.

Parameters

principal Specifies a principal that is to be granted all access. You need to give either this parameter or the *role* parameter.

role Specifies a role that is to be granted all access. You need to give either this parameter or the *role* parameter.

Examples

grantAll means that literally all permissions are granted to the given role or principal. In other words, these principals or roles will have unlimited access to everything. By default, the zope.app.securitypolicy package grants this kind of access to the [computeorutput] zope.Manager [/computeorutput] role with the following directive:

```
<grantAll role="zope.Manager" />
```

See also

zope:grant, zope:permission, zope:role, Chapter 18

zope:interface

Registers an interface as a utility and optionally makes it a type.

Parameters

interface The interface that is to be registered. This parameter is required.

type An interface type that the interface should be marked with. This interface type must be an interface extending IInterface.

Examples

Typically this directive is used to turn an interface into a type, for example a content type:

```
<interface
    interface=".interfaces.IRecipe"
    type="zope.app.content.interfaces.IContentType"
    />
```

See also

Chapter 5

zope:permission

Defines a new permission.

Parameters

id Identifier of the permission. This should a dotted name, usually starting with the name of the current package. This parameter is required.

title A short descriptive title that maybe used to describe the permission in user interfaces (rather than the identifier). This parameter is required.

description Longer narrative description for the permission. This parameter is optional.

Examples

Defining a permission is quite straight forward:

```
<permission
    id="worldcookery.ViewRecipes"
    title="View recipes"
    />
```

See also

zope:grant

zope:principal

Defines a global principal.

Parameters

id Identifier of the prinicipal. This needs to a dotted name; they usually start with the name of the current package. Note that prinicpal IDs need to be unique throughout a whole Zope instance. This parameter is required.

login Specifies the principal's username for login. This parameter is required.

password Specifies the principal's password for login. This parameter is required.

title Descriptive title for the principal. It usually describes the purpose of the principal (e.g. Sample Manager) or the full name of the person represented by the principal. This parameter is required.

description Longer narrative description of the principal. This parameter is optional.

Examples

This directive is usually only used during development and for emergencies since principal passwords are stored as clear text in the ZCML file. A typical example of a usage of this directive is the initial administrative user account that is created when the mkzopeinstance script is run:

```
<principal
    id="zope.manager"
    title="Manager"
    login="manager"
    password="secret"
    />
```

See also

zope:grant

zope:resource

Register a resource

Parameters

name The name under which the resource will be available. This parameter is required.

provides The interface the resource provides. This will cause the resource being registered as one providing this interface which will allow it to be looked up this way, too. This parameter is optional and defaults to `Interface`.

type Interface that specifies the request type this resource applies to. This parameter is required.

factory A factory (e.g. a class) that creates a new resource component. This is usually the class of the resource implementation, or some other callable that returns the resource object. This parameter is required.

layer The layer the resource is registered for. This parameter is optional and defaults to `default`.

permission The permission needed to use the resource. This parameter is required.

allowed_attributes A list of attributes that the *permission* should also apply to. By default, *permission* only applies to viewing resources, not accessing additional attributes of the resource component. This parameter is optional.

allowed_interface An interface that specifies a list of attributes that *permission* should also apply to. This parameter has the same effect of *allowed_attributes*. This parameter is optional.

Examples

Browser resources are generally much easier to register because the `browser:resource` accepts various parameters to directly create resource factories from either files, images or Page Templates. With the `zope:resource` directive, you have to pass a *factory* manually, which means that for each resource you register you would have to write a little piece of Python code.

This is why this directive is seldomly used. In cases where you want Python components be represented as resources, it is very useful, though:

```
<resource
    name="worldcookery.css"
    factory=".resource.WorldcookeryCSS"
    type="zope.publisher.interfaces.browser
.IBrowserRequest"
    layer="worldcookery"
    permission="zope.Public"
    />
```

See also

browser:resource, zapi.getResource

zope:role

Defines a global role.

Parameters

id Identifier of the role. This should be a dotted name, usually starting with the name of the current package. This parameter is required.

title Descriptive title of the role. This should be the full name of the role as it may appear in a user interface. This parameter is required.

description Longer narrative description of the role. This parameter is optional.

Examples

From the example application:

```
<role
    id="worldcookery.Visitor"
    title="Visitor of the WorldCookery website"
    />
```

See also

zope:grant, zope:principal, Chapter 18

zope:securityPolicy

Sets the security policy of a Zope instance.

Parameters

component The security policy component. This should be a callable object that provides ISecurityPolicy itself. When called it should return objects providing IInteraction. Usually, this is the implementation class of interactions. This parameter is required.

Examples

The security policy for a Zope instance can be configured in the etc/securitypolicy.zcml file. The default security policy implementation that comes with Zope resides in the zope.app.securitypolicy package which is why normally this file includes that package. In that package's configure.zcml, the security policy is set by using the appopriate directive:

```
<securityPolicy
    component=".zopepolicy.ZopeSecurityPolicy"
    />
```

See also

Chapter 18

zope:service

Registers a service.

Parameters

serviceType The type of service to be registered. This must be a service name previously registered with the serviceType directive. This parameter is required.

component Service component that is to be registered. This should be an instance that will be registered as it is. Either this or the *factory* parameter needs to be specified.

factory A factory that creates the service component. Use this parameter if you want ZCML to instanciate the service component from the factory for you. Note that unlike with views and other factory-dependent component types, service factories are called *once* upon registration. Then the created singleton instance is registered.

permission The permission that is required to use the service. This parameter is optional. If not specified, the service will be available to anyone.

Examples

When you want to register a service, you first have to register the service type. That is the name by which the service will then later be looked up. Each service name corresponds to a service interface which characterizes the service:

```
<serviceType
    id="Utilities"
    interface="zope.component.interfaces
.IUtilityService"
    />
```

```
<service
    serviceType="Utilities"
    permission="zope.Public"
    factory="zope.component.utility
.GlobalUtilityService"
    />
```

See also

zope:serviceType, zapi.getService, zapi.getGlobalService

zope:serviceType

Parameters

id Identifier of the service, also known as the service type or service name. The corresponding service will be looked up by this name. This parameter is required.

interface Interface that corresponds to the service type. Services registered for this service type should provide this interface. This parameter is required.

Examples

See the examples for the `service` directive.

See also

`zope:service, zapi.getServiceDefinitions`

zope:unauthenticatedPrincipal

Defines an unauthenticated principal.

Parameters

id Identifier of the prinicpial. This needs to be a dotted name. This parameter is required.

title Descriptive title of the principal. It usually describes the purpose of the principal (e.g. Anonymous User). This parameter is required.

description Longer narrative description of the prinicpal. This parameter is optional.

Examples

Note that there may only be one unauthenticated principal defined in a Zope instance. By default, an entry of the following already exists in etc/principals.zcml:

```
<unauthenticatedPrincipal
  id="zope.anybody"
  title="Unauthenticated User" />
```

See also

zope:principal

zope:utility

Registers a global utility

Parameters

provides The interface that the utility provides. It will be registered and looked up by this interface. This parameter is required.

component A component that is to be registered as the utility. This should be an instance providing the interface specified under *provides*. You have to specify either this parameter or a factory from which the utility component is created by using the *factory* parameter.

factory A callable that creates the utility object. This is often just a class with the utility implementation. The returned object should provide the interface that is specified under *provided*. You need to specify this parameter if you do not pass the *component* parameter. Note that unlike with views and other factory-dependent component types, utility factories are called *once* upon registration, not with every lookup.

name The name of the utility. If given, the utility is registered as a named utility with the value of this parameter being its name. This parameter is optional and defaults to an empty string (unnamed utility).

permission The permission needed to use the utility. This parameter is optional. If is not specified, the component will be available to anyone.

Examples

From the example application:

```
<utility
    provides=".interfaces.IKitchenTools"
    factory=".kitchentools.KitchenToolsFromFile"
    />
```

See also

zapi.getUtility, zapi.getUtilitiesFor

zope:view

Register a view for a component

Parameters

for The interface the view is registered for. This can also be a list of interfaces in which case a multi-view is registered. This parameter is required.

name The name under which the view will be available. This parameter is
optional and defaults to an empty string in which case the view will be
registered as an unnamed one.

provides The interface the view provides. This will cause the view being
registered as one providing this interface which will affect the way it
has to be looked up as well. This parameter is optional and defaults to
Interface.

type Interface that specifies the request type which the view applies to. This
parameter is required.

factory A factory that creates the view component upon request. This is
usually the class providing the view implementation itself. This parameter
is required.

layer The layer the resource is registered for. This parameter is optional
and defaults to default.

permission The permission needed to use the view. This parameter is
required.

allowed_attributes A list of attributes that the *permission* should
also apply to. By default, *permission* only applies to viewing views, not
accessing additional attributes of the view component. This parameter is
optional.

allowed_interface An interface that specifies a list of attributes that
permission should also apply to. This parameter has the same effect
of *allowed_attributes*. This parameter is optional.

Examples

In the example application, we register a view for recipes that is very general
with respect to the type of request it is registered for (the most general

request interface is IRequest). Since it provides certain functionality, it is registered as a a view providing an interface. In that respect, it is very much like an adapter:

```
<view
     for="worldcookery.interfaces.IRecipe"
     provides=".interfaces.IPDFPresentation"
     type="zope.publisher.interfaces.IRequest"
     factory=".recipe.RecipePDF"
     />
```

See also

browser:view, xmlrpc:view, zapi.getView,
zapi.getViewProviding, zapi.getMultiView

zope:vocabulary

Registers a voculabary

Parameters

name The vocabulary's name. The vocabulary will be referenced using this name, e.g. in a Choice field of a schema. This parameter is required.

factory A callable that returns an instance of the vocabulary. This is usually the class of the vocabulary implementation. The callable needs to accept at least one argument, the context in which the vocabulary is looked up (since vocabulary terms may be context-dependent). The callable may also take arbitrary keyword arguments directly passed through additional parameters of this directive.

Apart from the ones defined above, this directive takes arbitrary parameters. These will be passed on to the vocabulary *factory* as keyword arguments.

Examples

The following lines from the example application give an example of a regular vocabulary configuration without any extra parameters:

```
<vocabulary
    name="Kitchen Tools"
    factory=".kitchentools.kitchenToolVocabulary"
    />
```

Sometimes it is useful to provide generic vocabulary implementations that can be initialized with parameters from the vocabulary directive. The often used UtilityVocabulary is such a case. Here, the parameters *interface* and *nameOnly* are passed on to the UtilityVocabulary factory which can use them to constraint the number of terms inside the created vocabulary, for instance:

```
<vocabulary
    name="Roles"
    factory="zope.app.utility.vocabulary
.UtilityVocabulary"
    interface="zope.app.securitypolicy.interfaces
.IRole"
    nameOnly="True"
    />
```

See also

Chapter 16

References

1. (2001) Apache Software License 2.0. Apache Software Foundation website <http://apache.org/licenses/LICENSE-2.0.txt>
2. Zope 3 Coding standards. Zope development home <http://dev.zope.org/Zope3/CodingStyle>
3. Pilgrim M (2004) Dive Into Python. Dive Into Python website <http://diveintopython.org>
4. (2003) Dublin Core Metadata Element Set, Version 1.1: Reference Description. Dublin Core Metadata Initiative website <http://dublincore.org/documents/2003/06/02/dces/>
5. GNU gettext manual. GNU website <http://www.gnu.org/software/gettext/manual/gettext.html>
6. Bernstein M (1998) Maildir – directory for incoming mail messages. QMail website <http://www.qmail.org/man/man5/maildir.html>
7. Perence B (2004) The Open Source Definition. Open Source Initiative website <http://opensource.org/docs/definition.php>
8. van Rossum G (2001) Style Guide for Python Code. Python website <http://www.python.org/peps/pep-0008.html>
9. van Rossum G, Drake F L, (2004) Python Tutorial. Python website <http://python.org/doc/current/tut/tut.html>
10. Freed N, Borenstein N, (1996) Multipurpose Internet Mail Extensions (MIME) Part One. Internet Engineering Task Force (IETF) <http://www.ietf.org/rfc/rfc2045.txt>
11. Weibel S, Kunze J, Lagoze C, Wolf M, (1998) Dublin Core Metadata for Resource Discovery. Internet Engineering Task Force (IETF) <http://www.ietf.org/rfc/rfc2413.txt>
12. Goland Y, Whitehead E, Faizi A, Carter S R, Jensen D, (1999) HTTP Extensions for Distributed Authoring. Internet Engineering Task Force (IETF) <http://www.ietf.org/rfc/rfc2518.txt>
13. Resnick P (2001) Internet Message Format. Internet Engineering Task Force (IETF) <http://www.ietf.org/rfc/rfc2822.txt>
14. Crocker D (1982) Standard for the Format of ARPA Internet Text Messages. Internet Engineering Task Force (IETF) <http://www.ietf.org/rfc/rfc822.txt>

15. ReportLab API Reference. ReportLab website <http://www.reportlab.org/doc/reference.pdf>

16. ReportLab User Guide. ReportLab website <http://www.reportlab.org/rsrc/userguide.pdf>

17. Everitt P An Introduction to StructuredText. Zope community website <http://www.zope.org/Documentation/Articles/STX>

18. Test-driven Development. Wikipedia <http://en.wikipedia.org/wiki/Test-driven_development>

19. Kuchling A M What's New in Python 2.2. Python website <http://www.python.org/doc/2.2.3/whatsnew/whatsnew22.html>

20. Winter D (1998-2004) XML-RPC specification. XML-RPC website <http://xmlrpc.com/spec>

21. (2004) Zope Public License 2.1. Zope community website <http://zope.org/Resources/License/ZPL-2.1>

22. A reStructuredText Primer. Docutils website <http://docutils.sourceforge.net/docs/user/rst/quickstart.html>

Epilogue

I came to Zope in the early 2.x days when I needed a software tool that would allow me to collaborate on a school website project. It was the time of DTML Documents and Python Methods and neither the CMF nor Plone and Silva existed. What was even worse was that documentation was scarce. Fortunately, the first Zope book to be published in English was being written by two Digital Creations employees, Amos Latteier and Michel Pelletier.

Then, over a year later, everything had changed. Now there were many books about Zope, some even in French, German, and other languages. Though that was not surprising because Zope seemed gain a lot of momentum in Europe. Zope also hit the big market at that point. NATO probably was the most advertised Zope customer at the time and maybe still is. However, most importantly, DTML stopped being cool and Page Templates began their long path to victory.

What always has been great about Zope is its community. Maybe this is why I stuck with Zope after all and did not go back to PHP or moved on to Java. I still enjoy hanging out on IRC (#zope at irc.freenode.net) because that is where you can feel the heart beat of the Zope community. It is also where I met all of the people that I ended up working with for some years now – before actually having met them in person. Now that Zope and its offspring Plone are even more successful, we can afford to hold our own conferences and actually see each other in person. Only sometimes I wish the old times back when he had those barbecues in Berlin with no more than 40 people.

Before the second barbecue in 2002, I participated in a Zope 3 sprint[1]. That was the time when I first got involved into Zope 3 development. It was exciting to help redesigning the framework I had been using for some

---

[1] A sprint is a meeting of developers at which the software product in question is developed intensely for a couple of days.

time personally. During many "geddons"[2], I did not only have the pleasure of getting to know the Zope 3 source code inside out, I also was able to watch Zope 3 grow up and gain more momentum with every new feature, new geddon, or new event.

In late 2003 I was invited to Düsseldorf to give a tutorial on Zope 3 for the local Zope user group. At that event I realized that the new version of Zope needed good documentation from the start, otherwise it would have to overcome from the same initial hurdles of Zope 2 back then. Therefore, my goal was to provide an easy, but not too simple, a gradual, but not too horizontal introduction to Zope 3. I hope I have achieved that goal in this book. However, it would not have been possible without the community and their contributions to Zope and this book.

Special thanks goes to

- Hermann Engesser of Springer-Verlag for believing in Zope and this book.
- Jan Smith and Sidnei da Silva for their exceptional effort of reviewing the book. Thanks for everything, guys, that was incredible! I could not have done this without you.
- Róman Joost for his design of the World Cookery application skin as well as important feedback.
- Fred L. Drake for his advice during the initial phase of the book and for providing technical guidance.
- Jim Fulton for being a great mentor during the initial development phase of Zope 3.
- Stephan Richter for encouraging me to write a book in competition to his and some last-minute LaTeX help.
- Aroldo Souza-Leite for inviting me to Düsseldorf where it all started.
- Kit Blake, Martijn Faassen and the Infrae crew for their invaluable support.
- Paul Everitt for his support and the foreword to the book. Keep up the good work, Paul!
- Marius Gedminas and Joe Geldart for technical advice.
- Philipp Latzel for being a good friend at my side and carrying me through difficult school assignments more than once.
- My roommates Max and Gregor for their patience with me during the hot phase of the writing period.

Thanks for the music of Frank Sinatra, James Darren, and Natalie Cole which kept me in a good mood throughout the whole writing and editing period. *It don't mean a thing if it ain't got that swing!*

This book was written 100% with the help of Open Source software! Originally written in DocBook XML using GNU Emacs and James Clark's nxml-mode, it was converted to LaTeX using an extended version of Ramon Casellas's and James Devenish's db2latex stylesheet package. The DocBook

---

[2] Merciless refactorings, derived from the word arma*geddon*.

files and the source code to the example application were revision controlled in a subversion repository. Roundup, an issue tracking software written in Python, was heavily used during the review process. The browser shown in most screenshots is Mozilla Firefox 1.0 (preview) for Mac OS X.

Index

++apidoc++   393
++etc++site   292, *see also* site
    managers
++resource++   99, 114
++skin++   106, 304
++vh++   304
++view++   31, 304
@@   31

absolute URLs   234, 304, 353
adapters   32, 147, 357, 433
    customizing existing   157
    file representation   *see* file represen-
        tation
    multi-adapters   188, 364
    named   155, 356
    size   147
    trusted   227
annotations   211, 267, 319
    events   260
    IAnnotatable   297
    IAttributeAnnotatable   212, 297
    principals   342
Apache webserver   305
Archetypes   52
authentication   323

browser icons   117, 404
browser menus   197
    add menu   73, 80, 197, 394
    configuration   197, 406, 407, 409
    zmi_actions   197
    zmi_views   80, 94, 197

browser resources   99, 116, 371
    configuration   415, 445
browser tools   294, 302
browser views
    configuration   93, 411, 413, 420
    default view name   92
    enhanced   185
    Python   188
    supplementary class   185
BTrees   77
    container   239
    principal source   330

CamelCase   42
catalog   10
choices   279
CMF   23, 27
    Dublin Core   223
    file representation   157
    members   39
    portal type   59
    sites   295
    skins   108
    tools   295
    views   31
CMS   5, 211
Component Architecture   25
components
    configuration   35
    content   29
    global, local   292
    introduction   25
configuration   *see* instance

configure.zcml   35
containers   233
    constraints, preconditions   239
    contained proxies   237
    containment   235
    events   260
    file representation   250
    IContained   235, 297, 368
    names   245, 399
content   55
    configuration   63, 435
    factories   *see* factories
    management   5
    schema-based   59
    security   63
    types   *see* content types
content types   55
    IContentType   55
conventions
    examples   9
    interfaces   42
    naming   35
    packages   80
    zapi   351
cookies   324
credentials   323
CSS stylesheets   116

Data.fs   19
databases
    object vs. relational   29
    relational   10, 71
datetime   144
DAV   *see* WebDAV
debugger   *see* pdb
doctests   167
    DocFileSuite   170
    DocTestSuite   169
    flags   274
    functional   176
    FunctionalDocFileSuite   180
dotted names   35
DTML   90
Dublin Core   215, 262
    permissions   219

ECMAScript   96
email   266, 347, 427–430
events   257
    object events   259
examples
    application   8
    download   8
    installation   22
    introduction   8
expressions
    TALES   *see* TALES

factories   65, 355, 360, 361, 439
    from class   65, 435
    IFactory   67
FieldProperty   62
fields   50
    access   61
    parameters   51
    validation   60
file representation   151, 202
    containers   250
folder   291
folders   239, *see also* containers
ForbiddenAttribute   312
forms   79, 416
    adapted edit forms   347
    adding and editing   80, 396, 402
    customizing   94
FTP   250
    port   19
    request   31
    server   19
    views   151
functional tests   172
    doctests   176

generators   289
granting   440, 441
    local grants   318
    roles   318
groups   317
gtranslator   139

HTML
    generating   82

HTTP
    Accept-Language header   123, 158,
       174
    Basic authentication   325
    Host header   303
    port   19, 303
    protocols   201
    PUT   152, 202
    request   31
    server   19, 303
HTTPS   305

i18n   *see* internationalization
installation   13
    additional packages   21
    compilation   15
    download   15
    Python   13
    requirements   13
instance
    configuration   19
    controlling...   18
    creating   16
    restart   20
integration tests   172
interactions   310
interfaces   27, 41
    attributes   44
    browsing   57
    declaring   45
    defining   42
    deriving   42
    IInterface   47, 56
    implementing   45
    jargon   41
    location   42
    marker   56, 211, 247, 299
    schemas   *see* schemas
    semantics   28, 41
    type   55, 382
    verifying   48
internationalization   121
    message catalogs   137
    messages   122
    Page Templates   128
    Python code   127

ZCML   133
internationlization
    message catalogs   423
Internet Explorer   97

Java   6, 25
    XML-RPC client   207

KBabel   139
kitchen tools   286, 296

l10n   *see* localization
layers   105, 405
LDAP   36
Linux   13
local utilities   295
    deleting   302
    registration   298
localization   121, 141, 220
location   233, 367, 368, 370

Mac OS X   13, 157
mail   *see* email
menus   *see* browser menus
meta type   59
metadata   211
    custom   223
    principals   342
METAL   109
mkzopeinstance   17
Mozilla   97
MVC   25

new-style classes   62

Opera   97
overrides.zcml   107, 159, 175
overrides_ftesting.zcml   175

Page Templates   82, 185
    commands   *see* TAL
    expressions   *see* TALES
    global variables   87
    macros   *see also* METAL
    namespace adapters   220
    scopes   86
    viewing off of the filesystem   90
    Zope 2   90

participations   310
pdb   182
PDF   188, 276
permissions   36, 310, 315, 443
  vocabulary   284
persistency   71
  making persistent objects   72
  Persistent   72
  rules   75
  volatile attributes   75
PersistentDict   77
PersistentList   77
PIL/Imaging   189
PlacelessSetup   165, 169, 258
Plone   6, 27, 52
pluggableauth   323, 330
poEdit   139
portal type   59
preview   93
principal annotations   342
principal sources   330
principals   36, 310, 323, 444
  managing   330
  signing up   331
products   23
proxies
  contained   237
  security   311, 380
PyPI   7, 192
Python
  installation   13
  interpreter   8, 167
  Programming Language   6
  TALES expressions   85
PYTHONPATH   9, 164
PyUnit   163

quality assurance   3, 161

rating   223, 261
registrations   294, 300
  IRegisterable   297
  registration manager   294
renderers   186, 360
ReportLab   189
resources   see browser resources
reStructuredText   186

rewriting URLs   304
roles   38, 317, 447
  local roles   318
Rotterdam   106
runzope   18

schemas   49
  defining   51
  fields   see fields
  introspecting   51
  validation   60
security   36, 309, 323
  checkers   311
  high-level   310
  low-level   311
  policy   37, 310, 448
  proxies   311, 380
services   34
  acquiring   199
  adapters   258
  browser menus   198
  configuration   449, 450
  global   362, 363
  local   330
  look up   362, 363, 373–375, 383
  principal annotations   342
  testing   165
sessions   10
signup   331
Silva   6, 23
site managers   292
site-management folders   294
sites   291, 340
skins   105, 418
  customizing   111
  default   400
  Rotterdam   see Rotterdam
SSL   304
StructuredText   186
subscribers   257, 384

TAL   83
  commands   84
  namespace   83
  namespace prefix   91
TALES   84

expression modifiers   85
expressions   84
tcpwatch   176
term   281
test runner   180
testing   161
token   281
tool   419
tools   *see* browser tools
translation   *see* internationalization
translation domains   123

Unauthorized   313
   default view   324
unit tests   163
user management   323
UserError   246, 387
users   *see* principals
utilities   33, 358, 377, 452
   local   *see* local utilities
   named   33, 358, 376
   singletons   33
   vocabularies   284

views   30, 79, 185
   browser   *see* browser views
   configuration   453
   default view name   359, 401, 438
   look up   95, 105, 378, 379
   multi-views   366
   providing an interface   95, 188
   schema-based   79
virtual hosting   303
vocabularies   279, 455
   utility vocabularies   284

WebDAV   31, 201, 250
   file representation   156
   metadata   219

widgets   95
   configuration   102
   IInputWidget   96
Windows   13
   command prompt   17
   running tests   164
workflow   10
WYSIWYG   83

XHTML   83
XML   10, 35, 83
XML-RPC   31, 203, 221, 431

yield   289

zapi   34, 186, 199, 351, 352
ZCML   21, 35, 391
   complex directive   63
   including files   80
   overriding directives   107, 159
ZEO   72
ZMI   20, 23, 57, 140
ZODB   29, 71
   Zope 2   74
Zope
   configuration   *see* instance
   download   15
   history   6
   instance   *see* instance
   What is...   3
Zope Corporation   3
Zope Management Interface   *see* ZMI
Zope Public License, ZPL   4
Zope X3   5, 10
zopectl   18
ZPT   *see* Page Templates
ZPT Page   109
ztapi   124, 172, 258, 388

Printing: Krips bv, Meppel
Binding: Litges & Dopf, Heppenheim